MW01474024

Pirates of Empire

The suppression of piracy and other forms of maritime violence was a keystone in the colonisation of Southeast Asia. Focusing on what was seen in the nineteenth century as the three most pirate-infested areas in the region – the Sulu Sea, the Strait of Malacca and Indochina – this comparative study in colonial history explores how piracy was defined, contested and used to resist or justify colonial expansion, particularly during the most intense phase of imperial expansion in Southeast Asia from c. 1850 to c. 1920. In doing so, it demonstrates that piratical activity continued to occur in many parts of Southeast Asia well beyond the mid nineteenth century, when most existing studies of piracy in the region end their period of investigation. It also points to the changes over time in how piracy was conceptualised and dealt with by each of the major colonial powers in the region, Britain, France, the Netherlands, Spain and the United States. This title is also available as Open Access on Cambridge Core.

STEFAN EKLÖF AMIRELL is Associate Professor in History at Linnaeus University, Sweden. He is also the President of the Swedish Historical Association and Sweden's delegate to the International Committee of Historical Sciences (ICHS/CISH). Among his previous works are *Pirates in Paradise: A Modern History of Southeast Asia's Maritime Marauders* and several articles on piracy in Southeast Asia.

Pirates of Empire

*Colonisation and Maritime Violence
in Southeast Asia*

Stefan Eklöf Amirell
Linnaeus University

CAMBRIDGE
UNIVERSITY PRESS

CAMBRIDGE
UNIVERSITY PRESS

University Printing House, Cambridge CB2 8BS, United Kingdom

One Liberty Plaza, 20th Floor, New York, NY 10006, USA

477 Williamstown Road, Port Melbourne, VIC 3207, Australia

314–321, 3rd Floor, Plot 3, Splendor Forum, Jasola District Centre,
New Delhi – 110025, India

79 Anson Road, #06–04/06, Singapore 079906

Cambridge University Press is part of the University of Cambridge.

It furthers the University's mission by disseminating knowledge in the pursuit of education, learning, and research at the highest international levels of excellence.

www.cambridge.org
Information on this title: www.cambridge.org/9781108484213
DOI: 10.1017/9781108594516

© Stefan Eklöf Amirell 2019

This work is in copyright. It is subject to statutory exceptions and to the provisions of relevant licensing agreements; with the exception of the Creative Commons version the link for which is provided below, no reproduction of any part of this work may take place without the written permission of Cambridge University Press.

An online version of this work is published at doi.org/10.1017/9781108594516 under a Creative Commons Open Access license CC-BY-NC-ND 4.0 which permits re-use, distribution and reproduction in any medium for non-commercial purposes providing appropriate credit to the original work is given. You may not distribute derivative works without permission. To view a copy of this license, visit https://creativecommons.org/licenses/by-nc-nd/4.0

All versions of this work may contain content reproduced under license from third parties. Permission to reproduce this third-party content must be obtained from these third-parties directly.

When citing this work, please include a reference to the
DOI 10.1017/9781108594516

First published 2019

Printed in the United Kingdom by TJ International Ltd, Padstow Cornwall

A catalogue record for this publication is available from the British Library.

Library of Congress Cataloging-in-Publication Data
Names: Eklöf Amirell, Stefan, 1968- author.
Title: Pirates of empire : colonisation and maritime violence in Southeast Asia / Stefan Eklöf Amirell.
Description: Cambridge, United Kingdom : Cambridge University Press, 2019. | Includes bibliographical references and index.
Identifiers: LCCN 2019008719 | ISBN 9781108484213 (hardback ; alk. paper) | ISBN 9781108706100 (pbk. ; alk. paper)
Subjects: LCSH: Piracy–Southeast Asia–History–19th century. | Piracy–Southeast Asia–History–20th century. | Maritime history–Southeast Asia–History–19th century. | Maritime history–Southeast Asia–History–20th century. | Colonies–Asia–History–19th century. | Colonies–Asia–History–20th century.
Classification: LCC HV6433.786.S64 E35 2019 | DDC 364.16/4–dc23
LC record available at https://lccn.loc.gov/2019008719

ISBN 978-1-108-48421-3 Hardback

Cambridge University Press has no responsibility for the persistence or accuracy of URLs for external or third-party internet websites referred to in this publication and does not guarantee that any content on such websites is, or will remain, accurate or appropriate.

Contents

List of Maps	*page* vi
Preface	vii
Acknowledgements	ix
Introduction	1
1 Piracy in Global and Southeast Asian History	21
2 The Sulu Sea	42
3 The Strait of Malacca	96
4 Indochina	161
Conclusion	209
Epilogue: Piracy and the End of Empire	232
Bibliography	236
Index	257

Maps

1 Map of Southeast Asia	*page* 4
2 Map of the Sulu Sea	43
3 Map of the Strait of Malacca	97
4 Map of Indochina	162

Preface

Professionally, my interest in piracy began in the 1990s when I was doing research for my PhD thesis in Southeast Asia. Piracy and armed robbery against ships was relatively common in the region at the time, and just about every week the regional newspapers reported about commercial vessels being attacked by pirates in the Strait of Malacca, the South China Sea or Indonesian ports. To be honest, many of the incidents were trifling affairs that hardly seemed to justify the dramatic label 'piracy'. However, some of the attacks were serious crimes, including well-organised operations in which large ships, such as oil tankers and bulk vessels, were hijacked at sea and their crews, in some cases, ruthlessly shot or hacked to death and thrown overboard.

Piracy, I came to realise, was not a thing of the past, and the reality was a far cry from the romantic image of *Treasure Island* or *Pirates of the Caribbean*. As a historian, moreover, I began to wonder whether piracy, which seemed to have been so prevalent in Southeast Asia in precolonial and early colonial times, had really been stamped out in the nineteenth century and only recently returned, or if it had in fact never disappeared but only temporarily moved out of sight.

My attempts to make sense of contemporary piracy in Southeast Asia resulted in a postdoctoral research project at the Centre for East and South-East Asian Studies at Lund University in Sweden and eventually, in 2006, a book about the modern history of piracy in Southeast Asia, perhaps somewhat romantically entitled *Pirates in Paradise*. The focus was on the period from 1975 to 2005, which meant that I went further back in time than most studies of contemporary piracy published around the same time. Nonetheless, the question of what happened in the period from the middle of the nineteenth century until the last quarter of the twentieth century remained largely unexplored, not only by me but also by most other members of the small community of pirate historians.

The present study is an attempt to fill that gap. Although the period under study is long, going back to the onset of the European maritime expansion in Asia, the focus is on the period from around the middle of the nineteenth century, when most existing studies of the history of piracy and other forms of maritime raiding in Southeast Asia end their period of investigation, until the beginning of the twentieth century, when piracy, for the most part, had been efficiently suppressed in the region.

Above all, the book sets out to relate the phenomenon of maritime violence to the intensified colonisation of Southeast Asia in the second half of the nineteenth century and the first years of the twentieth century. In doing so, it compares the policies and interests of the five major colonial powers in the region at the time, Britain, France, the Netherlands, Spain and the United States. The book also aims, as far as possible, to highlight the perspectives of those who were accused of piracy or in other ways were affected by the efforts of the colonial powers to establish maritime security and commercial and political hegemony in maritime Southeast Asia. The book thereby draws attention to the central role that 'piracy', however defined, played, not only in the extension and legitimisation of empire, but also in the anti-imperialist critique of colonial expansion in the nineteenth and early twentieth centuries.

The title *Pirates of Empire* has been chosen in order to capture some of the ambiguity and the multiple meanings attached to the label *piracy* in Southeast Asia's age of empire. Piracy was a multifaceted and often useful concept, both for those who advocated imperial expansion and for those who resisted it, whether in Southeast Asia, Europe or the United States. The concept also changed its meaning and use over the long history of the overseas European expansion. Hopefully this book will contribute to a better understanding of how the imperial past and its pirates – whether Asian, European or American – all took part in shaping the global maritime security regime that still is a cornerstone of global commerce and the international political order.

The spelling of personal and place names follows, as far as possible, the Internet edition of the *Encyclopedia Britannica*. All translations into English from the cited sources and literature are, unless otherwise stated, by the author.

Acknowledgements

This book is the result of a research grant in history, financed by the Swedish Foundation for Humanities and Social Sciences (Riksbankens Jubileumsfond), which also has provided funding for publishing the book with full open access. Research for the book was carried out between 2013 and 2018, mainly at the Department of History, Lund University, which also cofunded part of the project. In December 2016 I joined Linnaeus University and its Centre for Concurrences in Colonial and Postcolonial Studies, where the project was concluded with generous support from the Centre. I am most grateful to all of these institutions for their support and for providing me with the facilities and favourable conditions for carrying out the research for this book.

Numerous people have contributed directly or indirectly to the book. I would like to thank all my colleagues at Lund University, where the Global History Seminar Series, coordinated by Joachim Östlund and myself, generated many stimulating discussions, and the Linnaeus University Centre for Concurrences, which is one of the most interesting research environments today for a researcher working on colonialism and colonial history. I also want to thank the generally helpful and competent staff at libraries and archives in Sweden, Britain, France, the Netherlands, Singapore and the United States, who over the years have helped me locate the sources and literature on which the book is founded.

Several colleagues have read and commented on various parts of the manuscript. I especially want to thank Bruce Buchan, Griffith University, and Gunnel Cederlöf and Hans Hägerdal, both at Linnaeus University, for their valuable comments and suggestions on different parts of the text. Needless to say, any omissions or mistakes are entirely my own responsibility.

Last but not least I am obliged to my family – Isabella, Miriam, Erik, Leo and Vincent – for their continuous moral support and encouragement throughout the duration of the project. They have often had little choice but to share my interest in piracy as a cultural and historical phenomenon, and I am happy to say that they have generally done so with great enthusiasm.

Introduction

It is often assumed that piracy in Southeast Asia – as in most other parts of the world – came to an end around the middle of the nineteenth century as a result of the resolute efforts of the expanding colonial powers and their navies. Aided by steam navigation and their increasingly superior military technology, the European naval forces were, at long last, able to suppress the large-scale piracy and other forms of maritime raiding that seemed to have plagued maritime Southeast Asia since the dawn of history. As the colonial regimes took control over most of the land in the region, the Malay, Chinese and other Asian pirates were deprived of their markets and safe havens on land. At the same time, increasingly frequent patrols by the colonial navies and other maritime forces made piratical ventures ever more difficult and precarious. The anarchy of the past gave way to the modern regime of relative security at sea, allowing for the freedom of navigation and the progress of maritime commerce, economic development and civilisation.[1]

For the advocates of colonisation the suppression of piracy was (and sometimes still is) hailed as a major achievement and a manifestation of the civilising and benevolent influence of Europe's and the United States' imperial expansion.[2] Colonisation, from this point of view, did not only mean the imposition of law and order on land, but also at sea, enabling people and goods to travel unmolested across the water. Meanwhile, the need to suppress piracy was often used as a rationale for colonial expansion. Sovereignty and the suppression of piracy were intimately linked with one another, albeit in varying and often complex and contested ways.

---

[1] E.g., Tarling, *Piracy and Politics*, 228; Blue, 'Piracy on the China Coast', 75; Trocki, *Prince of Pirates*, 123, n. 1; Brooke, 'Piracy', 299; Glete, *Navies and Nations*, 419; Young, *Contemporary Maritime Piracy*; Reid, 'Violence at Sea', 15; Andaya and Andaya, *History of Malaysia*, 3rd edn, 140.

[2] E.g., Lloyd, *Navy and the Slave Trade*, xi, calls the British Navy's suppression of piracy and the slave trade around the world in the nineteenth century '[p]erhaps the most admirable work it ever performed'. Cf. also Layton, 'Discourses of Piracy', 81; Dickinson, 'Is the Crime of Piracy Obsolete?', 334–60.

This book investigates the role of what Europeans, Americans and Asians of different nationalities called 'piracy' in the context of the modern imperial expansion in Southeast Asia. The origins of the colonial discourses and practices associated with piracy are traced to the onset of the European maritime expansion in the early modern period, but the focus of the study is on the period from around 1850 to 1920. This focus is in part motivated by the relative scarcity of studies of piracy and other forms of maritime violence in the region beyond the 1850s. Apart from some important studies of the Dutch East Indies, which deal with all or most of the nineteenth century, most full-length studies of piracy in Southeast Asia to date focus on the first half of the nineteenth century or earlier periods in history.[3]

The fact that organised piracy and maritime raiding were brought largely under control around the middle of the nineteenth century, however, does not render the study of the phenomenon obsolete for the remainder of the century or the twentieth century. For one thing, maritime raiding continued to cause problems in parts of maritime Southeast Asia and the South China Sea throughout the nineteenth century and, in some parts of the region, well into the twentieth century. For the most part the victims were Asian seafarers or coastal populations, including Chinese merchants, Malay fishermen, Vietnamese coastal populations and Japanese and other Asian pearl fishers. In addition, some of the attacks that befell Europeans or Americans attracted widespread attention, not only in the region but also in the colonial metropoles.[4]

Second, and most important for our present purposes, the suppression of piracy continued to be an important rationale for colonial expansion even though maritime raiding in itself, for the most part, had ceased to constitute a major security threat for the colonial authorities when imperial territorial expansion began to intensify in the region from the 1870s. As noted by Eric Tagliacozzo, with reference to Dutch and British writers and statesmen at the time, the threat of piracy was most immediate in the decades leading up to 1865, when it constituted a real impediment to the progress of commerce and administrative stabilisation on the peripheries of the Dutch and British colonial possessions in Southeast Asia.[5] Maritime raiding, however, did not cease in 1865, and the threat of piracy continued to be invoked throughout the rest of

---

[3] E.g., Antony, *Like Froth*; Tarling, *Piracy and Politics*; Graham, *Great Britain in the Indian Ocean*, esp. 362–90; Trocki, *Prince of Pirates*. Warren, *Iranun and Balangingi*, covers the second half of the nineteenth century but deals mainly with the period up until 1848, as does his earlier major study on the subject, *The Sulu Zone 1768–1898*. The most comprehensive study of piracy in the Dutch East Indies in the nineteenth century is Teitler, van Dissel and à Campo, *Zeeroof*; see also Tagliacozzo, 'Kettle on a Slow Boil'; Tagliacozzo, *Secret Trades*, 108–27.

[4] E.g., à Campo, 'Patronen, processen en periodisering', 78–107; Tagliacozzo, *Secret Trades*, 113–16; Eklöf Amirell, 'Pirates and Pearls', 1–24; Lessard, *Human Trafficking*.

[5] Tagliacozzo, *Secret Trades*, 109.

the nineteenth century and, in some cases, well into the twentieth century. The suppression of piracy – whether real, alleged or imagined – was thus an integrated part of the intensified process of colonisation in much of Southeast Asia in the second half of the nineteenth century. The perceived threat was not confined to maritime parts of the region but was also invoked in mainland Southeast Asia, particularly by the French in Indochina.

Against this background, piracy can be used as a lens through which the processes of imperial expansion and colonisation and the encounters between fundamentally different economic, social, political and cultural systems can be studied. In doing so the present study aims to provide fresh comparative insights into one of the most formative periods in the modern history of Southeast Asia and the world.

Piracy and Colonial Expansion in Southeast Asia

One of the first questions to ask in an investigation of piracy in Southeast Asia is what actually constituted piracy in the eyes of the actors involved. The terms *pirates* and *piracy* appear frequently in early modern and nineteenth-century sources pertaining to maritime Southeast Asia, but what were the reasons for using these and related terms to refer to the various types of illicit activities that usually – but not always – occurred at sea? A central purpose of this book is to highlight the different perceptions of 'piracy' held by contemporary Europeans, Americans and Asians of different nationalities, vocations and political convictions. To what extent and under what circumstances were piratical activities seen as troublesome, barbaric or horrific, and to what extent were they seen as trifling, legitimate or even honourable, depending on the point of view of the beholder? When and why did piracy begin (or cease) to be seen as a major security threat by, for example, the colonial authorities, the governments and general public in the colonial metropoles, Asian sovereigns and notables or merchants of different nationalities? Did the problem subside or disappear, and, if so, when and for what reasons? In what measure did the suppression of piracy, from the point of view of the colonial powers, necessitate the conquest of territory and the demise of local rulers and states? Put otherwise, were conquest and colonisation necessary in order to uphold security and the freedom of navigation, or should the invocation of piracy as a security threat or a barbaric practice be understood primarily as a fig leaf meant to conceal other, less honourable, motives for colonial expansion, such as the quest for land and natural resources, or strategic and commercial advantages?

To answer these questions, three allegedly pirate-infested areas in Southeast Asia are analysed comparatively with regard to how piracy was talked about, suppressed and used to motivate colonial expansion (Map 1). The first of these is the Sulu Sea in the southern Philippines. The region was the homeland of the

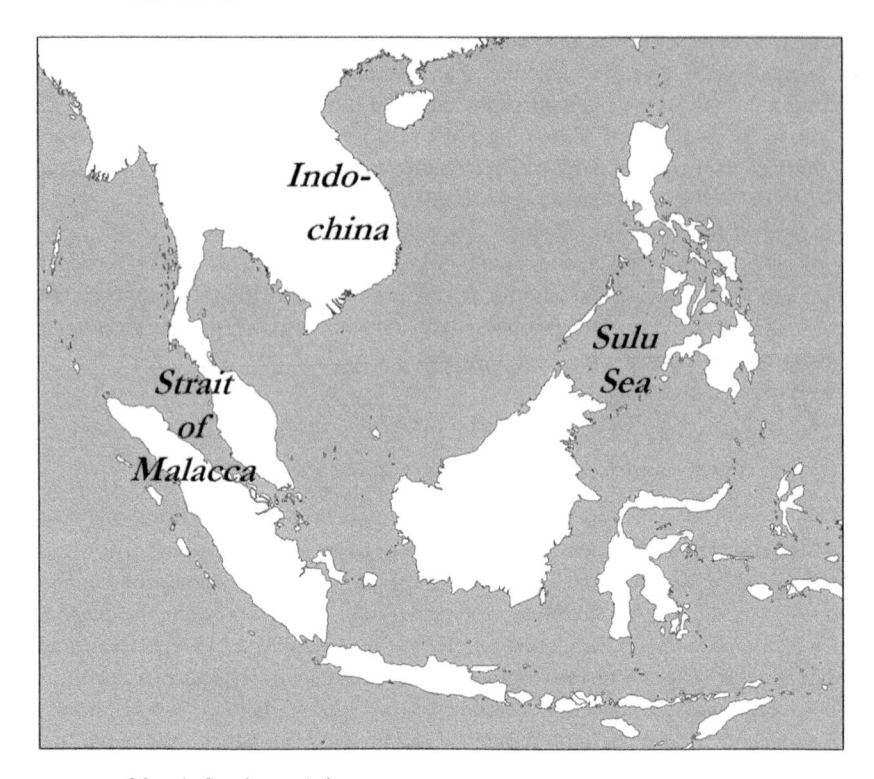

Map 1: Southeast Asia

feared Iranun and other maritime raiders, whose depredations surged in the second half of the eighteenth century and reached a climax in the first half of the following century. From around the middle of the nineteenth century, the Spanish naval forces, like the British and Dutch in other parts of maritime Southeast Asia, began to gain the upper hand in the fight against the Sulu raiders, and particularly from the 1860s a more permanent Spanish naval presence in the southern Philippines brought large-scale maritime raiding under control. Attacks on local vessels at sea and coastal raids on neighbouring islands for the purpose of capturing slaves nevertheless continued throughout the Spanish colonial period and during the first decade of the American colonial period from 1899.

The second area is the Strait of Malacca and the shipping lanes around Singapore and the Riau-Lingga Archipelago, where Malay and Chinese raiders attacked local trading and fishing boats and occasionally large cargo steamers as well. Even though British and Dutch gunboats were able in principle to control the major sea-lanes of communication from around the middle of the nineteenth century, plunder and extortion of riverine traffic, coastal raids and violent attacks at sea, targeting mainly small local vessels, continued for the remainder of the century and, occasionally, beyond. Civil and colonial wars and political instability in the autonomous Malay states bordering the Strait seemed on several occasions to lead to outbreaks of piratical activity throughout the nineteenth century.

The third region is the northwest part of the South China Sea and the rivers of Indochina, where Chinese and Vietnamese pirates and other bandits attacked local vessels at sea and on rivers, and raided villages and settlements on the coast and inland, mainly for the purpose of abducting humans for trafficking. Maritime violence at sea and coastal raiding were largely brought under control by a series of French naval expeditions in the 1870s, but extortion and plunder on Vietnamese rivers and other forms of banditry, as well as anticolonial resistance – all of which was labelled piracy by the French colonists – continued largely unchecked until the last decade of the nineteenth century and resurfaced sporadically even in the early twentieth century.

Several similarities between the three zones provide the rationale for the comparative study. First, the natural geography of all three regions was (and still is in many places) favourable for maritime raiding, a circumstance that was frequently noted by nineteenth-century observers. The coastlines were often thickly forested, and there were many small islands, sheltered bays and hidden passages that provided maritime raiders with safe havens and suitable bases from which to launch their attacks. Many rivers were also navigable inland for vessels of shallow draft and could serve as a means of quick refuge for the perpetrators after raids at sea or on the coast. By controlling strategic points along the rivers, pirates and other brigands, often supported by local strongmen, could control riverine traffic and demand tolls from or plunder trading vessels navigating on the river. As a crossroad for Eurasian maritime commerce, moreover, Southeast Asia has throughout history been amply supplied with richly laden targets for violent attacks. Combined with the seafaring skills of many of the peoples of maritime Southeast Asia, these factors go a long way to explain why the region has figured so prominently in the global history of piracy and why it at times has been regarded as one of the most dangerous regions of the world with regard to piracy and armed robbery against ships – not only in the past, but also in recent years.[6]

Second, most of the coasts and lands of all of the three zones were still by the middle of the nineteenth century governed, at least nominally, by

---

[6] Teitler, 'Piracy in Southeast Asia', 67–83; Eklöf, *Pirates in Paradise*. The term 'piracy and armed robbery against ships' is used for statistical purposes by, among others, the International Maritime Bureau and the International Maritime Organization, taking into account violent attacks against vessels both on the high seas and in waters under the jurisdiction of a state; see further Beckman and Page, 'Piracy and Armed Robbery against Ships', 234–55.

indigenous rulers: the Sultans of Aceh, Siak, Kedah, Perak, Selangor and Johor in the Strait of Malacca region; the kings of Vietnam and Cambodia in Indochina; and the sultan of Sulu in the Sulu Archipelago. However, European colonial powers had begun to make incursions into all of the three zones during the first half of the nineteenth century or earlier and continued to strengthen their presence after the middle of the century. European advances contributed to the destabilisation and decline of the indigenous states, although internal political developments and the repercussions of global and regional dynamics also were consequential. Regardless of the underlying reasons, the decline of the indigenous states and the ensuing disorder and lack of central control paved the way for the imposition of colonial rule in one form or another over most of the three zones between the 1850s and 1870s: by the British in the Malay Peninsula, the Dutch in northern Sumatra, the French in Indochina, and Spain and later the United States in the Sulu Archipelago. In all three zones European advances were met with armed resistance that led to protracted violent conflicts, particularly in the Sulu Archipelago and other parts of the southern Philippines, in Aceh in northern Sumatra and in Tonkin in northern Vietnam.

The third similarity concerns the preoccupation of the colonial powers with the problem of piracy. In all of the three zones, colonial officials and other agents of imperial expansion accused indigenous perpetrators, including not only obvious outlaws and renegades, but also members of the ruling families and other notables, of engaging in or sponsoring piratical activities. The precise nature and frequency of these accusations and the activities they concerned varied, however, and the question of whether the label *piracy* was appropriate in the different Southeast Asian contexts was the object of considerable contestation by nineteenth-century actors and observers. On the one hand, labelling entire nations and ethnic groups as piratical could serve to motivate European or American military intervention and colonisation. On the other hand, the opponents of colonial expansion, both in Southeast Asia and in the colonial metropoles in Europe and the United States, readily pointed to the flaws of such rhetoric and often rejected any claims that piracy justified colonial wars or the subjugation of indigenous populations. The response of the indigenous rulers of Southeast Asia, meanwhile, varied from active sponsorship of maritime raiding, often as a means of enhancing their own status, wealth and political power, to compliance and cooperation with the colonial authorities in suppressing piracy. Some Asian rulers, such as the sultan of Selangor, seemed indifferent to the problem, whereas others, such as the Vietnamese Emperor Tu Duc, turned the allegation around and accused the French of piracy.[7] The lines of

---

[7] Swettenham, *British Malaya*, 183; Retord, 'Lettre de Mgr Retord', 226; see Chapter 4 below.

division in the struggle to define piracy and to identify the best measures, if any, to curb it were thus not neatly drawn between colonisers and colonised, nor between a 'European' and an 'Asian' understanding of piracy and maritime raiding.

Fourth, and finally, for the nineteenth- and early twentieth-century Europeans and Americans who regarded piracy as a serious problem, allegations of piracy were often linked to presumably 'innate' ethnic or racial, traits of character associated with certain indigenous groups of Southeast Asia. This was particularly the case with regard to the coastal Malays throughout the archipelago and the formidable maritime raiders of the southern Philippines, such as the Tausug, Iranun and Sama, all of whom by the nineteenth century had acquired a reputation among Europeans for being more or less pirates by nature.[8]

Piracy in Southeast Asia and elsewhere was thus often held up by those in favour of colonisation as a manifestation of the presumed lack of civilisation among the nations and peoples concerned. The failure on the part of indigenous rulers to control illicit maritime violence both within their jurisdiction and emanating from their territories meant that they failed to meet the so-called standard of civilisation, which was the benchmark used by nineteenth-century European lawyers and statesmen to determine whether a state was civilised or not. Lacking the proper laws against piracy and other forms of illicit maritime violence or being unable to control non-state-sanctioned violence within or emanating from its territory disqualified a state from being recognised as a full member of the international community of nations.[9]

Such notions provided a rationale for European and American colonisers' efforts not only to subjugate but also to 'civilise' indigenous peoples in Southeast Asia and other parts of the world. The civilising mission, as put by Jürgen Osterhammel, involved the self-proclaimed right and duty of European and American colonisers to propagate and actively introduce their norms and institutions to other peoples and societies, based on the firm conviction of the inherent superiority of their own culture and society.[10] In this sense, the civilising mission enjoyed its most widespread influence during the period in focus for the present study, as the economic, political and technological superiority of the

---

[8] See Reber, 'The Sulu World', 2–4, for what she calls the 'innate' theory of piracy put forward by Thomas Stamford Raffles. Cf. McNair, *Perak and the Malays*, 269. This image was cemented and dispersed in Europe through popular fiction, including novels by Joseph Conrad and other British authors, as well as various purportedly true accounts of peoples and events in the Malay Archipelago, including those by James Brooke and Alfred Russell Wallace; see further Wagner, 'Piracy and the Ends of Romantic Commercialism'.

[9] Gong, *The Standard of 'Civilisation'*; Thomson, *Mercenaries, Pirates and Sovereigns*; cf. Koskenniemi, *The Gentle Civilizer of Nations*.

[10] Osterhammel, 'Approaches to Global History', 14; cf. Barth and Osterhammel (eds.), *Zivilisierungsmissionen*.

8   Introduction

West in relation to the rest of the world culminated between the mid nineteenth century and the outbreak of the Great War in 1914. The colonial discourse about and the antipiracy operations in Southeast Asia should thus be understood against the backdrop of the apparent triumph of Western modernity and civilisation at the time and the accompanying conviction on the part of many (but far from all) contemporary observers in both Western and non-Western countries that it was the manifest obligation of Europeans and Americans to civilise and to bring order, progress and prosperity to the rest of the world.[11]

Piracy in the Colonial Lens

The colonisation of Southeast Asia, including the three zones under study here, has been extensively researched ever since the nineteenth century, as have the subjects of maritime violence and the suppression of piracy in many parts of the region, particularly the Strait of Malacca and the Sulu Sea. Historians of French Indochina, by contrast, have shown less interest in the subject of piracy as such, at least with regard to modern historiography.[12]

Despite the obvious differences between the national historiographies of the countries concerned in the present context – including not only the former colonial powers Britain, France, the Netherlands, Spain and the United States, but also the postcolonial states of Cambodia, Indonesia, Malaysia, the Philippines, Singapore and Vietnam – some general features of how the history of colonisation and the suppression of piracy has been written since the nineteenth century can be discerned.

The first historical studies of the colonisation of Southeast Asia were written as the events in question were still unfolding, or shortly thereafter, often by military officers or colonial civil servants who themselves took part, in one capacity or another, in the developments concerned. Much of this colonial-era literature was, as put by Nicholas Tarling, 'cast in a heroic and imperialist mould', but there were significant exceptions.[13] Some European observers were highly critical of imperial expansion and colonialism, or at the very least of certain aspects of it, such as the use of dubious allegations of piracy in order to motivate territorial expansion or the use of indiscriminate violence against militarily inferior enemies.[14] Read critically, nineteenth-century historiography

---

[11] See further Eklöf Amirell, 'Civilizing Pirates'.
[12] An exception is Chérif, 'Pirates, rebelles et ordre colonial'. See also Lessard, *Human Trafficking*, who discusses piracy in colonial Vietnam with a focus on abductions and trafficking.
[13] Tarling, 'The Establishment', 73.
[14] E.g., Maxwell, *Our Malay Conquests*; 'The Expansion of the Empire', *The Economist* (13 December 1884). For examples of anti-imperialist texts from France and the United States written at the zenith of modern Western imperial expansion, see, respectively, Ageron, *L'Anticolonialisme en France*; Bresnahan, *In Time of Hesitation*.

also contains many valuable clues for understanding the actions and decisions taken by the agents of history from their point of view and for understanding the *Zeitgeist* of the age of empire in Southeast Asia.

Piracy was a prominent topic of analysis and discussion among nineteenth-century European writers, statesmen, politicians, colonial officials and naval officers in Southeast Asia. Their writings show that the term *piracy* was not, for the most part, applied unreflectedly to the Southeast Asian context but that it was often highly contested, particularly in the British colonial context. Some texts demonstrate that their authors had substantial knowledge about the historical, cultural and legal aspects of piracy and other forms of maritime violence, both in Southeast Asia and in global historical perspective. Many observers analysed the phenomenon with reference to broader temporal and cross-cultural frameworks, frequently comparing contemporary Southeast Asian piracy and maritime violence with earlier periods in classical and European history.[15] Although such analyses sometimes were imbued with Eurocentrism, stadial theory and racism, they could also be sincere efforts to understand, and not just condemn or suppress, indigenous piracy and other forms of maritime violence in Southeast Asia.

Without defending the often brutal methods used in the colonial efforts to suppress piracy, it is also important not to lose sight of the fact that, in contrast to latter-day scholars who study piracy in retrospect and from a distance, colonial officials and military officers in the field had to make decisions that had a real effect on people's lives. They also frequently had to argue for their preferred course of action, not only from legal or pragmatic perspectives, but also from a moral point of view. Writing in 1849, James Richardson Logan, a British lawyer and newspaper editor in the Straits Settlements, described the moral dilemma between taking the side of the perpetrators of maritime violence or that of their victims:

> Piracy is doubtless less reprehensible morally in those who have never been taught to look upon it as a crime, but that is no reason why every severity *necessary* for its extirpation should not be resorted to. A tiger is even less reprehensible in this point of view than a professional pirate 'to the manner born'. But we must do what is necessary to prevent injury to others from piratical habits, before we can indulge in compassion for the pirate. Our sympathy must be first with the victims and the endangered; with the murdered before the murderer, the slave before the slave dealer.[16]

Although allegations of piracy frequently were deployed for opportunistic reasons, there were strong moral arguments for acting against the large-scale and often brutal maritime raids that affected large parts of the Malay

---

[15] E.g., Raffles, *Memoir of the Life*, 180; Crawfurd, *Descriptive Dictionary*, 353–4; Maxwell, *Our Malay Conquests*, 5–6.
[16] Logan, 'Malay Amoks and Piracies', 466; italics in original.

Archipelago in the nineteenth century. The raids often involved the killing, abduction and robbery of innocent victims, including men, women and children, many of whom were forced to endure terrible abuse and hardship. From this perspective – and notwithstanding that other, less noble, motives frequently were decisive in the formulation of colonial policies, and that the measures adopted were at times excessively brutal – it is difficult to see the decline of maritime raiding in Southeast Asian waters from the middle of the nineteenth century as an altogether negative development.

Moral Relativism and Cross-Cultural Perspectives

Compared with most historians of the colonial era, their successors in the wake of the decolonisation of Southeast Asia from the 1940s have for the most part been much less favourable in their assessments of colonial efforts to suppress piracy in the region and of colonialism in general. The use of the very terms *piracy* and *pirate* in the Southeast Asian context has been one of the main points of criticism. Among the first scholars to draw attention to the problem was J. C. van Leur, a Dutch historian and colonial official in the Dutch East Indies during the final years of the colonial period. In an article originally published in 1940, Van Leur criticised the tendency of European scholars and observers to belittle Asian civilisations and to pass value judgements on precolonial states in Southeast Asia based on condescending notions drawn from European history and society:

> Even without knowing further details, it seems to me inaccurate to dispose of such Indonesian states as Palembang, Siak, Achin, or Johore with the qualifications corrupt despotisms, pirate states, and slave states, hotbeds of political danger and decay. Inaccurate, if for no other reason, because despotism, piracy, and slavery are historical terms, and history is not written with value judgements.[17]

Building on Van Leur's and other critical views of colonialism that emerged during the interwar years, the 1950s and early 1960s saw the rise of new historiographical frameworks with regard to colonial and imperial history imbued by a more professional historical ethos and methods. Profiting from the greater availability of primary sources, particularly in the form of colonial archives, the efforts to write imperial history tended to focus on political and administrative developments in London, Paris, Madrid and other colonial metropoles. The focus was often on official policy and less on the impact of the policies and the adopted measures in the colonies. Prominent themes included political debates and policy processes and the relations between different branches of the government, the military and the colonial

---

[17] Van Leur, *Indonesian Trade and Society*, 276; originally Van Leur, 'Eenige aanteekeningen'.

administration. The personal capacity and accomplishments of prominent figures, such as ministers, governors and other senior colonial officials and military officers, were often emphasised, whereas the perspective of the colonised, as in the earlier historiography, rarely was given much prominence, possibly with the exception of the members of the indigenous elites who were in direct contact with the Europeans. Despite the shortcomings of these studies, many of them are still valuable, particularly for their detailed mapping of political and military events based on the careful analysis of voluminous colonial archives and other primary sources.[18]

The foremost authority on piracy in colonial Southeast Asia to emerge in the context of this new paradigm was the British historian Nicholas Tarling. In his early studies of British efforts to suppress piracy in the Malay Archipelago in the first half of the nineteenth century, he took the cue from Van Leur and warned against unreflectedly describing acts of maritime violence undertaken by Asians as piracy.[19] Tarling noted that piracy carried 'from its European context certain shades of meaning and overtones which render inexact its application even to ostensibly comparable Asian phenomena'. Because his focus was on British policy, he nevertheless argued that the term *piracy* was relevant and that it was 'necessary to be fair to the Europeans who believed they were suppressing piracy', as it was not unreasonable, in the nineteenth-century context, to consider many of the acts of violence that took place in Southeast Asian waters as piracy.[20] Thus content with studying piracy, as the term was defined by contemporary British colonial officials, Tarling argued that it would be inadvisable for the historian to attempt to decide what was or was not really piracy in the Southeast Asian context. Neither did he think it would be meaningful or valuable to try to apply the term *piracy* interculturally, but rather that it was 'necessary to avoid commitment to irrelevant notions of international law and morality'.[21]

Both Van Leur and Tarling represent what Patricia Risso has called a 'position of moral relativism' with regard to the definition of piracy, in contrast to the absolutist (and often disparaging) position taken by most colonial observers.[22] The dichotomy between the two positions, however, precedes by far the modern historiography of piracy in Southeast Asia. Its origins can be traced to classical Antiquity, and it has a long intellectual history in Europe. Whereas the absolutist view of piracy can be traced to Cicero's writings in the first century BCE, the relativist position was most influentially formulated by

---

[18] Some examples of studies in this tradition include Parkinson, *British Intervention*; Cowan, *Nineteenth-Century Malaya*; Priestley, *France Overseas*.
[19] Tarling, *Piracy and Politics*. Other seminal studies by Tarling in which piracy figures prominently include *Anglo–Dutch Rivalry*; *Britain, the Brookes and Brunei*; *Sulu and Sabah*.
[20] Tarling, *Piracy and Politics*, 1–2; cit., 1.   [21] Ibid., 1.
[22] Risso, 'Cross-Cultural Perceptions', 294–6; cit., 294.

St Augustine of Hippo in the early fifth century CE. His well-known story of the pirate and the emperor is arguably still one of the most eloquent attempts to capture the essence of the relativist position:

> Indeed, that was an apt and true reply which was given to Alexander the Great by a pirate who had been seized. For when that king had asked the man what he meant by keeping hostile possession of the sea, he answered with bold pride, 'What do you mean by seizing the whole earth; but because I do it with a petty ship, I am called a robber, while you who do it with a great fleet are styled emperor.'[23]

The relativist position has been at the heart of the dominating paradigm in the historiography of piracy and maritime raiding in Southeast Asia (and other parts of the world) for most of the post–World War II era. The thrust of the argument is that the term *piracy* was inappropriately applied by European colonisers to indigenous maritime warfare and efforts aimed at state-building, as well as to malign commercial rivals. The effort by the colonial powers to suppress piracy should, from this perspective, above all be understood as a 'tool in commercial competition and in the building of empire – bad means to a bad end', as put by Risso.[24] Taking the argument one step further, historian Anthony Reid has suggested that the European discourse on piracy in Asia be understood as a form of 'organized hypocrisy'.[25]

Such analyses, however, are no less imbued with value judgements than the colonial historiography that Van Leur criticised close to eighty years ago. Just as the inaccurate descriptions of the indigenous Malay states as 'pirate states' failed to capture the complexity of the social, political and cultural systems in which maritime raiding played a central part, the more recent condemnations of colonial efforts to suppress piracy serve to obscure the nuances and diversity of various forms of maritime violence in the context of the European expansion in Asia from the turn of the sixteenth to the early twentieth century. Not taking the colonial discussions and debates about the problem into account, moreover, gives a distorted picture of the intellectual and political climate of the colonial period and risks producing overbearing claims to having exposed the alleged hypocrisy or high-handed and Eurocentric attitudes of colonial agents rather than trying to understand their attitudes and motivations in the proper historical context.

A further problem with the relativist position is that it is imbued with the very Orientalist assumptions that it purports to overcome.[26] By positing a

---

[23] Augustine of Hippo, *City of God*, 101 [4:4]. The story can be traced to Cicero, who provides an earlier version of it in *De Republica* [On the Republic]. Cf. also Pérotin-Dumon, 'The Pirate and the Emperor'; Chomsky, *Pirates and Emperors*, who uses it as a starting point for discussing international terrorism.

[24] Risso, 'Cross-Cultural Perceptions', 296. [25] Reid, 'Violence at Sea', 15.

[26] Said, *Orientalism*.

dichotomy between a presumptive European and a presumptive Asian (or Chinese, Malay or Southeast Asian, etc.) understanding of piracy, and by portraying the latter as more or less static before the onset of the European expansion, the idea of an Asian understanding of piracy serves above all as a counterimage to the European concept.

The Orientalist bias is even more evident in the exoticising and romanticising claims of piracy as a cultural tradition and an honourable vocation among the Malays and certain other ethnic groups. For example, although Sultan Hussein Shah of Johor may very well have been sincere when he, in the early nineteenth century, supposedly told Thomas Stamford Raffles that what Europeans called piracy 'brings no disgrace to a Malay ruler', taking such a statement as emblematic of a presumptive 'Malay' attitude to piracy shows a troubling lack of source criticism.[27] Doing so may even contribute to reproducing colonial stereotypes of the allegedly piratical 'nature' or 'instincts' of the Malays. Numerous testimonies by indigenous Southeast Asians who became victims of piratical attacks and maritime raids, by contrast, clearly demonstrate that far from all Malays or other Southeast Asians shared such positive attitudes with regard to maritime violence and depredations.[28]

Toward a Connected History of Piracy

From the late 1960s, in the context of decolonisation, the rise of Marxist historiography and a general surge in interest in the history of ordinary people and everyday life, colonial history began to concern itself more with the experiences and perspectives of the colonised. Many scholars were critical of the Eurocentric bias in earlier colonial historiography and tried to redress the balance by writing more Asia-, Africa- and Latin America-centred histories, focusing on, for example, the economic exploitation and oppression of indigenous people and the rise of anticolonial and national liberation movements. Dependency theory and world systems theory also influenced the writing of colonial history, aiming to provide a comprehensive analytical and conceptual framework for understanding the relations between colonies, semicolonies and metropoles. Another source of inspiration for this new colonial history was the emerging field of ethnohistory, which emphasised anthropological methods and the exploration of alternative sources, such as oral history and cultural expressions, in order to highlight the experiences of non-Europeans.

---

[27] Reid, 'Violence at Sea', referring to an unattributed citation by Andaya and Andaya, *History of Malaysia*, 1st edn, 130. It has not been possible to locate the citation. For another example of such colonial stereotypes, see Saleeby, *History of Sulu*, 157–8, citing an 'intelligent Dutch writer'.

[28] E.g., Warren, *The Sulu Zone 1768–1898*, 237–51; see also Warren, *Iranun and Balangingi*, 309–42.

In the context of maritime Southeast Asia, James Francis Warren's work on the Sulu Zone from the 1980s combined elements of both ethnohistory and world systems theory, and in doing so he succeeded in providing a much-enhanced understanding of the role of maritime raiding in Southeast Asia in relation to the expanding global commercial exchange in the eighteenth and nineteenth centuries.[29] Warren, like Van Leur half a century before him, rejected the characterisation of indigenous Malay polities as pirate states, not so much because of the value judgement associated with the term *piracy*, but because the label *piracy* tended to obscure the complex fabric of trade, slavery and raiding that characterised the Sulu Sultanate and its dependencies from the late eighteenth until the middle of the nineteenth century.[30]

In his later writings, Warren also tried to overcome the dichotomy between the absolute and relativist positions by arguing for the need to understand the phenomenon of piracy and maritime raiding from both perspectives. Avoiding passing value judgements on either Europeans or Asians, he has argued that it is possible both to understand why the colonial authorities, in view of the devastating effects of maritime raiding in the region, condemned such raiding and labelled it piracy and, at the same time, to realise that such activities, from the point of view of the sultan and coastal chiefs of Sulu, were an important means for them to consolidate their economic base and political power.[31]

Building on Warren's and others' attempts to define the concept of piracy from an intercultural historical perspective, a working definition of piracy for our present purposes is

any act of unprovoked violence or detention, or any act of depredation, done upon the ocean or unappropriated lands or within the territory of a state, through descent from the sea and with the capability to use force in the furtherance of these acts.[32]

This definition is intentionally broad in order to encompass the great variety of different forms of maritime violence perpetrated by European as well as Asian navigators throughout the early modern and modern periods. It also seeks to avoid passing a priori value judgements on the perpetrators. In contrast to most definitions of piracy, it also intentionally leaves out the provision that piracy be limited to acts done for private ends, as this raises difficult questions about sovereignty, *raison d'état* and what defines a legitimate state, questions that

---

[29] Warren, *The Sulu Zone, 1768–1898*; see also his later works on the subject, particularly *The Sulu Zone*; *Iranun and Balangingi*.
[30] E.g., Warren, *The Sulu Zone, 1768–1898*, 252–3.   [31] Warren, 'Balangingi Samal', 46.
[32] This definition combines parts of the current definition of piracy according to the United Nations Convention on the Law of the Sea (Article 101) and the broader definition used by Ormerod in his classic study, *Piracy in the Ancient World*, 60.

cannot be answered a priori, at least not without passing value judgements, with regard to maritime Southeast Asia during the period under study.[33]

The shift from a Eurocentric to a more Asia-centric or globally balanced perspective on the modern history of Southeast Asia has been one of the most important lasting developments in the region's historiography in recent decades. By comparison, the influence of postcolonial studies has been more limited, at least in comparison with other non-European regions such as South Asia, the Middle East and Latin America. The influence is mainly discernible in the greater interest of historians in previously occluded aspects of colonialism, such as race, ethnicity, gender, and perceptions of time and space.[34] Following the publication of Edward Said's book *Orientalism* in 1978, historians of Southeast Asia also began to take a more critical approach to the Western sources and literature about the region. Consequently, one of the most important influences of postcolonial studies in the field of Southeast Asian history has been the reconsideration of the historian's relationship to the archives and other colonial sources. As Ann Laura Stoler has pointed out, archives tend to draw the historian into their internal logic, language and areas of interest, while leaving out other aspects that may be at least as important from an academic and historical point of view.[35] The reassessment of colonial sources and the attempts to use them for answering new types of questions about popular culture and social practices has also been accompanied by a new interest in the examination or reexamination of Asian sources. Several scholars from Southeast Asia, such as Cesar Adib Majul, Thongchai Winichakul and Adrian B. Lapian, have made important contributions to these efforts.[36]

Since around 1990, global or transnational history has emerged as one of the most dynamic fields of historical research and has, in the view of some of the leading proponents of the field, led to a paradigmatic shift in the way in which history is written and apprehended.[37] The emergence of New Imperial History in the United States and Britain was a part of this development, while at the same time showing strong influences from postcolonial studies. The New Imperial History turn has meant that historians now take a greater interest in the social and cultural impact of colonisation, both in the colonies and the colonial metropoles, and try to put domestic and imperial historiographies into conversation with one another.[38] As such, the New Imperial History bears a

---

[33] Warren, *Iranun and Balangingi*, 3, also seems to concur with this position in adopting a similar definition of piracy from an ethnohistorical perspective.
[34] Cf. Reynolds, 'New Look at Old Southeast Asia'.
[35] Stoler, *Duress*, esp. ch. 1; cf Stoler, *Along the Archival Grain*; Bonura and Sears, 'Introduction', 25.
[36] Tarling, 'The Establishment', 73–4; Majul, *Muslims in the Philippines*; Winichakul, *Siam Mapped*; Lapian, *Orang laut*. Cf. also Sachsenmaier, *Global Perspectives*.
[37] E.g., Manning, *Navigating World History*. [38] E.g., Howe, *New Imperial Histories Reader*.

resemblance to the so-called *histoire croisée*-approach, as developed, originally for the purpose of studying transnational processes in the modern history of continental Europe, by Michael Werner and Bénédicte Zimmermann.[39]

The present study is influenced by the New Imperial History turn, and in particular by a recently proposed approach called 'Connected Histories of Empire'.[40] Inspired by postcolonial scholars such as Sanjay Subrahmanyam, Ann Laura Stoler and Natalie Zemon Davis, the approach seeks to uncover the complex and more or less obscure links that operated both within and across the borders of empires. At the heart of the attempt to write connected histories of empire are novel spatial frameworks that focus on the frontiers or borderlands of empires. The interaction and encounters in the contact zones are linked analytically to the developments in both the colonial metropoles and regional centres or nodes of empire, such as Singapore, Saigon and Manila. Influences did not only run between the metropoles, colonies and borderlands of a single empire, but also between the colonies and the often overlapping borderlands of different empires. In focusing on these multiple relations and comparisons between borderlands, colonies and metropoles, the approach seeks to understand Western colonisation and expansion in Southeast Asia as more contested, unstable, undetermined and mutually constitutive than earlier historiography.

The connected histories approach implies that imperialism and colonial domination did not just arise from the relentless spread of global capitalism or the increasing political and military superiority of the West in the nineteenth century. Colonialism was at least as much conditioned by the development of 'shifting conceptual apparatuses that made certain kinds of action seem possible, logical, and even inevitable to state officials, entrepreneurs, missionaries, and other agents of colonization while others were excluded from the realm of possibility', as it is put by Ann Laura Stoler and Frederick Cooper.[41] What was imaginable, moreover, was conditioned both by economic and political circumstances and public opinion in distant metropoles and by the immediate opportunities and constraints in the colonies and their borderlands. These opportunities and constraints, in their turn, were conditioned not only by the relations between colonisers and colonised (or to-be-colonised) peoples, but also by the relations with other colonial governments and indigenous states and centres of power.

In order to grapple with these complex relations and processes, the theoretical framework of Concurrences, as developed by Gunlög Fur and colleagues

---

[39] Werner and Zimmermann, 'Beyond Comparison'.
[40] Potter and Saha, 'Global History'; cf. Lester, 'Imperial Circuits'; Doyle, 'Inter-imperiality'; Barth and Cvetkovski (eds.), *Imperial Co-operation*.
[41] Stoler and Cooper, 'Preface', vii.

at Linnaeus University, is useful.[42] Concurrences implies both the temporal property of two or more things happening at the same time, and competition, taking into account both entanglements and tensions. In doing so, it points to a way of avoiding one of the major pitfalls in the writing of global history: the tendency to overemphasise connectivity and convergence, resulting in a deterministic and even celebratory grand narrative of globalisation.[43] As a heuristic point of departure, Concurrences directs attention to the universalising perspectives contained in colonialist claims and civilising imperatives, and highlights how such claims and imperatives frequently attempt to subsume or co-opt alternatives, regardless of their validity or influence. By moving beyond an understanding of imperial expansion in terms of simplistic binaries between active agents and passive victims, the historical process of colonial expansion can be fruitfully studied as a series of simultaneous and competing stories of exchange, cooperation, transculturation and appropriation, where non-Europeans always retain a measure of agency. The historian can thereby challenge established historical narratives while remaining alive to the significance of alternative voices and understandings of the world.

These points of departure serve to question the dualism that characterises many studies of piracy and colonial expansion, according to which misleading divisions are drawn between coloniser and colonised, or between Asian and European understandings of piracy and other concepts. The colonial experience is instead understood as conditioned by a series of entangled historical processes that were mutually shaped in engagement, attraction and opposition. For our present purposes, these processes involve both indigenous Southeast Asian rulers and populations and a multitude of European, American and Asians actors.[44] Despite attempts by historians to label and categorise these actors as, for example, colonisers, naval officers, missionaries, merchants, indigenous rulers, mandarins or pirates, no group of actors was homogenous. To the extent that the categories corresponded to a social, economic, political or cultural reality, there was, as we shall see, great heterogeneity in terms of opinion, interest and outlook within each group.

Method and Sources

Even though this book is based primarily on colonial firsthand sources, it is also deeply indebted to the work of earlier historians. Most of the existing

---

[42] The most comprehensive treatment of the framework to date is Brydon, Forsgren and Fur (eds.), *Concurrent Imaginaries*. This summary of Concurrences as a methodological concept is based on Fur, 'Concurrences as a Methodology'.

[43] For a critique of these tendencies in the writing of global history, see Fillafer, 'A World Connecting?'

[44] Stoler and Cooper, 'Preface', vii–viii; cit., viii.

literature — with the exception of general surveys of the history of the region — deal in principal with one particular colonial power or part of Southeast Asia. There are also significant differences in the state of the field with regard to the different colonies and colonial powers in the region. For example, whereas the British colonies in many respects have been thoroughly studied, the Spanish colonial period in the Philippines is less well studied, as is the American period.[45] Moreover, in contrast to the historiography of precolonial maritime Southeast Asia, there have as of yet been relatively few attempts to write more comprehensive or comparative studies or syntheses of the region's modern history.[46] Against this background, this book aims to contribute to a more nuanced comparative understanding of what role piracy played in the colonisation of different parts of Southeast Asia.

A central point of departure for the analysis is the concept of securitisation as developed by the Copenhagen School of Security Studies.[47] In the present context, studying piracy from a securitisation perspective means paying attention to how different actors – such as colonial officials, local merchants, missionaries, journalists and politicians – tried to draw attention to the problem of piracy and describe it as a major security threat. If successful, such securitising moves led to the implementation of extraordinary measures to deal decisively with the problem, such as punitive military expeditions, colonial wars of conquest, the wholesale destruction of alleged pirate fleets and villages or the annexation of territories believed to harbour pirates.

Studying the process of securitisation helps to highlight why the label *piracy*, as a legal, political and rhetorical concept, was so prominent in all three zones under study. The purpose is to explain the differences as well as the similarities in how piracy was defined, used and contested in different colonial contexts and at different points of time. In doing so, this book seeks to highlight the influence of the colonial discourses and practices with regard to piracy on the processes of colonisation as well as anticolonial resistance.

The contemporary sources consist of a wide range of conventional colonial sources, including both published and unpublished material, with some emphasis on the former. In contrast to an argument recently made in relation to methods in global history, this book has thus not done away with primary sources as the basis for empirical investigation.[48] The argument for leaving out primary research would be that multiple archival research would be too

---

[45] Slack, 'Philippines under Spanish Rule'.
[46] Seminal works on precolonial maritime Southeast Asia include Hal, *Maritime Trade*; Reid, *Southeast Asia*, 1–2; Lieberman, *Strange Parallels*, 2, esp. Chapter 7.
[47] Buzan, Wæver and de Wilde, *Security*; see also Stritzel, *Security in Translation*, 11–37, for the influence of the Copenhagen School.
[48] Myrdal, 'On Source Criticism'. Myrdal argues for the use of secondary or even tertiary sources (or literature) in the writing of global historical syntheses.

time-consuming and extensive for a single researcher to cope with in reasonable time. However, whereas there is some merit to that argument, it is feasible for a single historian to consult extensive collections of published sources, including those from different national and colonial contexts, particularly when these have been digitized and are accessible through online databases and repositories. In fact, this book could probably not have been written before the digital revolution in the discipline of history and other branches of the humanities in recent years, at least not within a few years and by a single researcher.[49]

The interpretation of the sources is in many cases relatively straightforward because the arguments by colonial officials, military officers and other actors in relation to piratical or allegedly piratical activities in different parts of Southeast Asia are generally explicit. The understandings of the problem of piracy and the appropriate ways of dealing with it from the colonial point of view can thus be studied comparatively and in depth with relative ease through the firsthand sources. What is less visible in most of the source material, however, are the concurrent understandings of piracy and maritime raiding held by indigenous rulers, noblemen, merchants, captives and other victims of piracy. Their voices are represented to some extent in the colonial archives and printed contemporary sources – for example, in official letters and transcripts of meetings and interviews – but for the most part their words are filtered through the eyes of European or American interpreters, negotiators and interrogators. In interpreting such pieces of information, the challenge is to read the texts against the grain in order to catch a glimpse of the non-European perspectives and understandings of the limits of legitimate maritime violence. In the absence, by and large, of indigenous sources of relevance to the subject at hand, doing so is often the only way of gaining some access (imperfect and patchy as it may be) to the indigenous perspectives on piracy in Southeast Asia's age of empire.

Disposition of the Book

This remainder of this book consists of four main chapters and a conclusion. In Chapter 1, which provides a conceptual platform and a historical background for the three subsequent chapters, the concept of piracy is analysed in global historical perspective, and its etymology and intellectual origins in Europe are traced to classical Antiquity. The role of piracy in European expansion is highlighted, with a special focus on the encounters between Asian and European understandings of piracy and other forms of maritime violence during the early modern period.

---

[49] Cf. Sinn and Soares, 'Historians' Use'; Putnam, 'The Transnational'.

The subsequent three chapters make up the core of the empirical investigation. Each chapter deals with one of the geographic areas under study and focuses on one or two of the five major colonial powers in Southeast Asia in the nineteenth and early twentieth centuries. Chapter 2 deals with Spanish and American understandings of and policies with regard to the allegedly piratical Moros of the Sulu Archipelago, particularly from the middle of the nineteenth until the early twentieth century. Chapter 3 analyses British and Dutch uses of the concept of piracy in the context of their commercial and political expansion in and around the Strait of Malacca with an emphasis on the third quarter of the nineteenth century. Chapter 4, finally, deals with French discourse and practices in relation to piracy and other forms of banditry and anticolonial resistance in Indochina from the time of the intensified French expansion in the region in the mid nineteenth century until the 1890s. A summary at the end of each chapter highlights the main comparative insights and conclusions from the study of each region. Finally, the Conclusion draws together the main results of the investigation as a whole, and the Epilogue briefly reflects on the resurgence of piracy in the post–World War II era in the light of the colonial system and its demise around the middle of the twentieth century.

1 Piracy in Global and Southeast Asian History

The term *piracy* can be traced to Greece and the third century BCE, but the modern understanding of the concept developed only from the sixteenth century, concurrent with European expansion across the Atlantic and Indian Oceans and the interaction between Christian and Muslim navigators in the Mediterranean. As such, its meaning changed over time, and it took on different connotations and functions in different cultural and political settings, not only in Europe, but also in Asia, Africa and the Americas. The European understanding of piracy was thus not, as has been claimed, static or 'consistent over centuries', neither as a legal nor as a vernacular concept.[1] As Alfred P. Rubin and others have demonstrated, the concept of piracy evolved historically over a long period of time in Europe, particularly from the turn of the sixteenth century, when the classic discussion of the concept was rediscovered in Cicero's writings. From around the same time, moreover, European overseas expansion gave rise to new challenges in the maritime sphere, including how to define and deal with illicit and unregulated forms of maritime violence in distant seas and coastal areas.[2]

Classical and Mediaeval European Understandings of Piracy

Etymologically, the modern word *pirate* can be traced to the Classical Greek word *peiratēs* (πειρατής), with its earliest attestation from the mid third century BCE.[3] The root of the word is *pēr-* (περ-), which means to try, risk or attempt, and which also – probably not by coincidence, as illustrated by St Augustine's story of the pirate and the emperor – is the root for the words em*pir*e and

---

[1] Risso, 'Cross-Cultural Perceptions', 298; cf. Reid, 'Violence at Sea', 19.
[2] Rubin, *Law of Piracy*; see also Heller-Roazen, *Enemy of All*; Thomson, *Mercenaries, Pirates, and Sovereigns*; Benton, *Search for Sovereignty*; Paige, 'Piracy and Universal Jurisdiction'; Kempe, '"Even in the Remotest Corners of the World"'.
[3] de Souza, *Piracy in the Graeco-Roman World*, 3; cf. Ormerud, *Piracy in the Ancient World*, 59. Earlier Greek texts, such as those by Homer and Thucydides, generally referred to what in modern translations are called 'pirates' as *lēistēs* (λῃστής); see further McKechnie, *Outsiders in the Greek Cities*, 101–41.

imperialism.[4] Originally, in Hellenistic times, however, there was no specific association between the term *peiratēs* and maritime depredations, but the word meant bandit or brigand in general, regardless of whether the activities took place on land or at sea.[5]

The Latin form of the word *pirate* was first used by Cicero, when he, writing in 44 BCE, famously claimed that a pirate (*pirata*) is the 'common enemy of all' (*communis hostis omnium*).[6] In so doing, Cicero echoed the words of the Greek historian Polybius, who in the previous century had singled out the Illyrians, a group of people based on the eastern shores of the Adriatic and reputed for maritime raiding, as the 'common enemies of all peoples'. Cicero, however, developed the concept beyond that of Polybius by drawing a distinction between lawful enemies in war and pirates. The laws of war did not apply to pirates, according to Cicero, and because they were the common enemies of all, there ought to be no obligation to keep an oath sworn to a pirate.[7]

From the time of Cicero – and largely as a consequence of Cicero's writings on the subject – pirates in the Roman Mediterranean world came to be associated specifically with maritime depredations rather than with brigandage in general. In contrast to the Greek meaning of the word, thus, the Latin word *pirata* only ever meant pirate in the sense of maritime raider and was not used to refer to land-based robbers or thieves.[8]

Cicero's earlier writings and speeches about the Cilicians were in large part responsible for this development, because they established a firm association between piracy and subversive maritime activities with grave security implications. In his defence of the Senate's decision to grant extraordinary military powers to the statesman and general Gnaeus Pompeius Magnus in 68 BCE, Cicero represented the situation in the Mediterranean at the time as one of unprecedented crisis, with the seas allegedly being overrun by fleets of Cilician marauders. The situation thus required immediate and decisive military action, and Rome, according to Cicero, was saved only by Pompeius, who supposedly cleared the Mediterranean of pirates in just three months.[9]

Pirates were thus from the outset described in highly securitising terms. Further prefiguring the modern development of the concept in Europe, pirates also became associated in the Roman imagination with exotic and uncivilised

---

[4] Rubin, *Law of Piracy*, 345–6.   [5] Heller-Roazen, *Enemy of All*, 35.
[6] Cicero, *De Officiis* [On Duties] 3.107.
[7] Polybius, *Historíai* [Histories] 2.12.4–6; cf. de Souza, *Piracy in the Graeco-Roman World*, 80.
[8] de Souza, 'Piracy in Classical Antiquity', 49, n. 67.
[9] Ibid., 39–40. In these instances, however, Cicero uses the word *praedones* (robbers, thieves) rather than *piratae*, and it was only in *De Officiis*, written in 44 BCE, that he first used the latinised form of the Greek word *peiratēs*.

outlaws, not unlike the image that dominates in Western popular culture today.[10] Whole villages and communities were labelled piratical by the Romans because their activities and way of life interfered with the new political and commercial order that Rome, at the height of her power from the first century BCE to the second century CE, sought to establish over the Mediterranean. In contrast to how the concept developed in Europe much later, however, piracy was not a specific legal term in Roman law.[11]

It is generally believed that the words *piracy* and *pirate* fell into disuse after Roman times, only to come back in the European context toward the end of the Middle Ages and particularly during the sixteenth century.[12] However, whereas it is true that other words were often used to describe, for example, the Vikings of northern Europe and various marauders who plagued shipping and coastal areas in the Mediterranean in mediaeval times, several laws from different parts of Europe from as early as the eleventh century had provisions that mentioned piracy or pirates, either in Latin or vernacular languages.[13] The principal source of maritime law in Europe in the High Middle Ages, the Rolls of Oléron from the twelfth century, for example, mentions pirates in the context of the obligation of land owners (*seigneurs*) to assist mariners who had been shipwrecked and landed on their shores. The obligation, however, did not include ships 'exercising the profession of piracy' (*exerçant le mestier de piraterie*) or sailors who were 'pirates or scums of the sea' (*pyrates ou escumeurs de mer*). In such cases – and particularly if the pirates were enemies of the Catholic faith – anyone could treat them as dogs and take possession of their property without punishment.[14]

Subsequent mediaeval laws and other texts also mentioned piracy and pirates, and at least from the thirteenth century a number of words apparently synonymous with the term *pirate* appear in the vernacular literature, such as the French *larrons de mer*, the English *sea thieves* and the German *Seeräuber*.[15] In Romance languages, the words for piracy (e.g., Fr. *piraterie*, Sp. *piratería*, It. *pirateria*) and pirate (*pirate, pirata,* etc.) were generally borrowed from Latin. In addition, the words meaning corsair (from mediaeval Latin *cursarius*, derived from *cursus*, raid) seem to have been used more or less synonymously with vernacular words for piracy in Romance languages in mediaeval times.[16] Most Germanic languages, by contrast, developed compound words in the vernacular that literally meant 'sea robbery' (e.g., Germ.

---

[10] de Souza, 'Piracy in Classical Antiquity', 43.   [11] Rubin, *Law of Piracy*, 8.
[12] E.g., ibid., 13; Paige, 'Piracy and Universal Jurisdiction', 134.
[13] For examples, see Weatley, 'Historical Sketch of the Law of Piracy', 540–2.
[14] Guyon, 'Les Coutumes pénales', 341.
[15] Prétou, 'Du "larron écumeur de mer" aux "pirathes"', 40–1.
[16] E.g., Rigaud (ed.), *Pirates et corsaires*, 32.

Seeraub, Dutch *zeerof*, Sw. *sjöröveri*) or 'sea robber' (*Seeräuber, zeerover, sjörövare*) to denote piratical activities or persons.

Toward the end of the Middle Ages, there were thus several, largely synonymous, terms in the European languages that set robbery at sea apart from its counterpart on land. This conceptual framework formed the basis for the subsequent legal, political and intellectual discussions in Europe during the early modern period about the precise definition and limits of piracy, understood broadly as illicit or unauthorized robbery at sea.

Piracy and the European Overseas Expansion

With the consolidation of the principal European states and the onset of European overseas expansion toward the end of the fifteenth century, piracy took on a much greater legal and political significance in Europe compared with earlier centuries. As European sovereigns acquired large fleets of heavily armed vessels capable of projecting their power to distant seas, European kings and queens began to make extensive claims to sovereignty and jurisdiction at sea, both in adjacent maritime zones and – particularly in the case of Spain and Portugal – over vast distant oceans and waterways. Such claims, however, were promptly challenged, not only by other states and commercial competitors, but also by pirates, now understood, in principle, as maritime raiders who operated without the authorisation of a lawful sovereign. With the exception of the Mediterranean, such pirates were, for the most part, of European origin, and although non-European pirates occasionally are mentioned in sixteenth- and seventeenth-century European sources, the pirates that caused by far the most concern for European governments and trading companies came from the same continent.

The operations of early modern European pirates occurred mainly in American, African and Asian waters, where the sea power of European governments was generally weaker than in Europe. The victims were not only European vessels but frequently those of Asian, African or American origin. The lack of sophisticated maritime legislation, both national and international, combined with the widespread use of privateers by European states, also created a vast grey zone between outright piracy and what was considered to be lawful prize-taking.[17]

Meanwhile, in the Mediterranean, piracy and corsairing shaped the commercial and political relations between Europe and the Ottoman Empire and the so-called Barbary States of North Africa (Morocco, Algiers, Tunis and Tripoli) for much of the period, from the second half of the sixteenth until the

---

[17] Rubin, *Law of Piracy*; Benton, 'Legal Spaces of Empire'.

beginning of the nineteenth century. The legal status and character of the Barbary States – particularly with regard to the question of whether they should be understood and treated as lawful political entities or illegitimate piratical nations – was one of the central aspects of the discussions about piracy in early modern Europe and had a great impact on how the European concept of piracy developed.[18]

The global maritime encounters that followed as a result of European expansion had a profound influence on how piracy was understood and defined, not only in Europe but in other parts of the world as well. As Lauren Benton has argued, studying the global legal discourse on piracy is not a question of choosing between, on the one hand, a Eurocentric narrative according to which an international legal community of nation states emerged in seventeenth-century Europe and then spread around the world and, on the other, a narrative that exaggerates the autonomy and resilience of non-European legal orders.[19] Benton instead argues – and demonstrates in her empirical historical work – that it is artificial to separate European from non-European legal cultures and that they should instead be understood as mutually constituting one another.[20]

Overseas expansion led European lawyers and intellectuals to take a great interest in the concept of piracy and its legal and political implications in the contemporary global context. Among the central questions that were debated, sometimes with great intensity, were: how to define piracy; whether there was such a thing as a piratical state or nation and, if so, how one should be treated; who was invested with the authority to define who was a pirate; what difference there was between a pirate, a criminal and a lawful enemy; to what extent piracy was a crime according to natural or positivist law; whether piracy was, or should be, a crime according international or national law (or both); and how far beyond his shores the jurisdiction of a sovereign extended with regard to the right and obligation to suppress piracy.[21]

In grappling with these and other questions, European intellectuals naturally turned to Cicero, whose *De Officiis* was more or less compulsory reading for young European men of the higher classes during the Renaissance. Cicero's discussion of piracy seemed to be of particular relevance in the sixteenth-century context of maritime expansion and the ensuing need to regulate maritime spaces. Jurists such as Pierino Belli and Alberico Gentili tried to find a legal definition of pirates based on Cicero, and toward the end of the century

---

[18] See Kaiser and Calafat, 'Violence, Protection and Commerce'; see also White, *Piracy and Law* for the Ottoman perspective on piracy in the early modern Mediterranean.
[19] Benton, 'Legal Spaces of Empire', 722.   [20] Ibid., 723; cf. 715–16.
[21] See Rubin, *Law of Piracy*, esp. 13–113, for a detailed discussion of these and other questions relating to piracy in early modern Europe.

pirates began to be widely described as the 'enemies of mankind' (*hostis humani generis*), a paraphrase of Cicero's formulation *communis hostis omnium* with approximately the same meaning.[22] Even though jurists continued to debate the exact definitions of piracy in the following century, the notion that pirates were the enemies of mankind was firmly established in European legal treaties and debates from the turn of the seventeenth century.

According to Gentili, the right to define who was a pirate belonged to the sovereign, who was authorised to deploy indiscriminate violence against pirates regardless of where they were found. This doctrine, as has been pointed out by Alfred P. Rubin, put a tool of enormous power in the hands of established sovereigns.[23] It served to legitimise the extension of European claims to sovereignty and jurisdiction overseas and could, combined with superior seapower, be used not just to chase pirates but also to further the commercial and political interests of European states and state-sponsored ventures, such as trading companies, overseas.

The jurisprudence on piracy was also implemented in the laws and regulations of European states and sovereigns. For example, in 1569 England's Queen Elizabeth I proclaimed pirates 'to be out of her protection, and lawfully to be by any person taken, punished, and suppressed with extremity'.[24] The result of this and other proclamations and legal practices that developed in England toward the end of the sixteenth century was that alleged pirates were often summarily executed by hanging in ports around the world.[25] Other European states, such as France and Spain, also passed laws that prohibited piratical activity and prescribed capital punishment for piracy from around the turn of the seventeenth century.[26]

The attempts to outlaw and suppress piracy in early modern Europe, however, did not include privateering, that is, the commissioning of private vessels to attack enemy ships in times of war. This practice was used to varying degrees by European governments throughout the early modern period and contributed unintentionally to condoning piratical activity and to perpetuating a vast legal grey zone in which piracy could be given a quasi-legal status. Privateering also stimulated piracy, as many privateers turned pirates when

---

[22] See ibid., 55 n. 61, on the possible origins of the phrase, which generally is attributed to the English jurist Edward Coke. According to Paige, 'Piracy and Universal Jurisdiction', 136, however, the phrase was coined by Gentili in 1598.
[23] Rubin, *Law of Piracy*, 19–26; cit., 21.   [24] Ibid., 40; Harding, 'Hostis Humani Generis'.
[25] Paige, 'Piracy and Universal Jurisdiction', 135.
[26] In France, an edict issued by Henri IV in 1584 prescribed the death penalty and the breaking of the offender's body on the wheel for robbery at sea, although it seems that the term *piracy* was not used before the seventeenth century; see Mathonnet, 'L'Évolution du droit'; Isambert, *Recueil général*, 575. For Spanish laws relating to 'the corsairs and pirates' (*los cosarios, y piratas*) in the Spanish colonies, dating mainly from the late sixteenth and early seventeenth centuries, see *Recopilación* 2, 64–6.

their commissions expired, leading to cycles of increased piratical activity in the wake of major inter-European wars, such as the Anglo–Spanish War (1585–1604), the Nine Years War (1688–97) and the War of the Spanish Succession (1701–14).[27]

Piratical Imperialism

The legal and intellectual discourse on piracy in Europe was literally a world apart from the reality of maritime encounters in the Indian Ocean and in East and Southeast Asia. Portuguese, Spanish, Dutch, English and French navigators all pursued ruthless policies to further their strategic and commercial interests in these and other eastern waters. With few goods to trade in exchange for the spices, textiles, porcelain, tea and other Asian commodities that Europeans craved, the main competitive advantage of the latter was their superior maritime power. Europeans thus made frequent use of maritime violence and coercion in order to force their will upon Asian sovereigns and communities and to eliminate any commercial competitors, whether European, Asian or African.

Historian Peter Earle has – provocatively, but nonetheless less appropriately – termed such use of maritime violence 'piratical imperialism', thereby highlighting the dubious legality and morality of early modern European maritime expansion in Asia and the Atlantic world. Earle concludes that piratical imperialism was even more apparent in the Indian Ocean than in most other theatres of European maritime expansion at the time, such as the Atlantic, the Caribbean and the Mediterranean.[28] Maritime violence thus reached unprecedented heights in the Indian Ocean in the two centuries that followed on from Vasco da Gama's arrival in India in 1498.[29]

In the early sixteenth century, the Portuguese introduced the infamous system of *cartazes* in the Indian Ocean. These were passes of safe passage issued by the Portuguese authorities, and all Asian ships navigating the Indian Ocean were required to carry a *cartaz* in order to avoid seizure or destruction by the Portuguese vessels that patrolled the ocean's coasts and sea-lanes. Essentially an institutionalised system of plunder and extortion, the policy was justified by a prominent Portuguese historian at the time, João de Barros, with reference to a combination of Portuguese sea power and Christian doctrine:

It is true that there does exist a common right to all to navigate the seas, and in Europe we acknowledge the rights which others hold against us, but this right does not extend

---

[27] Starkey, 'Pirates and Markets', 111; cf. Ritchie, 'Government Measures', 17–19.
[28] Earle, *Pirate Wars*, 111.   [29] Yazdani, *India, Modernity*, 544–5.

beyond Europe, and therefore the Portuguese as lords of the sea by the strength of their fleets are justified in compelling all Moors and Gentiles [heathens] to take out safe-conducts under pain of confiscation and death. The Moors and Gentiles are outside the law of Jesus Christ, which is the true law that everyone has to keep under pain of damnation to eternal fire. If then the soul be so condemned, what right has the body to the privileges of our laws?[30]

Even the possession of a *cartaz*, however, did not guarantee safe passage, and there was significant mistrust on the part of Indian and other Asian merchants with regard to the sincerity of the Portuguese and their willingness to keep their promises not to harm a licensed vessel at sea or in port. Demands for compensation for losses incurred because a ship had been molested despite possessing a valid *cartaz* – either by Portuguese naval vessels or by pirates, including Portuguese and other European freebooters – were generally rejected by the Portuguese on formal or technical grounds.[31] At the same time, plunder and booty were a way for the Portuguese state to pay its sailors, and when a ship was taken there were stipulations as to how large a share each individual was to receive.[32] Such provisions obviously stimulated the use of maritime violence, and in Bengal the memory of the brutality of the Portuguese lives on to this day in ballads about the piratical *harmads*, a word meaning Portuguese, derived from *armada*.[33]

With the arrival in Asia of the Dutch and English around the turn of the seventeenth century, maritime violence in the Indian Ocean, the East and South China Seas, and the Malay Archipelago reached new heights. Both the Dutch and English East India Companies pursued aggressive commercial policies directed at European as well as Asian commercial competitors. The Portuguese *cartazes* did not provide protection from attacks and harassment by the newcomers, and Asian merchants were often required to buy licences from all three maritime powers in order to navigate with some degree of security. On several occasions, moreover, both the English and the Dutch plundered Asian vessels at sea in order to force local rulers to comply with their demands for trading privileges or as compensation for losses allegedly inflicted by Indian officials or subjects.[34] In Southeast Asia, the Dutch East India Company used similar coercive tactics to obtain trading privileges and to establish a monopoly on the production of and trade in spices and other commodities, all to the detriment of indigenous traders and communities.[35]

---

[30] Quoted in Whiteway, *Rise of Portuguese Power*, 21. See also Nambiar, *Kunjalis,* 35–42, for the piratical activities of Vasco da Gama in Indian waters.
[31] Anjum, 'Indian Shipping and Security', 161–2.   [32] Pearson, 'Piracy in Asian Waters', 16.
[33] Subramanian, 'Of Pirates and Potentates', 28–9.
[34] Clulow, 'European Maritime Violence'.
[35] Reid, *Southeast Asia*, 2; see also Crawfurd, *History of the Indian Archipelago*, 3, 219ff.

The legally and morally dubious character of such practices did not go unnoticed by contemporary observers, European as well as Asian. In 1621, for example, a Dutch merchant in Surat, Pieter van den Broecke, worried that the navigators of the Dutch East India Company would be seen in India as 'pirates and worse as sea-rovers' due to their violent maritime practices.[36] His fears seem to have been confirmed by the fact that in the Bengal language the word *olandez* (from Hollanders) came to take on the generic meaning of pirate.[37] Further to the east, Chinese officials likewise often compared the Dutch to *wokou* – a term generally translated into English as pirates – because of the fear and hostility that their actions inspired along the Chinese coast.[38] In Japan, Tokugawa officials also frequently referred to the Dutch as pirates (*bahan*) or robbers (*nusum-ibito*). Such notions were part of the reasons for the adoption of the policy of *sakoku* (closed country) from the 1630s, which for more than two centuries succeeded in limiting the incursions of the Dutch and other European powers in Japan.[39]

The piratical reputation of the English in Asia seems to have been even worse than that of the Dutch. Toward the end of the seventeenth century a common assumption in India was that all European pirates were English and that the English East India Company colluded with them.[40] In part this notion was due to Dutch propaganda, which made out that the English were a 'nation of pirates', but it was also due to the depredations in the Indian Ocean and Red Sea by English pirates and privateers based, for the most part, in the Caribbean or the British colonies in North America. These acts of piracy culminated with the brutal attacks committed by Henry Avery and William Kidd on two Indian ships – the *Gang-i-Sawai* and the *Quedagh Merchant* – in 1695 and 1698, respectively. The attacks caused great anger in India and contributed to forcing the hand of the English government to take measures against the acts of piracy committed in Asian seas by its subjects, many of whom even carried letters of marque issued by the English crown. The English authorities thus took decisive measures from the turn of the eighteenth century, including the strengthening of the Royal Navy, intensified antipiracy operations, particularly in the Indian Ocean and the Caribbean, and the passing of new laws and regulations with regard to piracy, all of which were meant to deal with the problem and to restore England's international reputation and her relations with the Moghul court.[41]

---

[36] Cited in Kempe, '"Even in the Remotest Corners"', 360.
[37] Van Schendel, 'Asian Studies in Amsterdam', 1; see further Yazdani, *India, Modernity*, 532–4, about the background of the Indian perception of European navigators as pirates.
[38] Calanca, 'Wokou', 77.   [39] Clulow, 'European Maritime Violence', 91, n. 2.
[40] Rodger, *Command of the Ocean*, 162; Earle, *Pirate Wars*, 120.   [41] Ibid., 111ff.

In retrospect, the turn of the eighteenth century stands out as a sea-change of global significance, as England swiftly shed its reputation in India and elsewhere as a nation of pirates and instead began to take the lead in the efforts to suppress piracy worldwide. The new policy followed on from the English victories over the Netherlands in the three Anglo-Dutch Wars in the second half of the seventeenth century, which greatly strengthened the naval power of England, thereby giving her increased means by which to suppress piracy overseas.

England also adopted a series of legal positions that in effect extended the jurisdiction of English municipal law to the world's oceans. In 1700 the English Parliament passed an Act for the more Effectual Suppression of Piracy, thereby introducing 'piracy' and 'pirates' as statutory words of art in English law and prescribing severe punishments for pirates. The act expanded the definition of *piracy* compared with earlier laws and authorised the holding of Admiralty Commissions to try pirates outside England, thus disposing of the need to send suspected perpetrators home for trial.[42]

In the early eighteenth century the English government tried to appease the Moghuls and set an example by bringing Kidd and Avery and their crews to justice. The outcome was that Kidd was found guilty of piracy and executed, as were several members of both his crew and that of Avery. Avery, however, managed to evade capture, and his fate after 1696 is unknown. Through the trials, which were closely observed by the Moghul authorities, and the executions, the English government tried to convey the message to India and the world in general — as well as to domestic potential pirates — that they did not condone piracy and that they would do their utmost to exterminate the enemies of mankind, 'even in the remotest Corners of the World', as Leoline Jenkins, a leading judge of the High Court of the Admiralty around that time, put it.[43]

English efforts to suppress piracy were soon eclipsed by the outbreak of the War of the Spanish Succession (1701–14), however. England (and Britain from 1707) and other belligerents recruited large numbers of privateers, many of whom turned pirates after the end of the war, triggering the wave of piracy known as the Golden Age of Atlantic Piracy from around 1714 to 1726. In the face of this surge in piracy, which affected not only the Atlantic but also the western Indian Ocean, the Royal Navy again took the lead in chasing the pirates and managed to put an end to the large-scale European piracy that had accompanied European overseas expansion since the sixteenth century.

The result was that for close to a century, from around 1730 until the end of the Napoleonic Wars in 1815, there was relatively little piratical activity

---

[42] Rubin, *Law of Piracy*, 100–1; see 362–9 for the full text of the statute.
[43] Kempe, '"Even in the Remotest Corners"', 370; Burgess Jr., 'Piracy in the Public Sphere', 894.

perpetrated by Europeans and targeting European shipping around the world.[44] At the same time the levels of maritime violence in the Mediterranean also receded as diplomacy gained more prominence and the Ottoman Navy was centralised and modernised, leaving less opportunity for maritime raiding for Christian as well as Muslim corsairs.[45]

The Rise of the Piratical Paradigm

The fact that there was little piratical activity affecting European shipping between c.1730 and the beginning of the nineteenth century did not mean that Europe's now centuries-old preoccupation with pirates declined. On the contrary, the eighteenth century was crucial for the establishment of what Daniel Heller-Roazen has called the 'piratical paradigm'.[46] Moreover, as we shall see, from the middle of the eighteenth century, European concerns over piratical activities perpetrated by non-Europeans increased, and piracy started increasingly to be seen as a threat to the commerce and security of European colonies and maritime commerce in eastern waters, particularly in Southeast Asia.

The exploits of early modern European pirates and privateers not only attracted the interest of jurists and naval officers charged with the task of suppressing piracy: they also evoked the interest of the general public and gave rise to a popular culture in which pirates were portrayed as both heinous criminals and as daring, romantic or patriotic heroes. Some noted pirates or privateers, such as Francis Drake (c.1540–96) and Henry Morgan (c.1635–88), belonged to the pantheon of English 'noble pirates', as Douglas R. Burgess Jr. puts it, already in their own lifetime, long before the eighteenth century. However, it was in the latter century that many of the stereotypes still associated with pirates in Western popular culture were established, based in part on actual historical events and characters and in part on fictive accounts, sometimes loosely based on authentic events and personalities.

The fate of Henry Avery in the wake of his escape from justice in 1696 is illustrative of how pirates were conceived in the popular imagination in Europe. Although the English authorities wanted Avery to serve as a warning to other would-be pirates, they were unable to effectively counter the heroic image that he acquired among ordinary Englishmen. There was great public interest in the trials of Avery and his crew, and pamphlets summarising the proceedings were printed and circulated in great numbers, both in England

---

[44] On the Golden Age of Atlantic Piracy, see Rediker, *Villains of All Nations*, and on this and the subsequent wave of piracy between 1815 and 1835, see Earle, *Pirate Wars*; Starkey, 'Pirates and Markets'.
[45] White, *Piracy and Law*, 177–9, 268–70. [46] Heller-Roazen, *Enemy of All*, 11.

and in the colonies. The purpose of the pamphlets was to spread the message that piracy would be taken seriously and be severely punished, but many people instead read them as entertaining stories of heroism and adventure. Avery became the subject of poems and ballads, as well as a popular theatre play in London, *The Successful Pyrate*, written by Charles Johnson.[47] William Kidd was romanticised in similar ways, and their personas contributed significantly to the establishment of the classic image of the swashbuckling pirate.[48]

Public fascination with pirates was not limited to England or the British Isles, although they seem to have commanded a particular fascination there. Seventeenth-century French and Dutch buccaneers, such as Robert Chevalier, dit de Beauchêne, and Laurens de Graaf, were also popular figures in their respective home countries, as was the privateer and putative pirate Lars Gatenhielm in Sweden.[49]

Apart from poems, ballads and plays, the stories of the exploits of the most infamous European pirates were disseminated in two purportedly true accounts of the lives and deeds of a number of notorious pirates, both of which came to exercise great influence on the picture of piracy in Europe. The first was Alexandre Exquemelin's book *De Americaensche zee-rovers* (The Buccaneers of America), which was first published in Amsterdam in 1678.[50] Exquemelin had, by his own account, sailed with several of the most famous English and French buccaneers in the Caribbean, including François l'Olonnais and Henry Morgan. The original manuscript for the book seems to have been based on the author's firsthand experiences, but Exquemelin's publisher took the liberty of heavily editing the text and adding several anecdotes and stories to make it more exciting. The book became an instant bestseller and was within a few years translated into German, Spanish, English and French, and was widely read across Europe. Each time the book was published in a new language, it was further edited to suit the different tastes of the respective national audiences, thus further adding to the mythical aura of the main characters in the book.[51]

The second, and in the long run more influential, book was Charles Johnson's *A General History of the Robberies and Murders of the Most Notorious Pyrates*, first published in London in 1724. Like Exquemelin's book, Johnson's *General History* was a great success and was translated into several European languages. The stories and legends of many of the most notorious pirates during the so-called Golden Age of Atlantic Piracy

---

[47] Burgess, 'Piracy in the Public Sphere', 888. Cf. also Netzloff, 'Sir Francis Drake's Ghost'.
[48] Ritchie, *Captain Kidd*, 237–8.
[49] E.g., Bessire, 'Le Beauchêne de Lesage'; Ericson Wolke, *Lasse i Gatan*.
[50] Exquemelin, *Americaensche zee-rovers*.
[51] Konstam and Kean, *Pirates*, 92; see also Ouellet, 'Fiction et réalité'.

are based on Johnson's account, including those of Edward Teach (Blackbeard), Bartholomew Roberts, Samuel Bellamy and Calico Jack Rackham. Unlike Exquemelin, however, there is no indication that Johnson had firsthand experience of the pirates or the piratical communities he described. Whereas some of the individuals and events described in the book can be corroborated by other sources, the author seems to have embellished his stories significantly, and some of the characters are probably entirely fictional.[52]

Building on centuries of legal discussions and reports of the exploits of European pirates around the world, the success and transnational dissemination of Exquemelin's and Johnson's books cemented the common European notion of piracy. This piratical paradigm, which was firmly established by the middle of the eighteenth century, influenced public perceptions of maritime raiding and violence around the world and frequently had a strong impact on policies related to piracy and its suppression, not only in Europe or involving Europeans, but also in other contexts around the world such as those of North Africa, the Persian Gulf, the South China Sea and the Malay Archipelago. Put otherwise, the ideas about pirates and piracy in European culture from the eighteenth century onward meant that any allusion to piracy, regardless of the context, would have particular cultural, as well as legal and political, significance in Europe.

In the context of the piratical paradigm, piracy, as a complex but popular vernacular concept, was associated with, among other things, excessive violence, cruelty, cunning, debauchery, political subversion, social protest, liberty and romance. Pirates could thus on the one hand be seen as monstrous enemies of mankind and on the other as social bandits, in Eric Hobsbawm's sense of the term.[53] Although such social bandits can be found in many cultures around the world, the association between social protest and piracy seems to be peculiar to European culture. Its origins can be traced to the last decades of the seventeenth century and was consolidated in the first half of the eighteenth century. It was further reinforced in the nineteenth and twentieth centuries through fictional as well as nonfictional writings, and through other cultural expressions such as plays, illustrations and films.[54]

The history of piracy and its imagery, as it developed in the course of the early modern period, influenced the understanding of the concept of piracy in complex and heterogeneous ways. When confronted with the spectre of maritime violence in nineteenth-century Southeast Asia, European colonisers and

---

[52] Johnson and Cordingly, *General History*.
[53] Hobsbawm, *Bandits*. Hobsbawm, however, only mentions pirates briefly in his book. Rediker, *Villains of All Nations*, by contrast, pursues the theme at greater length, as does Hill, 'Radical Pirates?'. See also Pennell, 'Introduction', 8–10, for a critical discussion of social banditry in relation to Atlantic piracy.
[54] Turley, *Rum, Sodomy and the Lash*; Moore (ed.), *Pirates and Mutineers*.

observers readily interpreted the situation in terms of the long-standing piratical paradigm as manifested within their respective (European) national and cultural context. In doing so they simultaneously influenced the piratical paradigm, giving rise to new understandings of piracy and maritime violence, linked to maritime commerce, territorial expansion, military power, maritime jurisdiction, race, religion, civilisation and human rights. In some respects, there were common themes in these developments, but in other respects there were significant national and regional differences, both between different colonial powers and between colonies and metropoles. There were also significant differences between different Asian languages and cultures with regard to the laws and norms that defined what was lawful and accepted maritime violence.

Asian and European Concepts of Piracy

Although the term *piracy* may not have a direct equivalent in most Asian languages – except to the extent that the European term has entered the languages in question in modern times – several Asian languages have terms that signify various types of illicit maritime violence. These terms may on the surface seem similar to the European concept of piracy, but they carry connotations that set them more or less apart, both from each other and from European understandings of piracy. European maritime expansion in Asia from the turn of the sixteenth century gave rise to numerous encounters between such concurrent concepts of piracy and other forms of maritime violence, and these encounters were often central to the processes of colonisation, commercial expansion and the suppression of piracy by the colonial powers in maritime Southeast Asia.

Compared with Europe the connotations of the various Asian words translated as 'piracy' in the nineteenth century show a great variety. In many languages the closest approximation to the term *pirate* was a compound word that can be literally translated as 'sea robber', such as the Arabic *liss al-bahr* or the Persian equivalent *duzd darya'i*.[55] Like *pirate*, these terms denoted a person who committed violence at sea outside the context of war and for private gain, in contrast, for example, to a *qursan*, an Arabic term derived from the Italian word *corsale* (corsair), meaning a state licensed privateer.[56]

This distinction between *liss al-bahr* and *qursan* in Arabic resembles the distinction between *pirate* and *privateer* that developed in Europe in the early modern period, and as in Europe there was an obligation according to Muslim law for states to combat pirates and protect shipping in coastal waters. In

---

[55] Risso, 'Cross-Cultural Perceptions', 300; cf. Pearson, 'Piracy in Asian Waters'.
[56] Pelner Cosman and Jones, *Handbook*, 1, 216.

contrast to the Portuguese position, which, as we have seen, only set out to protect Christian (that is, Catholic) shipping, this obligation also included non-Muslim shipping, at least in theory.[57] Arabic concepts of piracy and privateering, like those of European Romance languages, developed mainly in the context of the interaction between Christian and Muslim shipping and maritime warfare in the Mediterranean. Against that background, and against the background of the common influences of Roman law on both Christian and Muslim jurisprudence in the Mediterranean, the similarities between Arabic and European distinctions between legal and illegal maritime violence are not surprising.

The Mandarin words normally used to refer to what Europeans called 'pirates' – *haidao*, *haizei*, *haifei* or *haikou* – literally meant 'sea bandit' but could also be translated as 'sea rebel' or 'sea traitor'. The term *haifei* was particularly condescending, with the suffix *fei* being an absolute negative implying the denial of humanity and the absence of the right of a person so described to exist.[58] Like the European concept of piracy, the Chinese terms could thus have subversive and dehumanising connotations that in some respects were similar to the European understanding of pirates as the enemies of all. The terminology and associations were similar in other countries where Chinese cultural influences were strong, such as in Japan, Korea and Vietnam.[59]

The other common Mandarin term frequently translated into European languages as pirate, *wokou* (Jap. *wakō*; Kor. *waegu*), was also associated with subversion and incursion. The affix *wo* in Mandarin was a derogatory term meaning approximately 'dwarf', which had been used since Han times to describe the Japanese. In China and Korea, thus, *wokou* was associated with Japanese maritime marauders, although the majority of the *wokou* seem in fact to have been Chinese.[60] As in Europe, the labelling of both *wokou* and *haifei* as subversive implied that they were a threat to the social and political order. The problem was thus securitised, which justified the implementation of extraordinary measures to suppress and exterminate the perpetrators.[61] The frequent comparisons by Chinese officials of Europeans to *wokou* should be understood against this background too.

One of the extraordinary measures deployed by both the Ming and Qing Dynasties was the authorising of private vessels to take part in naval warfare in exchange for material rewards, a practice that strongly resembled the European

---

[57] Pearson, 'Piracy in Asian Waters', 19; see further Khalilieh, *Islamic Maritime Law*, 128–48.
[58] Antony, 'Introduction', 7–8. See also Chappell, 'Maritime Raiding', 4–5, for the different Chinese understandings of piracy.
[59] E.g., Antony, 'Introduction', 7; Antony, *Like Froth*, 39; Antony, 'Maritime Violence', 114.
[60] Higgins, 'Japanese Piracy', 261.
[61] Cf. Buzan et al., *Security*, and the discussion in the Introduction above.

practice of privateering during the early modern era. In the sixteenth century, for example, the Ming authorities enlisted both Chinese junk traders and Portuguese merchants based in Macau to fight the *wokou* who ravaged the Chinese coast.[62] Although these measures proved largely inefficient, privateering continued in China throughout the late imperial period. As in Europe, such activities tended to encourage nonauthorised maritime violence in the wake of major conflicts, particularly after the end of the Opium War (1839–42), when many junks that had been enlisted in the war as privateers by the Chinese authorities took to piracy.[63]

Neither was piracy, in the sense of armed robbery at sea or on rivers, an unknown legal category in China before the nineteenth century. In 1727 piratical activities were explicitly outlawed in Chinese law in an article related to 'theft with violence' (*qiangdao*). According to the article, those who committed armed robbery on the Yangtze or at sea were to be executed immediately by decapitation and have their heads exposed in public.[64] For particularly serious acts of piracy, such as those involving the killing of officials or soldiers or attacks against foreign merchant ships, the punishment was to be death by slicing.[65] A substatute enacted in 1740, moreover, listed piracy as one of nine particularly serious crimes for which the courts were not to take into account any mitigating circumstances.[66]

In the Malay Archipelago there were several terms that were normally translated into European languages as piracy. One of the most common was the Malay verb *merampas* (from the root *rampas*), which did not, however, specifically refer to maritime activities. It could be translated as 'to rob' or 'to loot' but also 'to confiscate' or 'to take by law or force'. The word did not carry any inherent illegal or moral connotations, and *merampas* was often seen as a legitimate activity for traditional Malay chiefs and noblemen. The distinction between trading and looting or other forms of securing wealth – such as taxation, extortion, gambling and even magic – seems to have been relatively unimportant and, above all, not a question of morality. Such attitudes were reflected in the traditional Malay chronicles, in which there are no signs of moral repugnance or surprise in relation to maritime raiding.[67] Malay rulers also frequently encouraged young men of high rank to take to raiding, which was regarded as a suitable occupation for a prince of insufficient means, and

---

[62] Wei-chung Cheng, *War, Trade and Piracy*, 15.
[63] Antony, 'Piracy on the South China Coast', 36, 42. [64] Calanca, 'Wokou', 78.
[65] Antony, 'Suppression of Pirates', 98–9.
[66] MacCormack, 'Studies in Traditional Chinese Law', 234. Similar provisions were made in 1780 and 1855; ibid., 236–7. See also Fox, *British Admirals*, 83, about Chinese laws on piracy.
[67] Milner, *Kerajaan*, 19–20.

also had the advantage of relieving the ruler of the obligation to provide for the prince and his followers.[68]

In 1856 the Scotsman John Crawfurd – who was widely regarded as the leading British authority on Malay history and culture in the mid nineteenth century – observed that many Malay princes looked upon piracy as a 'fair and regular branch of their incomes'.[69] Crawfurd also noted the resemblance between the attitude of contemporary Malay sea-rovers and that of the early Greeks, as described by Thucydides. Piracy brought no disgrace to them, the Greek historian claimed, but was rather seen as an honourable vocation that was practised by the leading men in society.[70]

Another similarity between the early Greek and Malay concept of piracy was the association between risk-taking and piracy. Just like the root of the Greek word, *pēr-*, meaning 'to risk or attempt', a euphemism for piracy on the island of Banka was 'to seek one's fortune' (*mencari rezeki*), and a similar association seems to have been central to the understanding of maritime raiding in the Sulu Archipelago.[71]

Such attitudes, however, were not necessarily shared by all Malays, and almost certainly not by the victims of piracy and other forms of maritime violence. The chronicles, like the statements made by Malay chiefs and nobles to colonial officials defending piracy and raiding from a culturally relativist point of view, reflect the warrior ethos of the political and military elites of the traditional Malay world. As such, they should obviously not be taken as representative of Malay attitudes in general, particularly not in view of the considerable cultural variation between different groups of Malays. Many eighteenth- and nineteenth-century sources bear testimony to the horror and destruction that befell the coastal villages throughout much of maritime Southeast Asia due to the depredations of the Iranun, Sama and other maritime raiders emanating from the Sulu Archipelago. Large parts of the coastal regions of Java and Sumatra and other islands were depopulated as villagers abandoned their homes and resettled inland, where the threat of raiding was less immediate. Tales of piratical raids still survive in the oral traditions of many parts of the region today.[72] These circumstances indicate that piracy and other forms of maritime raiding were seen as far from right or just by the majority of the Malay population.

Although it may seem remarkable that there is no mention of illegal maritime robbery in the preserved texts of the Maritime Laws of Melaka

---

[68] B. Andaya, 'Anak Raja', 167.   [69] Crawfurd, *Descriptive Dictionary*, 354.
[70] Ibid., 353–4; cf. Raffles, *Memoir*, 180. For the passage from Thucydides, see *History of the Peloponnesian War*, 1:1 §4.
[71] B. Andaya, 'Anak Raja', 167; Kiefer, *Tausug*, 83–5; cf. Ahmad, *Precious Gift*, 355.
[72] E.g., B. Andaya, *To Live as Brothers*, 225–6; Velthoen, 'Pirates in the Periphery', 215; Warren, *Iranun and Balangingi*; Gaynor, *Intertidal History*.

(compiled between the fifteenth and nineteenth centuries), the Laws of Melaka (first compiled in the mid fifteenth century) did conceptualise illegal attacks on ships and property at sea. The law, for example, established punishments for stealing a ship and then selling or secreting it. However, the punishment – a fine of ten *emas* (gold coins), in addition to returning the value of the ship to the owner – seems relatively mild, particularly in comparison with early modern European and Chinese punishments for piracy.[73] Coastal raids involving the taking of slaves, on the other hand, were deemed to be a more serious crime:

> If a ruler's slave is stolen, the thief must be killed and (all) his property confiscated. Even in the case of a Sea-Captain (committing the theft), the rule is the same. If the slave (stolen) belongs to a high dignitary or the Chief Minister, the thief is also to be killed; likewise, if a Sea Captain is guilty of such an offence, the ruling is the same. If a slave belonging to an ordinary soldier or subject is stolen by a Sea-Captain, the ruling is that he (the Sea-Captain) shall either be killed or be fined 10¼ *tahil*. This is left to the discretion of the judge.[74]

These provisions in the Laws of Melaka demonstrate that there were laws against certain, if not all, forms of maritime raiding in the precolonial Malay world. There were also terms in the Malay language that signified illegal forms of maritime raiding and violence, and they resembled, at least in some respects, European understandings of piracy. The observation that notions of illegal maritime violence were understood in the precolonial Malay world is also corroborated by the studies of Carl A. Trocki and Adrian B. Lapian, both of whom argue that Malays in general recognised a distinction between legitimate and illegitimate peoples and power at sea.[75]

The most common terms in Malay for what Europeans called *pirates* seem to have been *bajak (laut)*, *perompak* and *lanun*.[76] Of these, the term that most closely resembles the English term *pirate* is the first, *bajak laut*, which can be translated as 'sea pirate'. The word seems to have been widely used throughout the Malay Archipelago well before the mid nineteenth century, and, like the European term, *bajak laut* signified unauthorised maritime violence or, in the words of Lapian, 'every kind of violence committed at sea without the sanction

---

[73] Abel, 'Covert War at Sea', 30; Liaw Yock Fang, *Undang-undang Melaka*, 81; cf. Winstedt and De Josselin De Jong, 'Maritime Laws of Malacca'.
[74] Liaw Yock Fang, *Undang-undang Melaka*, 121, 123.
[75] Trocki, *Prince of Pirates*, 69; Lapian, 'Violence and Armed Robbery', 132–7. See also Teitler, *Zeeroof*, 123; Ahmad, *Precious Gift*, 262.
[76] In addition, there are several other words (apart from *lanun*) that at different times and in different parts of the Malay Archipelago have been translated as *pirate*. Most of these referred to certain ethnic groups that engaged in maritime raiding, such as the Maguindanao, Tobelo, Papuans and Tidong; Lapian, 'Violence and Armed Robbery', 134–5; Gaynor, 'Piracy in the Offing', 846–50.

Asian and European Concepts of Piracy

of the local authority'.[77] Although the qualification *laut* (sea) was frequently added, moreover, *bajak* in itself implied an activity occurring at sea or close to the sea, as opposed to terrestrial raiding or violence.[78]

Second, the word *perompak*, from the root *rompak*, also meant 'pirate' and seems to have been largely synonymous with *bajak laut*, that is, meaning raiders operating at sea or close to the sea without the sanction of a legitimate political authority.[79] According to Trocki, *perompak* were groups of sea nomads (*orang laut*) who were not under the authority of a recognised chief. They consisted of 'wanderers and renegades who included hereditary outlaw bands with no fixed abode', as well as 'temporary bands of outlaws under down-on-their-luck rajas and foreign adventurers'. These were illegitimate raiders, distinct from the sea peoples whose patrol activities on behalf of a recognised ruler were seen as legitimate naval operations and part of the Malay political system.[80]

Finally, the word *lanun*, derived from the name Illanun (Iranun), is a contraction of *I-lanaw-en*, a Maguindanao term meaning 'people from the lake'. It was the name given by the lowland Maguindanaos of Mindanao in the southern Philippines to the Maranao-speaking people who migrated to the coast of Illana Bay from their traditional homelands in the highland lake country of Mindanao following a volcanic eruption around 1765. As James Warren has shown, Illanun or Iranun emerged as the name of a distinct ethnic group in the last decades of the eighteenth century and the beginning of the nineteenth century. Although the Iranun were relatively few, they quickly acquired a reputation as formidable maritime raiders, not only in the southern Philippines, but throughout maritime Southeast Asia. In that context, the

---

[77] Lapian, 'Violence and Armed Robbery', 134.

[78] See Tim Penysun Kamus, *Kamus besar Bahasa Indonesia*, s.v. 'bajak' (2), 79, for the contemporary meaning of the word in Indonesian. A Dutch–Malay dictionary from 1841 likewise translates the Dutch word *Zeeroover* as *badjak* (and *orang per-oempak*); de Wilde, *Nederduitsch–Maleisch*, 213. The British naturalist Alfred Russell Wallace, moreover, reported from a visit to Aru in the Eastern Indonesian Archipelago in 1857 that he was alarmed one evening by his hosts crying 'Bajak! bajak!', and although the alarm proved false that time, there were apparently real fears on the part of the Arunese of coastal raids conducted by *bajak-bajak*; see Wallace, *Malay Archipelago*, 502. See further Gaynor, *Intertidal History*, 44–5, 158, for the complicated etymology of the word.

[79] Crawfurd writes that there was no 'name in Malay and Javanese, or indeed in any other native language, for piracy or robbery on the high seas', and says that the usual name for piracy was *perompakan*, from *rompak*, which he claims meant to 'rob or plunder generally'; Crawfurd, *Descriptive Dictionary*, s.v. 'Piracy and Pirate', 353. Crawfurd's claim, however, is contradicted by de Wilde's dictionary, in which the first translation of *Zeeroover* is *per-oempak*; De Wilde, *Nederduitsch–Maleisch*, 213; cf also s.v. 'Roover, struikroover', 133, which is not translated as *perompak*.

[80] Trocki, *Prince of Pirates*, 68. Trocki also notes that the breakdown of central power and legitimate authority in the Riau-Johor Archipelago between 1787 and 1795 meant that everyone was a *perompak*, but that this was an exceptional period in Malay history.

term Illanun and its cognates were, somewhat inaccurately, extended to include not only the Iranun migrant population of Illana Bay, but also the non-Maranao-speaking people of southern Mindanao, as well as Tausug and Sama raiders and navigators of the Sulu Archipelago.[81] By the early nineteenth century the term *lanun*, according to Raffles, had been stretched to become synonymous with 'almost all the sea-rovers of the east'.[82]

Summary

Following the critical discussion of the absolutist and relativist understandings of piracy in the Introduction, this chapter has argued that a cross-cultural study of the concept of piracy can be fruitful as a point of departure for studying maritime violence in colonial Southeast Asia. The question of defining the limits of legitimate maritime violence is something that maritime cultures have had to grapple with throughout history, and there are several terms in Asian languages, including in Arabic, Persian, Bengal, Mandarin, Japanese and Malay, that have been used, to varying degrees, to correspond to the European notion of piracy. However, Europe's strong and long-standing interest in piracy in its various forms stands out as unique in comparison with other cultures.

There seem to have been attempts to conceptualise illicit maritime violence and raiding in Arab, Indian, Malay, Chinese and other non-European languages before the onset of European expansion, but the increased maritime interaction and violence in the Indian Ocean and other Asian seas from the sixteenth century brought the problem to the fore in unprecedented ways. As a consequence, Chinese, Indians and Malays all developed concepts and laws to define and regulate illicit maritime violence. Several contemporary observers also noted that European navigators were frequently seen as pirates, even to the point of being associated with piratical behaviour through generic terms in Asian languages.

These developments took place concurrently with the establishment in Europe of the so-called piratical paradigm, a complex cluster of political ideas, jurisprudence and cultural notions, which was firmly in place by the mid eighteenth century. Although the paradigm has not been static, it has survived in modified form to date, and continues to be reproduced in contemporary popular culture, news media, international law, naval policies and maritime security operations. The establishment of the piratical paradigm was not an autochthonous European development, however. Like Asian notions of

---

[81] Kuder, 'Moros in the Philippines', 123; cf. Warren, *The Sulu Zone, 1768–1898*, 149; Warren, *Iranun and Balangingi*.
[82] Raffles, *Memoir*, 45; published in 1830, the report was written in 1811.

illegitimate maritime violence, the European concept of piracy was shaped by the global maritime interaction in the early modern era.

The concept of piracy only makes sense in relation to states and their claim to have a monopoly on legitimate violence, but state attitudes toward piracy have varied greatly throughout history, ranging from open sponsorship to violent opposition and suppression.[83] In the course of the early modern period, European states and trading companies moved gradually from perpetrating acts of piracy and other forms of illicit maritime violence in Asian (and other) waters to policies of suppression and nontolerance of piracy and maritime raiding. However, regardless of whether European navigators used their superior sea power to perpetrate acts of extortion, piracy and maritime raiding, or to suppress such activities undertaken by Asians or other Europeans, their deployment of maritime violence in Asia was always used to their own advantage, commercially and politically. This observation is valid with regard to the entire history of European maritime expansion and colonisation in Asia, even as England, from the turn of the eighteenth century, shifted from being widely seen as an infamous 'nation of pirates' to take the lead in the global fight against piracy, with other European nations following suit. For England and other European nations in the early modern era and later, both the perpetration of piratical activities and their suppression served to further their commercial and political interests in Asia and elsewhere around the world.

---

[83] Eklöf Amirell and Müller, 'Introduction', 12–16.

2 The Sulu Sea

Of the three regions under study here, the Sulu Sea was the most strongly associated with piracy in the eyes of nineteenth-century observers. The raiders from Sulu were also, for good reason, the most feared by the coastal populations of Southeast Asia, who comprised by far most of the victims of the depredations.

Maritime raiding in the Philippines predated the first Spanish incursions in the region in the sixteenth century but was aggravated by the protracted conflict between the Spanish colonisers and the Muslims of the southern Philippines from 1565 to 1898, as well as by the region's integration into the global commercial systems of the early modern period and the influx of European firearms to the region. All of these factors initially served to strengthen the two major powers of the southern Philippines, the Sultanate of Maguindanao and – particularly from the second half of the eighteenth century – the Sulu Sultanate. Spain never managed to assert authority over the southern Philippines, and effective imperial control over the region was established only by the US Army after a series of bloody campaigns at the beginning of the twentieth century. Throughout the three and half centuries of conflicts between the Spanish and the populations of the southern Philippines, maritime raiding played a key role, not only for the accumulation of wealth and slaves, but also as a means of warfare and anticolonial resistance.

Piracy, Raiding and the Moro Wars

With few exceptions, relations between the Spanish colonisers in the northern Philippines and the predominantly Muslim population of the southern parts of the archipelago were characterised by hostility and mutual detestation and distrust. The Muslims fiercely resisted Spanish attempts to convert them to Christianity and to take control over their lands and waters. For close to three centuries, until the mid nineteenth century, this resistance effectively checked Spanish colonial ambitions in the southern Philippines.

The Spanish interpreted their protracted struggle with the Muslims in the south by analogy with the *Reconquista*, the effort of the Christian Iberian

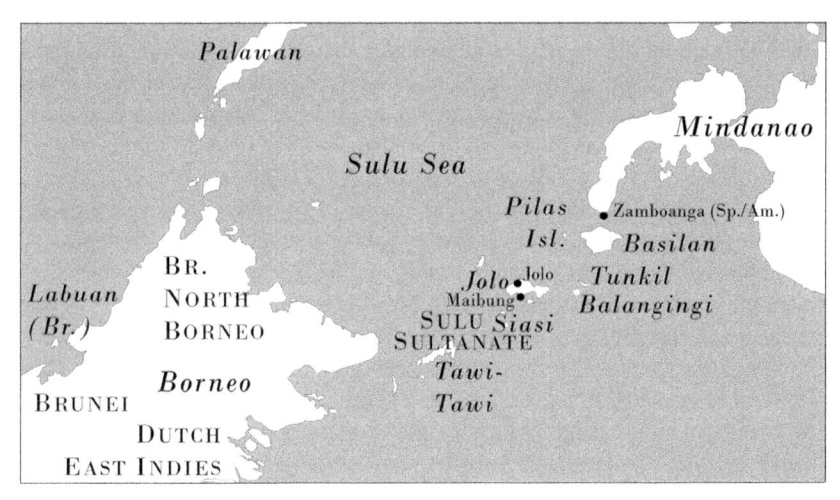

Map 2: The Sulu Sea

kingdoms to expel Muslims from the Iberian Peninsula from the eleventh to the fifteenth centuries. The Spanish consequently labelled their Muslim adversaries in the Philippines 'Moros', a condescending term for Muslims derived from the Mediterranean and Iberian context. From the point of view of the Spanish, and to some extent also from the point of view of the Moros, the protracted conflict was interpreted as part of a long-standing global struggle between Christianity and Islam.[1] In the course of this struggle, and as a result of increased contacts with the wider world from the sixteenth to the nineteenth centuries, the Muslim identity of the Moros was strengthened, largely in opposition to the Spanish incursions and their attempts to propagate the Christian faith.[2]

The religious dimension was thus at the heart of the so-called Moro Wars, a series of wars and hostilities fought with varying intensity throughout the Spanish colonial period in the Philippines from 1565 to 1899. In the context of these wars maritime raiding, including attacks on the enemy's commercial vessels and coastal raids for the purpose of taking slaves and booty, and as a means of reprisal, was undertaken by both parties. As the Moros generally lacked the strength and concentration of sea power to combat the Spanish

---

[1] Majul, *Muslims in the Philippines*, esp. 39–88; Hawkley, 'Reviving the Reconquista'. The term *Moro* is no longer regarded as condescending, as demonstrated by the inclusion of the term in the name of the two leading secessionist movements in the southern Philippines since the 1970s, the Moro National Liberation Front and the Moro Islamic Liberation Front.

[2] Federspiel, 'Islam and Muslims', 340–1; see further Majul, *Muslims in the Philippines*.

naval vessels or troops directly, Moro warfare principally took the form of maritime raiding, focusing on soft targets, such as Christian Filipino seafarers and coastal populations. Although material gain, principally in the form of human captives, was an important aspect of the raids, they should thus not be understood primarily as motivated by private gain, but as a part of the religious and political war that the Moros fought against the Spanish.[3]

Such an understanding of maritime raiding in the Philippines in the early modern period is probably close to how the Spanish colonisers interpreted the phenomenon during their first two centuries in the archipelago. As we have seen, maritime raiding was frequently used as a means of warfare in the European context, and the raiding of enemy vessels and settlements was a regular part of European wars at sea.[4] The boundaries between pirates and privateers were also far from clear-cut in European legal and political doctrine. For example, in the Spanish Laws of the Indies, which was first compiled in the seventeenth century, the terms *pirates* (*piratas*) and *privateers* (*corsarios*) were used interchangeably.[5]

Maritime violence in the context of the Moro Wars thus included Spanish raids on the coasts and islands of the southern Philippines. In the middle of the eighteenth century, for example, the Spanish governor in Manila authorised the use of privateers to capture and enslave all Sulu men, women and children who could be seized, and to confiscate or destroy their property.[6]

Allegations of piracy were at times used by the Spanish against the Muslims of the southern Philippines and north Borneo (particularly Brunei) from the earliest days of the Spanish colonial period, but it was not a principal reason for the onset of the Moro Wars, nor a prominent part of Spanish discourse about the Moros during the first two hundred years of the Spanish presence in the Philippines.[7] To the extent that the terms *pirate* (*pirata*) or *privateer* (*corsario*), or their cognates, are mentioned in the digitized records of the Audiencia de Filipinas from the late sixteenth to the middle of the eighteenth centuries, they deal above all with European or Chinese navigators whose activities were deemed to be illegal by the Spanish colonisers.[8] Maritime

---

[3] Ibid., esp. 121–89; Scott, *Slavery in the Spanish Philippines*, 54.
[4] E.g., Glete, *Warfare at Sea*; Starkey, van Eyck, van Hesling and de Moor, *Pirates and Privateers*.
[5] *Recopilación*, 64–6. On the early 'antipiracy' campaigns of the Spanish, see Mallari, 'Spanish Navy in the Philippines'.
[6] Majul, *Muslims in the Philippines*, 281; Bando del gobernor de Filipinas, in Montero y Vidal, *Historia de la piratería*, 2, Appendices, 29–31. According to Montero y Vidal, 299, the order was illegal because slavery was not permitted in the Philippines according to Spanish law; cf. Scott, *Slavery in the Spanish Philippines*, who discusses several ambiguities in relation to the Spanish laws on slavery and their implementation in the Philippines.
[7] Saleeby, *History of Sulu*, 168–71.
[8] Website of the Portal de Archivos Españoles (PARES), searches for *corsario*, *pirata* and *piratería* in the Archivos General de Indias, Audiencia de Filipinas between 1565 and 1800, rendering 46, 14 and 3 hits, respectively (30 March 2017).

violence emanating from the southern Philippines, by contrast, was not for the most part labelled piracy or even raiding, but simply described as attacks by enemies from various islands outside the control of the Spanish, such as Borneo, Ternate, Sangir, Jolo and Mindanao.[9]

In the second half of the eighteenth century a shift in the pattern of maritime violence emanating from the southern Philippines occurred as raids conducted by certain ethnic groups in the region, particularly Iranun and Sama, increased, and Sulu overtook Maguindanao as the principal centre for slave raiding.[10] The surge in slave raiding was associated with the increase in the China trade from the eighteenth century, which gave rise to a great demand for natural products from the Sulu Archipelago and other parts of the Malay Archipelago. The much sought-after products from the southern Philippines and eastern Indonesia included pearls, mother-of-pearl, sea cucumber, wax, bird's nests, shark fins and tortoise shells, all of which were exported in exchange for textiles, opium and firearms. The Sulu Sultanate was strategically located to benefit from the trade boom, and Jolo emerged toward the end of the eighteenth century as an important market for both slaves and natural products and other commodities. The main sponsors and beneficiaries of the slave raids were the *datus* (chiefs or headmen) of the Sulu Sultanate, who used part of the income from the bourgeoning trade to equip ever larger and well-armed raiding expeditions. With the integration of the slave- and raid-based economy of the Sulu Archipelago in the global commercial system during the second half of the eighteenth century, the Sulu Sultanate prospered and overtook Maguindanao as the major Muslim power in the region.[11]

From the second half of the eighteenth century the label *piracy* began to be used more frequently by Spanish officials to describe Moro raiding, and the efforts to contain or suppress such activities were stepped up.[12] In 1754 the governor-general of the Philippines, Marquis Francisco José de Ovando, proposed the conquest of Jolo and Mindanao in order to put an end to the 'piracy and grave evils' (*piratería y gravísimos males*) that the Moros from these islands visited upon the Spanish colony every year.[13] When peace was negotiated between Spain and the sultan of Sulu later the same year, moreover, the latter promised to punish any of his subjects who carried out

---

[9] Scott, *Slavery in the Spanish Philippines*, 53.
[10] Warren, 'Moro Wars', 40; see further Warren, *Iranun and Balangingi*, 25–40.
[11] Warren, *The Sulu Zone, 1768–1898*.
[12] Cf. Vlekke, *Nusantara*, 198, according to whom Europeans only began to distinguish between indigenous pirates and honest traders in the Malay Archipelago in the eighteenth century, whereas they had not made the same distinction in the sixteenth and seventeenth centuries.
[13] Carta del marqués de Ovando sobre necesidades para la conquista de Joló y Mindanao, 1753–55, ES.41091.AGI/23.6.277//FILIPINAS,385,N.25, Archivo General de Indias (PARES).

raids against the Spanish territories, although the actual word *piracy* (*piratería*) or any of its cognates were not mentioned in the Spanish treaty text.[14]

The treaty notwithstanding, maritime raiding emanating from the southern Philippines continued and increased during the last decades of the eighteenth century, driven, ironically, in part by Spanish efforts to develop the commerce of the colony.[15] The beginning of the nineteenth century created further opportunities for maritime raiding in Southeast Asia, in part because of the decline of European naval power in Southeast Asia during the Napoleonic Wars. Iranun and Sama raiders formed large bands who undertook annual raiding expeditions, not only to the Spanish colony in the northern Philippines, but also to the Dutch East Indies, the Strait of Malacca and north Borneo. In the Philippines, the raiders ventured as far north as Luzon and even conducted raids close to the centre of Spanish power in the region, in Manila Bay, carrying off hundreds and sometimes thousands of slaves from different parts of the Spanish colony every year. The Spanish sent several punitive expeditions to the Sulu Archipelago and tried to enforce a blockade on Sulu's trade with China and Manila, but despite the damage occasionally inflicted on the Iranun, Sama and other groups involved in the raids by Spanish naval forces, they were unable to put an end to the depredations.[16]

The increase in Sulu raiding coincided with greater commercial interest in the region, not only on the part of the Spanish, but also of the British and Dutch, all of whom saw the raids as a serious impediment to their commercial and territorial interests. The problem of maritime security thus took on a new importance, and the Sulu Sultanate was identified as a pirate state and the major sponsor of the raids. The term *Moro*, which for more than two hundred years had been used pejoratively by the Spanish, also came to be understood by Europeans in the region as more or less synonymous with *pirate*. The Spanish now consistently began to describe Moro raiding as piracy, and they often linked the practice to the influence of Islam, as well as to ethnic or racial deficiencies associated with the Moros.[17]

Such notions were not unique to the Spanish but were frequently expressed by other European observers as well. However, against the background of the protracted Moro Wars, the association between piracy and Islam seems to have been more emphasised by Spanish observers and officials than by their British and Dutch counterparts. Proselytisation among the Moros was at times promoted by Spanish colonial officials as a means of weaning the Moros

---

[14] Majul, *Muslims in the Philippines*, 284–5; for the original Spanish text of the treaty, see Montero y Vidal, *Historia de la piratería* 2, Appendices, 31–3.
[15] Scott, *Slavery in the Spanish Philippines*, 56. [16] Warren, *Iranun and Balangingi*, 86–123.
[17] Ibid., 23; Frake, 'Genesis of Kinds of People', 314–15.

from their piratical habits, although such efforts were on the whole unsuccessful.[18]

In the 1820s, several naval expeditions were dispatched by the Spanish to the Sulu Archipelago and Mindanao with the aim of destroying the mainland bases and vessels of the raiders. The expeditions, however, proved largely inefficient due to the limited naval power of the Spanish. The authorities in Manila then changed their tactics – partly also in response to the increased interest in the region shown by other colonial powers – and began instead to encourage more friendly commercial relations with the Sulu Sultanate. In 1836 two treaties were signed between Spain and the Sultanate, a commercial treaty and a treaty of friendship and alliance. The purpose of the first treaty was to discourage the Moros from engaging in piratical activity, or at least to make them refrain from attacking Spanish shipping and territory, and to encourage them to take up more peaceful pursuits. The main purpose of the second treaty was to keep other European powers from gaining a foothold in the region. In particular, the Spanish worried that Great Britain or the Netherlands might try to extend their influence in the East Indies to the Sulu Archipelago if the piratical incursions from the area were allowed to continue unchecked.[19] The risk of intervention by other European countries was demonstrated in 1845, when France made an attempt to acquire the island of Basilan from the sultan of Sulu. The venture was abandoned only after King Louis Philippe rejected the proposition in order to maintain good relations in Europe with Spain.[20] The incident seemed to display Spain's weak control over the southern Philippines, but even more worrying for the Spanish were the British designs on Sulu, particularly in view of Great Britain's superior naval strength, the British advances in north Borneo in the 1840s and the interest that the British had shown in the Sulu Sea since the eighteenth century.[21]

These developments, combined with the fact that the annual maritime raids emanating from the Sulu Sultanate continued more or less unchecked, cast doubts on Spain's claim to sovereignty over the southern Philippines. As Janice E. Thomson has shown, a fundamental requirement for the acknowledgement of sovereignty in the international context since the nineteenth century has been that the sovereign is able to control extraterritorial violence emanating from his or her territory.[22] In order to enforce her claim to the Philippine Archipelago, Spain thus had to put an end to the piratical depredations of the Sulu raiders. For the first time in history, moreover, Spain began to acquire the naval strength to do so, largely because of the arrival of steam navigation.

---

[18] Cf. Majul, *Muslims in the Philippines*, 321.   [19] Ibid., 318–19.
[20] Nardin, 'Français à Basilan'.   [21] Tarling, *Sulu and Sabah*, 9–44.
[22] Thomson, *Mercenaries, Pirates and Sovereigns*.

The Suppression of Piracy in Sulu

In 1848 a large Spanish naval expedition, which included three English-built steamboats, attacked and destroyed the Sama settlement on the island of Balangingi in the Sulu Archipelago, which was considered by the Europeans in the region to be the most formidable pirate base in the Malay Archipelago. On the eve of the attack, the island had a population of some 10,000 people, most of whom were engaged directly or indirectly in maritime raiding, and a fleet of 200 *prahus* (traditional Malay outrigger boats). The attack resulted in the death of more than 450 Sama raiders, along with some 200 women and children. Those who survived – apart from those who escaped or were out on raiding expeditions at the time of the attack – were deported to the Cagayan Valley in northern Luzon, where they were to be turned into farmers. The Spanish also took measures to prevent the Sama from re-establishing themselves on Balangingi by destroying 4 forts, 7 villages, 150 vessels and thousands of coconut trees, thereby making the island unfit for habitation for many years to come.[23]

The destruction of Balangingi signalled the beginning of the end of the great raiding expeditions emanating from the Sulu Archipelago and other parts of the southern Philippines. In contrast to most earlier Spanish attempts to put an end to the maritime raiding emanating from Sulu, the attack had the desired effect of bringing about a drastic decline in slave raiding. As in other parts of Southeast Asia at the time, the main reason for the newly found strength of the colonial navies vis-à-vis the raiders was the arrival of steam gunboats, combined with improved intelligence about the composition, location and *modus operandi* of the perpetrators.

The victory strengthened the position of the Spanish in the southern Philippines, but it failed to remove the threat of other colonial powers gaining a foothold in the region. The main threat to Spanish hegemony in the southern Philippines came from the two neighbouring colonial powers, the British and the Dutch, both of whom seemed determined to increase their commercial activities and political influence in the Sulu Archipelago. In 1849 rumours of an impending Dutch attempt to take possession of north Borneo and Sulu prompted James Brooke – a British soldier and adventurer, who in 1841 had been installed by the sultan of Brunei as Raja of Sarawak in north Borneo – to sail to Jolo and negotiate a treaty of friendship and commerce with Sultan Muhammad Fadl Pulalun (r. 1844–62). The destruction of Balangingi the year

---

[23] Warren, 'Balangingi Samal', 46–7, 49, 54; Warren, *The Sulu Zone, 1768–1898*, 192; see also Majul, *Muslims in the Philippines*, 324–7; Warren, *Iranun and Balangingi*, 343–78. A Sulu chief, Datu Tampang, nonetheless tried to establish himself and constructed a fort at Balangingi in December 1848, but was dislodged by the Spanish; Saleeby, *History of Sulu*, 204.

before had convinced the Sultan and the majority of the Sulu nobility of the necessity of rapprochement with Great Britain in order to counter the Spanish assaults. The result was that a treaty was signed in which the Sultan, among other things, agreed to do all in his power to suppress piracy and not to harbour or protect any persons or vessels engaged in piratical activities. Controversially from the Spanish point of view, the Sultan also agreed not to cede any portion of his territory to a foreign power or to acknowledge the sovereignty of any other power without the consent of Great Britain.[24]

The news of the treaty was received with alarm in Manila. The Spanish claimed that it violated the treaty between Spain and Sulu from 1836, according to which Sultan Pulalun's predecessor had pledged not to enter into an alliance with a foreign power without the consent of Spain. The Brooke treaty was ratified by the British Parliament shortly after its conclusion, but the ratifications were not exchanged, and therefore the treaty did not formally come into force, and the British government did not pursue the issue for fear of provoking an open conflict with Spain. However, the unclear status of Sulu continued to poison relations between Britain and Spain for several decades, and hampered any initiatives to cooperate in the efforts to suppress maritime raiding emanating from the region.[25]

The Brooke treaty, combined with Spain's greatly improved naval strength, triggered further Spanish interventions in Sulu. The destruction of Balangingi in 1848 had brought about a decline in large-scale organised raiding, and between 1848 and 1851 there were few reported slave raids in the Philippines. Piratical activity emanating from Sulu and affecting the Dutch East Indies also declined substantially in the years after 1848.[26]

These circumstances notwithstanding, allegations of piracy continued to be used as a justification for further Spanish advances in the southern Philippines. The reputation that Sulu had by now acquired as a hotbed of piracy and slavery made the charges seem credible to other European powers, regardless of their actual substance.[27] Piratical activity, moreover, continued, with smaller raids emanating from various other parts of the Sulu Archipelago, including the small islands of Tunkil, Bukutua and Bulan. To the colonial authorities, these raids provided a pretext not only for wiping out the alleged pirate bases on these islands, but also for attacking Jolo, the capital of the Sulu Sultanate located on the north coast of the island with the same name. The purpose was to enforce the Spanish claim to sovereignty over the Sultanate and to take control over its trade.[28] In justifying the attack, the Spanish, among other

---

[24] Warren, *The Sulu Zone, 1768–1898*, 104–5; see ibid., 283–4 for the full text of the treaty.
[25] Ibid., 104–5; see further Tarling, *Sulu and Sabah*, 52–94.
[26] Warren, *The Sulu Zone, 1768–1898*, 193–4.
[27] Majul, *Muslims in the Philippines*, 330–2. [28] Warren, *The Sulu Zone, 1768–1898*, 105.

wrongdoings, pointed to the robbery, desolation, death and slavery that the Sulu pirates throughout history had visited upon the population of the Spanish islands.[29] In the context of Europe's piratical paradigm, such rhetoric served to place the sultan and his subjects among the generic enemies of mankind and make them liable to subjugation and destruction.

In December 1850 the governor of the Philippines, Don Antonio Urbiztondo, left Manila in command of a naval expedition that proceeded first to Zamboanga and then to the Sulu Archipelago, where they visited several islands, burning houses and vessels and killing several people. Upon arrival in the Sulu capital at Jolo the expedition was met with hostility and failed to obtain any concessions from the sultan. As Urbiztondo estimated that he did not have the strength to invade the fortified capital, he sailed for Tunkil, where Spanish troops conducted a raid that left twenty-five Moros dead. They also burnt down 1,000 houses and destroyed 106 boats before the expedition returned to Zamboanga.[30]

Early the following year the Spanish returned to Jolo with a heavily reinforced expedition, which now consisted of a corvette, a brigantine, three steamboats, two gunboats, nine tenders, nine transports and twenty-one smaller sailing boats (*barangay*), carrying altogether around four thousand regular and voluntary troops. Despite fierce resistance on the part of the Joloanos, the Spanish captured the town in a battle that lasted two days and left around three hundred Moros and thirty-six Spanish troops dead. The rest of the population fled, and the town was burnt to ashes. Having thus accomplished their aim of destroying the Sulu capital, the Spanish left without leaving a garrison on the island. The Joloanos promptly returned to the site of the battle and started to rebuild the capital.[31]

In April 1851 a treaty between the sultan and the Spanish was signed, according to which the sultan – at least in the Spanish text of the treaty – recognised Spanish sovereignty over the Sulu Sultanate and its dependencies and, among other things, agreed to allow the Spanish to establish a trading factory and a naval station on Jolo.[32] Neither of the signatories upheld the provisions of the treaty, however, and as Najeeb Saleeby has observed, it did not receive as much attention in Jolo as it did in Madrid or London. The Spanish and Tausug texts of the treaty also differed significantly, a circumstance that Saleeby – based on his close examination of both versions of the treaty – put down to the interpreters' insufficient knowledge of the Tausug language.[33] It seems likely, however, that certain words and passages

---

[29] Ayala, *Discurso*, 8.   [30] Saleeby, *History of Sulu*, 204, 206–7.   [31] Ibid., 208.
[32] Ibid., 205–14, where English translations of the treaty (from both the Spanish and Sulu texts) are given; Warren, *The Sulu Zone 1768–1898*, 105–6.
[33] Saleeby, *History of Sulu*, 214, 209.

that no doubt would have been difficult to accept for the sultan and the leading *datus* of Sulu were deliberately omitted from the Tausug version of the treaty. In particular, this seems to have been the case with regard to Article 3, where Spain's rights over the entire Sulu Archipelago were described in the Spanish treaty text as 'ancient and indispensable' (*antiguos é indispensables*), a phrase that was omitted from the Tausug text.[34] British sources from the years following the signing of the treaty also indicate that the sultan did not think that he had surrendered his sovereignty over Sulu to the Spanish.[35]

The 1851 treaty also contained an article dealing with the suppression of piracy, but there were differences in the Sulu and Spanish versions in this respect as well. Article 4 of the treaty text in Sulu, as translated into English by Saleeby, read:

New promise: Pirates shall not be allowed at all here in Sulu. Should they commit any crime they shall be punished wherever they may be.[36]

The corresponding article in Spanish, by contrast, was more exhaustive:

They [the Sultan and *datus*] renew the solemn promise not to carry on piracy or allow anybody to carry on piracy within the dominions of Sulu, and to run down those who follow this infamous calling, declaring themselves enemies of all islands that are enemies of Spain and allies of her friends.[37]

The reference to a renewed promise in the Spanish (but not in the Tausug) text of the treaty referred to the 1836 Treaty of Peace, Protection and Commerce, according to which Spain and Sulu offered mutual protection for the vessels of the other country in its waters and territories. Article 5 of that treaty read:

The Sultan and Datus of Sulu pledge themselves to prevent the piracies of the Ilanuns [Iranuns] and Samals in the Philippines, and if they are unable, the Sultan shall so report in order that the Spanish Government may afford assistance or undertake the task alone.[38]

The 1851 treaty thus extended the promise of the sultan to suppress piracy to include not only the raids of the Iranun and Sama against the Spanish colony, but also any form of piracy emanating from Sulu, without limitation in terms of location or ethnicity of the perpetrators. In contrast to the formulation in the treaty from 1836, the Spanish text of the 1851 treaty clearly resonated with the

---

[34] Ibid., 210, 213; Spanish text from Montero y Vidal, *Historia de la piratería*, 2, Appendices, 54, where the Spanish text of the treaty is rendered.
[35] Earl of Derby to Lord Odo Russell, 17 January 1876, in *Philippine Claim to North Borneo*, 1, 25.
[36] Saleeby, *History of Sulu*, 213.
[37] Ibid., 210; for the original Spanish text, see Montero y Vidal, *Historia de la piratería*, 2, Appendices, 54.
[38] Saleeby, *History of Sulu*, 198; transl. by Saleeby from the Spanish text of the treaty.

European understanding of pirates as the enemies of mankind. In that sense the treaty served as a signal to other colonial powers that Spain was committed to the suppression of piracy emanating from its territory and affecting the neighbouring British and Dutch colonies.

Traditionally, Sulu noblemen had a radically different understanding of piracy from that of the Spanish, particularly as formulated in the treaty of 1851. Before the destruction of Balangingi in 1848, the Sultan and *datus* of Sulu had thrived on the slave raids conducted by the Iranun and Sama but sponsored by the Tausug *datus*. Not only did the Sulu nobility regard raiding as a legitimate and potentially honourable activity, it also formed the basis for the economic prosperity and political power of the Sulu Sultanate, and the slaves and material wealth that the raids brought enhanced the power and social status of the nobility. As James Warren has shown, the raiding economy of the Sulu Sultanate flourished from the last decades of the eighteenth century largely as a result of the region's integration into the global capitalist economy, but raiding and slavery had a long history, not only in the southern Philippines but also throughout the archipelago.[39]

From the 1840s, however, the system began to decline. The Sulu Sultanate came under pressure to end its sponsorship of maritime raiding, not only from the Spanish but also from the British and Dutch. The British, for example, attacked Jolo in 1846, and a couple of years later the Dutch utterly destroyed by fire a portion of the town, which was built on piles in the sea.[40] The most serious blow to the raiding system was the destruction of Balangingi by the Spanish in 1848, and subsequent Spanish naval expeditions and attacks seemed to indicate that the system was coming to an end.

In response to these developments the Sulu Sultanate began to reorient its economy from an emphasis on raiding to trade. The latter had all along been an important foundation for the Sultanate, but the Spanish onslaught made the promotion of trade, particularly with the British in north Borneo, more important. From the second half of the 1840s Sultan Fadl Pulalun began, at least superficially, to distance himself from the Iranun and Sama raiders and declare his commitment to the suppression of piracy. The sultan was aware of the Spanish intention to use accusations of piracy as a pretext for waging war on his country and to assert Spanish sovereignty over Sulu. In order to avert the Spanish threat, the sultan sent his brother to negotiate with Manila, and he tried to placate the Spanish by banning the Iranun and Sama raiders from bringing their captives to his capital at Jolo.[41] In the wake of the destruction of

---

[39] E.g., Warren, *The Sulu Zone, 1768–1898*; Junker, *Raiding, Trading, and Feasting*; Scott, *Slavery in the Spanish Philippines*, 50–2. See also Jansen, 'Aanteekeningen'.
[40] St John, *Life of Sir James Brooke*, 150; Teitler et al., *Zeeroof*, 284.
[41] Majul, *Muslims of the Philippines*, 338; Warren, 'Port of Jolo', 185. The sultan nonetheless maintained contacts with the Iranun and plotted to attack Spanish interests in the southern Philippines; ibid., 185–6.

Balangingi, moreover, the sultan and the leading headmen of Sulu rejected proposals from one of the Sama chiefs who had escaped the Spanish attack, Panglima Julano Taupan, to attack to the Spanish in order to liberate the prisoners from the raid on Balangingi.[42]

The Spanish obviously did not believe – and probably did not want to believe – that the sultan and his followers were committed to the suppression of piracy. The British, however, were of a different opinion. According to Henry Keppel, the Royal Navy officer who commanded the frigate *Maeander*, which carried James Brooke on a visit to Jolo in 1849, the sultan was sincere in his wish to cooperate with the colonial navies in the suppression of piracy, but he was hampered in his efforts by Spanish aggression:

> The Sultan, under the influence and counsel of the Rajah of Sarāwak [James Brooke], had become opposed to piracy, and anxious for its suppression. His fortified position gave him weight, which he had frequently thrown into the scale of humanity: and it must now be feared that many, whom he was able to hold in check, will again follow their evil propensities unrestrained, as they did under previous dynasties.[43]

The reason for the military weakness of the sultan was to some extent due to the Spanish attacks, but the Sulu Sultanate was also a segmentary state, in which the political influence of the sultan depended on his ability to form strategic alliances and enlist the support of the leading *datus* and other influential groups.[44] On his own, thus, the sultan could only muster a small armed force, and he had few means by which to impose his authority in the remote parts of the Sulu Archipelago. The naval attacks, not only by the Spanish but also by the British and Dutch, contributed to weaken whatever power the sultan previously had to restrain the raiders dispersed around the archipelago, regardless of his level of commitment to do so.[45]

Imperial Rivalry

The Spanish victory at Balangingi in 1848 had broken the back of the large raiding expeditions emanating from Sulu, but it did not put an end to piratical activity. At the time of the attack more than half of the male population had been out on raids, and hundreds of others managed to escape. Many of those who were thus displaced by the Spanish destruction of Balangingi and other naval campaigns around the middle of the nineteenth century took refuge in the borderlands between the Sulu Sultanate and the British, Dutch and Spanish

---

[42] Warren, 'Balangingi Samal', 55.
[43] Keppel, *Visit to the Indian Archipelago* 1, 58; cf. Tarling, *Sulu and Sabah*, 83–4.
[44] For the political system of the Sulu Sultanate and the concept of 'segmentary state' in that context, see Kiefer, 'Tausug Polity'; cf. Majul, *Muslims in the Philippines*, 377–402.
[45] Keppel, *Visit to the Indian Archipelago*, 1, 58.

colonies, where colonial naval power and political control were weak and hampered by imperial rivalry. The borderland region included the western parts of the Sulu Archipelago, south Palawan, northeast Borneo and the eastern islands of the Dutch East Indies, including Sulawesi, the Moluccas and Flores. From their new bases the raiders continued to harass maritime traffic and neighbouring coastal settlements, albeit generally on a smaller scale than before.[46]

In the aftermath of the destruction of Balangingi in 1848, the Sama chief Julano Taupan first continued to lead raids on trading boats and to conduct raids on the coasts of Samar and Leyte to the north of Mindanao. Followed by some of the most militant of the survivors from Balangingi, Taupan settled in Tawi-Tawi, a group of small islands located in the western part of the Sulu Archipelago. From 1852 Taupan's band scaled up their depredations, and they triggered a 'general sea war', as James Warren put it, which for six years affected the region, costing the Spanish colonial government large sums of money and resulting in many casualties, both on the side of the victims – most of whom were Filipinos, as well as coastal populations and seafarers in the Dutch East Indies and north Borneo – and on the side of the raiders.[47] Taupan's followers became known in European sources as 'Tawi-Tawi pirates', and at times they joined forces with Sama and Iranun raiders from other parts of the Sulu Archipelago. In doing so they were occasionally able to assemble fleets of between sixty and one hundred *prahus*.[48] The depredations were facilitated by the decrease in antipiracy operations by the British Navy in the region following criticism in London of the brutality of the operations, which often resulted in the killing of hundreds of alleged pirates.[49]

By the mid 1850s attacks on the Philippines and the southeast coast of Borneo, Sulawesi and the Moluccas had become so frequent as to prompt the Dutch and British to try to bring about an international agreement with Spain in order to combat piracy. Madrid, however, was loath to allow the navies of other European powers to operate in Philippine waters, because it might compromise the Spanish claim to sovereignty over the southern Philippines, a claim that was not formally recognised by the neighbouring colonial powers. Spain thus rejected the proposed naval cooperation, claiming that Spanish forces had already succeeded in suppressing Sulu piracy and that the obligation to cooperate with Great Britain and the Netherlands would restrain their hand in dealing with the pirates. The Spanish also warned the Dutch and the British

---

[46] Tarling, *Sulu and Sabah*, 95, 98; Warren, *The Sulu Zone, 1768–1898*, 194–5; Teitler et al., *Zeeroof*, 289; see also Jansen, 'Aanteekeningen', 218, for a list of the main islands harbouring Sulu raiders in the 1850s.
[47] Warren, 'Balangingi Samal', 56.
[48] Warren, *The Sulu Zone, 1768–1898*, 194–5; Warren, *Iranun and Balangingi*, 362–6.
[49] Tarling, *Sulu and Sabah*, 96; see further Chapter 3.

not to give chase to pirates within Spain's maritime zone or to attack the pirates on land in areas over which Spain claimed sovereignty. The British and Dutch consequently went ahead without Spanish cooperation and increased their naval presence in the waters adjacent to the Spanish colony. They tried to some extent to coordinate their operations against the Tawi-Tawi (and other) pirates, and the patrols were successful in bringing about a decline in raids affecting Dutch and British interests in the region from the early 1860s.[50]

The Spanish refusal to cooperate with the Dutch and the British again demonstrated that the main concern for the Spanish was not the suppression of piracy but the assertion of their control over the Sulu Archipelago. For the Spanish, naval cooperation with Great Britain or the Netherlands was out of the question as long as Spain's claim to the Sulu Archipelago – which also implied north-east Borneo (Sabah), an area over which the sultan of Sulu had exercised at least nominal sovereignty – was not internationally recognised.

The commercial and territorial rivalry was particularly strong between Great Britain and Spain. The destruction of Balangingi in 1848, as we have seen, pushed the Sulu Sultanate to seek closer relations with the British in order to fend off the threat of further Spanish aggression. The British, for their part, were interested in expanding their commerce in the region, particularly after Labuan off the coast of Brunei was established as a British coaling station in 1847 with the intention of developing it into a hub of trade in the region. After a slow start, trade between Sulu and Labuan developed rapidly after the middle of the 1850s, and Labuan emerged as an important entrepôt for the trade between Sulu and Singapore. For the Sulu Sultanate the trade with Labuan was very advantageous, and it provided the nearest alternative trading station to the Spanish-controlled ports at Zamboanga and Balabac. The commercial boom also helped to reestablish the domestic authority of Sultan Fadl Pulalun, which had suffered as a result of the Spanish attacks in the middle of the century.[51]

The Spanish, however, were not happy with the commercial competition from the British, and they claimed that the trade between Sulu and Labuan violated the treaty of 1851. The Spanish tried, mostly ineffectively, to enforce their monopoly on the trade of the Sulu Sultanate. Spanish naval vessels patrolled the Sulu Sea in order to assert sovereignty and to enforce Spain's commercial monopoly. The patrols also tried to suppress piracy and maritime raiding, and in 1858 the Spanish won a major victory when Taupan and two of his close lieutenants were captured and sent off to exile in the northern Philippines. Thus ended the exploits of the man whom the Spaniards considered to be the last of the great raiding chiefs of the Moros.[52]

---

[50] Ibid., 105–6. [51] Warren, *The Sulu Zone, 1768–1898*, 104–14.
[52] Warren, 'Balangingi Samal', 56–7.

The Spanish were still largely unable to check petty acts of piracy effectively, however, and further measures were deemed necessary in order to assert Spain's de facto sovereignty and control over the Sulu Archipelago. To this effect the Spanish Governor-General, Fernando Norzagaray, issued a proclamation in 1858 according to which anyone would receive 10 pesos for each captured or killed pirate, provided the latter had been caught in the act, whereas a pirate leader commanded a reward of 50 pesos. The incentive seems to have had some effect, at least on paper, and over the subsequent years thousands of pesos were paid by the Spanish authorities to Moros for their efforts to suppress piracy, although it is far from certain that all of those for whom rewards were paid were indeed pirates.[53] Overall, these and other measures taken by the Spanish authorities did little to bring an end to petty piracy and coastal raiding in the Sulu Archipelago and the neighbouring parts of the Spanish colony. From the Spanish point of view, the problem was exacerbated by the relative efficiency of Dutch and British efforts to suppress piracy in the adjacent waters, one effect of which was to push the Sulu raiders to increase their operations in Philippine waters.[54]

The situation changed only in 1861, when the Spanish government purchased eighteen small gunboats, by means of which they, for the first time, were able to extend regular patrols to all parts of the Sulu Sea. The main tasks of the gunboats were to chase after pirates and to enforce a Spanish embargo on the importation of firearms and ammunition to the Sulu Archipelago. The embargo was difficult to control, however, and was compromised by the influx of arms via Labuan.[55]

By means of their new superior naval and military capacity, the Spanish managed over the course of the 1860s to put an end to most of the remaining piratical activity and slave-raiding in and emanating from the Sulu Archipelago.[56] The measures deployed were harsh and often arbitrary, however, and, according to British observers, the cruel and destructive naval warfare of the Spanish provoked bitter hatred among the Moros.[57] In July 1871, the British commander of the steamer *Nassau* reported from a visit to the Sulu capital at Jolo:

There is now a Spanish war vessel stationed at Sulu, and occasionally a gunboat, to punish Pirates. They have just returned from a tour round Tawi-Tawi, where they have shot 25, burnt their villages and destroyed their cocoanut trees, releasing 9 Bisayans. They go ... to the South of Tawi to destroy the building yard Balingki (I think) where all the large Boats are built and fitted out. This is unfortunate for us.

---

[53] Llanos, 'Piratas y cautivos', 49, n. 82. Hurley, *Swish of the Kris*, 147, claims that the Sultan used the provision as a convenient way to dispose of individuals who had lost royal favour.
[54] Saleeby, *History of Sulu*, 214; Tarling, *Sulu and Sabah*, 95, 98.
[55] Saleeby, *History of Sulu*, 214, 221; Tregonning, *History of Modern Sabah*, 10; Tarling, *Sulu and Sabah*, 101.
[56] Saleeby, *History of Sulu*, 214, 221.   [57] Tarling, *Sulu and Sabah*, 140.

The Sultan of Sulu is very civil to us, and wanted me to hoist the English flag to protect himself against the Spaniards, who will no doubt eventually take the whole group, that being their object clearly ...

While we lay here 30 June, there are 3 Spanish steam Vessels of war, a sloop and two gunboats, one has just arrived with 5 Boats in tow, and having on board 34 men and women chained to their steam chain. They are Pirates. They were captured (having no arms) off Siassi 30 miles South of Sulu doing nothing. One of the Boats belongs to the Sultan. Two days after they all sail for Tawi where a trial takes place, a witness has been obtained who saw them some years since in the act of piracy – kidnapping. They are guilty; are taken to Zamboanga to work as convicts for life. The Sultan ... says the men are all quiet, harmless persons and that whenever women and children are found in Boats with the men there is no mischief intended.[58]

In suppressing piracy and other forms of subversion on the part of the Moros the Spanish relied on tactics that were not very different in character and effect from those of the Moro raids they aimed to suppress. The Spanish frequently attacked Moro settlements that were suspected of serving as pirate bases. Typically, the Moro forces were defeated, some of the inhabitants killed or sentenced to transportation, and the houses, trees and other property were burnt, after which the Spanish withdrew. By and large, these tactics were similar to the ones that the Spanish had deployed during the three centuries that the Moro Wars had been fought. Meanwhile, the Moros, just as earlier, retaliated by making war on the Spanish, mainly by raiding Spanish or Christian coastal settlements and vessels.[59]

The outcome was that the already bitter relations between Spain and the Sulu Sultanate deteriorated further as a consequence of the increased Spanish naval activity in the Sulu Sea. The sultan, meanwhile, considered the 1851 treaty with Spain 'null and void', as he and his chiefs allegedly had not received their annual salaries during the previous ten years. The Sultan's salary was 1,500 pesos a year according to the agreement and was intended as compensation for the loss of his palace and fort, which were burnt to the ground in the Spanish attack of 1851.[60]

Although the Spanish, by means of their gunboat flotilla, were able to uphold a reasonable degree of maritime security in the Sulu Archipelago, sporadic acts of piracy and coastal raids continued to occur. For example, in 1870, pirates preyed on the maritime traffic through the San Bernardino Strait separating Luzon from Samar and raided several islands on the southwest coast of Luzon. The Spanish colonial government accused the sultan of Sulu of not fulfilling his obligations according to the 1851 treaty of suppressing piracy,

---

[58] Extracts from a letter from the Commander of the 'Nassau', Sulu, 1 July 1871, FO 71/2, The National Archives of Great Britain, Kew (TNA).
[59] Saleeby, *History of Sulu*, 221–2; Warren, *The Sulu Zone, 1768–1898*, 119.
[60] Commander of the 'Nassau', 1 July 1871; Saleeby, *History of Sulu*, 214.

and of importing arms without licence, which also was a violation of the treaty.[61] The British, however, were of the opinion that the Spanish brought up the accusation of piracy as a pretext for intervention and that their real aim was to extend their control over the Sulu Sea and to convert the Moros to Christianity. The British Consul in Manila, George Thorne Ricketts – who, like most British officials, was clearly no admirer of the Spanish colonial administration – wrote:

> The suppression of piracy can then only be regarded as the ostensible cause, and a desire to propagate the doctrines of the Roman Catholic faith and exterminate Islamism in the South, a love of aggrandisement, the creation of new places for the support of a certain number of officials, a jealousy of foreign influence obtaining any footing within the zone of Spanish rule, and the exclusion of foreign vessels from trading freely with the Sultan's people are, we may rest assured, the real causes which prompt Spain to aim at this extension of her territory.[62]

In the eyes of the Spanish, however, religion could not be separated from the problem of piracy. In 1859 a royal edict claimed that 'piracy was an occupation that found religious basis and was viewed not as an act arising from moral degradation but rather, lack of civilisation'.[63] Proselytisation, thus, did not only serve religious purposes but was also seen as a means of bringing civilisation to the Moros and thereby ending their addiction to the practice of piracy. The suppression of piracy may not have been the primary objective of conquering Sulu from the Spanish perspective, but doing so, it was hoped, would make it possible for the Spanish to civilise and convert the Joloanos and thereby make them give up their piratical habits.

Naval Destruction

From the 1870s the Spanish began to pursue their claim to sovereignty over the southern Philippines even more aggressively. They increased their naval presence in the region to thirty-two ships of different sizes, and Spanish gunboats constantly patrolled the Sulu Archipelago, not only to suppress piracy but also, and primarily, to enforce the blockade on Sulu's foreign trade with Labuan and Singapore.[64] The Spanish claimed to have the right to visit all ships, both Sulu and foreign, in the archipelago, and they seized vessels and cargoes deemed to be in violation of the embargo. At the same

---

[61] Tarling, *Sulu and Sabah*, 118–19.
[62] Ricketts to Earl Granville, 16 October 1871, FO 71/2 (TNA), cf. Tarling, *Piracy and Politics*, 183. Majul, *Muslims in the Philippines*, 341–2, makes a similar assessment of the Spanish motives for conquering Sulu.
[63] Cit. by Warren, 'Balangingi Samal', 58.
[64] Consul-General, Labuan to Earl Granville, 27 April 1872, FO71/2 (TNA).

time interimperial rivalry also increased. The British undertook to survey the archipelago, and there were signs of increasing German interest in the region, all of which served to strengthen the Spanish resolve to take firm control over the Sulu Sultanate.[65]

In 1872 a Spanish naval commander, Santiago Patero – who apparently had some understanding of the social and economic conditions of the Sulu Sultanate – published a policy paper entitled 'A Suitable System for Putting an End to Piracy'. Santiago Patero made fifteen recommendations with regard to Spanish policy in Sulu, including occupying the capital at Jolo and dispatching as many Catholic missionaries as possible to the archipelago. He also recommended establishing forward naval bases in the area and the increased use of steam power in order to destroy all Sulu craft and facilities for boat-building. The principal idea, according to Santiago Patero, was to let the natives go through a transitional period of 'proper and marked humility' [*conveniente y marcada humildad*], which would serve completely to ruin their commerce, destroy their boats, make them lose their capacity to build them, and to turn the natives, by force or by necessity, to the agricultural life.[66]

The programme was promptly adopted as the blueprint for Spanish naval policy in the Sulu Archipelago. After an incident in which Sultan Jamal ul-Azam (1862–81) refused to fly the Spanish flag in his capital and instead had the flag burnt in public, the Spanish declared Sulu to be in open rebellion.[67] Citing the need to prevent raiding on the Philippine coasts, the Commander of the Spanish Naval Station in the Philippines, Rear Admiral Juan Antequera, in August 1873, issued a regulation that declared all Muslim shipping in the Sulu Sea illegal. All Spanish vessels were to observe the following orders:

1st. Every vessel coming from the Soloo Archipelago and manned by Moors shall be destroyed, and its crew and passengers destined to labour on public works on the northerly islands of the Archipelago.

2nd. If the vessels referred to in the former article be armed, they shall, as our laws direct, be held as pirates and their crews be tried by court martial according to the provisions of the Penal Code.

3rd. Every vessel, although it may not be manned, belonging to Moors of the islands of Soloo and Tawi Tawi shall be destroyed by the cruisers.

4th. Vessels referred to in the former articles, which do not acknowledge the authority of the Sultan and do not carry on piracy, shall, when they endeavour to sail from other islands than those of Soloo and Tawi Tawi, be conducted by the cruisers to the islands whence they had come.

---

[65] Majul, *Muslims of the Philippines*, 344–5; Warren, *The Sulu Zone, 1768–1898*, 116–18.

[66] Santiago Patero, *Sistema que conviene adoptar*, 39–40; cit. 40; italics in original; my transl. from Spanish. See also Warren, *The Sulu Zone, 1768–1898*, 118, on the influence of Santiago Patero's book on Spanish policy.

[67] Majul, *Muslims in the Philippines*, 290.

5th. In the islands whence the vessels referred to in the previous article may proceed, fishing will be permitted under restrictions deemed desirable by the Commander of the Division.[68]

The implementation of the declaration did great harm to Sulu trade and fishing but failed to force the Sultanate into submission. The trade embargo was circumvented by Sulu traders, aided by Chinese, German and British smugglers, who brought food and other necessities, as well arms and munitions, to Jolo from Singapore and Labuan.[69]

The governor-general of the Philippines, José Malcampo y Monge, was convinced that the only way to enforce Spain's claim to sovereignty over the Sulu Archipelago was once and for all to conquer and occupy Jolo, as recommended by Santiago Patero. For the first time in more than 300 years of Spanish colonial presence in the Philippines, moreover, it seemed possible, in view of Spain's enhanced military and naval supremacy, not only to defeat the Moros but also to take control over the Sulu Archipelago and the rest of the southern Philippines.

In February 1876 a large military expedition, consisting of nine thousand troops conveyed in ten steamboats and eleven transports, and escorted by a fleet of twelve gunboats, left Zamboanga for Sulu in order to conquer and occupy Jolo. The expedition succeeded in conquering the capital at Jolo and destroyed several other alleged pirate nests in the archipelago. A Spanish garrison was established at Jolo, and further expeditions were dispatched to search for alleged pirate bases around the Sulu Archipelago. A medal was struck for each of the participants in the campaign, and Malcampo was given the title 'Count of Jolo'.[70] The victory was widely celebrated in Spain, and Malcampo was hailed as a hero.[71] There seems to have been little or no questioning of the use of the word *pirate* to describe the Moros, and the Spanish press reported enthusiastically the Spanish Navy's heroic encounters with the piratical Moros.[72]

Two years later a book entitled *Piratical Wars of the Philippines against the Mindanaos and Joloanos* was published by Vicente Barrantes, a Spanish writer and poet who had worked for several years in the colonial administration in the Philippines. The work dealt with the Moro Wars up until the early nineteenth century, and the purpose, as stated by the author, was to 'demonstrate the perverse behaviour of the Moro along with our prudence, in order now to win their friendship and to contain their piracies'.[73]

---

[68] Appendix L: Regulation Declaring all Muslim Shipping Illegal in the Sulu Sea, in Warren, *The Sulu Zone, 1768–1898*, 288; transl. by Warren.
[69] Ibid., 120–1, 129.   [70] Saleeby, *History of Sulu*, 222–3.
[71] Montero y Vidal, *Historia de la piratería* 2, 520–1.
[72] See, for example, the report of an encounter between the Spanish corvette *Santa Lucia* and an allegedly piratical banca in 1876; *El Globo* (4 March 1876).
[73] Barrantes, *Guerras piráticas*, 4.

A more comprehensive study of Moro piracy in two volumes appeared ten years later, written by José Montero y Vidal, a Spanish author and politician, who, like Barrantes, had served for several years as an official in the Philippine colonial administration. The title of Montero y Vidal's work was *The History of the Malay-Muslim Piracy in Mindanao, Jolo and Borneo*, and it covered the whole history of the Moro Wars, from the sixteenth century until the present. It was possibly even more negative in its assessment of the Moros than Barrantes' work, describing them as 'cruel, vengeful, devious, treacherous, deceitful and false'. 'War is his element; piracy his only occupation; slavery his wealth', according to Montero y Vidal.[74]

The works of Barrantes and Montero y Vidal were examples of a colonial historiography 'cast in a heroic and imperialist mould', in the words of Nicholas Tarling.[75] The image of the Muslims of the southern Philippines as piratical by nature and of the Moro Wars as a series of heroic Spanish efforts to suppress piracy was part of colonial propaganda and seems to have gone more or less unchallenged in Spain. Such notions, however, were not limited to Spanish colonial historiography but were prevalent in other colonial histories and assessments of the Moros (and other Malays) as well. A few years after the Spanish conquest of Jolo an Austrian ethnographer, Ferd. Blumentritt, published a map and a survey of the peoples of the Philippines in which he lumped all ethnic groups of the southern Philippines together under the label 'pirate tribes' (*Piratenstämme*).[76] His writings would come to exercise a great influence on American understandings of Moro culture and society as the United States acquired Spain's Philippines colony in 1899.[77]

Moro Resistance

The Joloanos regarded the establishment of the Spanish garrison at Jolo as an intrusion and a humiliation, and they continued, encouraged by Sultan Jamal ul-Azam and the leading *datus*, to wage a guerrilla war that inflicted many casualties on the Spanish troops. Spanish soldiers and Christian Filipinos were frequently ambushed and killed or became victims of assaults by

---

[74] Montero y Vidal, *Historia de la piratería*, 1, vii.   [75] Tarling, 'Establishment', 73.
[76] Blumentritt, 'Versuch einer Ethnographie der Philippinen', 52, encl. map. References to the Moros as being piratical by nature are also frequent in American colonial sources well into the twentieth century; e.g., *Annual Report of the Governor of the Moro Province* [henceforth *ARGMP*] (1908), 23, and the discussion below. See also Warren, 'Moro Wars', for the different perspectives and historiographical perspectives on the Moros and the Moro Wars.
[77] Amoroso, 'Inheriting the "Moro Problem"', 125; cf. Brinton, 'Professor Blumentritt's Studies', 122–5.

juramentados, suicide attackers, usually armed with a dagger, sword or spear, who ventured to kill as many Spaniards or other Christians as possible before they, in most cases, were themselves killed. On several occasions the Moros also made concerted attacks on the Spanish garrison at Jolo but were repelled with heavy losses.[78]

After more than two years of hostilities, one of the leading Sulu *datus*, Harun ar-Rashid, convinced the sultan that peace and submission to Spanish suzerainty were preferable to continued fighting, which looked likely to bring about the complete ruin of the Sultanate. Negotiations followed, with the result that the sultan accepted Spanish sovereignty in exchange for an annual salary and full autonomy in matters concerning internal administration, customs, law and religion. The status of the Sulu Sultanate in the 1878 treaty thus resembled more that of a protectorate than a dependency or a fully integrated part of the Philippines, as the Spanish claimed it was.[79]

The Sultan's earlier promise in the 1851 agreement not to permit or engage in piracy and to punish those who attempted to do so was developed further in the 1878 treaty. According to Article 8:

We will try to suppress all pirates; but in case we are unable to do so we will notify the Govenor of their location. But in case we do not know where they are, we can not be held responsible for such information. We will also aid the Government with as many men as we can afford to bring together, and we shall be pleased to give guides who can tell the hiding places of such pirates.[80]

The treaty did not immediately put an end to hostilities, however. The sultan's power was dependent upon the loyalty and support of the local *datus*, whose allegiance to the sultan often was little more than nominal and whose relations with the Spanish were frequently outright hostile and contemptuous. After the death of Sultan Jamal ul-Azam in 1881, hostilities between the Spanish and Sulu Moros led by discontented *datus* once again surged. The Spanish had no control over the island of Jolo beyond their garrison, and small parties of soldiers who ventured outside were frequently ambushed and killed. The unleashing of *juramentados* seems to have been encouraged and used as a military tactic for the purpose of striking fear into the hearts of the Spanish soldiers and the Chinese and Christian Filipinos who resided in the garrisoned

---

[78] Ewing, 'Juramentado', 148–55; Majul, *Muslims in the Philippines*, 353–60; Saleeby, *History of Sulu*, 224. See also Hurley, *Swish of the Kris*, 139–40, for several reports of *juramentado* attacks in Jolo toward the end of the Spanish colonial period.

[79] Saleeby, *History of Sulu*, 231; for English translations of the treaty, see 227–31.

[80] Ibid., 230; transl. by Saleeby. For the Spanish text, see Montero y Vidal, *Historia de la piratería*, 2, Appendices, 82. Compared with earlier treaties, the Spanish and Sulu texts of the 1878 treaty were relatively similar.

town of Jolo.[81] An American scientist, Dean Conant Worcester, who visited the island in 1891, described the situation: 'Hardly a night passed during our stay at Sulu that marauders were not in evidence near the town. They took pot-shots at the sentries, stole cattle, and made themselves generally disagreeable.'[82] The journalist and amateur historian Vic Hurley – possibly with a flair for the dramatic – likewise claimed that a 'reign of terror persisted in Jolo without respite until the town was finally evacuated to the American forces in 1899'.[83] General John C. Bates, who shortly after the American takeover of the Philippines in 1899 led a mission to establish an agreement between the United States and the sultan of Sulu, concluded from his studies of Spanish records of their activity in the Sulu Archipelago that:

> Spain never announced nor conceived a definite, fixed policy of control over the archipelago which looked to improvement and permanency. Its frequent recorded actions seem to have been the result of a desire to temporarily meet difficulties growing out of some strained relationship with the Moros existing at the time, accompanied by the evident fixed purpose to maintain a sufficient number of troops in the archipelago to show to Europe that occupation in fact which would demonstrate Spanish sovereignty.[84]

If the Spanish never succeeded in establishing more than nominal control over Jolo and the other islands of the Sulu Archipelago, they were eventually, toward the end of the Spanish colonial period, relatively successful in upholding maritime security in the archipelago. In addition to the garrison at Jolo, the Spanish established ports and a military presence in Siasi and Tawi-Tawi, both in order to overcome Moro resistance to Spanish rule and to assert Spanish sovereignty over the region *vis-à-vis* other colonial powers. As a result of the increased Spanish naval presence, there seem to have been few cases of piracy in or emanating from the Sulu Archipelago during the last years of the Spanish colonial period.

In 1885 Great Britain and Germany officially recognised Spanish sovereignty over the Sulu Archipelago, both with regard to the effectively occupied parts and those not yet occupied.[85] Spain had thus, after more than 300 years, finally achieved most of her main objectives in the Sulu Archipelago, that is, to

---

[81] Saleeby, *History of Sulu*, 233–45. On his detailed map of the Philippines, published in 1882, Blumentritt noted that in Jolo the Spanish only had direct control of the close surroundings of Fort Alfonso XII and that the rest of the island was under the control of the sultan of Sulu; Blumentritt, 'Versuch einer Ethnographie', encl. map. The situation remained the same until the end of the Spanish presence in Sulu; see the report of the commanding officer of US troops upon his arrival in Jolo in May 1899, in US War Department, *Annual Reports of the War Department* (henceforth *ARWD*) 2 (1899), 133.
[82] Worcester, *Philippine Islands*, 175. [83] Hurley, *Swish of the Kris*, 144.
[84] *ARWD* 2 (1899), 155.
[85] See Saleeby, *History of Sulu*, 367–73 for the full text of the protocols. See further Tarling, *Sulu and Sabah*, 95–179, 239–51, for the background and negotiations surrounding the protocols.

put an end to the raids and warfare that affected the northern islands and to assert her sovereignty, at least nominally, over the Sulu Sultanate. The conversion of the Moros to Christianity, however, did not make any significant progress despite the establishment of a Catholic mission at Jolo following the 1876 conquest of the town.

The sultan, meanwhile, continued to hold his title and was allowed considerable autonomy in legal, religious and cultural affairs, but his authority was nonetheless severely weakened. In the course of a generation, the Spanish expansion in Sulu had not only ended the maritime raiding system on which the Sultanate had thrived before the middle of the nineteenth century: it had also destroyed much of the maritime commerce of the Moros, and indigenous traders found themselves increasingly marginalised or pushed out of business by European and Chinese competitors.[86] These developments would brew up further resentment against both colonial rule and foreigners in the Sulu Archipelago, which eventually would lead to a renewed wave of piratical activity in the region in the early twentieth century.

The United States and the Philippines

In April 1898 war broke out between Spain and the United States, and in just ten weeks the Spanish forces had been soundly defeated, both in the Caribbean and the Philippines. In the peace treaty, Spain was forced to transfer sovereignty over the Philippines to the United States, giving the latter country a foothold in Asia and a commercial gateway to the Chinese market. American businessmen and policymakers hoped that the commercial opportunities that would follow colonial expansion would help alleviate the economic, social and political ills caused by the Industrial Revolution in the United States. There was also a conviction that the United States needed strategic bases in Asia if American companies were to be able to compete successfully with European enterprises.[87]

The Philippines was by far the largest of the overseas territories that the United States acquired as a result of the war with Spain. It was the most remote of the new territories and was at the time virtually unknown, not only to ordinary Americans, but also to most of the civil and military officials who were charged with the task of governing the new colony.[88] Moreover, America's colonial expansion in Asia was vigorously opposed, both in the colony itself and in the United States. In the Philippines, Spain's harsh repression of even relatively moderate nationalist aspirations had triggered

---

[86] Warren, *The Sulu Zone, 1768–1898*, 126–34.   [87] LaFeber, *New Empire*, 412.
[88] Amoroso, 'Inheriting the "Moro Problem"', 118. See also Mark Twain's satirical sketch 'The Philippine Incident' (1901) in Zwick, *Mark Twain's Weapons of Satire*, 57–60.

an armed uprising in 1896, and although a truce was concluded the following year, nationalist sentiments and demands for independence continued to be strong among Christian Filipinos. When the Spanish–American War broke out, Philippine nationalists, led by Emilio Aguinaldo, joined forces with the Americans in the hope that the United States would grant independence to the Philippines. Encouraged by the Americans, who counted on the support of the nationalists to weaken Spain's control over the colony, Aguinaldo declared independence for the Philippines in June 1898.[89]

After the war, however, the US government had no intention of allowing independence for the Philippines.[90] In February 1899, after much controversy, Congress barely voted to ratify the peace treaty with Spain and thus to approve the annexation of the Philippines. Philippine nationalists, who at the time were in control of most of the archipelago, with the exception of Manila and the southern Philippines, however, refused to recognize American sovereignty, and a three-year armed struggle for independence, the Philippine–American War, followed. The United States was substantially in control of most of the islands by 1900, but fighting and brigandage continued in a number of locations for several years.[91]

In the United States colonial expansion was opposed by prominent public figures, including politicians, intellectuals, artists and writers, who formed a vigorous anti-imperialist faction. American anti-imperialism was linked, ideologically as well as genealogically, to the antislavery movement from before the Civil War, and many of the leading anti-imperialists saw colonisation as another form of enslavement and thus as unconstitutional.[92] The anti-imperialists also claimed that imperialism was a flagrant violation of the fundamental principles on which the United States was founded, as colonial domination was incompatible with the principles of freedom, democracy and every nation's right to self-government.[93]

American policy in the Philippines from the conclusion of the Philippine–American War of 1902 up until the outbreak of the Pacific War in 1941 was to a great extent shaped by the tension between, on the one hand, the commercial and geopolitical arguments for continued colonial administration and, on the

---

[89] This summary of events is based on Kratoska and Batson, 'Nationalism and Modernist Reform', 253–6; see also Smith, *Spanish–American War*.
[90] See Brands, *Bound to Empire*, 20–35, for a rebuttal of the argument that American colonial expansion happened by coincidence.
[91] Kratoska and Batson, 'Nationalism and Modernist Reform', 253–7; see further Linn, *Philippine War*.
[92] Salman, *Embarrassment of Slavery*, 33, 40, 43.
[93] Tompkins, *Anti-imperialist in the United States*, 2; Harrington, 'Anti-imperialist Movement', 211.

other, Filipino nationalist aspirations and the sympathy that those aspirations commanded among anti-imperialists in the United States.

Transfer of Power in the South

It took several months after the ratification of the peace treaty by Congress before the United States could muster enough troops to occupy the Spanish posts in the southern Philippines. According to the American Military governor of the Philippines, Major-General Elwell Stephen Otis, who relied on reports from the Spanish acting governor of the southern Philippines, the situation in the region was very unsatisfactory, and Otis hesitated to dispatch the few troops he could spare into the area. He was particularly concerned that if the troops were too few they would not be able to secure and hold the necessary positions there given the hostility of the local population. Moreover, not only had the northern and northeastern coasts of Mindanao fallen to Philippine nationalist rebels after the Spanish troops on the island had withdrawn to Zamboanga, but control by the Spanish military had also been relaxed in the Sulu Archipelago, and gunboat patrols had practically ceased. The Spanish had deserted the smaller military posts in the area, such as the one at Siasi, and withdrawn its troops in Sulu to the main garrison at Jolo. Meanwhile, it was reported that the sultan and the *datus* of Sulu were gathering large supplies of arms and ammunition from abroad and that they planned to oppose any American attempts to assert their sovereignty over the Sultanate.[94]

A further blow to American ambitions in Sulu came in March 1899, when most of the Spanish gunboat flotilla – thirteen vessels in all – that had been used to patrol the Sulu Archipelago and adjacent seas was hijacked by Mindanao nationalists. The boats were eventually recovered and escorted to Manila by the Spanish Navy, but not before the nationalists had stripped them of arms and munitions.[95] Once in American hands, the fate of the gunboats became the object of a controversy between the Army and the Navy. Governor Otis intended for the gunboats to be commissioned with Army personnel and used to stop illicit trade between the Philippine Islands, but he was told by Admiral George Dewey, Commander of the US Navy's Asiatic Squadron, that the Army had no authority to operate gunboats. Should they nevertheless attempt to do so, Dewey said, the Navy would consider them to be pirates

---

[94] Annual Report of Maj. Gen. E. S. Otis, USV commanding the Department of the Pacific and Eighth Army Corps, and Military Governor of the Philippine Islands, 29 August 1898–31 August 1899, in *ARWD* 2 (1899), 130.
[95] Otis, Annual Report, in *ARWD* 2 (1899), 130–1; cf. Sawyer, *Inhabitants of the Philippines*, 117.

and run down the gunboats and sink them.[96] The outcome of the standoff was that the Navy took the seagoing gunboats while the Army was allowed to keep ten shallow-draft steamers, some of which were equipped with heavy cannon and machine guns, to support military operations. As a consequence, the Army's maritime capacity in the southern Philippines was strictly limited and insufficient to uphold maritime security.[97]

In the middle of May 1899 the situation for the Spanish troops in Zamboanga became untenable after the garrison was attacked by nationalists who managed to cut off their water supply. The Spanish then decided to evacuate both the garrisons at Zamboanga and Jolo immediately and requested that the Americans relieve them. The latter, unable to spare enough troops to take control of both major garrisons in the South, decided to concentrate their forces on Jolo and let Zamboanga fall into the hands of the nationalists, despite the greater strategic importance of the latter town and garrison. According to Otis, there was a significant risk that if the Jolo garrison was abandoned, the Moros would destroy the fortifications and turn the guns on the Americans once they arrived. In order to avoid this Otis dispatched a force of 700 troops to occupy the fort at Jolo.[98]

Upon arrival in Jolo, the Americans learnt that the Spanish had already turned over the small garrison at Siasi to Sultan Jamalul Kiram II (r. 1894–1936) and that they had planned to leave him the garrison at Jolo as well. The sultan was reportedly very disappointed when the Americans arrived and prevented him from taking control of the garrison. The sultan and the leading *datus* had seen the departure of the Spanish as an opportunity to restore the sovereignty of the Sulu Sultanate.[99] Against this background, the delicate task for the Americans during their first weeks in the Sulu Archipelago was to convince the sultan and his chiefs to accept American sovereignty and to try to establish friendly relations with the Moros.

When the Americans first arrived in the southern Philippines they knew virtually nothing about the Moros, 'save that they professed the Mohammedan religion and were a warlike people who had always resisted the domination of Spain', as a contemporary official report put it.[100] Their military strength was not insignificant, as it was estimated that the Sulu Sultanate could put 20,000 fighting men in the field. This figure did not include the fighting capacity of

---

[96] W. H. Standley to F. H. Sawyer, 1945, Subject File 00: Operations of Gunboats in the Philippines, 1900–02, Box 469, RG 45, National Archives and Records Administration (NARA), Washington, DC.

[97] Linn, *Philippine War*, 132. The arrangement seems mainly to have been aimed at supporting the American effort to win the Philippine–American War, however, and at least before 1902 there were few gunboats in operation in the Sulu Archipelago.

[98] Otis, Annual Report, in *ARWD* 2 (1899), 132–3.   [99] Ibid., 133, 153–4.

[100] Philippine Commission, *Fifth Annual Report of the Philippine Commission 1904*, 1, 6.

other Moros in the southern Philippines, such as in Mindanao and Basilan. Against this background, Governor Otis was of the opinion that hostilities would be unfortunate for all parties concerned and risked being very costly to the United States in terms of money and troops.[101] The situation was particularly critical in view of the Philippine–American War, which stretched the military capacity of the Americans, who thus had strong incentives to try to win the hearts and minds of the Muslims in the southern Philippines in order to avoid having to fight a double war, as well as an incentive to weaken the predominantly Christian Philippine nationalist movement.

Against this background, rather than opting for direct rule in the Sulu Archipelago, the Americans sought to establish indirect rule on terms similar to those of the 1878 treaty between Spain and the Sultanate. The sultan was to be given a large degree of autonomy in matters concerning religion, custom, law and internal administration in exchange for his acknowledgement of American sovereignty. To this effect, a mission led by Brigadier General John C. Bates was sent to Sulu in mid 1899 with instructions to negotiate an agreement with the sultan and the leading *datus*. Several of the latter were reportedly favourably disposed toward the Americans, but the sultan was initially reluctant to negotiate with the American delegation.[102] After six weeks, however, in August 1899 he was persuaded to sign the agreement, largely on the terms proposed by the Americans.

With the signing of the so-called Bates Agreement the American military seemed to have covered its back in the Sulu Archipelago for the coming years and could concentrate its efforts on the task of fighting the nationalists. In the United States, however, the agreement caused an uproar, because it seemed to imply that the American authorities in the Philippines condoned slavery. Article 10 of the agreement stated that '[a]ny slave in the archipelago of Jolo shall have the right to purchase freedom by paying to the master the usual market value'.[103] For American anti-imperialists, this provision seemed to confirm their worst fears in connection with the American takeover of the Philippines, and the opponents of colonial expansion readily seized on what they saw both as a violation of the Thirteenth Amendment to the Constitution, which abolished slavery in the United States or any place subject to its jurisdiction, and as evidence that colonialism in itself was a form of slavery.[104]

The controversy over the Bates Agreement seems to have come as a surprise to the senior military officers in the Philippines. Slavery, or its abolition in the Sulu Sultanate, was not mentioned in Otis's instructions to Bates, and several statements and observations by leading military officials in the Philippines

---

[101] Otis, Annual Report, in *ARWD* 2 (1899), 157. [102] Ibid., 156.
[103] Gowing, 'Mandate in Moroland', 849. [104] Salman, *Embarrassment of Slavery*, 27–8, 36.

indicate that they did not consider Moro slavery to be a problem. Many leading American military officers in the Philippines at the time claimed that Moro slavery was in fact not slavery at all, at least not in the common (that is, American) sense of the word. In order thus to distinguish Moro slavery from the chattel slavery of the American South before the Civil War they tended to use less offensive terms in official reports, such as 'peonage' or 'a species of serfdom', to describe the phenomenon.[105] The military governor of the Department of Mindanao and Sulu, Brigadier General W. A. Kobbé, even went so far as to claim that the 'slaves belong to the same race as the masters, appear to live with them on equal social terms and, as far as is known, have no hard labor to perform'.[106]

Petty Piracy

In contrast to slavery, piracy was mentioned by Otis in his instructions to Bates, indicating American concerns over the issue from the outset of their administration in the Sulu Archipelago. Occasional acts of piracy and slave raiding emanating from Sulu and affecting Mindanao and other Philippine islands, as well as the east coast of Borneo, occurred throughout the first years of American rule in the Philippines. Although piracy was not a major problem for the Americans, it soured relations between the American authorities and the Moros.

In his instructions to General Bates in mid 1899, Governor Otis pointed out that it was necessary for the military to take control over strategic points in the Sulu Archipelago in order to undertake 'naval and military operations against foreign aggression or to disperse attempted piratical excursions'. He instructed Bates to get the sultan and his chiefs to promise that they would not 'permit acts of piracy by their people on its waters, and to assist the United States Government to suppress and abolish this crime by whomsoever attempts to commit it, whether American, inhabitant, or alien'.[107]

The issue of piracy did not generate any longer discussion in the negotiations between Bates and the sultan of Sulu, and seems to have been of minor concern to both sides.[108] In their respective drafts for the agreement text, both sides proposed an article that provided for cooperation to suppress piracy, but

---

[105] Otis, Annual Report, in *ARWD* 2 (1899), 153–5; cit., 157; Kobbé, Annual Report, in *ARWD* 3 (1900), 269–70.

[106] Appendix P: Report of Commanding General Department of Mindanao and Jolo, in *Annual Report of Major General Arthur MacArthur, U.S. Army, Commanding, Division of the Philippines*, 1 (1901), 5. On changing American perceptions of Sulu slavery, see further Eklöf Amirell, '"An Extremely Mild Form of Slavery"'.

[107] Otis to Bates, 3 July 1899, in Otis, Annual Report, in *ARWD* 2 (1899), 155.

[108] US Congress, *Treaty with the Sultan of Sulu*, 49; cf. Salman, *Embarrassment of Slavery*, 73.

the sultan readily agreed to use the American version in the final text of the agreement. The article, which was somewhat less specific than the corresponding one in the 1878 treaty between Spain and Sulu, read: 'Piracy must be suppressed, and the sultan and his datos agree to heartily cooperate with the United States authorities to that end, and to make every possible effort to arrest and bring to justice all persons engaged in piracy.'[109]

Despite the apparent commitment of the sultan and his headmen to cooperate in the suppression of piracy, their sincerity was soon doubted by the American officers charged with the task of governing the Sulu Archipelago and the rest of the military department of Mindanao and Jolo. Less than a year after the signing of the Bates Agreement, General Kobbé expressed his doubts about the value of the cooperation against piracy. Such cooperation could not be controlled, he claimed, and was 'believed to be perfunctory and valueless, because piracy has existed in one form or another for many years and is considered by the average Moro a perfectly fair game'.[110] The commander of Jolo Garrison, Major Owen J. Sweet, likewise reported that everything was 'smooth and complacent on the surface', but that there was no desire or intention on the part of the sultan or his chiefs to cooperate with the Americans in order to improve the condition of the people or to stop acts of robbery or piracy. The sultan, Sweet claimed, would put two or three hundred armed men in the field to collect a fine but would not care, or would plead inability, when asked, to arrest pirates or thieves wanted by the US authorities.[111]

Piratical activity and other forms of banditry, both on land and at sea, increased during the first years of American rule in the Sulu Archipelago as a result of the lapse in security in connection with the withdrawal of Spanish troops and the discontinuation of gunboat patrols.[112] The departure of Spanish gunboats, which, as we have seen, were transferred to the US Navy and were used mainly in the Philippine–American War in the north, rendered the effective suppression of piracy and other forms of criminal or insurgent activities difficult in the Sulu Archipelago and other parts of the southern Philippines.[113]

---

[109] US Congress, *Treaty with the Sultan of Sulu*, 49, 26–7; for the Sultan's suggestion, see 67.
[110] Annual Report of Brig. Gen. W. A. Kobbé, USV, commanding Department of Mindanao and Jolo, in *ARWD* 3 (1900), 257.
[111] Ibid., 267.
[112] *ARGMP* (1904), 6–7; see also 'The humble petition of the residents, traders, and natives of Bongao, Tawi Tawi', 1 October 1903, cited in Report of General Wood as to abrogation of Bates Treaty, 16 December 1903, in *Annual Report of the Philippine Commission* [henceforth *ARPC*] 1 (1903), 508–9.
[113] *Annual Reports of the Navy Department 1900: Report of the Secretary of the Navy: Miscellaneous Reports* [henceforth *ARSN*] (1900), 3; *ARSN* 1 (1901), 608; Col. W. M. Wallace, Report Commanding Officer, Jolo, 2 June 1902, *ARWD* 9 (1902), 530; Maj. James S. Pettit, Report Commanding Officer Zamboanga, 16 September 1901, *ARWD* 9 (1902), 555.

At first the situation was seen by the American authorities as quite satisfactory. In 1902, the Commander of the Seventh Brigade, which was charged with the administration of the Department of Mindanao and Sulu, reported that after the Spanish gunboats had delivered the death knell to the Sulu pirates, 'these whilom sea rovers limit their forays to an occasional assault on other Moro boats, but the merchant vessels of all nations are as secure in the Sulu Sea as in the Atlantic Ocean'.[114] In general, the American assessment of the situation was that piratical activities now only occurred sporadically. According to the 1899–1900 Annual Report of the Department of Mindanao and Sulu, the inhabitants of Tawi-Tawi – all of whom, it was claimed, were either 'pirates, ex-pirates, or descendants of pirates' – now only rarely engaged in piracy and then only on each other.[115] This claim implied that the Tawi-Tawi pirates supposedly only attacked local vessels, owned and crewed by Moros, and not American-, European- or Chinese-owned vessels. As a consequence, the petty piracies that still occurred were of little concern to the colonial authorities.[116]

To the extent that the piratical activity and slave-raiding emanating from the Philippines affected other countries or colonies, however, it did cause the authorities concern. In May 1900 an attack occurred in which six Moros from the Sulu Archipelago killed five Moros and one Chinese from the Dutch East Indies near the island of Kulan, off the east coast of Borneo. The vessel of the victims was sunk, and the pirates got away with $6,000 (US) in cash and $20,000 (US) worth of merchandise. The Americans were informed by the Dutch authorities that the perpetrators were hiding in a village on Jolo. Sultan Jamalul Kiram II was asked to cooperate with American forces in order to capture the perpetrators, to which he reportedly only agreed reluctantly. The Sultan's followers, together with American troops, surrounded the village and tried to arrest the suspects, but five of them escaped and only one was apprehended. The American officer in command of the operation was convinced that those who managed to escape did so with the aid of the Sultan's fighting men and that the arrested Moro in fact was a mere scapegoat.[117]

A few months later a small outrigger canoe (*banca*) with two Chinese and four Moros, or Filipinos dressed as Moros, and a cargo of goods worth $2,000 (US) was attacked near Bunbun after they had left Jolo for Zamboanga. The entire crew was killed, except for one of the Moros, who escaped.

---

[114] Report of Brig. Gen. George W. Davis, USA, commanding Seventh Separate Brigade, 1 August 1902, *ARWD* 9 (1902), 501.
[115] Kobbé, Annual Report, *ARWD* 3 (1900), 266; see also Davis, Report, *ARWD* 9 (1902), 495.
[116] On one occasion, in September 1899, however, a dinghy belonging to the US Navy and sailed by a crew of four American officers and enlisted men was chased by pirates who set out from Tawi-Tawi; *New York Times* (12 November 1899). The dinghy managed to get away.
[117] Kobbé, Annual Report, in *ARWD* 3 (1900), 257.

Investigations by the US military pointed to a certain Sabudin, a chief from Lapingan, as the instigator of the attack, and the Americans asked the sultan to assist in capturing the perpetrators. According to the commander of the Jolo garrison, Major Sweet, however, such help was not forthcoming.[118]

To the Americans, this and other similar incidents seemed to prove that Sultan Jamalul Kiram II was not sincere in his commitment to suppress piracy. As during the Spanish colonial period, however, the sultan had limited means by which to suppress it or other forms of banditry, and was dependent on the support of the *datus*, some of whom were only nominally loyal to the sultan.[119] Moreover, although the sultan had pledged to combat piracy, both to the Spanish and the Americans, piracy or maritime raiding was not a crime according to Sulu law. Theft and abduction were criminal offences, but it was not stated in the law that they were punishable if committed outside the jurisdiction of the Sulu Sultanate or against foreigners. Moreover, the Sultan's power and authority to implement the law waned in principle with increasing distance from the capital and was particularly weak in the more remote parts of the Sulu Archipelago. In places such as Tawi-Tawi, he thus had very limited means at his disposal by which to suppress piracy without the support of the local headmen.[120]

The Americans understood piracy as a natural phenomenon in the Sulu Archipelago and an integral part of Moro culture, but as long as the victims were other Moros or Chinese merchants based in the region, the problem was not seen as a major security issue. The number of attacks was probably significantly underreported, and no attempt was made to collect information systematically or to assess the true scope of the problem.[121] Officers in the region, however, were aware that maritime security in the Sulu Archipelago was deficient. In July 1900 Major Sweet reported of the situation in the Sulu Archipelago:

The natives of the islands are natural pirates, the multitude of small reefs and islands favoring them. These piracies are committed against each other or against Chinamen. When boats and their crews disappear, the natives take it as a matter of course; it is only another case of piracy. No reports of piracy against whites have been received, but from

---

[118] Sweet to Sultan of Sulu, 23 November 1900 [Extract], cited in Wood, Report, *ARPC* 1 (1903), 509.

[119] The Americans seem gradually to have realised that the Sultan's power was limited; e.g., Wallace to Wood, 17 August 1903, Hugh Lenox Scott Papers (HLSP) 55, Manuscript Division, Library of Congress (MDLC), Washington, DC (henceforth MDLC).

[120] For the Sulu Codes, see Saleeby, *Studies in Moro History*, 89–100. For the political system of the Sulu Sultanate, see Kiefer, 'Tausug Polity'. Cf. also the report by the District Governor of Sulu, H. L. Scott, 12 October 1903, *ARPC* 1 (1903), 490.

[121] The lack of interisland transport and telegraph cables connecting some outlying military posts, including Bongao, contributed to a lack of intelligence about what was going on in the more remote parts of the Southern Philippines, particularly in many of the smaller islands of the Sulu Archipelago; Davis, Report, 1 August 1902, *ARWD* 9 (1902), 507; Wallace, Report, 2 June 1902, *ARWD* 9 (1902), 530.

Petty Piracy 73

evidence found by Captain Cloman in the Selungan affair, it would appear that piracies against Sandakan traders have been committed recently.[122]

Selungun was the leader of a band of Sulu pirates who were responsible for a number of attacks on local fishing boats and traders in the archipelago in the first years of the twentieth century. According to official reports, he was a 'slave dealer' and a 'bad Jolo Moro', but Captain Sydney A. Cloman, the commander of the garrison at Bongao, who eventually arrested and interviewed him, was impressed by his charismatic personality and described the pirate chief as 'magnificent', 'well-built, dignified and fearless'.[123] The description may have been influenced by a penchant for literary flair, but in addition, the opportunity to catch an illustrious and notorious pirate probably provided a welcome distraction from the routine and boredom of daily life at the isolated military post at Bongao.[124] Chasing pirates could still be seen as something of an adventurous and romantic pursuit for American soldiers in the Philippines at the beginning of the twentieth century.

Apart from carrying out petty pirate attacks against local traders and fishermen, Selungun and his band undertook slave raids to Mindanao and possibly other islands. Pablo, a Filipino who escaped from enslavement in Jolo in 1901, gave the following testimony of how he was abducted by Selungun and his followers from his home in Cotabato, Mindanao, and brought to Sulu, where he was sold as a slave:

I was walking about in a jungle very close to Cotabato, some one called out to me to wait; I waited; three men came up and caught hold of me and tied my hands behind my back and took me to a small boat, and I was then taken to a large boat that brought me to Jolo Island. Eleven besides myself were brought to this island as slaves – 3 women and 3 children (females), 6 males (2 boys and 4 grown men), all were brought from near Cotabato ... We came from Cotabato and landed at Patotol, where 8 were sold; from Patotol we left for Parang; Selungan met Akir and asked him to sell the slaves; there were 12 slaves then; we were all taken to Wuolo by Akir, who sold some of them, 6 (3 women and 1 girl child, 1 man, and 1 boy). One woman was sold in Tapul; 1 girl child was sold in Siassi; 1 woman, 1 man, and 1 boy were sold in Look; 1 young girl was sold at Bual. One grown-up boy escaped over to the town of Siassi ...[125]

---

[122] Maj. O. J. Sweet, Twenty-Third Infantry: Report No. 12: Jolo, I., 19 July 1900 [Extract], cited in Wood, Report, *ARPC* 1 (1903), 496.
[123] Maj. Lea Febiger, Report of the commanding officer at Cotabato, 4 June 1902, *ARWD* 9 (1902), 525; Pettit, Report, 16 September 1901, *ARWD* 9 (1902), 555; Cloman, *Myself and a Few Moros*, 90; see also 96.
[124] See Cloman's vivid description of the boredom at Bongao in Kobbé, Annual Report, in *ARWD* 3 (1900), 266. In his book from 1923, by contrast, he wrote that 'all days seemed like holidays at Bongao'; Cloman, *Myself and a Few Moros*, 111.
[125] Captain W. H. Sage, Investigation in connection with suspicion of stealing slave from Mindanao..., cited in Wood, Report, in *ARPC* 1 (1903), 533.

A couple of months later, in August 1901, a small sailing boat (*vinta*) was attacked close to Tukuran by a gang of pirates linked to Selungun. The attackers killed one of the men on board and abducted another man and two women, all of whom were sold as slaves to Selungun, who in turn seems to have sold them on. The Americans, who began to investigate the matter upon receiving a complaint by the owner of the boat, were initially unable to catch the perpetrators, but they destroyed the house of one of Selungun's accomplices, *Datu* Malalis, at Dinas in South Mindanao. Malalis and another suspect named Sulug were subsequently tricked by a *datu* who was friendly to the Americans to come to Cotabato, where they were arrested and sentenced to prison terms of four and three years respectively. The arrests and the destruction of *Datu* Malalis's house reportedly dealt a serious blow to the slave market at Dinas.[126]

Selungun himself still evaded capture, however, and he was believed to have taken refuge in Tawi-Tawi. The Commander of Jolo Garrison thus asked the Sultan to arrest Selungun and arrange for the slaves to be returned to Mindanao. In connection with this request, Captain Cloman, the commander of the Bongao station, received a letter from the Sultan asking for permission to capture and punish Selungun. According to Cloman's – somewhat fanciful – later account of his service in the Sulu Archipelago, the letter accused Selungun of an attack on a boat belonging to a rich trader who was a friend of the Sultan. Three people were reportedly killed, the cargo was seized and the boat burned. Cloman claimed that he then, with the assistance of the Sultan's men, managed to find and arrest Selungun, but that he later escaped en route to Maibung, the capital of the Sultan. Selungun subsequently – with the connivance of the Sultan, according to Cloman – made his way to Celebes (Sulawesi) in the Dutch East Indies, from where he continued his piratical depredations. Despite the joint efforts of the Americans, the British and the Dutch, Selungun seems never to have been captured.

The depredations of Selungun's band brought to the fore the need for gunboats to patrol the coasts and waters of the southern Philippines. The Commander of the Zamboanga garrison, Major James S. Pettit, was convinced that the lax security measures under American rule compared with the last decades of the Spanish era was the reason for the surge in piratical activities and human trafficking:

We would have broken up this nefarious business before this, but did not have the boat transportation. I will repeat a recommendation I have made, that one or two gunboats should be constantly on patrol duty between Marigosa, Punta Flecha, and the mouth of the Rio Grande and down the coast for about 40 miles, with instructions to overhaul

---

[126] Febiger, Report, 4 June 1902, in *ARWD* 9 (1902), 525.

every vinta and capture and destroy all those containing arms or slaves without a permit from some commanding officer. The Spaniards never permitted them to engage in that sort of traffic, and they expect to be harshly dealt with when caught. A half dozen captures would probably break up the business.[127]

Gunboat patrols were intensified, particularly after the United States managed to gain the upper hand in the Philippine–American War. From 1902 between two and six or eight naval vessels constantly cruised the waters of the Department of the Mindanao and Sulu. They reportedly provided efficient service and were very valuable in policing the seas against illicit trade and for 'furnishing to evil-minded Moros a manifestation of vigilance and national power'.[128] The patrols continued over the following years and seem to have been instrumental in the suppression of piracy, human trafficking and smuggling, as well as in improving the general conditions of peace and security in the Sulu Archipelago and other parts of the southern Philippines. The mere presence of the gunboats reportedly had a deterrent effect even if they did not have recourse to violence. The 1903 annual report of the Navy's Asiatic Squadron claimed that the Moro coastal tribes had 'great fear of and respect for a gunboat', although subsequent developments indicated that this claim may have been somewhat too optimistic.[129]

Colonial Rule and Economic Expansion

After the demise of Selungun's band, security conditions at sea and around the coasts of the archipelago improved. Piracy, coastal raiding and the maritime slave trade were virtually brought to an end, and for three and a half years, from the beginning of 1903 until the middle of 1906, there is no mention in the annual reports of the region of any piratical activity.[130]

The increased patrols coincided with a policy shift on the part of the United States in the southern Philippines. From 1899 until 1903, the military administration, in keeping with the Bates Agreement, pursued, as far as possible, a policy of noninterference with regard to the Moros. Army activities were limited in principle to the suppression of piracy, slave-raiding and human trafficking, and to trying to keep major conflicts among the Moros within bounds. The Sulu Sultanate had great autonomy in matters concerning internal

---

[127] Pettit, Report, 16 September 1901, *ARWD* 9 (1902), 555.
[128] Report of Brig. Gen. George W. Davis, USA, commanding Seventh Separate Brigade, *ARWD* 9 (1902), 501. Despite the 1899 controversy over the command of the gunboats acquired from Spain, local army commanders and gunboat captains for the most part cooperated efficiently; Linn, *Philippine War*, 132.
[129] *ARSN* (1903), 476.
[130] *ARGMP* (1903–06); in particular *ARGMP* (1904), 6, 16; *ARGMP* (1905), 29; *ARGMP* (1906), 12, 13, 31.

administration and justice, leading to a double system of justice in Sulu – one for Moros and one for Americans, Filipinos and others – with many anomalies and conflicting or overlapping laws and practices.[131]

Many of the commanding officers in the southern Philippines believed that the policy of noninterference and indirect rule encouraged banditry and general anarchy and disorder. Gradually a consensus emerged among most American officers who had firsthand experience of interaction with the Moros that the only way to end the unrest and violence and to create favourable conditions for developing the region, economically as well as socially and culturally, was to impose direct colonial rule. Many officers were also eager to take a direct hand in the project of civilising the Moros, both in the Sulu Sultanate and other parts of the southern Philippines.[132]

After the end of the Philippine–American War in 1902 the American colonial authorities were able to divert more resources to the south, and the need to maintain friendly relations with the Moros by means of noninterference became subordinated to the goal of developing and modernising the region. These goals involved the exploitation of the natural resources of the southern Philippines, such as fish, pearls, mother-of-pearl and timber. With increasing self-confidence, the American colonisers thus began to assert their sovereignty over all parts of the Philippine Islands and set about bringing Western civilisation to the Moros and other purportedly backward peoples of the colony. The civilising measures, particularly the abolition of slavery, were also important in order to legitimise American colonial rule in the Philippines, not only internationally but also domestically, particularly in the face of continuing strong anti-imperialist sentiments in the United States.

A first step toward abolishing indirect rule over the southern Philippines was the creation of Moro Province in 1903. It was still kept under military command, and Major General Leonard Wood, a headstrong and progressive army officer and medical doctor, was appointed as the first governor because of his administrative skills in both civil and military affairs. Wood was convinced that a strong authoritarian government would bring Sulu and other unruly parts of the southern Philippines under American control. He had no hesitation about imposing such a government by firm military action and to set clear examples to the Moros. To Wood, the problems of Moro Province seemed straightforward enough. Shortly after his arrival there, he wrote to the governor-general in Manila, William Howard Taft: 'A good many people have been looking at the Moro question through magnifying glasses, and taking it altogether too seriously ... What is needed is the establishment

---

[131] Gowing, 'Muslim–American Relations', 374–5; Wood, Third Annual Report, in *ARGMP* (1906), 12.

[132] Gowing, 'Muslim–American Relations', 374–5.

immediately of such simple and patriarchal government as will adapt itself to their present conditions.'[133]

One of Wood's first priorities as governor was to bring about the abrogation of the Bates Agreement. To this effect he submitted a report to the colonial authorities in Manila in December 1903, in which he recommended that the treaty be abrogated immediately and even retroactively, from 30 October, and that all payments to the Sultan and the *datus* of Sulu be stopped. Wood listed eight reasons why the treaty was detrimental, including: the inability of the Sultan and the *datus* who signed the agreement to fulfil their obligations; the treaty's recognition of the 'authority of a class of men whom we have found to be corrupt, licentious, and cruel'; the frequent *juramentado* attacks on Jolo Garrison; the continuation of slave-raiding; the stealing of government property by Moros; the general condition of anarchy and impunity; the deficient and allegedly barbarian laws of the Sulu Sultanate; and a recent armed uprising in Jolo led by Panglima Hassan.[134] The Moros, Wood summarised, 'are nothing more or less than an unimportant collection of pirates and highwaymen, living under laws which are intolerable, and there is no reason, in view of the numerous acts of bad faith on their part, why the so-called Bates agreement should be longer continued'.[135]

Most of the report's fifty pages consisted of extracts from official reports and correspondence from the previous three years. Wood cited them in order to demonstrate the general condition of insecurity and anarchy in the Sulu Archipelago. Several of the extracts mentioned piratical activities, particularly the raids of Selungun before his exile in 1902.[136] In relation to the other reported disturbances, however, piracy and maritime raiding were not particularly prominent in the reports. The governor and his staff had presumably studied the official documents of the preceding years carefully in their search for arguments for the abrogation of the Bates Agreement, and the fact that there were relatively few cases of piracy must be taken as an indication that piracy had in fact not been a significant problem for the colonial authorities in the preceding years. There is no evidence, moreover, that the Sultan or the leading Sulu *datus* would have sponsored or tacitly tolerated piratical activities, although Wood claimed that the Sultan and the other signatories to the Bates Agreement were incapable of fulfilling their part of the agreement with regard to, among other things, the suppression of piracy.

The report was well received by Governor Taft and the government in Washington, and in March 1904 President Theodore Roosevelt unilaterally

---

[133] Cited in Lane, *Armed Progressive*, 120.
[134] Report of General Wood as to abrogation of the Bates Treaty, in *ARPC* 1 (1903), 489–90; cit., 489.
[135] Wood, Report, *ARPC* 1 (1903), 490.
[136] Ibid., 496, 497, 509, 533–5. Most of these cases have been discussed earlier.

abrogated the Bates Agreement on behalf of the United States. General Wood notified Sultan Jamalul Kiram II of the abrogation, and although the Sultan was displeased, he acquiesced, along with most of the major *datus* of Jolo. The Sultan was still to be given an allowance by the Americans, and was to continue to enjoy a position of dignity as the symbolic head and religious leader of the Sulu Moros. Although slavery was formally abolished, manumission was to be achieved only gradually and involve some form of monetary compensation for the slave owners. It is uncertain, however, how the Sultan and the leading headmen of Sulu interpreted the new arrangements, particularly with regard to the separation of the political from the religious leadership.[137]

Governor Wood now set about imposing direct colonial rule, establishing law and order and modernising Moro society. A new legal code was adopted to replace the traditional Moro laws, and an unpopular Spanish-era head tax known as the *cedula* was restored. These and other policies met with opposition and resentment from many Sulu Moros, including several *datus* whose power and social status were threatened by the abolition of slavery and the imposition of direct colonial rule and administration of justice. Many Moros, both in Mindanao and Sulu, refused to recognize American rule, and attacked American military posts and soldiers. The military answered with a series of punitive expeditions designed to break the resistance, and in Sulu these culminated in a massacre in March 1906 of close to 1,000 Moros, including many women and children, who had garrisoned themselves in the crater of an extinct volcano, Bud Dajo, in Jolo. The assault, which was carried out with the support of the Sultan and most leading *datus* of Sulu, broke the back of anti-American resistance in the Sulu Archipelago, although at a very high cost in human lives.[138]

Piracy Resurgent

Parallel with the military campaigns against the Moros the colonial authorities started to implement measures to develop the region in areas such as education, healthcare, infrastructure and commerce. Regular markets were set up from 1904 in order to facilitate trade and to stimulate the growth of a commercial fishing industry. Efforts were also launched to increase agricultural output, and American settlers were encouraged to invest in plantations and other export-oriented businesses.[139] The result of these policies was that the export of

---

[137] Gowing, 'Mandate in Moroland', 405, 408.
[138] Byler, 'Pacifying the Moros', 42–3; see also Gowing, 'Mandate in Moroland', 449–94; Lane, *Armed Progressive*, 123–31.
[139] Finley, 'Commercial Awakening', 325–34; Miller, 'American Military Strategy', 46; Gowing, 'Mandate in Moroland', 412–20.

natural resources and agricultural products, including fish, mother-of-pearl, rubber, lumber, cocoanut, sugar cane and hemp, increased rapidly. The economic opportunities attracted not only American settlers but also Europeans, Chinese, Japanese and Christian Filipinos to Moro Province.[140]

The commercial expansion also led to an increase in maritime traffic that provided increased opportunities for piratical activities. On the whole, however, the authorities were successful in maintaining maritime security, and, as noted earlier, there were virtually no reports of piracies from the beginning of 1903 until the middle of 1906. This period approximately coincided with Wood's term as governor of the province, and his iron-fisted rule and the frequent military campaigns probably served as a deterrent to would-be pirates. American gunboats, moreover, provided interisland transport in the Sulu Archipelago, and although they were not primarily charged with the task of suppressing piracy, they provided protection for local traders from piratical attacks.[141]

In April 1906 Wood was replaced as governor of Moro Province by Brigadier General Tasker Howard Bliss. In contrast to his predecessor, Bliss preferred diplomatic to military solutions for dealing with the unrest in the province. Bliss thus discontinued Wood's practice of conducting sweeping punitive military expeditions in favour of more targeted actions aimed at punishing individual wrongdoers rather than entire communities.[142] In Bliss's opinion, raids, killings and tribal feuds among the Moros should be treated as criminal actions and not as security problems or challenges to American sovereignty.[143]

Around the time that Bliss assumed the position of governor, however, piracy began to resurge in the Sulu Archipelago, and within a couple of years the problem had, for the first time since the 1860s, developed to become a serious security problem.[144] From the middle of 1906 scattered piratical attacks, mainly on local vessels, began to be reported. The *Manila Times*, for example, reported that the inhabitants of South Ubian in Tawi-Tawi had turned to piracy because of the deteriorating economic conditions on the island and that they undertook coastal raids on towns and villages in British North Borneo. The provincial authorities, concerned about the risk that these acts

---

[140] Ibid., 422; Wood, Third Annual Report, 1 July 1905–16 April 1906, *ARGMP*, 6 (1906).
[141] Miller, 'American Military Strategy', 98; cf. *ARGMP* (1908), 23.
[142] Byler, 'Pacifying the Moros', 43; see further Thompson, 'Governors of the Moro Province', about the differences between Wood and Bliss.
[143] Linn, *Guardians of Empire*, 39–40.
[144] The fact that acts of piracy, particularly around Basilan, increased already from 1906 is rarely noted; e.g., Gowing, 'Mandate in Moroland', 517–23; Arnold, *Moro War*, 182–7. Tan, 'Sulu under American Military Rule', 75–80, and Hurley, *Swish of the Kris*, 194, note in passing that there was piratical activity in the months preceding the major wave of piracy from the end of 1907.

of piracy might disturb relations with the British, promptly sent a customs cutter and two quartermaster launches to Tawi-Tawi to stop further depredations.[145] The result seems to have been that the piratical activity shifted to Palawan, and in the following year the governor of Palawan reported that entire fleets of *vintas* from Tawi-Tawi, Samal and Siasi had come to the island for the purpose of fishing and committing piracy and that they were responsible for several attacks around the coasts of the island.[146]

This piracy was initially not seen as a major problem by the authorities. Despite the complaints of piracy around Tawi-Tawi and Palawan, the 1907 Annual Report of the Philippine Commission stated that '[s]ince April of this year complete tranquillity has prevailed in every part of the archipelago, inclusive of the Moro province'.[147] This apparent tranquillity seems to have prompted the military to withdraw the gunboats that since 1902 had assisted the Army in patrolling Moro Province, although the main reason for the decision was the rising tension between the United States and Japan during the so-called Japanese War Scare of 1906–07.[148]

The tranquility turned out to be short-lived, however, as the increased seaborne commerce, particularly between Jolo and Zamboanga, provided new opportunities for piratical activity. Traders based in Jolo were attracted to the newly established Zamboanga Exchange, where they were able to sell their products, such as fruit and pearl shells, at higher prices than in the Sulu Archipelago. In order to avoid strong currents in the vicinity of Basilan the traders had to steer north and pass through the Pilas Islands, which, according to the colonial newspaper in Moro Province, the *Mindanao Herald*, was 'famous in history and song as the rendezvous of daring pirates'. Toward the end of 1906 the paper also reported that pirates from Pilas were harassing Jolo traders on the route between Zamboanga and Jolo. Several *vintas* with traders bringing the proceeds of their sales back to Jolo had reportedly disappeared at sea close to the islands, presumably as a result of pirate attacks that had left all of the victims dead. In December 1906, however, a Jolo *vinta* managed to escape after being chased by pirates for some 40 miles. Complaints were made to the American authorities, who stepped up their efforts to suppress the depredations.[149]

In the early months of 1907 it seemed that the repressive measures taken by the provincial authorities, aided by friendly local *datus*, were having the desired effect of bringing the piracies under control. It was believed that most

---

[145] *Manila Times* (15 June 1906), cit. in Tan, 'Sulu under American Rule', 75–6.
[146] Edw. Y. Miller, Report of the Governor of Palawan, 15 July 1907, in *ARPC* 1 (1907), 425–6.
[147] Ibid., 44.   [148] *ARGMP* (1908), 23.
[149] *Mindanao Herald* (22 December 1906); Report on Tribal Ward No. 1, 2 May 1908, Tasker Howard Bliss Papers (THBP) 91 (MDLC).

Piracy Resurgent 81

of the depredations were the doings of a single small band of pirates from Jolo based in Pilas. They were reportedly led by a one-eyed Moro named Tahil, and the authorities estimated that the capture or elimination of the band was close at hand. In March a detachment led by the headmen of the tribal ward at Basilan, *Datu* Gabino, killed two members of the band and captured another two. The *datu* had the two dead outlaws decapitated and sent their heads to the district governor of Basilan, Major John Finley, for the purpose of identification – a practice that, according to the *Mindanao Herald*, was an old Moro custom that had been common during the Spanish colonial period. Governor Finley, however, strongly objected and 'most forcibly' informed *Datu* Gabino that such gruesome methods would not be tolerated.[150]

Despite this and other successful measures, the hope that the piracies around Basilan would be brought to a swift end was confounded as the year 1907 progressed. In May a *vinta* with two Moro pearl fishers was attacked near Pilas, and one of the victims was abducted and the other wounded.[151] In September a Chinese pearl trader was stabbed and robbed by the crew of a small vessel that he had chartered to take him, his mother and a young cousin from Basilan to Zamboanga.[152] A few weeks later, at the beginning of November, a Chinese trader, Tao Tila, and three Moro crew members on route from Jolo to Zamboanga were attacked off the north coast of Jolo and Tao Tila, and two crew members were killed. The aggressors made off with the cargo of merchandise worth about 1,000 pesos. The only remaining crew member, however, escaped by jumping into the water and was subsequently able to bring the news of the attack to the attention of the authorities and the colonial press.[153]

According to the *Mindanao Herald*, Basilan was now 'becoming a rendezvous for all the bad characters of the Sulu Archipelago'.[154] The band of outlaws led by Tahil – who was still at large despite the efforts to apprehend him – was constantly being enlarged by renegade Moros from Jolo and nearby islands. A hostile local Muslim leader in Basilan, Salip Aguil, was suspected of protecting them. A military expedition, reinforced with thirty constabulary soldiers from Zamboanga, tried to chase down the suspected pirates, but the

---

[150] *Mindanao Herald* (30 March 1907); cf. (20 April 1907).
[151] *Mindanao Herald* (25 May 1907). Arnold, *Moro War*, 183, seems to attribute this attack to Jikiri, but he does not state where this information came from or even which attack he refers to. The earliest raid that can safely be attributed to Jikiri seems to be the attack on Tao Tila on 1 November 1907; *Mindanao Herald* (25 January 1908); see also below. Hurley, *Swish of the Kris*, 199, who in addition to newspaper reports relied on oral sources, seems to be of the same opinion, although he elsewhere states that Jikiri's depredations started in the middle of 1907; ibid., 198.
[152] *Mindanao Herald* (21 September 1907). [153] *Mindanao Herald* (25 January 1908).
[154] *Mindanao Herald* (14 September 1907).

82   The Sulu Sea

operation only resulted in the killing of one man, a Yakan, who turned out probably not to have been a member of Tahil's band.[155]

The surge in piratical activity around Basilan coincided with increased efforts on the part of the American authorities to develop the island economically. Basilan was believed to have great economic potential, particularly for the production of timber, rubber, hemp and other staple products, and the population was generally seen as peaceful and amenably disposed to American rule.[156] Most of the island was covered by forest, and American settlers had in the previous years set up logging camps and other businesses on the island.

Despite the depredations of the Jolo outlaws affecting the local traders around Basilan, it looked as if the risk of an attack against white settlers or traders was small or even inconceivable. American soldiers were occasionally attacked by Moros in certain parts of Moro Province, particularly in Jolo and the Lanao District in Mindanao, but otherwise the life and property of American and European colonisers – in contrast to Chinese traders – seemed on the whole to be secure. This assessment probably contributed to the relative lack of interest on the part of the authorities in suppressing piratical activity, despite the apparent increase from 1906.[157]

Jikiri and the Last Wave of Sulu Piracy

On Christmas Eve 1907, Kopagu, a logging camp on the east coast of Basilan, was attacked by a group of Moros who descended on the camp from the sea.[158] After landing on the beach, the raiders sneaked up on the three men in the camp – one American, one Dutchman and one Chinese – and killed them, almost simultaneously, by hacking them to pieces with machetes (*barongs*). In addition, the wife of one of the men received a deep cut across her back and barely survived. After having taken control of the camp the raiders proceeded to carry off everything of value, including, it seems, a substantial amount of cash.[159]

The raiders had come to Kopagu by boat, but it was initially suspected that they had come from the nearby village of Ucbung, the home of Salip Aguil, an Islamic leader whom the Americans suspected of sponsoring Jolo pirates.

---

[155] *Mindanao Herald* (21 September 1907). See also Tan, 'Sulu under American Rule', 76–7.
[156] E.g., *ARGMP* (1908), 25; *Mindanao Herald* (15 February 1908).
[157] The *Mindanao Herald* (28 December 1907), for example, noted that although there had been numerous attacks on the peaceful Moros of Basilan throughout 1907, the marauders had not, until the end of the year, been so bold as to attack white men.
[158] This is a condensed account of Jikiri's depredations, based on Eklöf Amirell, 'Pirates and Pearls'.
[159] Memorandum for Major Finley and Captain Muir, 3 January 1908, THBP 88 (MDLC); *Mindanao Herald* (28 December 1907).

Ucbung was also believed to be the centre for the piratical depredations that for more than a year had affected the waters around Basilan.[160]

The news of the murders caused a great uproar in the colonial community in Zamboanga. The two white men were well-known and apparently much-liked figures among the Europeans and Americans of Moro Province.[161] In the week after the raid, two well-attended public meetings were held for the purpose of supporting the government in the capture of the perpetrators and assisting the survivors of the attack. The meetings, among other things, discussed how to improve security for the white settlers in the region. The consensus was that Moros should not be allowed to carry any arms except smaller machetes (*bolos*) and only when engaged in labour requiring them. They should not be allowed to enter any town or village carrying knives or other arms. American and European colonialists, by contrast, were to be sufficiently armed to defend themselves from attacks by Moros, and demands were made for the government to facilitate the procuring of arms by white settlers in the province. The meetings focused on the protection of the white community in Moro Province, whereas there is no indication in the newspaper reports of the events that the protection of Chinese, Filipino or other Asian traders and settlers was discussed, despite the fact that one of the murdered men was Chinese and both the widows of the two other slain men were Japanese.[162]

The tragic event brought much latent racist sentiment to the fore. The *Mindanao Herald* probably reflected the general mood when it editorialised that the raid revealed 'the Moro again in all the savage cruelty and treachery of his nature' and that the murders had 'stirred this community to a sense of the dangers which attend the isolated Americans and Europeans who are facing the wilderness with the spirit of the Western pioneers in an effort to push a little farther the bounds of our civilization'. The newspaper also called for prompt and resolute action by the government for a 'salutary lesson' to be taught to the 'murderous bands of vagabond Moros' who terrorised the Basilan coast. Ucbung and Malusu, another village suspected of harbouring pirates, should be wiped out, and every Joloano on Basilan should be made to go to work or be 'driven into the sea', according to the editorial. The operation on Bud Dajo in March 1906 was held up as a model for such prompt and resolute action.[163]

The murder of two white men by Moro pirates was thus immediately seen as a major security threat that demanded swift, extraordinary measures. Governor Bliss requested military reinforcements from Manila for the purpose of

---

[160] *Mindanao Herald* (28 December 1907); see also *ARGMP 1908*, 25, for Salip's role in sponsoring the perpetrators of the raid and other Jolo outlaws.
[161] Thompson, 'Governors of the Moro Province', 155–6.
[162] *Mindanao Herald* (4 January 1908).
[163] *Mindanao Herald* (28 December 1908; 4 January 1908).

bringing the perpetrators to account and restoring confidence in the ability of the authorities to uphold law and order in the province, and in early January 1908 a battalion of four infantry companies was dispatched to Basilan.[164] Their orders were to take Ucbung, where the perpetrators were believed to be still hiding, and to arrest Salip, who was suspected – wrongly, as it later turned out – to have been the mastermind behind the attack.[165] Meeting no resistance, American troops captured Ucbung, but Salip and his followers had already escaped, and only one man was arrested.

Although the authorities were convinced of Salip's complicity in the attack, they had little positive information about the identity and origin of the raiders beyond that they were from Sulu. By coincidence, however, more information was obtained through the arrest of a Moro implicated in the murder of the Chinese trader Tao Tila and two of his crew members two months earlier. The suspect confessed to taking part in the attack on Tao Tila and also revealed that the leader of the band responsible for the attack was Jikiri, a Moro from the small island of Patian, to the south of Jolo.[166] It also transpired that the raid on the logging camp was meant as revenge on the Americans for arresting their comrade.[167]

After the raid on Kopagu, Jikiri and his followers took refuge in Patian and then in Jolo, where they seem to have received assistance from *datus* hostile to the Americans. Successfully evading capture, Jikiri ventured forth occasionally to conduct several minor raids in the first months of 1908, before he, along with ten of his followers, in March, conducted a major raid on Maibung (Maimbung), the Sultan's capital on the south coast of Jolo. Three Chinese shop owners were killed and several other people were wounded, and every store in town was burned to the ground. Apart from Europeans and Americans, the Chinese who traded and operated small stores and businesses around the Sulu Archipelago were the main target of Jikiri and his band. Jikiri's aversion to the Chinese appears to have been based on his resentment against their commercial success in the colonial economic system, a success which was perceived as having come at the cost of Moro traders and producers. The Chinese, moreover, were an easy target because they often lacked the protection of the local population or local strongmen. Some of the Chinese merchants who survived the raid on Maibung even claimed that the Sultan had received warning of the impending raid but had failed to share it with them.[168]

---

[164] Report of the Department of Mindanao, *ARWD* 3 (1909), 271.
[165] Thompson, 'Governors of the Moro Province', 156.
[166] *Mindanao Herald* (25 January 1908).
[167] Report of the Department of Mindanao, *ARWD* 3 (1908), 272.
[168] Chinese Merchants of Jolo to Colonel Alexander Rogers, 5 May 1908, THBP 91 (MDLC).

By mid 1908 Jikiri had evaded capture for more than half a year and appeared to be growing increasingly confident, which allowed him to expand his operations and recruit more followers. In August his band reportedly consisted of dozens of armed men capable of attacking larger vessels, particularly pearling luggers, which was another main target for Jikiri and his followers. In the middle of August a pearling lugger was attacked by some forty armed men in four *vintas* off the island of Tunkil, between Jolo and Basilan. The attackers killed a Japanese pearl diver and four Moro crew members, and made off with half a ton of pearl shell, including several valuable blisters, and a supply of provisions.[169]

By this time, it was estimated that Jikiri had killed around forty people, most of whom were Chinese, and the failure of the authorities to kill or capture him was starting to draw criticism, not only because of the insecurity that the depredations brought on the region, but also because Jikiri reportedly had begun to acquire a heroic reputation among the Moros. As a consequence, it was feared that his depredations might develop into a full-scale rebellion against American rule.[170]

The Army was assisted in the manhunt by the Philippine Constabulary, a paramilitary force consisting of indigenous troops led by American officers. The rivalry between the Constabulary and the Army, however, hampered the efforts to defeat Jikiri and his band. The Chief of the Constabulary, General Harry Hill Bandholz, accused the Army of being incompetent in dealing with the situation and was convinced that his forces would have defeated Jikiri quicker and with far fewer losses than the military, had they been allowed to bring their small launches to the Sulu Archipelago.[171] Bandholtz's argument seemed convincing to the governor-general of the Philippines, William Cameron Forbes, who blamed the provincial governor and his inefficient management of Moro Province for the failure to catch Jikiri.[172]

The Constabulary troops, however, were on the whole no more successful than the Army in their efforts to kill or capture the outlaws. Captain F. S. De Witt of the Constabulary – who, in contrast to most Army officers, spoke the Joloano dialect fluently – tried to trace Jikiri with a small detachment, hoping to get information from the local population in order to catch him and his band off guard. In November 1908 De Witt believed that he had trapped Jikiri near Parang on the West coast of Jolo. An exchange of fire ensued, and four outlaws were killed, but Jikiri himself escaped.[173]

---

[169] Rodgers to Bliss, 15 August 1908, THBP 86 (MDLC); see also *Mindanao Herald* (22 August 1908).
[170] *Mindanao Herald* (22 August 1908). On Jikiri's attacks against Chinese, see also Tiana to Scott, 3 September 1908, HLSP 11 (MDLC).
[171] Coats, 'Philippine Constabulary', 24–5.
[172] Thompson, 'Governors of the Moro Province', 167–8.
[173] Bliss to Provsec, 24 August 1908; Bliss to Rodgers, 29 August 1908, THBP 86 (MDLC); *Mindanao Herald* (9 September 1908; 31 October 1908; 14 November 1908).

86   The Sulu Sea

In January 1909 Jikiri's band made their hitherto boldest attack when they assaulted a pearling fleet consisting of four luggers owned by a British businessman based in Zamboanga. The attack took place off Parang, on the west coast of Jolo, and was carried out by four *vintas* coming from the shore. Two of the pearlers managed to escape but the other two, *Ida* and *Nancy*, were surrounded by the raiders and looted, and *Ida* was sunk by the pirates. Most of the crew members managed to escape by swimming to the shore, but a Japanese diver and three crew members were killed. When American troops arrived at the scene the following day they were unable to catch any of the perpetrators, and they managed only to retrieve a lamp from *Nancy*, despite a thorough search operation in a nearby village, where Jikiri was believed to have disposed of the goods.[174]

By now the depredations were beginning to have palpable economic effects. Pearling luggers fishing in the Sulu Archipelago had difficulties recruiting local crews because of their fear of piratical attacks at sea.[175] Interisland trade and exports from the province declined sharply, with the period from July 1908 to April 1909 – which approximately coincided with Jikiri's most successful period of operation – showing a two-thirds decrease in customs returns at Jolo. According to the collector of customs at the port, the decrease was due to the insecurity of life and property throughout Sulu district owing to the depredations. Chinese businesses were particularly affected, and all but two Chinese merchants – one of whom was suspected of being an accomplice of Jikiri – stopped doing business in the area outside the garrisoned towns of Jolo, Siasi, Sitankai, Bongao and Jurata.[176]

Two days after the attack on the pearling fleet off Parang, Governor Bliss formally asked the aid of the Navy for assistance to suppress the piratical attacks by Jikiri and his band.[177] Bliss was convinced that the withdrawal of the gunboats in mid 1907 was the main reason for the renewed pirate activity in the province. In his annual report for the fiscal year 1907–08, he wrote:

Since the withdrawal, about a year ago, of the small, light-draft gunboats which were employed by the Spanish and American governments alike for the suppression of piracy in the Sulu seas, there has been a revival of lawlessness which nothing but the continued presence of these vessels will prevent. The Spanish Government made no progress in complying with its international obligations for the suppression of piracy until it built and maintained this fleet of small vessels. The American government found them here engaged in the performance of this international duty and continued to maintain them until about the close of the last fiscal year. So far as the government of this province knows, no question has ever been raised as to the necessity of their continued presence.

[174] Bliss to Smith, 28 January 1909, THBP 100 (MDLC); *Mindanao Herald* (30 January 1909).
[175] *Mindanao Herald* (30 January 1909).
[176] *Straits Times* (29 May 1909); *ARGMP* (1910), 6–7.
[177] Report of the Department of Mindanao, *ARWD* 3 (1909), 224.

It may be, though it is scarcely conceivable, that the maintenance of the peace for a couple of years, without any serious outbreak of hostility, has given rise to the belief that the Moro has changed his nature. The Joloano Moro is now just what he has always been—a warrior and a pirate.[178]

Bliss believed that a dozen gunboats were needed to keep Moro Province free from pirates, but he was only able to secure the aid of the *Arayat* and the *Paragua*, both of which arrived at the end of February. Operations around Basilan over the following weeks resulted in the capture of seventeen prisoners and the confiscation of a number of rifles, spears and other weapons, but those arrested turned out not to be members of Jikiri's band. The gunboats were then dispatched to the Sulu Archipelago, but again they failed to catch Jikiri, despite several close brushes with his band.[179] According to the commander in charge of the manhunt, Colonel Ralph W. Hoyt, the operation was hampered by 'scarcity of transportation, the numerous islands affording hiding places, and the utter impossibility of obtaining from the natives any information concerning the whereabouts of this band'.[180]

In this situation Jikiri launched a counteroffensive against the Americans. Shortly after the arrival of the gunboats, he attacked the Constabulary barracks at Siasi, where twenty-two troops were stationed under the command of Captain De Witt, apparently for the purpose of securing arms and ammunition. Over 600 bullets were fired into the barracks before the troops managed to repel the attack. Jikiri's band were forced to retreat, reportedly taking four dead comrades and a number of wounded with them.[181]

A few days later, after an unsuccessful attack on a Greek sponge fisher on the island of Latuan, Jikiri and his band landed on the small island of Simunul (Simonore) in Tawi-Tawi, where an English trader and a former American soldier were murdered. Both were killed in ways similar to those murdered in the attack on Kopagu, and the body of the Englishman was hacked into thirty-two pieces that were scattered over an area of several meters.[182]

The raid on Simunul was the last of Jikiri's spectacular attacks. The massive manhunt against him and his band – which by now was believed to consist of more than a hundred mostly well-armed men – finally began to bear fruit.[183]

---

[178] *ARGMP* (1908), 23. See also Bliss, Report of the Department of Mindanao, in *ARWD* 3 (1908), 294, for a further plea for the necessity of gunboat patrols in the Southern Philippines.

[179] *Straits Times* (26 February 1909); *Mindanao Herald* (6 March 1909); Report of the Department of Mindanao, *ARWD* 3 (1909), 208. For the initial reports of the raid at Lampinigan, when it was attributed to Jikiri, see *Mindanao Herald* (30 January 1909).

[180] Hoyt, Report of the Department of Mindanao, in *ARWD* 3 (1909), 208.

[181] *Mindanao Herald* (27 March 1909).

[182] Bliss to Smith, 22–23 March 1909, THBP 101 (MDLC); *Mindanao Herald* (27 March 1909).

[183] *Mindanao Herald*, 27 March 1909. The estimation is probably reasonable: in all, sixty-four of Jikiri's followers were known to have been killed during the long campaign against him and

The two gunboats relentlessly pursued the outlaws throughout the Sulu Archipelago, and throughout May and June military and constabulary troops killed dozens of members of Jikiri's band, including his closest lieutenants.[184] At the beginning of July Jikiri himself was cornered on Patian, where he barricaded himself in a cave with six men and three women. They were besieged for two days by troops from the Sixth Cavalry, supported by the Navy and Artillery, before they made a deliberately suicidal attempt to break out. Jikiri and all of his followers, men as well as women, were killed. The Americans also suffered heavy casualties, including four killed and twenty seriously wounded.[185]

A New Pearl-Fishing Regime

The unbridled violence and the hideous mutilations, combined with the swift and unexpected character of Jikiri's attacks, were designed to strike fear in the hearts and minds of Americans, Europeans and Chinese in the Sulu Archipelago. As such, Jikiri's tactics can be characterised as terroristic, and the authorities had obvious problems in eliminating him and his band. Not only did trade and pearl-fishing in the archipelago come to an almost complete stop for fear of the raids, but the killings also, as the *Mindanao Herald* put it, 'created a feeling among all white planters and traders that no one is safe'.[186] The fear that Jikiri's depredations provoked among foreigners also drew on a long-established image of the Moro as a violent and brutal pirate.[187]

Three main explanations as to the rise of Jikiri have dominated the literature to date. The first is the lack of naval patrols in Moro Province, particularly after the withdrawal of the Navy's gunboat patrols in mid 1907. As we have seen, Governor Bliss and other American officers in Moro Province believed that this was the major reason for the surge in piracy from the end of 1907. The explanation rests on the covertly racist assumption that the Joloano Moro was a pirate by nature, as Bliss argued, and the fact that piracy returned to the region as soon as the opportunity arose seemed to imply that the American – and earlier Spanish – attempts to make him change his ways and give up piracy for more peaceful pursuits had been largely unsuccessful. Essentially, this explanation was a variety of the so-called innate theory of piracy, which assumed that the propensity to carry out piratical depredations was an 'integral part of the

---

another forty were subsequently sentenced to prison; see Woods, 'Looking Back Thirty Years', 191; *Straits Times* (30 November 1909).

[184] *ARWD* 3 (1909), 208; see also *Straits Times* (4 May 1909); *Mindanao Herald* (29 May 1909, 19 June 1909).

[185] *Straits Times* (19 July 1909); Record of events, Post return: Post of Jolo Pl, July 1909. Returns from US Military Posts, 1800–1916; Microfilm M617, Roll: 53 (NARA); see also Davidson, 'Jikiri's Last Stand', 14–16, 71–2, for an eyewitness account.

[186] *Mindanao Herald* (27 March 1909).   [187] E.g., *ARGMP* (1908), 24.

Malays' behavior, if not an inherent defect in their character', as Anne Lindsey Reber put it in her analysis of Raffles's writings on piracy in the Malay Archipelago a century earlier.[188]

The second explanation as to Jikiri's depredations has been surprisingly persistent since it was first introduced by Vic Hurley, an American journalist and amateur historian, in 1936, despite – or possibly because of – its obviously fanciful character. According to this explanation, Jikiri turned to a life of banditry because of a physical defect. His otherwise striking appearance was allegedly marred by one eye being considerably larger than the other, and the ridicule that he suffered as a young man for his looks caused him to seek fame with his *kris*. 'The strength of my *kris* arm will comfort the women who now shun me', he allegedly told Jammang, one of his accomplices.[189] Aside from the obviously legendary character of the alleged explanation, it does not explain why Jikiri was able to carry out his depredations and evade capture by superior American forces for more than eighteen months. Hurley may have told the story of Jikiri's physical defect to add flair and character to the pirate chief, but it is remarkable that the explanation continues to be cited in scholarly literature.[190]

According to the third, and more plausible, explanation, Jikiri took to banditry because of the failure of the American colonial administration to respect the traditional rights of the Moros with regard to the pearl beds of the Sulu Archipelago. The explanation was first conveyed to the Americans by Sultan Jamalul Kiram II, when he met President William Howard Taft in Washington, DC, the year after Jikiri's defeat.[191] In his memoirs published in 1928, the district governor of Sulu from 1903 to 1906, Hugh Lenox Scott, also linked Jikiri's depredations to the loss of control over the pearl beds of Sulu:

There were several laws emanating from Manila, against which I protested in vain, that caused a vast amount of trouble and even bloodshed in Sulu. One was the confiscation of the pearl-beds by the government without compensation to the owners. Those pearl-beds had been owned by families for more than a hundred years, and were as much

---

[188] Reber, 'Sulu World', 2; Raffles, *Memoir*, 78.
[189] Hurley, *Swish of the Kris*, 198. In another book, *Jungle Patrol*, 302, which appeared two years later, however, Hurley instead cited Jikiri's personal skills as a war leader as the reason for his piratical depredations. These allegedly included a 'great personal magnetism, the cunning of a leopard, the ferocity of a boar, and the benefit of Arab blood to give him prestige', in addition to a tall and broad-shouldered physique.
[190] E.g., Gowing, 'Mandate in Moroland', 520; Arnold, *Moro War*, 183; Fulton, *Moroland*, 343.
[191] Col. Frank McIntyre to General John J. Pershing, 1 October 1910, John J. Pershing Papers 128 (MDLC). Mentions of this explanation are found in Gowing, 'Mandate in Moroland', 520; Thompson, 'Governors of the Moro Province', 157–8, J. V. Uckung, 'From Jikiri to Abu Sayyaf', *Philippine Inquirer* (9 June 2001).

personal property as the oyster-beds of New Jersey or Virginia. This brought on the war of Jikiri that culminated after I left.[192]

The pearl beds of the Sulu Archipelago were among the richest in Southeast Asia, and pearls and pearl shells had been exported from the region to the outside world for centuries. According to Moro custom, all of the land and sea belonged to the sultan, who granted his subjects the exclusive right to the pearling grounds that they found in exchange for the privilege of receiving the largest pearls. Such pearling grounds were handed down from generation to generation and thus, as noted by Scott, were considered family possessions.[193]

The economic significance of pearl-fishing increased in the second half of the nineteenth century as demand from merchants, based mainly in the Straits Settlements, increased, and the Spanish embargoes and attempts to destroy the commerce of the Sulu Sultanate made the population more dependent on the natural resources of the archipelago.[194] Toward the end of the Spanish period, however, the traditional pearl fisheries came under pressure as modern pearl luggers equipped with diving suits and air pumps began to operate in the Sulu Archipelago. In 1892 a firm owned by two Chinese businessmen, Leopoldo Canizato Tiana and Tan Benga, was established at Jolo, which then was in Spanish hands, and began to fish for pearls with six modern and fully equipped boats of about 10 tons each. According to a Protocol from 1885 between Britain, Germany and Spain, fishing in the Sulu Archipelago was free for all, and the firm consequently did not feel obliged to ask the sultan – who had not been consulted in the negotiations that led to the Anglo–German–Spanish agreement – for permission to fish for pearls in the waters off Jolo, nor to pay him for the privilege of doing so. The luggers were instead protected by the Spanish Navy and only fished in the vicinity of Jolo, literally under the Spanish guns. In the wake of the Spanish–American War of 1898, however, the Spanish garrison at Jolo was greatly reduced, and the colonial gunboats were no longer able to protect the operations of Tiana and Tan. The merchants were thus forced to make terms with the sultan and pay him 100 dollars a month for the right to fish in the Sulu Archipelago. Two other firms, one based in London and one in Singapore, also began pearling in Sulu around the same time, but in contrast to the Chinese firm they made agreements with the sultan from the start and did not need to fish under Spanish protection. In 1899, moreover, the Philippine Pearling and Trading Company, owned by a German long-term resident of Jolo, Eddie Schück, and his brother Charlie, signed an

---

[192] Scott, *Some Memories of a Soldier*, 370.
[193] Dalrymple, *Historical Collection* 1, 1, 11; Appendix: Notes and Reports on Mineral Resources, Mines and Mining, Pearl, Shell, and Sponge Fisheries: Statement made by the Sultan of Sulu relative to the Pearl Fisheries, *ARPC* 2 (1908), 529.
[194] Warren, *The Sulu Zone, 1768–1898*, 121.

A New Pearl-Fishing Regime 91

agreement with the sultan that gave them the exclusive rights to fish for pearls using boats with diving equipment around Jolo.[195]

In 1904, shortly after the abrogation of the Bates Agreement, a law was passed that opened up the Sulu Archipelago to pearl fishers of all nations. Licence fees for fishing were to be collected by the treasurer of Moro Province, whereas it was made illegal for any Moro – including the sultan and the leading *datus* of Sulu – to try to exact payment from pearl fishers. The law also stated that the governor of Sulu district was to 'investigate the alleged claims of certain Moros residing within his district to property rights in the shells of marine molluscs in the seas adjacent to their places of residence'. A sum equivalent to half of the proceeds of the licence fees during the first year and a half after the implementation of the law was to be set aside for the compensation of such claims. The payment was to be 'understood to be in full and final settlement of the supposed property rights of the Moros of the district of Sulu'.[196] However, as indicated both by Scott's description cited earlier and by the financial statement of Moro Province for the fiscal year 1906, the payment was never distributed.[197] From 1 January 1906, moreover, the exemption from paying the licence fee for vessels up to 15 tons owned, manned and operated wholly by Moros, as stipulated by the law, expired, thereby putting a new financial burden on local Moros engaged in pearl-fishing. The law also unintentionally imposed an additional hardship on the Moros because it prevented them from exchanging their shells for food and clothing, which the larger boats easily could have carried, had they not been prohibited from trading in pearl shells by the law.[198]

An attempt to investigate the claims to the pearling grounds in accordance with the law on pearl-fishing was undertaken by the local authorities in Jolo in September 1907. Scott's successor as district governor of Sulu, Colonel E. Z. Steever, convened a board for the purpose of carrying out the investigation of the traditional claims to the pearl beds. The move was rejected by Provincial Governor Bliss, however, who was of the opinion that because the investigations had not been carried out immediately after the law was passed, as

---

[195] *ARPC* 2 (1908), Appendix, 524, 526–7.
[196] Act no. 43 approved by the Philippine Commission 19 July 1904, *ARPC* 2 (1908), Appendix, 549–52; quotes, 551.
[197] *ARGMP* (1906), 47–50. The government collected 3,300 pesos in shell-fishing licences in Sulu district, equivalent to eleven first-class licences (each allowing the operation of one diver equipped with submarine armour), but there is no mention of the disbursement of the compensation among the expenditures for the year. It is also clear from subsequent official correspondence that the compensation was never paid; Governor of Moro Province to the District Governor of Sulu, 13 April 1908, THBP 90 (MDLC).
[198] *ARPC* 2 (1908), Appendix, 544–5, 551. The luggers were required to keep a log of their catches and testify to their accuracy before entering the port of Jolo or Zamboanga, thereby, in effect, prohibiting them from buying or selling pearl shells while operating in the archipelago.

prescribed by the law, the provisions therein had 'expired by the limitation imposed by its own terms', in the words of Bliss.[199] No compensation was thus to be paid to the Moros, according to the governor, who also thought that it was time for the Moros to start paying for their fishing licenses.

Shortly afterwards Steever was replaced as district governor by General C. L. Hodges, who – like his successor, Alexander Rodgers – did not pursue the issue of compensation. The failure of Steever's attempt to settle the compensation question occurred about a month before the first known attack by Jikiri in November 1907, and probably influenced his decision to take to piracy.

The changes in the pearl-fishing industry, combined with the abrogation of the Bates Agreement and the imposition of the deeply unpopular head tax, not only affected Jikiri and his band but all Sulu Moros as well. Consequently, it seems that the population of Sulu had little sympathy for the efforts of the authorities to hunt down Jikiri. Quite a few people – among them the hundred or so who joined him – may even have regarded Jikiri as a hero and something of an anticolonial resistance fighter. Although it is probably an exaggeration to claim that Jikiri's motives were political rather than economic – his actions, in fact, resembled more those of a desperado rather than a politically motivated resistance leader – his success in evading capture for more than a year and a half was to a great extent due to the general discontent among the Sulu Moros with the laws and policies of the American colonial administration after 1904. This popular discontent was an important reason for the difficulties that the authorities had in suppressing the most serious wave of piracy and coastal raiding in the Philippines throughout the American colonial period.

Maritime security conditions improved significantly in the Sulu Archipelago following the defeat of Jikiri and his band, and the exports from Jolo recovered.[200] Occasional pirate attacks and coastal raids nonetheless continued in the year following his death. In October 1909, as the trials against the surviving members of Jikiri's band were still going on, an American-owned plantation on Basilan was raided, and a large amount of moveable property was stolen. In the same week two pearling luggers were attacked off Jolo, probably by the same band, but the crews were able to fight off the raiders. In neither instance was anyone killed or wounded.[201]

---

[199] Governor of Moro Province to the District Governor of Sulu, 13 April 1908, THBP 90 (MDLC).

[200] Total exports from Jolo increased by almost 50 per cent between 1909 and 1910, and pearl shells by over 80 per cent; *ARGMP* (1910), 9–10.

[201] *Straits Times* (15 October 1909). In September 1909, a rumour that a British customs cutter had been pirated and the captain along with thirteen crew members murdered, however, proved to be false; *New York Times* (27 September 1909).

A more serious attack occurred in the following year, when seven Sulu Moros raided a settlement in Sulawesi and murdered and robbed two Dutch farmers. The raiders then took refuge on Manuc Manka, a small island near Bongao. The American colonial authorities – obviously fearful of a new wave of piracy – immediately dispatched the constabulary from Bongao, followed by four companies of infantry from Jolo. A Dutch gunboat assisted the troops by patrolling the adjacent seas, and, with the aid of the local population, six members of the band were arrested, whereas the leader was killed by the local Moros who assisted the colonial troops.[202]

After 1910, pirate attacks in or emanating from the Sulu Archipelago became even rarer and remained so for the duration of the American colonial period. Conditions of law and order improved steadily, in part because of an executive order issued by the provincial governor in 1911 that prohibited the unlicensed possession of firearms, as well as cutting and thrusting weapons. It is likely that unreported cases of petty piracy and coastal raids continued, but as far as is known the only documented case of piracy before the outbreak of World War II occurred in June 1920, when two boats with twelve Dutch subjects were attacked at sea by a band of twenty-four Moros in six *vintas* from South Ubian. The victims were robbed of their possessions, and two women were raped. The pirates then cut holes in the victims' boat in order for it to submerge, but the victims managed to mend the holes and save themselves. The perpetrators were subsequently identified and captured, and two of them were sentenced to death and executed in 1922, after the Supreme Court in Manila had rejected their appeals.[203]

Summary

Maritime raiding was an integral part of the social, economic and political fabric of the Philippine islands in precolonial times, but the expansion of the European colonial powers in maritime Southeast Asia from the sixteenth century stimulated piracy and maritime raiding in and emanating from the Sulu Archipelago in several ways. The Moro Wars, which shaped relations between the Muslims of the southern Philippines and the Spanish colonisers from 1565 to 1878, entailed a sharp increase in the level of maritime violence in the Philippines and neighbouring parts of the Malay Archipelago. Maritime raiding was used as a

---

[202] *ARGMP* (1910), 19–20; *Annual Report of the Director of the Constabulary* (1910), 9; *Straits Times* (1 June 1910). See also Tagliacozzo, *Secret Trades*, 115, for a summary of the same event based on Dutch sources.
[203] 'The People of the Philippine Islands vs. Lol-lo and Saraw', Supreme Court of the Republic of the Philippines, G.R. No. 17958 (27 February 1922), in Lauterpacht and Williams (eds.) *Annual Digest* (1932), 164–5; cf. Rubin, *Law of Piracy*, 318–19, who discusses the legal implications of the case.

tactic in the wars by the Spanish as well as the Moros, both for the purpose of damaging the enemy's economy and military capacity and for the purpose of material gain. As regards the latter, the main objective of the Moros and other raiders based in the southern Philippines was the capture of slaves.

Slavery was common throughout Southeast Asia, but its importance increased in the early modern period, both because of the Moro Wars and the strong demand for slaves in the European colonies, particularly in the Dutch East Indies. From the second half of the eighteenth century, slave-raiding was also stimulated by the increased demand for export products from the Sulu Archipelago, such as pearls, sea cucumbers, wax, bird's nests and tortoise shells, the provision of all of which was principally the work of slaves.

Before the middle of the eighteenth century Spanish sources rarely referred to raiders from Sulu and adjacent parts of the archipelago as pirates, but as the Sulu Sultanate rose to power toward the end of the century by successfully combining maritime raiding, the slave-based production of export commodities and trade, the Spanish – and other Europeans – began increasingly to describe the Sulu Moros as pirates. Under the influence of Enlightenment notions of race and civilisation, piracy became associated with certain ethnic groups, particularly the Muslim population of Sulu. Islam was seen as an important part of the explanation of the piratical habits of the Moros, which strengthened the case for proselytisation and the conversion of the Moros to Catholicism, particularly from the middle of the nineteenth century.

Allegations of piracy also served to justify Spanish military intervention in the Sulu Archipelago, particularly from the 1840s, when imperial rivalry, combined with increased Spanish naval power, led to a more aggressive policy of colonial expansion in the southern Philippines. As the European states grew economically, politically and militarily stronger, it became increasingly important for them to enforce their monopoly on violence, not only within their territory and colonies but also emanating from them. Against this background, and with imperial rivals, such as Great Britain, France, the Netherlands and Germany, showing greater interest in the southern Philippines over the course of the nineteenth century, it was of crucial importance for Spain to demonstrate sovereignty over the Sulu Sea and to enforce a monopoly on violence in the area. Suggestions for naval cooperation with the Dutch and British in order to suppress piracy were rejected by the Spanish because of worries that such cooperation might compromise the Spanish claim to sovereignty over Sulu, a claim that was not formally recognised by the other imperial European powers before 1885. Sovereignty, rather than the suppression of piracy, was thus the overriding concern for the Spanish as they increased their presence in the Sulu Archipelago from the 1840s, eventually leading to the conquest of Jolo in 1876.

With the establishment of regular Spanish naval patrols and of garrisons in Sulu, large-scale organised piracy in and emanating from the region came to an end. It is likely, however, that piracy would have come to an end even without the ruthless search-and-destroy strategy of the Spanish Navy from the 1870s. By the mid nineteenth century, the sultan of Sulu had begun to distance himself from the Iranun and Sama raiders and declared himself willing to collaborate with the colonial powers, particularly Britain, for the suppression of piracy. The Sulu Sultanate was in the process of restructuring its economy, from a focus on the slave trade and maritime raiding to trade in export commodities. However, Spanish monopolistic commercial policies and the use of maritime violence to eliminate indigenous maritime commerce hampered the transition. Moro traders, pearl fishers and producers of export commodities were replaced by European and Chinese merchants – largely because of their better access to capital and international commercial networks, but also because of Spanish trade embargoes and naval patrols targeting Moro shipping.

During the first years of the American colonial period sporadic piratical attacks occurred, targeting mainly local fishermen and coastal populations in the southern Philippines, Palawan and eastern north Borneo. As the American military established firmer control over the southern Philippines from 1903, however, piracy seems to have come to an almost complete stop, and for several years, until the middle of 1906, no pirate attacks were reported from Moro Province.

After the imposition of direct rule in 1904 the colonial authorities tried to stimulate commerce and the extraction of natural resources in Moro Province. These efforts included measures designed to improve conditions for indigenous traders and producers, for example by the establishment of regular markets. However, the intensified exploitation of the natural resources of the Sulu Archipelago, particularly in the pearl-fishing sector, seemed to benefit foreign economic interests at the expense of the local population. The economic marginalisation of the Moros and the opening up of the pearl beds of Sulu to outsiders without due compensation by the authorities thus led to much resentment and set the stage for a resurgence of maritime violence. In 1907–09 Jikiri and his band of at least 100 followers were responsible for a sustained wave of piracy, robbery and murder that the colonial authorities, only with difficulty and after a manhunt that lasted for more than a year and a half, were able to suppress.

Shortly after the defeat of Jikiri and his band, piracy in the southern Philippines seems to have come to an end, and for the remainder of the colonial era there were only a handful of sporadic pirate attacks in the region. It was not the definite end of piracy in the Sulu Archipelago, however, and in the wake of World War II, maritime raiding once again began to emanate from the region and affect the eastern coast of north Borneo, stimulated by the spread of firearms and the motorisation of sea transportation.

3   The Strait of Malacca

Next to the Sulu Sea the most pirate-infested region in Southeast Asia according to nineteenth-century colonial observers was the Strait of Malacca. The conditions for piratical activity were (and still are) in many ways formidable. The natural geography of the area, with many small islands, secluded bays, rivers and densely forested coastlines, was ideal for launching swift attacks and for evading capture afterwards. The southern part of the Strait of Malacca and the adjacent Strait of Singapore has throughout history been a bottleneck for regional and long-distance maritime commerce, which has provided raiders with a wealth of richly laden targets.

Given these circumstances it is unsurprising to find attestations of piratical activity in the Strait of Malacca since the earliest historical times.[1] Like elsewhere in the Malay Archipelago, piracy and maritime raiding in precolonial times were often linked to political processes, and the control of maritime violence and commerce was a key to political power as well as wealth. Piracy and maritime raiding thus fluctuated over time with political developments, and tended to increase in times of political instability and upheaval and, conversely, to decrease in times of political stability and centralisation.

The arrival of European navigators in the area from the turn of the sixteenth century triggered a period of political insecurity, characterised by an increase in piracy and maritime raiding perpetrated by both European and Malay navigators. In 1511 the Portuguese conquered Melaka (Malacca) on the west coast of the Malay Peninsula, the main commercial hub in Southeast Asia, which led to a dispersal of the trade previously centred on the port-city and a decline in its prosperity. The conquest also led to an increase in piratical activity in the Strait due to the demise of Melaka's sea power, which previously had checked the activities of local raiders, and due to the Portuguese raids on Arab, Indian, Malay and other Asian shipping, and on coastal settlements.

---

[1] The earliest mention of piracy in the Strait of Malacca is probably from the beginning of the fifth century, when the Chinese Buddhist monk Faxian reported that the 'sea is infested with pirates, to meet whom is death'; Fa-hsien, *Travels of Fa-hsien*, 77. See also Wheatley, *Golden Khersonese*, 82, for a fourteenth-century testimony.

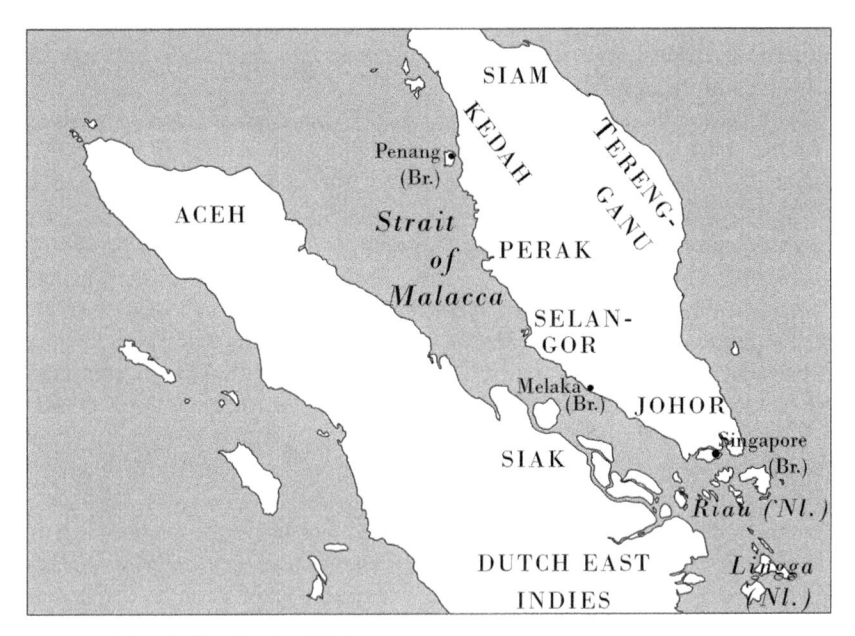

Map 3: The Strait of Malacca

As in the Indian Ocean, the Portuguese tried to establish the *cartaz* system in the Strait of Malacca (and other parts of maritime Southeast Asia), but they had too few ships at their disposal in order to enforce it efficiently. Meanwhile, the decline of Melaka paved the way for the rise of Aceh in northern Sumatra and for Johor in the Riau Archipelago, both of which competed fiercely for the remainder of the sixteenth century with the Portuguese and with each other for dominance in the Strait. As in the southern Philippines, maritime violence and raiding were the dominating form of warfare in the struggle for power in the Strait of Malacca throughout the early modern era.

Dutch Expansion and Notions of Piracy

From the turn of the seventeenth century the Portuguese were gradually pushed out of Southeast Asia by the Dutch and, to a lesser degree, the English. The Dutch East India Company established itself as the dominant power in the Strait of Malacca and much of the rest of the Malay Archipelago (except for the Philippines), particularly after they established a permanent base in Batavia (Jakarta) on the north coast of Java in 1619 and conquered Melaka from the Portuguese in 1641. The company's ruthless policy of conquering strategic ports and strongholds in the Indonesian Archipelago, killing or enslaving tens of thousands of people in the process, accelerated the decline of indigenous traders and rulers, and resulted in a sustained long-term drop in Southeast Asian commerce and prosperity.[2]

For most of the early modern period Malay piracy was not a major problem for the Dutch East India Company or other European navigators in Southeast Asia. The European vessels were generally larger and better armed than those of their Asian competitors, and they were thus less likely to be attacked. The prevalence of piracy and maritime raiding in the Strait of Malacca and other parts of the Malay Archipelago in fact often benefitted European navigators, both because it struck at their commercial competitors and because of the opportunities that such activities offered for trade with the raiders or their associates. The Dutch and other Europeans thus readily sold arms and munitions to Malay pirates in exchange for slaves, contraband and pirated goods.[3]

The fact that the Dutch thus indirectly thrived on piracy did not prevent them from using the word to discredit their enemies in the Malay Archipelago. For example, after the Dutch sack of Makassar in Sulawesi in 1669 large numbers of Makassarese and Bugis migrated and formed large fleets led by Bugis and Makassarese noblemen. They earned a reputation as formidable fighters and traders, and their services were welcomed by many indigenous rulers in the eastern parts of the Malay Archipelago.[4] They also engaged in maritime raiding, although piracy for private gain seems to have been relatively rare.[5] Dutch sources from the last decade of the seventeenth century nevertheless described the Makassarese raiders as full-fledged pirates, and decisive measures were taken in order to suppress them, even after most of the Makassarese diaspora had been repatriated to Sulawesi in 1680.[6]

Just as in England, the decades around the turn of the eighteenth century marked a shift in the Dutch attitude toward piracy and maritime raiding. In the Dutch case, moreover, the new policy was conditioned by the adverse effects that the slave raids had on Dutch settlements and interests in Southeast Asia. The raids mostly emanated from the southern Philippines and the eastern parts of the Indonesian Archipelago that were outside the control of the Dutch East India Company. From the beginning of the eighteenth century the Company began to take measures designed to suppress piratical activity, both in the eastern parts of the Indonesian Archipelago and in the west, in and around the Strait of Malacca. In 1705 the company issued a detailed regulation that limited the number of crew members and passengers that indigenous craft were allowed to carry, obviously without concern for the increased

---

[2] Reid, *Southeast Asia*, 2, 272–4.
[3] Kathirithamby-Wells and Hall, 'Age of Transition', 260–1. [4] Ibid., 260–1.
[5] L. Y. Andaya, *Heritage of Arung Palakka*, 208–28; 226.
[6] Hägerdal, *Hindu Rulers*, 77–80.

vulnerability that the restrictions entailed for indigenous traders. From the middle of the century three cruisers were engaged to keep the north coast of Java free from pirates, and during the rest of the century further measures were taken to ensure that the indigenous rulers with whom the Dutch had friendly relations would cooperate in order to suppress piracy in and emanating from their lands.[7]

Such measures notwithstanding, however, piracy and maritime raiding increased significantly, particularly after 1770, when raiding emanating from the Sulu Archipelago took off – stimulated, as we have seen, by the integration of the region into the commercial networks that connected Europe and East Asia and by the demand for slaves in the Dutch East Indies and other colonies.[8] The annual raids of the feared Iranun, or *lanun* (pirates), affected large parts of maritime Southeast Asia. Toward the end of eighteenth century the Iranun had also established forward bases in several places in the Strait of Malacca, including in Riau and along the east coast of Sumatra, and began to plunder the coasts and maritime traffic of the Strait systematically. The Iranun were drawn to the area by the opportunities for raiding offered by the burgeoning maritime traffic and by the power vacuum due to the decline of the Dutch East India Company and the political instability of the major indigenous power in the southern part of the Strait of Malacca, the Sultanate of Johor.[9]

The complex historical, social and political reasons behind the surge in maritime raiding in Southeast Asia from the end of the eighteenth century were not entirely understood by contemporary Dutch colonial administrators and observers. As among other Europeans, the explanations generally focused on racial, cultural and religious factors. With regard to the latter, Islam was believed to be instrumental in sanctioning piracy and slave-raiding among the Malays. Pieter Johannes Veth, who was one of the leading scholars on the geography, history and culture of the Dutch East Indies in the nineteenth century, argued, for example, that piracy in the archipelago to a large extent should be understood as a form of *jihad*.[10] The religious antagonism, however, was less pronounced in the context of the Dutch East Indies than in the Spanish Philippines, and the Dutch did not try to make the Malays abandon their piratical habits by converting them to Christianity.

There was some disagreement among Dutch colonial officials as to whether certain groups of Malays should be labelled piratical or not, and as to which policies were most efficient for bringing an end to maritime raiding. The report by a Malay translator for the Dutch colonial government, Johan Christiaan van

---

[7] Cornets de Groot, *Notices historiques*, 3.   [8] See Vink, "'World's Oldest Trade'".
[9] Vlekke, *Nusantara*, 197–8; Warren, *Iranun and Balangingi*, 58–9; cf. Trocki, *Prince of Pirates*, 68–9.
[10] Veth, 'Heilige oorlog', 175–6.

Angelbeek, from 1825, for example, presented an image of piracy in the Riau-Lingga Archipelago as a traditional way of life on the part the so-called Rayat Laut (lit. 'sea people'), embedded in regional patterns of dependency and servitude to Malay princes and headmen. Rather than suggesting a military solution to suppress piracy – which was the method of choice for most Dutch colonial administrators and military officers at the time – Van Angelbeek proposed that antipiracy measures focus on offering alternative sources of income to the pirates in order to wean them from their traditional way of life.[11]

For the most part Dutch efforts to deal with piracy in the first half of the nineteenth century focused on repressive measures. After the British handed back Java to the Netherlands at the end of the Napoleonic Wars the colonial authorities stepped up their efforts to enlist the support of indigenous sovereigns in an attempt to suppress piracy. The Malay rulers of several autonomous states in the archipelago, such as Lingga, Banjarmasin and Pontianak, signed, or confirmed, treaties of friendship with the Dutch government in which they, among other things, promised to punish pirates and not allow them to reside in their territory.[12] The Dutch, however, were aware that most indigenous rulers – to the extent that they were willing to cooperate in the suppression of piracy – had very limited means at their disposal, and the Dutch colonial government tended instead to rely above all on its own marine forces to suppress piracy and to prevent smuggling. Anglo–Dutch rivalry in the Strait of Malacca, moreover, provided a further rationale for strengthening Dutch naval power in the region, as did the Java War (1825–30), which brought about an increase in maritime raiding. As a consequence of these developments, Dutch forces in the Strait of Malacca, and in Southeast Asia in general, were much larger than the British. Dutch sea power was further strengthened in the 1830s, when a permanent coastguard was set up to suppress piracy and smuggling. In addition, several units of the Dutch Navy regularly cruised the colony's archipelagic waters throughout the nineteenth century.[13]

It seems that these efforts began to bear fruit from the 1840s, although it is not always immediately obvious which colonial power was responsible for the decline in piratical activity. In 1848, for example, there was a sharp falling-off in maritime raiding in the eastern parts of the Dutch East Indies. Dutch officials put this development down to the fear that the Dutch steamers aroused among those inhabitants of the colony who harboured piratical inclinations. It seems

---

[11] à Campo, 'Discourse without Discussion', 202–3; see further Teitler et al., *Zeeroof*, 35–8. The traditional way of life of the Rayat, or Orang Laut, were in decline at the time, however, in a process that had begun more than a century earlier; see Barnard, 'Celates, Rayat-Laut'.

[12] [Anonymous], 'Piracy and Slave Trade of the Indian Archipelago', 586; de Hollander (ed.), *Handleiding*, 88.

[13] Teitler et al., *Zeeroof*, 68, 95; cf. Somer, *Korte verklaring*. See also Tagliacozzo, *Secret Trades*, 58–62.

likely, however, that the Spanish destruction of the Sama base at Balangingi in the beginning of the year was at least as consequential in bringing about the decline in maritime raiding – possibly combined with the withdrawal of support and sponsorship by the Sulu Sultanate for the Iranun and Sama raiders.[14]

As in the Spanish colony, there was little questioning among the Dutch of the use of the label *piracy* to describe the various bands of Malays who were responsible for the maritime violence in the archipelago, particularly in the press and among the general public in the Netherlands. The Dutch discourse about piracy in the East Indies tended to label all forms of maritime violence perpetrated by Malays as piracy and thus illicit, whereas coercive and violent practices on the part of the colonial government and European and other foreign individuals were seen as legitimate and regarded as a buffer against indigenous piracy.[15] The Dutch media was above all concerned with the extent and efficiency of the antipiracy measures taken and less with questioning the rationale and motives for designating various ethnic groups as piratical.[16]

To the extent that criticism against the promiscuous use of the allegation of piracy and the excessive violence deployed to suppress it was voiced in the Dutch context, it came largely from government officials in the Dutch East Indies. In 1838, for example, the governor-general of the colony, J. C. Baud, complained to the Dutch government about a naval operation in Flores that had resulted in the destruction of fifty vessels and seven prosperous villages, and left 14,000 people homeless. A few years earlier the Resident of Riau had voiced similar apprehensions about the use of indiscriminate violence against alleged pirate communities.[17] Such voices were nonetheless rare and seem to have met with little sympathy in the Netherlands.

Piracy and British Expansion in Southeast Asia

Piracy, as we have seen, had been a topic of great public interest in Great Britain at least since the beginning of the eighteenth century. As the British expanded into Southeast Asia, particularly during the following century, piracy frequently became the object of considerable controversy in Great Britain, more so than in any of the other major four colonial powers in Southeast Asia in the nineteenth century. The great British interest in piracy can be explained by the importance of piracy in the country's history, particularly in British overseas expansion – both with regard to the piratical imperialism of the sixteenth and seventeenth centuries and to Britain's leading role in the struggle to suppress piracy from the turn of the eighteenth

---

[14] Teitler et al., *Zeeroof*, 96; de Moor, 'Warmakers in the Archipelago', 63. On the destruction of Balangingi, see Warren, *Iranun and Balangingi*, 343–78.
[15] Teitler et al., *Zeeroof*, 119. [16] Warren, *Iranun and Balangingi*, 86.
[17] Teitler et al., *Zeeroof*, 91–2.

century. The cultural fascination with pirates as fictional or semifictional characters also served to stimulate public interest in piracy in its various guises.

Many nineteenth-century Britons associated piracy with the trafficking of slaves. The background to this association can be traced to 1807, when Parliament prohibited the slave trade and the Royal Navy was charged with the task of intercepting ships of any nationality suspected of trafficking slaves across the Atlantic. The Navy declared slave-trading to be on a par with piracy, a feat that served as a legal justification for the self-proclaimed right of Britain to intercept and search foreign vessels on the high seas.[18]

Apart from the effort to suppress the transatlantic slave trade, British antipiracy operations in the first half of the nineteenth century were concentrated on the three areas where the problem seemed to be most serious: the Mediterranean, the Persian Gulf and the Malay Archipelago. In all three areas the vast majority of the alleged pirates were Muslims, and in line with the arguments made by contemporary Dutch and Spanish observers, Islam was seen as a corrupting force that encouraged both piracy and the abduction and trafficking of slaves. Piracy also began to be linked to the lack of civilisation on the part of certain nations or races, particularly Arabs and Malays.[19]

John Crawfurd, a Scottish colonial official and scholar, who served in several capacities in the British colonial administration in Southeast Asia in the first half of the nineteenth century, was a leading proponent of stadial theory, and influenced subsequent British perceptions and policies pertaining to piracy in Southeast Asia. According to Crawfurd, there were hardly any maritime peoples in the Malay Archipelago that had not at one time or another engaged in piracy, and the only ones who were not inclined to piracy, at least not in present times, were the agricultural peoples of Java, Bali, Lombok, Sumatra and the Philippines under Spanish control.[20]

British commercial interests in Southeast Asia can be traced to the beginning of the seventeenth century, but their presence in the region was for a long time limited to the west coast of Sumatra, where the English East India Company established a trading station at Benkulu (Bencoolen) in 1685. During the following century, British interests in Southeast Asia, particularly the Malay Peninsula, increased because of its strategic location between India and China, and its commodities, particularly tea and opium. In 1786 the company established a free port called George Town on the island of Penang

---

[18] Wilson, 'Some Principal Aspects', 506, n. 5.
[19] Eklöf Amirell, 'Civilizing Pirates'; Layton, 'Discourses of Piracy', 86; for examples of such racist discourses, see Raffles, *Memoir*, 73, 78; Keppel, *Visit to the Indian Archipelago*, 1, 127.
[20] Crawfurd, *Descriptive Dictionary*, 354. Comparing the inhabitants of the Malay Archipelago with the 'tribes of the deserts of Arabia', Crawfurd explained the prevalence of piracy and other forms of lawlessness by the uncivilised state of their societies; Crawfurd, *History of the Indian Archipelago*, 1, 72; cf. Knapman, *Race and British Colonialism*.

off the west coast of the Malay Peninsula. A major purpose of Penang was to compete with the declining Dutch East India Company for the trade in the area, and Penang developed rapidly during its first decades, attracting large numbers of Chinese, Indian, Malay and European traders.[21]

The founding of Penang coincided with a surge in maritime raiding in Southeast Asia after 1770 and the establishment of forward bases of the Iranun in Riau and the east coast of Sumatra in the 1780s. This maritime raiding, combined with the political instability of the Sultanate of Johor, led to a deterioration in maritime security, which threatened the commerce and prosperity of Penang. To a large extent these concerns explain the increase in British allusions to piracy in the Strait of Malacca from the end of the eighteenth century, but there were also pragmatic reasons for labelling the Malay raiders pirates. In 1784, the British Parliament had passed the East India Company Act, which aimed to bring the company's rule over India more firmly under London's control. The Act, among other things, cancelled the delegating of the presidencies subordinate to the governor-general in Calcutta to make war or negotiate treaties with foreign potentates without explicit permission from higher authorities, ultimately from London, except in the direst emergencies. The provision thus limited the scope for local initiative, and company officials in Southeast Asia began to look for a way to circumvent the restrictions. By extending the term *piracy* to include not only raids against ships for private gain but also naval operations and other forms of maritime violence sanctioned by indigenous sovereigns, British officials in Southeast Asia gave themselves *carte blanche* to take military action without seeking prior permission from London or Calcutta. British officials in the region also believed that the Malay nobility and others engaging in piratical activity had to be convinced that the British would not confine themselves to defensive measures but would be proactive in their efforts to uphold maritime security in the Strait of Malacca and other major sea-lanes of communication in the region.[22]

The blueprint for much of British policy in Southeast Asia during the nineteenth century was drawn up by Sir Thomas Stamford Raffles, who served as lieutenant-governor of Java during the British occupation of the island between 1811 and 1815, and who in 1819 founded Singapore. Although Raffles gave different explanations for the prevalence of piracy in the Malay Archipelago in his many speeches and writings, he principally believed that piracy was a consequence of the commercial and political decline of indigenous commerce and polities due to the long-standing, ruthless and monopolistic

---

[21] See Cowan, 'Early Penang'. [22] Rubin, *Law of Piracy*, 222.

commercial policies of the Dutch in the archipelago. Such policies, according to Raffles, were 'contrary to all principles of natural justice, and unworthy of any enlightened and civilised nation'.[23]

Like other British observers in the nineteenth century, Raffles did not necessarily see a contradiction between the historical and the racial or cultural explanations, or, in the words of Anne Lindsey Reber, the 'decay' and the 'innate' theories of piracy.[24] On the contrary: both explanations were consistent with stadial theory, and both also sat easily with the Orientalist trope of the decline and decay of formerly great Oriental civilisations. The attractive implication of this line of argument was that the British had a special obligation to bring civilisation and progress to the Malays and thus to end the decay imposed on them by two centuries of Dutch oppression. The best way to do so, according to Raffles, was to suppress piracy and slave-raiding by providing commercial opportunities:

> We may look forward to an early abolition of piracy and illicit traffic, when the seas shall be open to the free current of commerce, and when the British flag shall wave over them in protection of its freedom, and in promotion of its spirit. Restriction and oppression have too often converted their shores to scenes of rapine and violence, but an opposite policy and more enlightened principles will, ere long, subdue and remove the evil.[25]

Raffles further argued that the British should support the indigenous Malay rulers and strengthen their authority over their shores and over the lesser chiefs, who frequently were the instigators of piratical activities.[26]

Such policies were implemented in Raffles's lifetime and afterwards by means of so-called agreements or treaties of peace and friendship. Hundreds of such bilateral treaties were concluded in the course of the nineteenth century between Great Britain or the East India Company and Asian sovereigns of greater or lesser importance. The agreements typically regulated matters of sovereignty, jurisdiction and commerce, always to the advantage of the British, who invariably were the economically, politically and militarily stronger party. From around 1820 most of the treaties – like the corresponding Dutch and Spanish treaties with indigenous rulers in the archipelago – included one or several paragraphs in which both parties promised to do their best to suppress piracy in and around their territories. There was no explanation or legal definition of the words *piracy* or *pirate* in the treaties, however, a circumstance that served to give the British colonial officials and naval officers on the spot

---

[23] Raffles, *History of Java*, 1, 255.
[25] Raffles, *Memoir*, Appendix, 20.
[24] Reber, 'Sulu World', 2.
[26] Raffles, *Memoir*, 227.

great leeway in deciding what constituted piracy, and to deploy harsh and often arbitrary measures to suppress it.[27]

Anglo–Dutch Rivalry and the Suppression of Piracy

As in the Sulu Sea, the efforts of the colonial powers to suppress piracy and other forms of maritime violence in the Strait of Malacca in the nineteenth century were hampered by imperial rivalry. British expansion in the area was viewed unfavourably by the Dutch, who not only resented the commercial competition but also feared that that British might try to extend their territory and political influence to Sumatra, which the Dutch considered to be within their sphere of influence. The establishment of Singapore, which soon eclipsed Penang as the major British commercial and administrative hub in Southeast Asia, exacerbated these tensions, which in turn led to negotiations that eventually, in 1824, resulted in the Treaty of London between the two countries. The British ceded Benkulu to the Dutch in exchange for Melaka, and promised to respect Dutch sovereignty over Riau and other islands to the south of Singapore, whereas the Dutch withdrew their opposition to the establishment of Singapore. Both countries also agreed to take forceful measures to suppress piracy, but there was no concrete provision for naval cooperation or intelligence-sharing in the treaty.[28]

In 1826 the British merged their three colonies in the Malay Peninsula, Penang, Singapore and Melaka, to form the Straits Settlements, and six years later the administrative centre was moved from Penang to Singapore, which had undergone rapid economic and demographic growth since it was founded. The new colony was still a part of the East India Company's Indian possessions and subordinate to the governor-general in Calcutta. For almost fifty years, until 1874, official British policy was not to seek further territorial expansion in the Malay Peninsula or in other places around the Strait of Malacca. The emphasis was instead on maintaining friendly relations with the indigenous Malay Sultanates that controlled the rest of the peninsula, and on developing profitable commercial relations with merchants and producers regardless of origins or nationality. In contrast to the more aggressive policies pursued by the British in Burma, the policy in the Strait of Malacca before the 1870s was thus very much that of 'Imperialism of Free Trade', in the words of John Gallagher and Ronald Robinson. It was a policy that in many ways was advantageous to the British, as it relieved them of the burden of administering

---

[27] See Aitchison (ed.), *Collection of Treaties*, 1, 271, 280, 283, 313, for examples of articles related to the suppression of piracy in treaties between Malay rulers and the British; cf. also Belmessous (ed.), *Empire by Treaty*; Rubin, *Law of Piracy*, 206–11.
[28] Webster, *Gentlemen Capitalists*, 83–110; see further Tarling, *Anglo–Dutch Rivalry*.

vast territories populated by potentially unruly or hostile populations while at the same time bringing great commercial benefits to the British, such as access to markets and commodities.[29]

It was not only the British who profited from the country's free trade policy. The Straits Settlements also attracted large numbers of merchants and workers, including Chinese, mainly from Fujian and Liaoning (Kwangtung), Malays, Indians, Arabs and other Europeans. The population of Singapore multiplied in the decades following its foundation, and by the 1830s it had become the main commercial entrepôt in Southeast Asia.[30]

The Straits Settlements were vulnerable to piratical depredations, however, because they were an essentially maritime colony, the unity of which depended on the free flow of navigation in and out of the three settlements and between them.[31] Piracy and maritime raiding were a threat to the commerce of the colony and affected mainly the indigenous traders, whose small and weakly protected vessels were often easy targets for pirates. The problem was not alleviated by the Anglo-Dutch Treaty of 1824, despite the two countries' promise to act forcefully against pirates. Moreover, although Britain's Royal Navy was the most powerful in the world, her sea power in Asian waters was limited and generally insufficient for the purpose of suppressing piracy and slave-trafficking.[32] As a result, piracy continued unabated throughout the 1820s and most of the 1830s, leading the Straits government to worry that native trade in the region would eventually become extinct.[33]

The opportunities offered by the boom in maritime commerce combined with the lack of political control – on the part of both the colonial powers and the indigenous Malay states – made the Strait of Malacca a haven for maritime raiding. Marauders from around the archipelago were drawn to the area, including Malays from Johor, Riau-Lingga and Brunei, Bugis from Sulawesi, Dayaks from Borneo, Iranuns and Samas from the southern Philippines, and Acehnese from North Sumatra. In addition, Chinese pirates began to arrive in the region, particularly from the 1840s, as piracy surged in the aftermath of the Opium War. European and American adventurers also at times seized the opportunity and engaged in piratical raids.

Some of the pirates operated out of the Malay Peninsula, but most of them (apart from the Chinese) were based in Sumatra or the Riau-Lingga Archipelago, which was, at least nominally, under Dutch control. There were both small bands of freebooters and those who operated under the covert

---

[29] Gallagher and Robinson, 'Imperialism of Free Trade'.
[30] Turnbull, *History of Singapore*, 33–75; Ken, 'Trade of Singapore'; Annual Report of the Straits Settlements 1855–56, in Jarman (ed.), *Annual Reports*, 32.
[31] de Vere Allen, 'Colonial Office', 23.   [32] Graham, *Great Britain in the Indian Ocean*, 1.
[33] Mills, *British Malaya*, 263.

sponsorship of local Malay rulers, sometimes sponsored or led by members of a royal family or other notables. The predations of the major bands of pirates sometimes took the form of large-scale expeditions that could involve dozens of vessels and hundreds of men who attacked vessels at sea and in port and made coastal raids, mainly for the purpose of capturing slaves.

As among the Dutch, British knowledge about the identity and origins of the perpetrators was often scarce and confused, particularly before the 1830s. Moreover, despite the Treaty of 1824, mutual animosity and suspicion persisted between the Dutch and the British. These circumstances, combined with the lack of sea power on the part of the British, the region's natural geography, the navigational skills of the pirates, and the speed and shallow draft of their vessels, rendered the task of suppressing piracy and other forms of maritime violence difficult for the colonial authorities.[34]

Colonial officials tended to regard all Malays as more or less addicted to piracy, at least those who did not practise agriculture. Fishermen and others who lived on the coasts or around the estuaries of rivers were believed to be particularly prone to engage in piracy. According to Crawfurd, who was the resident of Singapore from 1823 to 1826, the maritime Malays were 'barbarous and poor, therefore rapacious, faithless, and sanguinary'. Piracy, Crawfurd thought, was part of their character.[35]

Despite such pervasive claims, which tended to regard Malays as pirates by nature, there were colonial and naval officials who expressed doubts about the sweeping use of the label *piracy* in the Malay context. In 1832 the commander-in-chief of British naval forces in the East Indies, Rear-Admiral Edward Owen, rejected the use of the term *pirates* to describe the Malay forces involved in a dynastic struggle in Kedah. To the dismay of the governor of the Straits Settlements, Robert Ibbetson, Owen said: 'I could not treat as pirates any against whom no acts of piracy had been specifically alleged, or proof obtained.'[36] A few years later the commander of a British gunboat in the Strait of Malacca, Sherard Osborne, likewise contested the East India Company's labelling of a fleet of forty Malay war-*prahus* as piratical:

This fleet of prahus, styled by us a piratical one, sailed under the colours of the ex-rajah of Quedah; and although many of the leaders were known and avowed pirates, still the

---

[34] Lombard, 'Regard nouveau'; cf. à Campo, 'Discourse without Discussion'; Tarling, *Piracy and Politics*. On the Dutch lack of intelligence about the pirates, see à Campo, 'Asymmetry, Disparity and Cyclicity', 43–4.

[35] Crawfurd, 'Malay Pirates', 243.

[36] Cited by the governor of the Straits Settlements, Robert Ibbetson, who, on the other hand, was disappointed by the lack of naval support for the suppression of what he considered piracy; see Kempe, '"Even in the Remotest Corners"', 371. Ibbetson himself, moreover, also rejected the use of the label *piracy* to justify political action; see Rubin, *Piracy, Paramountcy and Protectorates*, 17.

strong European party at Penang maintained that they were lawful belligerents battling to regain their own.

The East India Company and Lord Auckland, then governor-general of India, took however an adverse view of the Malay claim to Quedah, and declared them pirates, though upon what grounds no one seemed very well able to show.[37]

In the mid 1830s, however, the efforts to suppress piracy were stepped up, henceforth leaving little room for second thoughts as to who was a pirate and who was not. These renewed efforts had not only to do with the continued threat from piracy to the colony's commerce or the improved intelligence about the whereabouts and *modus operandi* of the perpetrators: it also gained strength from an Act, passed by Parliament in 1825, for encouraging the capture or destruction of piratical ships and vessels. The Act was originally passed for the purpose of suppressing piracy in the Caribbean during the Latin American wars of independence.[38] Most importantly in the present context, however, the Act established the practice of paying head money for the killing, capturing or dispersing of pirates:

[T]here shall be paid by the Treasurer of His Majesty's Navy ... unto the Officers, Seamen, Marines, Soldiers, and others, who shall have been actually on board any of His Majesty's Ships or Vessels of War, or hired armed Ships, at the actual taking, sinking, burning, or otherwise destroying of any Ship, Vessel, or Boat, manned by Pirates or Persons engaged in Acts of Piracy ... the Sum of Twenty Pounds for each and every such piratical Person, either taken and secured or killed during the Attack on such piratical Vessel, and then the Sum of Five Pounds for each and every other Man of the Crew not taken or killed, who shall have been alive on board such Pirate Vessel at the beginning of the Attack thereof.[39]

The Act did not require any adjudication of the criminality of alleged pirates, and killing them, rather than capturing or dispersing them, obviously facilitated the procedures for claiming the bounty, as there would be no one alive to dispute the accusation of piracy. Moreover, the stipulation that the reward for killing alleged pirates was four times that of dispersing them obviously encouraged the use of lethal violence and contributed to the brutality of British efforts to suppress piracy in Southeast Asia and elsewhere during the 1830s and 1840s.

---

[37] Osborne, *My Journal in Malayan Waters*, 22. The reluctance of the European community in Penang to intervene in the conflict was apparently linked to their commercial interests in Kedah; see Graham, *Great Britain in the Indian Ocean*, 375.

[38] Tarling, *Piracy and Politics*, 101. The Act was modelled on an Act from 1803 (superseded two years later but with the relevant provisions retained) meant to create incentives for British soldiers and sailors to fight in naval battles in the Napoleonic Wars. In contrast to the 1825 Act, however, the precursors did not differentiate between the remuneration for enemies killed, captured or dispersed; Rubin, *Law of Piracy*, 205.

[39] Ibid., 370, giving the full text of the Act (6 Geo. 4, c. 49).

The Act was not immediately implemented in Southeast Asia after it was passed in 1825, probably because of uncertainty about whether it was applicable in Asian waters and with regard to personnel serving on board the vessels of the East India Company. In 1836, however, a naval encounter with a fleet of alleged Malay pirates set a precedent.[40] The British frigate *HMS Andromache* encountered three *prahus* with about a hundred Malays from the Lingga Archipelago. A Scottish officer, Colin Mackenzie, who was on board ship as a passenger, described what happened after the British had fired their cannons and hit the Malay boats:

> The whole crew having in their desperation jumped into the sea, the work of slaughter began, with muskets, pikes, pistols, and cutlasses. I sickened at the sight, but it was dire necessity. They asked for no quarter, and received none; but the expression of despair on some of their faces, as, exhausted with diving and swimming, they turned them up towards us merely to receive the death-shot or thrust, froze my blood.[41]

A claim was subsequently submitted to the Admiralty for head money, and in following year the Admiralty paid £1,825 to the crew of the *Andromache* for defeating the alleged pirates. Remarkably, the bounty was paid despite the fact that nine alleged pirates, who were taken prisoner in the encounter, were acquitted of all charges because there was no evidence that they had undertaken or planned to undertake any act of piracy when they were attacked by the British. The advocate-general in Calcutta also noted that the Malays had not fired at the British before they were attacked by the *Andromache*, thus implying that the alleged pirates had in fact acted in self-defence.[42]

Another problematic circumstance (not raised by the advocate-general) was that, even if the three *prahus* had indeed been piratical, as defined by the British, only about one-third of those on board were likely to have been raiders or warriors. The majority of people on board a Malay *prahu* used for war or raiding were normally slaves, prisoners or hired hands whose task it was to row the boat and wait upon their masters.[43]

The risk of killing innocent people was obviously even greater when the British, soon after the massacre witnessed by Mackenzie, intensified their antipiracy campaigns and began to attack whole villages suspected of harbouring piratical persons. The main advocate for this policy was James Brooke, who was able to enlist the support of the Royal Navy in his campaigns against alleged pirates on the coast of north Borneo. Consciously stretching the definition of piracy and arguing that piracy in Asia was fundamentally different from European piracy, Brooke, in a memorandum of 1844, urged the

---

[40] Tarling, *Piracy and Politics*, 101; for the harsher measures employed by the British from 1836, see ibid. 81–90.
[41] Mackenzie, *Storms and Sunshine*, 64–5.   [42] Tarling, *Piracy and Politics*, 100.
[43] Teitler et al., *Zeeroof*, 79; cf. Warren, *Iranun and Balangingi*, 171–2, 175.

British government to burn and destroy all pirate haunts and disperse the pirate communities in order to eradicate the evil from the Malay Archipelago. The methods recommended by Brooke were diligently implemented during the remainder of the 1840s.[44]

The apparent discrepancy between, on the one hand, piracy in the legal sense of the word and, on the other, an allegation of piracy as a basis for claims to head money was resolved after a fashion by the High Court of Admiralty in 1845. In the so-called Serhassan case, named after a small island, Serasan, off the coast of northwest Borneo, where around thirty alleged pirates were killed and another twenty-five captured by a British naval expedition in 1843, the court ruled that the bounty claimed by those involved in the encounter was due, despite the lack of positive evidence that those killed or defeated were in fact pirates. In the opinion of High Admiralty judge Stephen Lushington, it was sufficient 'to clothe their conduct with a piratical character if they were armed and prepared to commence a piratical attack upon any other persons'.[45]

In the twelve years between 1836 and 1847 altogether £20,435 were paid for over 1,000 killed or (more rarely) captured Malay pirates, and £12,675 for some 2,500 dispersed pirates in Southeast Asian waters. During this time, the head money claimed from engagements in the Strait of Malacca and on the north coast of Borneo made up the bulk – more than 80 per cent – of total British payments for the capture and destruction of pirates worldwide.[46] The Admiralty, which paid the bounties, seemed to be of the opinion that if piracy was to be exterminated in the Malay Archipelago, there was little room for arguing about whether or not an attack had been justified or whether those killed were in fact pirates or innocent fishermen or traders.[47] Racial classification thus overrode other concerns, such as those pertaining to humanity and the rule of law, all under the colonial 'logic of the disposability of human life in the name of civilization and progress', as in another context Rolando Vazquez and Walter Mignolo put it.[48]

The antipiracy operations and the brutality used in them were controversial, however. In London, anti-imperialist politicians and humanitarian activists began to question the sweeping use of the term *piracy* in the Southeast Asian

---

[44] 'Mr Brooke's Memorandum on Piracy of the Malayan Archipelago', in Keppel, *Expedition to Borneo*, 302–14; cf. Knapman, *Race and British Colonialism*, 166–7.
[45] 'Serhassan (Pirates)' (1845), 2 W. Rob. 354, in *British International Law Cases*, 3, 779. See further Rubin, *Law of Piracy*, 230–2, for a fuller discussion of the court's decision and its implications.
[46] Pirates: Return of bounties paid for the capture and destruction of pirates, under the Act 6 Geo. 4, c. 49, Parliamentary Papers (PP) 114 (1850), 5. Mackenzie, *Storms and Sunshine*, 66, meanwhile, claims that 113 pirates were killed, 9 taken prisoner and 8 escaped in the engagement of May 1836.
[47] Graham, *Great Britain in the Indian Ocean*, 380–1.
[48] Vázquez and Mignolo, 'Decolonial Aesthesis', vii.

context and raised questions about who should be held responsible for the maritime violence and what the appropriate response of the British authorities should be. In particular, the brutal campaigns of James Brooke against the allegedly piratical communities of north Borneo began to draw sharp criticism in the press and in Parliament toward the end of the 1840s. Brooke was criticised, among other things, for designating as piracy what was actually intertribal warfare.[49] He was also chastised for the harsh measures employed to deal with the alleged pirates and the large-scale destruction of human life and property. With reference to the so-called Battle of Batang Marau in 1849, in which several villages were burned and some 500 alleged pirates killed, the Radical Member of Parliament Richard Cobden said: 'The loss of life was greater than in the case of the English at Trafalgar, Copenhagen, or Algiers, and yet it was thought to pass over such a loss of human life as if they were so many dogs; and, worse, to mix up professions of religion and adhesion to Christianity with the massacre.'[50]

The mass slaughter at Batang Marau led to a renewed effort to repeal the already criticised Bounty Act, a move that had begun a few years earlier, both for humanitarian and financial reasons. When the government, in 1850, demanded over £100,000 from Parliament to satisfy claims for head money – mainly for engagements in the South China Sea, but also including £20,700 for the 500 pirates who were killed and another 2,140 who were dispersed at Batang Marau – the process of changing the law was reinitiated.[51] The Act was repealed in 1850, although the practice of paying head money – now renamed 'prize money' – continued until 1948.[52]

While Brook and the Royal Navy campaigned against alleged pirates in north Borneo, piratical activity in the Strait of Malacca declined sharply, particularly during the second half of the 1840s. Between 1846 and 1849 there were only three reported attacks against British vessels committed by Malays or Dayaks, compared with twenty-two between 1840 and 1845: that is, a decline of 80 per cent on a yearly basis.[53] By the 1850s organised Malay

---

[49] Pringle, *Rajahs and Rebels*, 95; Walker, *Power and Prowess*, 232, n. 2; Knapman, *Race and British Colonialism*, 179–208. See also Keppel, *Visit to the Indian Archipelago*, 1–2, for a contemporary attempt to refute the allegations against Brooke.

[50] House of Commons Debate, 10 July 1851. Commons and Lords Hansard, Official Report of Debates in Parliament, vol. 118, cc 498–9. For the Battle of Batang Marau, see further Marshall, *Nemesis*, 208–15.

[51] Tarling, *Piracy and Politics*, 101, 139; Fox, *British Admirals*, 112.

[52] Rubin, *Law of Piracy*, 284, n. 168.

[53] Malay pirates. Return of the names of any British vessels attacked or plundered by Malay or Dyak pirates, from 1839 to 1849, PP HC 1850 (238).

piracy had ceased to be a security threat in the Strait of Malacca, even though occasional acts of petty piracy and coastal raiding continued to occur.[54]

It is doubtful to what extent the massacres of the 1830s and 1840s were responsible for the decline in piratical activity toward the middle of the century. John Crawfurd, who in 1825 had recommended that the most noted pirate haunts be destroyed by way of example, now advised against such methods:

> The destruction of the supposed haunts of the pirates by large and costly expeditions, seems by no means an expedient plan for the suppression of piracy. In such expeditions the innocent are punished with the guilty; and by the destruction of property which accompanies them, both parties are deprived of the future means of honest livelihood, and hence forced, as it were, to a continuance of their piratical habits. The total failure of all such expeditions on the part of the Spaniards, for a period of near three centuries, ought to be a sufficient warning against undertaking them.[55]

By contrast, Dutch efforts to suppress piracy, particularly in the Riau Archipelago, were of greater consequence. From the 1840s, the Dutch began to take firmer control over the Riau Archipelago, where most of the pirates were based, administratively, economically and militarily. The Dutch also began, on a limited scale, to promote indigenous trade as a means of weaning the Malay elites from engaging in or sponsoring piracy and to encourage them to take active part in the efforts to suppress piracy. The Dutch also intensified conventional antipiracy patrols, and, with improved intelligence and enhanced naval capacity, they were able to capture many of the perpetrators, often at their landbases. Thus deprived of their safe havens and protection from local rulers and strongmen, the pirates had little choice but to withdraw to more remote locations in the archipelago, or to take up other occupations.[56]

For the Dutch in the Strait of Malacca, like the Spanish in the Sulu Archipelago, it was of key importance to assert their sovereignty or hegemony over Sumatra and the Riau Archipelago by preventing maritime violence from emanating from Dutch territory or spheres of influence, and to affect British interests or international commerce. These concerns came to the fore in the early 1840s, when British naval vessels engaged in antipiracy operations violated Dutch territory on several occasions. In 1841, moreover, the British announced that they were considering abrogating the 1824 Treaty of London because of alleged commercial discrimination by the Dutch. By efficiently suppressing piracy emanating from its territory, the Dutch sought to alleviate the risk of further British intervention in the Dutch sphere and to weaken support for a more expansionist British policy in the Straits Settlements.[57]

---

[54] Crawfurd, *Descriptive Dictionary*, 355.   [55] Ibid., 355.   [56] Teitler et al., *Zeeroof*, 275.
[57] Ibid., 274–5.

Chinese Piracy

As the depredations by Malay pirates declined in the Strait of Malacca in the 1840s, a new type of piracy appeared, which soon came to constitute an even greater threat to the indigenous trade of the Straits Settlements than the earlier form. This new type of piracy was directly linked to social and political developments in China and the South China Sea. The Qing Dynasty enlisted large numbers of Chinese junks as armed privateers in the Opium War (1839–42) against the British, and after the end of the war many of them took to piracy. The Chinese authorities had little will or capacity to check the depredations of the pirates, most of whom were based in or around the major trading centres of southern China, such as Canton (Guangzhou), Hong Kong and Macau. Firearms and munitions were readily available in these ports, and the pirates could also easily acquire provisions and dispose of their booty there. The British authorities in Hong Kong were notoriously corrupt and inefficient in the colony's early years, and local officials at times even colluded with the pirates.[58]

The first reports of Chinese junks committing piracy in the Strait of Malacca in the 1840s led the Straits authorities to increase antipiracy patrols. There was no permanent British naval base in the region, however, and the colonial government itself had very limited ability to combat piracy. For most of the time there was only one British colonial steamer available for antipiracy operations in the Strait of Malacca. Piracy nevertheless declined in the second half of the 1840s – largely, as we have seen, as a result of the measures taken by the Dutch in Sumatra and Riau – which led the British to believe that their own efforts were sufficient to check both Chinese piracy and the depredations of the Malay raiders based in and around the Strait of Malacca.[59]

The decline in piratical activity in the second half of the 1840s was temporary, however, and once again events in China spilled over into Southeast Asia. In 1849 pirates from southern China robbed a junk belonging to a British subject and killed two British officers off the south coast of China, which led the Royal Navy to step up antipiracy operations in the South China Sea. At least in part as a result of these and subsequent naval operations, some of the perpetrators moved their operations to Singapore and the Malay Archipelago.[60] The upheaval of the Taiping Rebellion in southern China, which broke out in 1850, further contributed to the surge in piracy on the South China coast and in the major rivers of southern China. Pirates soon extended their

---

[58] Blue, 'Piracy on the China Coast', 71–2; Boxer, 'Piracy in the South China Sea', 44; Antony, 'Piracy on the South China Coast', 41–3; Fox, *British Admirals*, 86–7.
[59] Tarling, *Piracy and Politics*, 214.
[60] Antony, 'Piracy on the South China Coast', 42; Tarling, *Piracy and Politics*, 214.

operations further to the western parts of the South China Sea, including the waters off Vietnam, Cambodia, and the Gulf of Thailand. By the mid 1850s heavily armed junks also preyed on maritime commerce in the waters close to Singapore and in the Strait of Malacca.[61]

On average there were between one and two cases of piracy every month reported to the police in the Settlements between 1855 and 1860, with Singapore making up for more than half, or forty-nine out of a total of eighty-nine reported cases, followed by Penang with around 40 per cent, or thirty-six reported cases.[62] These figures, based on the number of cases reported to the Straits Settlements police, were only a fraction of the total number of pirate attacks committed, however, a circumstance of which the authorities were well aware.[63] Frequently none of the victims survived to report an attack to the police, and even if there were survivors, many attacks that occurred outside the jurisdiction (that is the ports and territorial waters) of any of the three settlements went unreported. Moreover, because of cultural differences and language barriers, it is likely that many victims of non-European nationality did not report attacks to the police. The local press, by contrast, was rife with horrific stories of piracy, and the Singapore newspapers featured reports of pirate attacks nearly every week for most of the 1850s.[64]

The main targets of the junk piracy were the small trading junks that plied the South China Sea between Singapore and Cochinchina (southern Vietnam). Unarmed or lightly armed junks carrying various types of cargo, such as opium, textiles, livestock and agricultural products, were boarded and robbed at sea, both in the waters near Singapore and along the east coast of the Malay Peninsula, and further to the north, in the waters around southern Vietnam and Cambodia. The level of violence varied depending on the *modus operandi* of the perpetrators and whether or not the victims offered resistance. Many attacks involved the use of indiscriminate and lethal violence.[65]

The depredations had a visible impact on the maritime trade between Singapore and Cochinchina. According to the Singapore Chamber of Commerce, the attacks brought about a sharp decrease in that trade in the junk season of 1853, an impression that is corroborated by official statistics. Between the fiscal years 1850–51 and 1853–54 the total number of junks arriving from or departing for Cochinchina declined from 255 to 156, that is,

---

[61] Elleman, 'The Taiping Rebellion', 53. See further Fox, *British Admirals*, about Chinese piracy and its suppression in the South China Sea in the mid nineteenth century.
[62] Numbers based on Jarman (ed.), *Annual Reports*, 40–1, 98–9, 173, 238, 292–3.
[63] E.g., Jarman (ed.), *Annual Reports*, 164, 188, 673.
[64] M. C. Turnbull, *History of Singapore*, 42.
[65] E.g., *Straits Times* (1 May 1855), 4. For an eyewitness account of a series of what seems to have been mainly nonviolent attacks by a pirate junk captured in 1859, see Jarman (ed.), *Annual Reports*, 202.

by close to 40 per cent.[66] According to contemporary newspaper reports, only half of the Asian vessels bound for Singapore from the east managed to reach their destination in 1854.[67]

The decrease, however, was not evident in the aggregate trade statistics for Singapore: the value of the total registered imports and exports of Singapore in fact increased by 46 per cent between the fiscal years 1851–52 and 1853–54. The volume of trade with other parts of Asia was not affected by the piratical activity, and the number of junks arriving from and departing for China and Siam increased substantially between the two fiscal years.[68] Moreover, the share of trade carried by square-rigged vessels – which in general were larger and more heavily armed than the small trading junks – increased and compensated for the decline in the junk trade.[69]

The Straits government received little support from Calcutta with regard to gunboats or other resources needed to suppress piracy. In 1855 the merchants of Singapore sent petitions to the governor-general of India, the Royal Navy and both Houses of Parliament, asking for naval protection and improved legislation to deal with the problem of piracy, but with no result.[70] Calcutta's apparent lack of interest in the maritime security and commerce of the Straits Settlements fed into a long-standing and widespread discontent in the colony with being subordinated to the English East India Company in India. In a petition to Parliament in 1857 a number of merchants complained – among a host of other things – about the failure of the company to take the problem of piracy in the Strait of Malacca seriously:

From the very first establishment of Singapore the trading vessels, and more especially the native craft, resorting to it, have been much exposed to the attacks of pirates. No systematic measures of protection have ever been adopted or carried out by the East India Company, who have been content to leave the service to be performed by the Royal Navy. Her Majesty's Naval forces being liable to be called away to other duties, can only act at intervals; and hence for long periods the neighbouring Seas have been left wholly or very slightly guarded and have at such times swarmed with pirates, to the great injury of the trade of this port.[71]

In view of the great risks of travelling by sea, many trading junks and other vessels were heavily armed with spears, swords, handguns, cannons and other weapons. According to the authorities, by the mid 1850s virtually all vessels leaving Singapore were heavily armed and appeared to have the means of committing piracy, but it was impossible to know whether they were armed for that purpose or for protection. Often the only times the authorities could be

---

[66] Ken, 'Trade of Singapore', 279; cf. Crawfurd, *Descriptive Dictionary*, 109–10.
[67] Turnbull, *History of Singapore*, 41.   [68] Ken, 'Trade of Singapore', 254, 276, 278.
[69] Trocki, *Prince of Pirates*, 99.   [70] Turnbull, *History of Singapore*, 42.
[71] *Straits Times* (13 October 1857), citing the full text of the petition.

certain were in the rare instances when pirates were caught red-handed committing a piratical attack at sea.[72]

The problem of identifying the pirates was not limited to the sea but was as pertinent on land. Singapore was in many respects an excellent base for fitting out and launching pirate expeditions, a circumstance that was frequently noted by contemporary observers.[73] In its early years, Singapore was even reputed to be a market for slaves captured by the Iranun and other raiders in Southeast Asia, despite the British commitment to the abolition of the slave trade.[74] By the middle of the century the Dutch resident in Riau, located just across the Singapore Strait, claimed that pirates had become both more deplorable and more frequent in Singapore than in Riau – which, as we have seen, until recently had reputedly been a pirate nest in the region – and that pirates based in both Singapore and Riau obtained their arms and munitions in British ports and sold their booty or exchanged it for ammunition there.[75]

Like Hong Kong in eastern Asia, Singapore was a major market for arms in Southeast Asia, and firearms and munitions were readily available for purchase. Moreover, there were no restrictions on the amount of armaments that a vessel could carry without being formally suspected of being a pirate vessel. The trade in arms was not regulated, and the importation of arms from Europe was an important part of the city's commerce. For example, in 1855, according to official figures, 3,659 iron guns, 15,259 muskets and 2,559 pairs of pistols were exported to Singapore, only from British and Dutch ports.[76] These figures did not include numerous unreported shipments of munitions. According to the governor of the Straits Settlements, Edmund Blundell, there was scarcely a mercantile firm in Singapore, regardless of nationality, that did not import large and small arms, military stores and ammunition.[77] Most of the arms were re-exported, particularly to China, where demand for arms and munitions was high because of civil unrest. Many weapons, however, also ended up on board pirate junks operating out of Singapore.

Besides the ready supply of arms, there were several other reasons Singapore was an excellent base for piratical operations. Unscrupulous crews could easily be hired, and information about the routes and cargoes of potential victims was easy to come by. Pirates could obtain passports and other papers from the Straits authorities by which they could pass themselves off as honest traders if they were visited by British, or any other nation's, vessels at sea. As a

---

[72] Jarman (ed.), *Annual Reports* (1855–56), 29–30; Tarling, *Piracy and Politics*, 214–27.
[73] E.g., Jarman (ed.), *Annual Reports* (1858–59), 164; cf. Stibbe, 'Zeeroof', 823–4.
[74] Mackenzie, *Storms and Sunshine*, 66.
[75] Cited by Keppel, *Visit to the Indian Archipelago*, 1, 279; see also Temminck, *Coup d'oeil général*, 2, 224, for similar analysis. Blundell's report from 1855, cited in Tarling, *Piracy and Politics*, 222, demonstrates that the British authorities also were aware of the problem.
[76] Jarman (ed.), *Annual Reports*, 29. [77] Chew, *Arming the Periphery*, 175.

port of free trade, Singapore was also a good place for the pirates to dispose of their booty with little risk of questions being asked about the provenance of the goods. As there were no tariffs or duties on imports or exports, there was little incentive or interest on the part of the authorities to keep records of the goods that changed hands, legally or illegally. The police, consequently, generally lacked the means by which to investigate reported cases of piracy through tracking down suspicious goods.[78]

The police sometimes searched suspected pirate junks in port, particularly those with heavy, offensive armaments and little cargo on board, but even when the indications of piratical intent were strong, there was little the authorities could do to stop the suspected marauders from setting out to sea. A police report from 1856, for example, gives the following account of an investigation in Singapore Harbour, which was conducted after rumours had reached the police that pirate vessels were being fitted out:

Junk No. 171 has twenty-three large Guns, most of them mounted; twenty-four Casks Gunpowder; number of Chinese Spears and Swords; a large quantity of shot, both small and large, with 13 Chests of Opium ... This Junk looks very suspicious; she is apparently a fast sailer, and with her large armament, would take, with ease, any Junk or Vessel that came in her way.

Junk No. 145 has thirty Guns, that is eleven large and nineteen small, all well mounted. She has also, in her hold, four very large Guns; they are lying right down in the centre of the hatch, and can easily be got up when wanted. Her powder is thirty-two piculs, with a large number of Shot of all sizes. Her cargo consists of sixteen Chests of Opium, Gambier and Shells in bags, with some empty boxes, and is ballasted with sand.

Junk No. 143 has fourteen Guns, nearly all large; forty kegs Gunpowder; a number of Boarding Pikes or Spears, and a large quantity of shot ...

The whole of the Junks mentioned have a very suspicious-looking appearance. At present they have but few men on board, but when they are about to leave to proceed to Sea, they generally take in a large number.[79]

The rudders were removed from the three suspected junks in order to prevent them from sailing, but they were returned after a few days because no proof could be presented of their intention to commit piracy. The owners of the junks, according to the report, 'of course, naturally argued that the armament was designed solely for defence'.[80]

Governor Blundell advised his superiors in Calcutta to pass new legislation in order to enable the authorities to take effective measures against the pirates. One of his proposed measures was to give the Straits authorities the right to detain in port suspect pirate vessels without the need to present concrete

---

[78] *Straits Times* (1 July 1851); Ken, 'Trade of Singapore', 6; Keppel, *Visit to the Indian Archipelago*, 1, 279; Chew, *Arming the Periphery*, 161.
[79] Jarman (ed.), *Annual Reports*, 29–30.   [80] Ibid., 30.

evidence of piratical intent.[81] The suggestion was controversial for the 'stretch of authority' that risked not only being inefficient but also bringing the government and the police into public contempt, as the *Singapore Free Press* opined.[82] Two years later a version of Blundell's suggestion was nonetheless passed into law in the form of the Indian Act XII of 1857 (Ordinance No. 7) on 'Piratical Native Vessels'. The Act stated that a native vessel could be seized and detained for up to six months by the authorities if there was reasonable cause to suspect that the vessel in question was a 'piratical vessel', 'belonged to pirates', 'intended to be used for piratical purposes or for the purpose of knowingly trading with or furnishing supplies to pirates'. The authorities were also invested with the power to order measures to prevent a vessel from going to sea if it was 'manned, armed, equipped, furnished or fitted out' in a manner deemed 'more than sufficient for the due navigation and protection thereof as a trading vessel'.[83]

The Act, however, did little to check the problem of piracy emanating from Singapore. In 1858, just like five years earlier, the authorities had to release six heavily armed junks, all of which had been detained on suspicions of piratical intentions under the Act. The junks were released after some 'Chinese merchants and shop-keepers of decided respectability' in Singapore had come forward and certified that the junks were peaceful traders.[84]

The law was in many respects a half-measure, and two of Blundell's more controversial suggestions in order to curb piratical activity around and emanating from the Straits Settlements were not adopted. One was the suggestion that the steamers and gunboats of the colonial government be given the right to visit, search and seize any suspect vessel, regardless of nationality, on the high seas. The governor argued for the legalisation of the 'apparently arbitrary seizures' which he believed were necessary, and he proposed that a powerful steamer, commanded by a 'young and active commander, manned by Malays and not encumbered with naval discipline and etiquette', nor with 'Common Law definitions of piracy' or the Admiralty's instructions to Her Majesty's Ships, be despatched to clear the Straits Settlements and its neighbourhood of all piratical vessels.[85] The suggestion was rejected by the Indian Government, however, on the grounds that it was beyond the colonial government's power to legislate on matters relating to the high seas and the law of nations.[86]

Although the governor failed to obtain legal sanction for some his proposed measures, antipiracy patrols and search operations were eventually stepped up

---

[81] Tarling, *Piracy and Politics*, 227.   [82] *Singapore Free Press* (11 November 1853).
[83] 'Piratical Native Vessels', Ordinance No. 7 [Indian Act XII of 1857; 29 May 1857], in *Laws of the Straits Settlements*, 1, 35–7. For the discussions preceding the passing of the ordinance, see Tarling, *Piracy and Politics*, 221–7.
[84] Jarman (ed.), *Annual Reports* (1858–59), 164–5.   [85] Tarling, *Piracy and Politics*, 223.
[86] Ibid., 224–5.

in order to suppress Chinese piracy. British vessels in the area – both the colonial steamers and the gunboats of the Royal Navy – interpreted their right to visit, search and seize suspected pirate vessels on the high seas generously. The antipiracy operations began to bear fruit toward the end of the 1850s. In May 1858 the colonial steamer *Hooghly* captured two suspected junks and brought them to Singapore, and in May the following year the Royal Navy's corvette *Esk* captured another two piratical junks, after they had managed to fight off the *Hooghly*. In each case there were about fifty Chinese on board, all of whom were convicted and sentenced to transportation to Bombay.[87]

Perhaps the most controversial of Blundell's suggestions was to curb the free trade in munitions (but not in arms) in the Straits Settlements, a trade that obviously stimulated piracy, not only in the Strait of Malacca and the Malay Archipelago in general, but also in China and the South China Sea. The problem was that the trade was extremely profitable and a cornerstone of the commercial success of the Strait Settlements. After the founding of the colony in 1826, the English East India Company had been given virtually free rein to trade in arms, even though there were strong concerns already at the time about the risk that arms and munitions that passed into Asian hands might be used in uprisings and piratical attacks. The company was nonetheless licensed to supply munitions to Asian buyers, but only in 'deserving' cases, including to indigenous rulers who ventured to suppress piracy and other disturbances in their territories. The scope of the licence was lavishly interpreted, however, and the second half of the 1820s saw an explosion in the colony's arms trade, which in turn fuelled the increase in piratical activity in the region at the time. In 1828 an attempt was made to restrict the arms trade in and out of Singapore, but the Board of Commissioners for the Affairs of India in London decided to abandon the attempt after protests from Singapore merchants. The argument was that the restrictions were useless because munitions were readily available in the archipelago from American and French traders.[88]

As thirty years earlier, thus, Blundell's suggestion to restrict the Singapore arms trade did not meet with approval, neither in the Straits Settlements nor in London or Calcutta. It was obviously deemed more important from the colony's and Britain's point of view that the lucrative trade continue to prosper than to curb the proliferation of arms that fuelled piratical activity. Free trade, in other words, took precedence over maritime security.

---

[87] Jarman (ed.), *Annual Reports*, p. 164; see also the appendices to the report, 197–202. For the trial of the pirates of the junks captured by the *Hooghly*, see *Straits Times* (10 July 1858). While on their way to Bombay, one of the pirate gangs killed their guard and tried to take control of the vessel, but were overpowered by the British troops on board; Jarman (ed.), *Annual Reports*, 208.

[88] Chew, *Arming the Periphery*, 174–5.

When the export of arms eventually was regulated, in 1863, it was not primarily for the purpose of discouraging piratical activity but mainly for the purpose of preventing wars and major uprisings directly affecting British interests in Asia. Concerns over such disturbances were aggravated, particularly in the wake of the Indian Rebellion (1857–58) and the Second Opium War (1856–60) in China, both of which involved armed violence against British citizens and interests.[89]

After 1860, junk piracy in the Straits largely subsided for several reasons. The arrest of two of the major bands of Chinese pirates operating out of Singapore in 1858–59 was of some consequence, but of greater importance were the political developments in China, particularly the end of the Second Opium War in 1860 and the defeat of the Taiping Rebellion in 1864. Around the same time China and Britain agreed to cooperate in the suppression of piracy and China agreed to support British warships in pursuit of pirates within Chinese territory.[90] From the 1860s the Chinese authorities also began to take more decisive measures to suppress piracy in and emanating from their territory as part of a broader attempt at the time to strengthen and modernise the military and civil administration. Taken together, these developments brought about a decline in Chinese piracy in the Strait of Malacca.

Chinese piracy did not disappear from Southeast Asia, however. Squeezed between the antipiracy operations of the Chinese, British, Dutch and other colonial powers, both in China and the South China Sea, and in the Malay Archipelago, Chinese pirates increasingly took refuge in the Gulf of Tonkin, where, as we shall see, they continued to wreak havoc.

'Highway Robbery at Sea'

Although Malay piracy had declined in the 1840s, it continued on a smaller scale far beyond the middle of the century, and it would, in the estimation of John Crawfurd, be as hopeless to exterminate it as it would be to put an end to 'burglary and theft in the best ordered states of society'.[91] An unintended consequence of the increased Dutch control over Riau was that many of the pirates moved and dispersed to various locations around the Strait of Malacca. Attacks thus continued to occur, not only in the vicinity of Singapore and in the southern parts of the Strait, but also along the east coast of Sumatra and along the west coast of the Malay Peninsula.

---

[89] Ibid., 176.
[90] 'Treaty of Peace, Friendship, and Commerce, between Great Britain and China', 6 June 1858, in Hertslet (ed.), *Hertslet's China Treaties*, 1, 35 (Art. 52–3). The treaty was ratified by China in 1860.
[91] Crawfurd, *Descriptive Dictionary*, 355.

Although they were less serious than the acts of Chinese piracy, the depredations of Malay pirates were a nuisance to traders and colonial officials in both the British and the Dutch colony. These were difficult to suppress, moreover, because information about the hideouts of the perpetrators was difficult to come by, and large expeditions were for the most part inefficient against the scattered pirates. When detected red-handed, the perpetrators of an attack were often able to make a swift escape into one of the many small rivers and creeks of the Malay Peninsula or Sumatra, where the large colonial steamers and gunboats could not follow them because of their deep draft. Cruising against the pirates was also difficult because of problems of recognition and, interpretation, and, while at sea, pirates were often indistinguishable from traders or fishermen.[92]

Many petty pirate attacks occurred in the vicinity of Singapore in the late 1850s and early 1860s. The perpetrators generally used small, inconspicuous boats, such as Malay *sampans* (small, flat-bottomed boats, usually with a shelter on board) and they tended to carry only light and inconspicuous armament, such as muskets and cutlasses. In contrast to the heavily armed pirate junks that were equipped with cannons, stinkpots, boarding pikes and other offensive weapons, there was thus little about the piratical *sampans* that a priori indicated criminal intent. Another circumstance that favoured the operations of the pirates was that they were able to dispose of their plunder quickly and in ways that were difficult for the authorities to detect. The loot from pirate attacks in British waters or against British vessels was often carried off to neighbouring islands beyond the jurisdiction of the British.[93]

This type of 'highway robbery' at sea, as it was labelled in an official report, was not a security threat to the Straits Settlements, and its frequency was not so great as to have a serious impact on trade in and out of the colony.[94] At the same time, however, the attacks were often violent and brutal. In several instances they involved the murder of the victims, even when they did not offer resistance. In the year between May 1859 and April 1860, for example, eight people were reportedly murdered by Malay pirates in various locations around the Straits colony.[95]

According to newspaper reports one particular gang of Malay pirates, based in the Riau Archipelago and led by a man from the island of Galang, Pak [Pah] Ranti, was responsible for the attacks. For several years Pak Ranti managed to avoid capture by the Straits Settlements police, despite several close brushes. In 1859, he attacked a police boat with a crew of six men and a Malay officer, killing the officer and three of the policemen, an event that led the police to intensify their efforts to defeat the band.[96] A series of unsuccessful operations and fruitless chases, accompanied by false reports of Pak Ranti's capture or

---

[92] Tarling, *Piracy and Politics*, 209–11, 213, 214.   [93] Jarman (ed.), *Annual Reports*, 165.
[94] Ibid., 164.   [95] Ibid., 164, 188, 210.   [96] Ibid., 210; *Straits Times* (21 September 1861).

defeat, however, led the police to be chastised in the Singapore press for its alleged incompetence and overzealous efforts in pursuing pirates. The *Straits Times*, in an editorial, argued that pirate-hunting seemed to be a 'pleasant and exciting [occupation] with a touch of [the] romantic about it' and that it too readily distracted the police from their 'dull routine duties'.[97] Such views demonstrated the extent to which piracy by the early 1860s had been desecuritised and was no longer seen as a major threat to the commerce and prosperity of the Straits Settlements, despite the violence and the risk that the attacks posed to local traders and fishermen.

If chasing pirates could be described as a romantic pursuit, there seems to have been little that was romantic about being a Malay pirate at the time. A captured member of Pak Ranti's gang confessed in 1861 to having been a pirate for three years, earning only his food and getting no share of the spoils. He and his comrades were frequently chased by the police and forced to hide in the jungle for several days. On several occasions members of the band were killed and their boats captured. Sometimes they lacked food, and most of the village chiefs in Riau, where the pirates were based, would have nothing to do with them.[98] This testimony shows the extent to which piracy and maritime raiding, in only a couple of decades since the mid 1840s, had ceased to be an attractive or even feasible occupation in and around the Strait of Malacca.

The Straits Settlements police, aided by the Raja of Johor, who was on friendly terms with the British, eventually succeeded in bringing the ravages of Pak Ranti to an end through their relentless pursuit of the pirates and the issue of a reward for any information that would lead to the capture of the pirate chief. At the end of 1861, he gave himself up to a local chief in Riau who was loyal to the Dutch. The reason, according to the British report, was the continual harassment that he and his followers had suffered for several years at the hands of the police.[99]

Following the capture of Pak Ranti the number of piracies reported to the Straits Settlements authorities declined, and only a few isolated attacks on small native crafts, most of them of a trifling nature, were reported in the following years.

In the long term, the successful suppression of small-scale Malay piracy in and around the Straits Settlements was in large part due to a new strategy on the part of the authorities. Regular patrols were launched, not only in the territorial waters of the Settlements and in the vicinity of its ports, but also

---

[97] *Straits Times* (7 December 1861); see also *Straits Times* (31 August 1861).
[98] *Straits Times* (21 September 1861).
[99] House of Commons, Statement Exhibiting the Moral and Material Progress and Condition of India, 1861–62 (1863), 646; Jarman (ed.), *Annual Reports*, 318; *Straits Times* (7 December 1861).

along the coast of the Malay Peninsula. *Tonze*, a former so-called penny ferry, which previously had been used to carry passengers on the Thames in London, was brought to the Straits Settlements and converted to a gunboat. She was attached to Melaka and employed to patrol the west coast of the Malay Peninsula and its many rivers and estuaries in order to deter any piratical activity.[100] Another, similar, vessel, the *Mohr*, was attached to Penang. Despite some initial doubts about the suitability of the penny ferries for military or law enforcement purposes, they proved able to perform their duties efficiently. They drew little water, which enabled them to cross the bars that existed at most river mouths in the peninsula and thus penetrate far into the interior, thereby making it more difficult for the pirates to elude pursuit by seeking shelter upstream.[101]

As a result of these efforts petty piracy could finally be effectively checked, and in 1864–65 only one incident was reported in British territorial waters, probably the lowest since the founding of the Straits Settlements almost forty years earlier. Outside the British jurisdiction, however, deadly pirate attacks continued to occur occasionally, as attested by the discovery of the dead bodies of three Siamese, who evidently had been murdered at sea, on the shore near Kuala Buka in Terengganu in 1865.[102]

Resurgence of Piracy in the North

The lull in piratical activity turned out to be temporary. From the end of the 1860s small-scale piratical activity resurged, now in the northern parts of the Malay Peninsula between Penang and Melaka. As earlier, many attacks went unreported by the colonial authorities because they occurred outside the British (or Dutch) jurisdiction. However, to the extent that the attacks befell British subjects – including merchants, shipowners, crew and passengers residing in the Straits Settlements but not necessarily of British nationality – or were attended with murder, the piracies were brought to the attention of the authorities as well as the general public.

The renewed wave of piracy was linked to the social and political upheaval in the Sultanates of Perak and Selangor. Initially it seemed that most of the pirates came from Perak in connection with an ongoing conflict over the control of the tin-mining district of Larut in Perak. After civil war broke out in Selangor in 1866, however, the main theatre of piratical activity in the Strait of Malacca seemed to shift, and Selangor soon gained a reputation among the British for being the most formidable pirates' nest in the region.[103]

---

[100] Jarman (ed.), *Annual Reports*, 487.   [101] Ibid., 336.   [102] Ibid., 560.
[103] Jarman (ed.), *Annual Reports*, 673; see also 777–8 for a summary of the antipiracy measures taken to suppress petty piracy.

The background to the unrest in Selangor was a dispute between two of the country's leading chiefs, Raja Abdullah and Raja Mahdi, over the control and taxation rights in the district of Klang in western Selangor. Both sides kept boats in the Strait of Malacca, off the coast of Selangor, by means of which they tried to cut off the communications and supply lines of the other side. In that context, some trading vessels from Melaka became victims of minor acts of plunder. Such incidents occurred with relative frequency, but they were for the most part relatively insignificant and did not involve the murder of crew and passengers.[104]

To the British the piratical activity emanating from Perak and Selangor seemed qualitatively different from the petty piracy that had taken place in the waters off Singapore a few years earlier. The new type of piracy appeared to be organised and sponsored by leading Malay chiefs, whose allegiance to the Sultans of Perak and Selangor, respectively, was but nominal. From the British perspective the chiefs seemed to believe that their rank gave them the right to rob and molest seafarers with impunity and that doing so could even be considered an honourable occupation. John McNair, a British colonial official who served in Singapore at the time, wrote with reference to Perak that 'piracies are, for the most part, chieftain-like raids. There is no petty thieving, but bold attacks upon vessels by men who seem to have considered that they had a right to mulct the travellers on the great highway of the sea at their will'.[105]

The resurgence of piracy in Perak and Selangor in the second half of the 1860s seemed, in this sense, to resemble traditional maritime raiding in the region, which was seen by the perpetrators – but not necessarily by the victims or the Malay population in general – as a legitimate and even honourable pursuit. Raja Mahdi was a particular scapegoat in British eyes, who was made out to be a pirate and a thoroughly bad character. At the same time, however, the British had reports that he was admired by his followers as a courageous and chivalrous 'Malay warrior of the old school', as Richard Wilkinson, a British colonial official and historian, put it.[106]

What was at stake for the British was not only the suppression of piracy and security for maritime traffic and commerce: British investors also looked at the Malay Peninsula with a view to exploiting the economic opportunities provided by the booming tin industry and other natural resources. The unstable political situation in Selangor and Perak was aggravated by the influx of rival Chinese societies involved in tin-mining. Political instability was thus increasingly seen as an obstacle to the economic interests of British and other

---

[104] Gullick, *History of Selangor*, 56–8.   [105] McNair, *Perak and the Malays*, 270.
[106] Wilkinson, *History of the Peninsular Malays*, 145–6; cit., 145; cf. Gullick, 'Tunku Kudin', 8.

businessmen based in the Straits Settlements. Toward the end of 1860s the traditional noninterventionist policy that the Indian government had adhered to in the region since the establishment of the Straits Settlements began to be regarded as obsolete by leading officials and merchants in the colony. Moreover, the case for a more expansionist British policy was strengthened by the rise of Germany as an imperial power and fears that the Germans might try to establish a naval station in the region.[107]

Against that background, the acting governor of the Straits Settlements, Colonel Edward Anson – who substituted for Governor Harry Ord, on leave at the time – took the initiative to appoint a committee to report on the colony's relations with the Malay states. The report, dated 19 May 1871, recommended the introduction of a residential system modelled on that used for indirect British rule in India. A British resident (or 'political agent') was to be appointed to the Malay Sultanates who would advise the Sultans on all policy matters of concern to the British, which, in principle, included everything except questions related to Malay religion and custom.[108]

In London, however, the Liberal government, led by Prime Minister William Ewart Gladstone, continued to maintain the policy of nonintervention, leaving little room for the Straits government – especially under the aegis of an acting governor – to exercise any influence over the developments in Perak and Selangor. For those in the colony who favoured a more interventionist policy, such as Anson, a resurgence in piratical activity in or emanating from the two states could be regarded as a welcome development that might provide the pretext for an intervention.[109]

The Selangor Incident

In June 1871 a particularly gruesome pirate attack, in which thirty-four men, women and children were murdered, reportedly took place in the Strait of Malacca. The alleged perpetrators were fourteen Chinese, who boarded the junk *Kim Seng Cheong*, bound for Larut in Perak, as passengers shortly after its departure from Penang. Apart from the passengers and crew, the junk was said to be carrying a general cargo worth about $7,000, including $3,000 in specie.[110]

---

[107] McIntyre, *Imperial Frontier*, 203; Webster, *Gentlemen Capitalists*.
[108] Cowan, *Nineteenth-Century Malaya*, 82–5; for the report, see Report of the Committee on Native States, 19 May 1871, CO 273/47 (TNA). See also Fisher, 'Indirect Rule', 423.
[109] Tarling, *Piracy and Politics*, 228–30.
[110] Anson to Earl of Kimberley, 14 July 1871, PP C.466 (1872), 1; newspaper clipping citing the *Penang Argus*, 1 July 1871, PP C.466 (1872), 14–15.

The attack on the *Kim Seng Cheong* – if, indeed, it happened as officially reported – was not just 'a simple case of piracy', as put by one historian.[111] It was the most lethal and ruthless known pirate attack in the Strait of Malacca for several decades, and it happened at a time when piratical activity seemed, once and for all, to have subsided. For nine months before the attack there had been no acts of piracy reported at all in the Straits Settlements.[112] As the attack on the *Kim Seng Cheong* befell a ship owned by a Chinese firm based in the British colony, and as the perpetrators had boarded the junk in the vicinity of a British port, governor Anson saw it as his duty to take action in order to apprehend the perpetrators and, if possible, recapture the junk and its cargo. At the same time, however, Anson's handling of the affair must also be understood against the background that he, like many other leading officials in the Straits Settlements, took a great personal interest in the problem of piracy and that he was in favour of a more interventionist colonial policy with regard to the Malay states.[113]

The general sequence of the ensuing events is well documented, both in contemporary sources and in the literature.[114] Upon receiving news of the missing junk and the suspected pirate attack, Governor Anson despatched the colonial steamer *Pluto* to search for her. Having secured, at least nominally, the cooperation of the Selangor government, as represented by the Sultan's eldest son, Raja Musa, the *Pluto* proceeded north along the coast of Selangor in search of the junk. Unexpectedly, according to Anson, the junk was found at anchor off the mouth of the Selangor River, an area that was under the control of Raja Mahdi, who, as we have seen, was accused by the British of being a pirate and a bad character in general. The junk was seized, and six suspected pirates who were on board were arrested. A detachment from the *Pluto* proceeded ashore to capture the remaining culprits and reclaim whatever part of the cargo they could find. They managed to arrest another three suspects, but

---

[111] Cowan, *Nineteenth-Century Malaya*, 85. There are several lapses and inconsistencies in the official documents and subsequent developments, which, taken together, cast doubt on the official version of what happened. There seems to be no record of who the thirty-four murdered people were, and no bodies appear to have been found at sea or been washed ashore in the weeks or months following the attack. Another conspicuous circumstance is that, although a number of suspected perpetrators were arrested soon after the attack, it is unclear whether the trial against them was ever held; cf. Rubin, *Law of Piracy*, 249.

[112] Acting Governor Anson to the Earl of Kimberley, 19 October 1871, in PP C.466 (1872), 37.

[113] Cowan, *Nineteenth-Century Malaya*, 83, n. 38; Robinson to Anson, 6 July 1871, PP C.466 (1872), 10.

[114] The main British sources are collected in PP C.466 (1872), and CO 273/48 (TNA) contains some additional relevant material. For the literature, see Cowan, *Nineteenth-Century Malaya*, 66–98; Parkinson, *British Intervention*, 47–58; the summary of events given here builds, unless otherwise stated, on the latter. See also MacIntyre, 'Britain's Intervention in Malaya', 57–9; de Vere Allen, 'Colonial Office', 22–3; Rubin, *Law of Piracy*, 245–58 for additional (critical) perspectives on the affair.

a fourth, believed to be the leader, escaped with the assistance of another Malay chief, Raja Mahmood. He assembled a large group of armed men and threatened to kill the British, who were forced to retreat, some of them swimming, back to the *Pluto*. The British left Selangor with the junk in tow under fire from Raja Mahdi's stockade.

Upon receiving the report of the confrontation, Anson requested the assistance of the Royal Navy's gunship *Rinaldo*. Anson's exact instructions are not known, but they obviously included the capture of the remaining six pirates and the retrieval of the stolen property from the *Kim Seng Cheong*. In addition, the Commander of the *Rinaldo*, Captain George Robinson, later claimed that the purpose of the operation was salutary, that is, 'to take such measures as may seem best for the punishment of those Malays who resisted the Colonial officers and men in their attempt to secure the pirates'.[115]

The *Rinaldo* met with the *Pluto* and proceeded to Selangor, where they anchored at the bar of the Selangor River. A detachment of troops, led by Robinson, proceeded up the river in small boats. As they went ashore to search for the suspected pirates, a skirmish occurred in which one British soldier was killed and six injured, which forced the party to retreat back to the *Rinaldo*.[116] The wounded soldiers were taken back to Penang on the *Pluto*. The following morning, at high tide, the *Rinaldo* proceeded across the bar and up the river, which reportedly was a risky undertaking given that it was not known whether the uncharted river was navigable for a ship of *Rinaldo*'s size and that there was no possibility of getting out, should the British find themselves under attack, before the next tide half a day later.

At 6.15 a.m., as the *Rinaldo* approached the Fort of Selangor at the entrance of the river, the British were fired upon from the fort and the opposite bank of the river. Three men were wounded, and the hull and rig of the *Rinaldo* were damaged, but the British returned the fire, whereupon the fire from the shore stopped. The *Rinaldo* returned with reinforcements the following day and landed at the fort, which they found deserted. Robinson reported:

> We spent the day in utterly destroying this nest of pirates. The town of Salangore is completely burnt down, the forts demolished, the guns spiked and broken up. Had it been possible to make terms with any one, I might have spared the town on the condition that the six pirates ... should be given up. I would also have inflicted a fine

---

[115] Robinson to Anson, 6 July 1871, PP C.466 (1872), 7. The latter instruction is not mentioned by Anson in his summary of the incident to the Secretary of State for the Colonies, although he included Robinson's report; see Anson to Earl of Kimberley, 14 July 1871, PP C.466 (1872), 1. The precise instructions that Anson gave, first to the Commander of the *Pluto*, E. Bradberry, and the Deputy Commissioner of the Police, George Cox, and later to Captain Robinson seem not to have been preserved or ever supplied to Anson's superiors in London; see Earl of Kimberley to Anson, 6 September 1871, PP C.466 (1872), 17.

[116] Robinson to Anson, 6 July 1871, PP C.466 (1872), 8.

to pay for the expenses of this expedition. Failing this, we have done all the damage we could, and it is not likely any act of piracy will take place hereabouts for some time to come.[117]

The expedition also burnt five heavily armed 'piratical prows', before withdrawing and returning to Singapore. Commander Robinson deemed that the object of the expedition had been well accomplished, even though the British had failed to capture the remaining pirates or retrieve any property from the pirated junk.[118]

The course of action taken by Anson met with great approval in the Straits Settlements, although he was questioned, both in the local press and by his superiors in London, for the decision to send in the lightly armed *Pluto* to chase after the pirates. In his defence – which eventually was found to be satisfactory by the Minister of Colonial Affairs – Anson claimed that he had not expected the pirates to be found on board the *Kim Seng Cheong* – nor indeed the junk ever to be found – or the pirates to offer resistance should they be found. He also pointed out that colonial steamers such as the *Pluto* had been used successfully in the past for the purpose of chasing pirates and that it was 'almost entirely by their means that piracy, once so rife in these waters, was put down'.[119]

Shortly afterwards Anson followed up on the *Rinaldo*'s intervention by sending a mission to Selangor, led by the Colonial Secretary of the Straits Settlements, J. W. W. Birch, and seconded by the Auditor-General, C. J. Irving. Birch brought a letter from Anson to the sultan of Selangor, Abdul Samad (r. 1857–98), in which he summarised the course of events from the piracy of the *Kim Seng Cheong* to the destruction of Selangor Fort. He also reminded the sultan of a treaty of 1825 between Great Britain and Selangor in which Abdul Samad's predecessor had promised not to permit any pirates to reside in Selangor, and to seize and return to Penang any offenders, such as pirates, robbers, murderers and others who might escape to Selangor.[120] Referring to the treaty, Anson asked that the sultan seize and deliver the six pirates who remained at large, together with Rajahs Mahdi and Mahmood. He further demanded that the sultan appoint 'some person in the office of Governor or Chief over the country about the Selangor River, whom this Government can trust to carry out the Treaty'.[121]

---

[117] Ibid., 10.   [118] Cowan, *Nineteenth-Century Malaya*, 83, n. 38.
[119] Anson to Kimberley, 19 October 1871; Kimberly to Anson, 9 December 1871, PP C.466 (1872), 37–8.
[120] Anson to Sultan of Salangore, [July 1871], PP C.466 (1872), 19–20. For the full text of the treaty, see Aitchison (ed.), *Collection of Treaties*, 275–7.
[121] Anson to Sultan of Salangore, [July 1871], PP C.466 (1872), 19–20.

Sultan Abdul Samad had limited means by which to fulfil the obligations of the 1825 Treaty, regardless of his will to do so. In his younger days, the sultan had been a great warrior and an influential chief, but by the early 1870s his authority had waned, mainly because of the conflict in Klang and, the British believed, because of excessive opium smoking. The sultan thus wielded little actual authority over large parts of his country, including the coast, where the British alleged that the pirates were based.

The British solution for bringing stability to Selangor was that Sultan Abdul Samad transfer de facto power to his son-in-law, Tunku Kudin (Tunku Dhiauddin Zainal Rashid), a nobleman from Kedah, who had had a British education and enjoyed the support of influential British and Chinese businessmen in the Straits Settlements. As an outsider with foreign, European clothes and manners, however, Tunku Kudin had little support among the other notables of Selangor. His followers, consisting of hundreds of Kedah men whom he had brought to Selangor, were viewed with suspicion, and the Sultan feared, already before the British intervention, that Tunku Kudin might try to usurp the throne.[122]

The Straits Government, by contrast, was convinced that Tunku Kudin was the only Malay chief who could be counted on to make a serious effort to suppress piracy and put an end to the civil war in Selangor. British support for him had not wavered even when he, only six months earlier, had been implicated in a piratical act that drew considerable public attention in the Straits Settlements. In December 1870 some of Kudin's followers from Kedah tried to enforce a blockade against Raja Mahdi at the mouth of the Selangor River, when a small schooner from Melaka, the *Sree Singapura*, anchored nearby. Some fifty of Kudin's men pulled out to her in three boats and found her guarded only by a handful of unarmed Indians. They robbed the passengers of their money and valuables of a total value of between about £30 and £40 before returning to the shore. Forty-nine perpetrators were subsequently arrested and put on trial in March 1871. The three leaders were sentenced to between seven and ten years' transportation, and forty-five others who had taken part in the robbery were sentenced to eighteen months' hard labour.[123] In view of the harsh sentences for what seems like a relatively trifling offence, it is remarkable that no shadow was allowed to fall on Kudin.

In order to ensure the success of the mission and to secure the compliance of Sultan Abdul Samad, Anson ordered the Royal Navy's gunboat *Teazer*, with a heavily armed escort on board, to take the colonial secretary with the letter up the Selangor River to the Sultan's residence. Upon entering the river, Birch

---

[122] Wilkinson, *History of the Peninsular Malays*, 144–5; see further Gullick, 'Tunku Kudin'.
[123] *Straits Times Overland Journal* (20 December 1870; 15, 29 March 1871); Maxwell, *Our Malay Conquests*, 121.

130   The Strait of Malacca

visited the ruins of Selangor Fort and noted, with obvious satisfaction, that the 'effect of the "Rinaldo's" fire was everywhere visible, not only in the destruction of the forts themselves and the large trees on the top of the hill, but in the general demeanour of the people'. Travelling further up the river, he observed that the women and children of the villages they passed fled into the jungle when they saw the British gunboat, whereas the men came down to the river banks unarmed – 'a very unusual practice for a Malay', according to the secretary.[124]

The British delegation was warmly welcomed by Abdul Samad, who told the British that he had already seized the remaining six pirates and sent them to Melaka. He also declared himself utterly without responsibility for the acts of Rajahs Mahdi and Mahmood and of another nobleman, Syed Mashoor, all of whom he called 'bad men and pirates who had long devastated his country'. The Sultan was not prepared to transfer power to Tunku Kudin, however, saying that he had to consult with his chiefs first, and that if the British would go away he would send a letter to Singapore communicating the result of the consultations. Birch, however, plainly rejected what he saw as a bid by the Sultan to gain time. Instead he told him that he required an answer within twenty-four hours and that any neglect in complying or an unsatisfactory reply would be 'attended by very serious consequences'. With the guns of the *Teazer* pointing at his palace, the Sultan was forced to yield and, at least in theory, transfer power to Tunku Kudin so that he could 'govern and open up' the country, as the British desired.[125]

Tunku Kudin appeared confident that he, with the support of the Straits Government, would shortly be able to establish his authority over all parts of Selangor, a belief he shared with the British. Auditor-General Irving, who was one of Kudin's strongest supporters in the Straits Settlements, lauded his 'intelligence and honesty of purpose'. He compared the disorder in Selangor with the relatively stable and prosperous southern Malay state of Johor, where the East Indian Government, in Irving's words, had 'selected the most intelligent of the Native Chiefs, the present Maharajah, and supported him by their advice and their influence'. Irving anticipated an equally or even more opulent future for the naturally well-endowed country of Selangor, if only security for life and property could be guaranteed.[126] Governor Anson concurred, and at the end of July he reported to London that he was very satisfied with the

---

[124] Birch to Anson, 26 July 1871, PP C.466 (1872), 20–23; cit., 20.
[125] Birch to Anson, 26 July 1871, PP C.466 (1872), 20–23; Power given to Tunku Dia Oodin, by the Sultan (translation); Sultan of Salangore to Birch, 22 July 1871, PP C.466 (1872), 24, 23, respectively. Of the six pirates seized by Abdul Samad, one reportedly died on the way, and his hair queue was cut off and sent in proof; Bloomfield to Kellett, 20 September 1871, PP C.466 (1872), 45.
[126] Irving to Anson, July 1871, PP C.466 (1872), 28.

outcome of the expedition and the transfer of power to Kudin: 'I think the affairs of Salangore are likely henceforth to be far more satisfactorily conducted than they have hitherto been, and the Tunku Dia Ooodin [Kudin] will have a sufficient force at his disposal with the aid of the steamer which he possesses, to prevent the harbouring of pirates in that territory in future.'[127]

The latter formulation was remarkable for two reasons. First, Kudin was entrusted with suppressing piracy in Selangor despite his implication in the recent case of piracy close to the Selangor coast. Second, the attack on the *Kim Seng Cheong*, which had triggered the British intervention in Selangor, was not launched from Selangor but from the vicinity of the British port of Penang, where the perpetrators had boarded the junk disguised as passengers. These perpetrators, moreover, were reportedly Chinese and not Selangor Malays, and their connection to Raja Mahdi or any other Selangor chiefs was not immediately obvious, nor backed by concrete evidence, apart from the circumstance that the junk had been found in Selangor.

Even though the junk had been located and all but one of the alleged perpetrators of the attack had been apprehended, the Straits police had obvious problems in producing tangible evidence against them. At first the pirates were expected to be tried by the Magistrate in Penang, but as essential evidence was lacking the trial was postponed, and the prisoners, on the orders of the colonial government, were transferred to Singapore. The lack of witnesses to the alleged attack hampered the prosecution, and the prisoners were detained for several months awaiting their trial while the police, apparently unsuccessfully, searched for evidence. By October, the Chinese owner of the junk had become tired of waiting for the trial to commence and wished to retire from the prosecution. Around the same time, the *Straits Times*, in an editorial, asked why the prisoners had not yet been brought to justice and deplored the political consequences and the loss of face for the British should the pirates be acquitted for lack of evidence.[128]

The further fate of the suspected pirates and the outcome of the trial are unclear. According to a small notice in the *Straits Times Overland Journal*, they were tried in Penang in late November and convicted, save two who were recommended to mercy.[129] No records of the trial seem to have survived, and no further details have been found in the newspapers or official correspondence.[130] Apparently the outcome of the trial was less than satisfactory from the

---

[127] Anson to Earl of Kimberley, 28 July 1871 PP C.466 (1872), 18–19; cit., 19.
[128] *Straits Times* (21 October 1871); see also *Straits Times Overland Journal* (23 September 1871), for an attempt by the police to secure evidence against the perpetrators.
[129] *Straits Times Overland Journal* (6 December 1871).
[130] Rubin, *Law of Piracy*, 249, came to the same conclusion.

colonial government's point of view, and the whole affair seems in the end to have been played down by the authorities.

The Aftermath of the Selangor Incident

The news of the British intervention in Selangor reached London at the end of August, and at the beginning of September an extract of Commander Robinson's official report describing the shelling of Fort Selangor and related events was published in *The Times*.[131] A week later, on 13 September 1871, a critical letter to the editor entitled the 'The destruction of Salangore' appeared in the same newspaper, signed by the recently retired Chief Justice of the Straits Settlements, Sir Peter Benson Maxwell. In contrast to the extract from Robinson's report, which only related the immediate events leading up to the destruction of the 'nest of pirates' at Selangor, Maxwell's article placed the events in a somewhat larger context, mentioning also the attack on the junk that had preceded the British intervention.

Maxwell had left the Straits Settlements shortly before the Selangor incident after having served in the colony's judiciary, first as a recorder and then as chief justice, for altogether fifteen years. He was a prominent and outspoken Irish lawyer who believed in the presumed perfections of British justice and saw it as a duty for the British to spread the rule of law among their Asian subjects.[132] During his tenure in the Straits Maxwell had consistently strived to defend the position and integrity of the courts against the executive, which had led to a poisoned relationship between the two branches of the colonial government.[133] As a leading official in the colony, Maxwell was well up on the relations of the Straits Settlements with the neighbouring Malay states and the political situation in Selangor. He was also well acquainted with the problem of piracy in the Strait of Malacca: six months earlier he had presided over the *Sree Singapura* piracy trial and had handed out the harsh sentences to Tunku Kudin's followers.

In his letter to *The Times*, Maxwell sharply criticised Governor Anson for his handling of the affair. The military intervention in Selangor was, in Maxwell's view, an unjustifiable act of war, ordered by an acting governor who had no authority to wage war on a sovereign state. The colonial police, Maxwell maintained, had no more right to arrest a suspected criminal on

---

[131] *The Times* (5 September 1871). For Robinson's full report, see PP C.466 (1872), 7–10. The report was received by the Colonial Office on 21 August; PP C.466 (1872), 1. Presumably the government had supplied the report to the newspaper for publication.
[132] Turnbull, 'Governor Blundell and Sir Benson Maxwell', 137, 160–1.
[133] Cowan, *Nineteenth-Century Malaya*, 95; See also Anson, *About Others*, 288–9, for the poisoned relationship between Anson and Maxwell long before the latter's critique in relation to the intervention in Selangor.

Malay territory than the French police had to arrest a Communist on the streets of London. The proper course of action would instead have been to demand the extradition of the alleged pirates, for which there were well-established procedures and a legal basis in the form of the 1825 treaty between Great Britain and Selangor. Maxwell also lambasted the gunboat diplomacy by which the colonial authorities, assisted by the Royal Navy, had forced Sultan Abdul Samad to appoint Tunku Kudin as his viceroy and thereby taken sides in the conflict in Selangor. The suppression of piracy, according to Maxwell, was a judicial matter and not a legitimate cause for hostilities or interference in the affairs of another state.

The former chief judge also rejected outright the allegation that Selangor was a piratical haunt or that its government or inhabitants would have committed any act of piracy. Quoting the *Straits Times*, he asserted that 'piracy has ceased to exist in the Malay Peninsula as a system', and he believed that there were no longer any *prahus* that were armed and manned as professional pirates – only occasional murders and robberies in the Malacca Straits, which should be handled by legal procedure, not by military interventions. Genuinely outraged, Maxwell concluded the article by condemning the inglorious deployment of modern European ships and artillery against Malay stockades and guns. Such 'unjust and wanton' executions, he wrote, 'can bring only discredit and hatred upon us, and if they are not sternly repudiated by our Government the face of England, in Oriental idiom, will be blackened, and her name will stink'.[134]

Maxwell's letter did not pass unnoticed. On 22 September an answer was published in *The Times*, signed 'A Singaporean' and obviously written by a person with good knowledge of the affairs of the Straits Settlements. The author expressed his support for the action taken by the Straits government and emphasised the severity and persistence of the piracy problem in Selangor. He quoted the *Straits Times* as saying that the 'Malays richly deserved the punishment they have got' and that the 'only way to deal with Malay pirates is to inflict summary punishment upon them'. The newspaper, as quoted by the anonymous letter writer, also called for the 'unqualified sanction of Her Majesty's Government' and opined that it was the government's duty to protect its citizens and commerce from the 'enemies of mankind', regardless of whether they be found on the high seas or in a stronghold located in the territory of a friendly state.[135]

---

[134] *The Times* (13 September 1871); cf. Cowan, *Nineteenth-Century Malaya*, 94–8; Rubin, *Law of Piracy*, 249–54.

[135] *The Times* (22 September 1871). For the original of the quoted passages from the *Straits Times*, see the *Straits Times Overland Journal* (14 July 1871). Maxwell also replied in a second letter in *The Times* (27 September 1871).

The Times, in an editorial published the same day, declined to take sides in the debate, given the scant information about what had actually happened. The editor, however, expressed his doubts about Maxwell's belief that the 'interesting natives' of Selangor had abandoned their former piratical habits. The editorial noted that the trigger of the incident indisputably was a shocking act of piracy committed against a vessel departing from a British port and probably owned by a British subject, and, as such, 'it became incumbent on the British authorities to take measures accordingly'. It was further noted that the sultan of Selangor, through his son Raja Musa, had granted the British search party the authority to pursue the suspected perpetrators in his territory, although the newspaper was unable to decide whether the violence deployed by the British, which probably involved some loss of innocent life, was really necessary.[136]

The *Straits Times* – which was quoted as an authority on the matter by both Maxwell and his Singaporean opponent – deplored Maxwell's public castigation of the government, even though the paper pointed out that it, in the past, had frequently sided with Maxwell when he, in his capacity as chief judge, had criticised the Straits government. The paper rejected Maxwell's argument that the police had no more right to arrest a suspected pirate in Selangor than the French police had to arrest a Communist in England – even if the law, abstractly, stipulated that the British intercourse with 'these petty Native states which surround us' should be guided by the same principles of form and ceremony as those with 'civilised governments', it was unrealistic to expect the sultan to deliver up the suspected pirates even if he had the will and power to do so. In the present circumstances, according to the paper, the pirates were shielded by 'vassals in open arms against their legitimate ruler' with whom no diplomatic intercourse was possible. The only practical course of action for the government, consequently, was to do what they did, namely to take matters into their own hands:

The piracy of a junk under British colours in the immediate neighbourhood of our own possessions – the butchery of over thirty men, women, and children – all of them probably our own subjects – are crimes of far too serious a magnitude to permit us to be trammelled with considerations of routine or the claims of Native dignity.[137]

In those circumstances, not taking decisive measures, the newspaper opined, would have made the British look weak and thereby – in contrast to the action taken – done great harm to the reputation of the British in the eyes of their Chinese and Malay subjects.

Maxwell's point of view did not meet with much sympathy from the government in London, whose main worry seemed to be that the intervention

---

[136] *The Times* (22 September 1871).   [137] *Straits Times* (21 October 1871).

might stir up public opinion and lead to criticism of the government's colonial policy. The intervention in Selangor obviously invited comparisons with James Brooke's and the Royal Navy's (far more brutal) campaigns in north Borneo a quarter of a century earlier, which, as we have seen, had drawn much criticism from humanitarians and radical and liberal opposition groups. Another, more recent, controversy in London over Governor Edward John Eyre's brutal repression of a labour revolt in Jamaica in 1865–66 probably also made the government wary of the risk of being accused of deploying unjust and brutal means to further British interests overseas.[138]

Prime Minister Gladstone, however, was assured by the Secretary of State for the Colonies, the Earl of Kimberley (John Wodehouse), that the Sultan's 'apparent approval' of the bombardment of the Fort of Selangor was adequate.[139] Rather than repudiating Anson for the intervention in Selangor, the Colonial Office internally expressed its support for it. The Colonial Secretary, in a despatch to Anson dated 6 September 1871 – that is, before the publication of Maxwell's letter in *The Times* – expressed his 'general approval of the zeal and courage' of all involved in the proceedings and only questioned Anson's decision to dispatch the *Pluto* rather than a warship to search for the pirates in the first instance.[140] The Colonial Office also sent letters to the Admiralty and the War Office expressing the Colonial Secretary's appreciation for the assistance rendered by the Royal Navy and the British soldiers who took part in the action, lauding the 'gallant manner in which the necessary operations were carried out'.[141]

Maxwell's letter nonetheless led Parliament to demand full documentation of the Selangor incident, and the controversy contributed to the adoption of a less interventionist British policy *vis-à-vis* the Malay states over the following years.[142] The plan to give active support to Tunku Kudin in order for him to take control over Selangor was abandoned, leaving the viceroy with little power to assert his authority. The Admiralty, meanwhile, decided that all piracy expeditions henceforth must be approved beforehand by the commander-in-chief of the Far East Station in Hong Kong, unless immediate action was called for and that, under all circumstances, all diplomatic and political affairs be carefully avoided.[143]

---

[138] See Semmel, *The Governor Eyre Controversy*.
[139] Cowan, *Nineteenth-Century Malaya*, 95. For criticism of Brooke's intervention in Sarawak, see Tarling, *Britain, the Brookes and Brunei*, 76ff.
[140] Earl of Kimberley to Anson, 6 September 1871, PP C.466 (1872), 17–18; cit., 18.
[141] Colonial Office to Admiralty, 6 September 1871; Colonial Office to War Office, 6 September 1871, PP C.466 (1872), 17.
[142] For the documentation, see PP C.466.
[143] Bloomfield to Kellett, 20 September 1871; Admiralty to Colonial Office, 16 December 1871, PP C.466 (1872), 44.

Even though there was no official repudiation of the intervention in Selangor, Maxwell's position, that piracy was to be treated as a judicial rather than as a security issue, thus prevailed in practice over subsequent years. The move by Anson and other senior colonial officials in the Straits Settlements to initiate a more interventionist policy with regard to the Malay states thus backfired, and the policy of noninterference was reconfirmed. The outcome was largely a result of Maxwell's angry letter to *The Times*, but it was conditioned by the controversies surrounding the British antipiracy campaigns in north Borneo a couple of decades earlier, as well as the Eyre controversy of the second half of the 1860s.

Strong commercial interests in the Straits Settlements – including British, Chinese and Malay merchants and businessmen – continued, however, to pressure the colonial government to do more to protect British lives, property and trade in the Strait of Malacca and the Malay Peninsula. In July 1872 a petition signed by thirty-four traders in Melaka complained of the lawlessness in Selangor and the British failure to support Tunku Kudin. They also demanded more decisive action on the part of the British authorities to protect trade from 'pirates and robbers' such as Raja Mahdi. The latter, the petitioners observed, was still at large, even though the authorities had had the opportunity to arrest him.[144] Colonial Secretary Birch, however, answered that:

> ... [I]t is the policy of Her Majesty's Government not to interfere in the affairs of these countries unless where it becomes necessary for the suppression of piracy or the punishment of aggression on our people or territories; and that, if traders, prompted by the prospect of large gains, choose to run the risk of placing their persons and property in the jeopardy which they are aware attends them in these countries under present circumstances, it is impossible for Government to be answerable for their protection or that of their property.[145]

This stance in turn invited a reply from the Singapore Chamber of Commerce in which it was pointed out that the Melaka traders had been induced to invest in Selangor 'upon the faith of the vigorous action of Government in July last year' that measures must be taken to suppress pirates in the area – including preventing Raja Mahdi and his allies from causing trouble – and that support should be given to Tunku Kudin. The Chamber also argued that even if the Melaka traders were motivated by the prospects of large profits, this did not alleviate the government from the duty of protecting them.[146]

---

[144] Petition of the Malacca Traders to the Chamber of Commerce, Singapore, 27 July 1872, PP C.1111 (1874), 5–6; cit., 5.
[145] Birch to Chamber of Commerce, 21 August 1872, PP C.1111 (1874), 6.
[146] Chamber of Commerce (W. H. Read) to the Colonial Secretary (Birch), 17 [September] 1872, PP C.1111 (1874), 6–7; cit., 7.

Although Raja Mahdi was widely seen by the British as an evil and cunning pirate chief and the cause of a great deal of the troubles in Selangor, the evidence that he was involved in piratical activities was circumstantial at best. When questioned by the colonial secretary in London over his failure to arrest Raja Mahdi, Governor Harry Ord – who had returned to his post as governor of the Straits Settlements in March 1872 – replied that although he was convinced that the Raja was a 'thoroughly bad man, capable of any treachery', there was no proof that he was guilty of piracy, nor that he was responsible for firing at the *Rinaldo*. The governor, based on his careful review of all the statements about Raja Mahdi in the context of the incident, concluded that the British possessed 'no evidence which could secure his conviction in our courts on any charge that could be preferred against him'.[147]

The attempt to use piracy as a pretext for increasing British influence in Selangor thus failed after the matter was brought to public attention in London. The government feared that the affair might stir widespread controversy, such as that surrounding James Brooke's antipiracy campaigns in the 1840s, and in subsequent years political and military interventions in the Malay states were avoided by the British. The outcome of the Selangor incident demonstrated that there were limits to the use of allegations of piracy to legitimise colonial expansion. Piracy could no longer be credibly constructed as a major security threat in the Strait of Malacca, and the attempt on the part of the colonial government to resecuritise the issue was, in the end, unsuccessful.

Piracy and Civil War in Perak

Shortly after the debacle surrounding the intervention in Selangor had subsided, the focus of attention with regard to piracy in the Strait of Malacca shifted to Perak, to the north of Selangor. Occasional piratical attacks occurred off the Perak coast and affected maritime commerce in and out of Penang. Even though the incidents were relatively few, the colonial government complained about the failure of Perak to apprehend and punish the perpetrators.[148]

In the early months of 1872 conflict over tin-mining rights in Larut began to escalate and spill over into the maritime sphere. Chinese and Malay traders reported piratical attacks or threats of attacks at the mouth of the Larut River to the British authorities in Penang, where Anson was now back as lieutenant-governor after his stint as acting governor. Anson referred the complaints to his superior, Governor Ord, who sent a letter to the local *Mantri* (governor) of Larut, Ngah Ibrahim, asking him to see to it that justice be done. Ord also

---

[147] Ord to the Earl of Kimberley, 27 October 1872, Correspondence relating to the affairs of certain native states of the Malay Peninsula [Confidential], 3–5; cit., 3, 4, CO 882/2 (TNA).
[148] Jarman (ed.), *Annual Reports*, 673.

expressly instructed Anson – obviously against the background of the events in Selangor the year before – that he was not to interfere in the administration of justice in Perak.[149]

Ngah Ibrahim's response, however, turned out to be less than satisfactory from the British point of view. He denied the allegations of the Penang traders, which fuelled suspicions among the British that he and his followers were in fact involved in piratical attacks. The British abstained from direct intervention in Larut, but the steamer *Zebra* was sent to patrol the area around the mouth of the Larut River, which seems, at least temporarily, to have brought about a decline in piratical activity in the area.[150]

Over the course of 1872, however, unrest in Perak grew worse, and open conflict over mining rights broke out between two competing Chinese factions, the Sin Heng and the Go Kwan, who between them controlled the mining industry in Larut. Ngah Ibrahim and his followers were driven out of Larut, and both the Sin Heng and the Go Kwan began to plunder any vessel they could lay hands on off the coast.[151] Fighting between the two rival Chinese factions also broke out toward the end of 1872 and during the first half of 1873, fuelled by a great influx of men, vessels and arms from Penang, Singapore and Macau.[152]

In December 1872, the British steamer *Fair Malacca* was attacked by eleven heavily armed junks belonging to the Sin Heng at the mouth of the Larut River. Thirty-five bullets were shot in the hull of the vessel, and a Chinese passenger was shot in the head. The captain and owner of the steamer petitioned to the governor for protection and for legal redress. He pointed out that the 'British flag has been insulted and fired upon by junks manned by British subjects' and that he had been heading for a friendly port in treaty with the British.[153] Governor Ord, however, in a letter to Anson, still rejected the suggestion that the British interfere and argued that the owner had brought the attack on himself:

> I do not find it clearly established from the Petition and the documents which you have attached to it, that this vessel was attacked in the open sea, or under circumstances which would justify a charge of piracy against the junks. The vessel appears to me to have gone on a trading voyage at a time when the petitioners had perfect cognizance of the fact that there was war in the river Laroot, and that they might fairly expect to find their presence obnoxious to one or other of the contending parties.

---

[149] A. Skinner, Précis of Perak Affairs, 10 January 1874, PP C.1111 (1874), 121.
[150] Ibid., 121.   [151] Ibid., 123.
[152] Ord to Earl of Kimberley, 27 July 1873, PP C.1111 (1874), 32–3.
[153] Petition, signed R. G. Jeremiah and S. Whate, 17 December 1872, PP C.1111 (1874), 22. For further details of the attack, see Statement of R. G. Jeremiah, master of the steam-ship "Fair Malacca", 13 December 1872, PP C.1111 (1874), 35–6.

By proceeding, then, under these circumstances, they have therefore deprived themselves of all claim to protection.[154]

Ord also asked the Solicitor-General, D. Logan, for his opinion as to whether the attack on the *Fair Malacca* could be considered piracy in the legal sense. Citing a leading authority on international law, Logan was of the opinion that the attack could not be defined as piracy because it had not occurred on the high seas but within the jurisdiction of a state.[155]

Two steamers, the *Zebra* and the *Hornet*, were nonetheless dispatched to the mouth of the Larut River to investigate the attack and, if possible, to apprehend the suspected perpetrators. The commander of the *Hornet*, A. D. S. Denison, was careful to explain to the representatives of Ngah Ibrahim and the warring Chinese factions that the British were not taking sides in the conflict and that he had come only as a 'policeman of the seas to seize a pirate', and that had Ngah Ibrahim not been a fugitive and been able to keep order in his own territory, the British would have turned to him for redress.

Bringing a witness to the assault with them, the British boarded several junks suspected of involvement in the assault on the *Fair Malacca*, and identified two of them. One of the suspect junks was reportedly 'full of men well-armed, and with stinkpots at their mast-heads, and boarding-nets ready'. There was also an English ensign on board. The British took the two junks in tow back to Penang, along with a number of their crew, for the purpose of bringing them to justice, although one of the junks sank on the way.[156]

Governor Ord, upon receiving Denison's report, asked the solicitor-general to reconsider his opinion as to whether the attack on the *Fair Malacca* had been a case of piracy that might justify the British intervention and the seizure of the junks. Apparently under pressure from the executive, Logan now opined that because the authority of the Raja of Larut had been superseded and that the junks had no lawful authority or right to commit the attack on the *Fair Malacca*, the British were entitled to send a man-of-war to enquire into the matter and, failing a satisfactory explanation, to take the junks to the nearest British port and bring the suspects to justice. The solicitor-general still refused, however, to call the junks piratical because doing so might 'justify any man-of-war in dealing with them in the most summary manner on the spot'.[157] Logan thus concurred with Maxwell's position that the rule of law should be upheld and that piratical attacks, regardless of where they occurred, be treated as normal crimes and not as security threats.

---

[154] Petition Respecting Attack on "Fair Malacca", 22–3.
[155] Solicitor-General's Opinion, 22 December 1872, PP C.1111 (1874), 24–5.
[156] Denison to Governor, 3 January 1873, PP C.1111 (1874), 23–4; cit., 23.
[157] Solicitor-General's Opinion, undated [22–25 December 1872], PP C.1111 (1874), 25.

The junk that was brought back to Penang was, according to the British, equipped and armed primarily for piracy or other aggressive purposes. It was larger than the usual trading junks in the area and seemed to have come directly from China.[158] Because none of the perpetrators of the attack on the *Fair Malacca* could be identified, however, the trial was cancelled, and all suspects were released upon arrival in Penang.[159] The seized junk was sold and the proceeds – a rather insignificant net sum of $71 – were paid to the Admiralty Court after the owners of the junk had failed to appear to claim the vessel after one year and one day, as prescribed by the law.[160]

Given the dubious legality of the seizure of the junk in Larut and the fresh memory of the debacle over the intervention in Selangor less than two years earlier, the quiet resolution of the affair was a relief both to the Straits Government and the Colonial Office in London. The latter was particularly concerned about the matter in view of a similar case of a seizure of an alleged pirate vessel, the *Telegrafo*, in the West Indies, which recently had resulted in large damages against Crown agents.[161]

The Sin Heng, however, bitterly resented the British intervention because it seemed to them that the British were taking sides in the conflict and supported Ngah Ibrahim.[162] The seizure of the two junks thereby limited the possibilities for the British to mediate and bring an end to the conflict in Larut and the piratical depredations. The conflict continued to escalate over the following months as Chinese fighting men and arms flowed into the area, both directly from China and through the Straits Settlements, particularly Penang. The British issued a ban on the export of arms and ammunitions to Larut, but it was not efficiently upheld.[163] In the middle of 1873, moreover, the fighting spread to Penang itself. On 20 August, Anson telegraphed to Ord: 'If Laroot disturbances not stopped, considered certain serious riots will break out Penang before many days. Can do nothing without man-of-war's boats. Can "Thalia" come here; further complaints of piracies.'[164]

Governor Ord secured the support not only of the *Thalia* but also of the *Midge*, and the two naval vessels undertook a thorough search operation to clear the Larut coast and rivers of pirates. The mission was reportedly 'most ably carried out' and resulted in welcome relief for the small local traders and

---

[158] Fox to Lieutenant-Governor, Prince of Wales Island, 14 December 1872, PP C.1111 (1874), 34–5.
[159] Ord to Earl of Kimberley, 24 July 1873, PP C.1111 (1874), 32–3.
[160] Bradford to Anson, 19 September 1873, PP C.1111 (1874), 50.
[161] Cowan, *Nineteenth-Century Malaya*, 118, n. 37.
[162] Clarke to Earl of Kimberley, 26 January 1874, PP C.1111 (1874), 70.
[163] Ord to Earl of Kimberley, 24 July 1873, PP C.1111 (1874), 32–3; Skinner, Précis of Perak Affairs, 123. See also Cowan, *Nineteenth-Century Malaya*, 116, on Ord's disapprobation of Anson for his failure to stop the disturbances in Larut.
[164] Cited in Ord to Earl of Kimberley, 21 August 1873, PP C.1111 (1874), 43.

fishermen on the coast, many of whom had not dared to venture out to sea because of the depredations. With regard to the number of suspected pirates who were captured, however, the results were less impressive. The pirates sent their large junks and vessels out to sea and concealed their smaller craft in the many shallow and overgrown bays and creeks along the coast and rivers.[165] Frank Swettenham, a British civil servant who took part in the operation for three weeks, also later described it in less positive terms:

> The duty was an excessively trying one, the men being exposed, without the smallest protection, to the terrible heat of the sun all day, with very often deluges of tropical rain all night ... It was impossible to land, for the coast was nothing but mangroves and mud, with here and there a fishing village, inhabited, no doubt, by pirates or their friends, but with nothing to prove their complicity. These mangrove flats were traversed in every direction, by deep-water lagoons, and whenever the pirates were sighted, as not infrequently happened, and chase was given, their faster boats pulled away from their pursuers with the greatest ease, and in a few minutes the pirates would be lost in a maze of water-ways, with nothing to indicate which turn they had taken ... The net result of these excursions was, that about fifty per cent of the crews of the gun-vessels were invalidated, and not a single pirate boat or man had been captured.[166]

Based on the idealised descriptions of the official reports, Governor Ord, on 9 September, told the Legal Council in Singapore that all apprehension of danger from piratical depredations was relieved. A week later, however, two Malay crafts were attacked in the Larut area, and several of their crew members were killed. To the extent that British patrols had any deterrent effect on the pirates, it was obviously highly temporary. The boats of the *Midge* were even fired on in the Larut River, and two officers were wounded. The British retaliated and shelled the stockades from where the fire had come, but the depredations against small local traders continued, as the British warships were unable to catch the small, quick row-boats that the perpetrators used.[167]

There was, among the British, some confusion about the roots and course of the conflict and consequently about the identity of the pirates. As the British understood the situation at the beginning of September 1873, the Sin Heng faction had taken control of the lower parts of Larut, including the coast and river mouths, whereas the Go Kwan controlled the interior of Larut, where most of the tin mines were located. The Sin Heng tried to blockade the interior, but the Go Kwan received supplies through a neutral group of Hokkien Chinese. Large numbers of Go Kwans, who had been driven out of Larut by the Sin Heng, had also taken refuge in Penang, where they threatened to kill

---

[165] Ord to Earl of Kimberley, 5 September 1873, PP C.1111 (1874), 43–4; cit., 44.
[166] Swettenham, *British Malaya*, 125–6.
[167] Skinner, Précis of Perak Affairs, PP C.1111 (1874), 124.

the brethren of the Sin Heng, should the latter attempt an attack on the Go Kwan.[168] It was, under all circumstances, clear to the British that the piratical activity was closely related to the conflict between the Sin Heng and the Go Kwan, with the perpetrators mostly, or possibly even exclusively, belonging to the former faction.

The situation deteriorated further in November, and the British, despite the presence of several warships in the area, were unable to stop the increasingly bold piratical attacks. In some cases the marauders seem to have fallen out among themselves in quarrels over the booty, and they were reportedly becoming desperate as food, due to the disturbances and the large number of fighting men in the area, was becoming increasingly scarce.[169]

On 10 November a Malay trader was attacked by three piratical row-boats off a British settlement on the island of Pangkor, within sight of the Royal Navy's ship *Avon*, which tried in vain to avert the attack. Six Malays were 'barbarously hacked', in the words of the *Penang Guardian*, and at least two of them subsequently died. The perpetrators escaped in fast row-boats and proceeded to attack another three vessels the same day, murdering most of the crew and carrying off the cargo before making their escape up the Perak River. By mid November, ruthless pirate attacks in which the crews were hacked and hewn to death were a more or less daily occurrence, and the depredations continued throughout 1873 and the beginning of 1874.[170] It was the most serious sustained wave of piratical violence affecting the Straits Settlements since the Chinese junk piracy had come to an end in the late 1850s.

Intervention in Perak

The terrifying accounts of murder and robbery at sea and the negative economic consequences of the conflict in Larut once again began to tip the balance in favour of a more interventionist British policy. The commander-in-chief of the Royal Navy's Far East Station, Vice-Admiral Chas Shadwell, was convinced that such intervention was long overdue:

The lawless state of affairs in the Laroot district has for some time past been a cause of great trouble and annoyance, seriously interfering with legitimate trade in the Straits of Malacca, and producing excitement and disquietude among the native populations of Penang and Singapore. I have long since foreseen that, sooner or later, it would be

---

[168] Extract of Legislative Council Proceedings, 9 September 1873, PP C.1111 (1874), 73–4.
[169] Skinner, Précis of Perak Affairs, PP C.1111 (1874), 124.
[170] 'Penang "Guardian" Extraordinary', (14 November 1873), CO 882/2 (TNA), 72; Skinner, Précis of Perak Affairs, PP C.1111 (1874), 124.

absolutely necessary to interfere in a decided manner as soon as a legitimate cause for action should arise. That opportunity has at length occurred.[171]

Public opinion in the Straits Settlements was also strongly in favour of firmer security measures in order to protect the colony's trade and British economic interests in the Malay Peninsula. Virtually all politically significant groups in the colony – British and Chinese businessmen, leading military officers, civil servants and the press – seemed to support interventions in both Perak and Selangor for the purpose of reestablishing law and order. There was also widespread discontent in the colony (and in London) with Governor Ord's allegedly high-handed behaviour and failure to protect British commercial and political interests. Against this background, the news of the replacement of Ord by Lieutenant-Colonel Andrew Clarke, who was reputed to be a man of action and an experienced military officer, was greeted cheerfully. According to the *Straits Times*:

> Sir Harry Ord, jealous of his own personal dignity, and too egotistical to learn anything from those who had spent years in the place, and were thoroughly acquainted with the various phases of the petty quarrels that constantly agitate the small native states, chose to draw his own deductions and to mark out a line of policy for himself, by which, instead of developing, he has narrowed, the limits of the trade with the native territories; and by his now notorious declaration that British subjects who venture out of the Colony on trading excursions need expect no protection from their Government, he has effectually checked the enterprise that has been the mainspring of the success of this Settlement as the commercial emporium of the states by which it is surrounded ...
>
> We earnestly trust that the day for this passiveness is now drawing to a close, and that the line of policy shadowed forth in the speech of Sir Andrew Clarke will shortly be inaugurated; and that instead of sitting still with his hands folded, the Governor of this Colony will, by well-timed, determined intervention, resume his proper position as an arbitrator and mediator between the petty rajahs, and firmly prevent them from paralyzing trade and jeopardizing the lives and property of traders from the Colony.[172]

In November 1873 Clarke was installed as governor of the Straits Settlements. He carried with him a much clearer and more far-reaching mandate for intervention from the Colonial Office in London than any of his predecessors had held. Although the British government – still under Gladstone – did not openly declare its intention to interfere in the Malay states, it had come to the conclusion that some form of intervention was needed in order to protect British interests in the region. In part the new policy had come about as a result of pressure from influential groups of politicians and businessmen in London and the Straits Settlements. As in 1870, there were also worries in

---

[171] Shadwell to the Secretary of the Admiralty, 27 October 1873, PP C.1111 (1874), 58.
[172] *Straits Times* (13 September 1873).

London that the rising German Empire might seek to establish a foothold in the region.[173]

Clarke's instructions from the colonial secretary were to carefully assess the conditions of each Malay state and report whether any steps could 'properly be taken by the colonial government to promote the restoration of peace and order, and to secure protection to trade and commerce with the native territories'. In particular, the Secretary asked Clarke to consider whether it would be advisable to appoint a British officer to reside in any of the states – a suggestion that, as we have seen, Anson's Committee on Native States had advocated in 1871.[174]

Equipped with these instructions Clarke was in a much stronger position than his predecessor to deal with the unrest in Perak and other Malay states such as Selangor. His appointment marked the beginning of a more thorough British colonisation of the Malay Peninsula, in contrast to the noninterventionist policy of the previous decades. In relation to the conflict in Larut it was also of some consequence that Clarke could distance himself from his predecessor's obviously inefficient policy and the earlier British interventions that had alienated the Sin Heng.[175]

The new governor immediately set to work to bring about a solution to the instability in Perak, and in less than three months, by January 1874, he had managed to bring the fighting among the Sin Heng and the Go Kwan and the contenders in the dynastic struggle to an end by the so-called Pangkor Engagement, which consisted of two separate agreements. One settled the dispute over the throne of Perak, in which one of the main contenders, the British-friendly Abdullah Muhammad Shah, was recognised as the legitimate ruler on condition that he accept a British advisor residing at his court. The other agreement formally ended the conflict between the Go Kwan and the Sin Heng over mining rights in Perak.[176] The combined result was that the piratical depredations swiftly came to an end, and that relative order was reestablished in Larut, although rivalry and sporadic clashes between the two Chinese societies continued in the following years.

The success of Clarke's initiative to end acts of piracy in Perak was above all achieved through mediation and appeasement, backed up by unmistakable threats of violence. The peace negotiations were facilitated, Clarke believed, by a weariness on both sides of the ruinous struggle, which had already cost thousands of lives and which threatened to intensify over the coming months

---

[173] Tarling, 'The Establishment of the Colonial Régimes', 28–9.
[174] Earl of Kimberley to Clarke, 20 September 1873, PP C.1111 (1874), 38–9; cit., 39.
[175] Pickering to Governor, 5 January 1874, PP C.1111 (1874), 153–4. See further Parkinson, *British Intervention*, 119–20, on Clarke's reversal of his predecessor's policies and leadership.
[176] See Wilkinson, *History of the Peninsular Malays*, 115–22, for a summary of the Pangkor Treaty and the conditions surrounding its establishment.

due to the arrival of more junks and men from China, particularly on the side of the Go Kwan.[177] The Sin Heng were in a tight spot, pressured not only by the Go Kwan, but also by the Royal Navy on the coast and by a blockade on land, led by the former superintendent of police in Penang, Tristram (Captain) Speedy, an eccentric adventurer and explorer who commanded a contingent of 110 Punjabis and Pathans brought to Larut from India to deal with the upheaval.[178]

For the British the object of the Pangkor Engagement was to reestablish law and order in Perak and to create favourable conditions for trade and economic development, while at the same time keeping British military commitments and costs to a minimum. Restoring law and order, Clarke hoped, would provide those responsible for the piracy and fighting with alternative sources of livelihood. He also believed that without the negotiation of a sustainable peace between the Sin Heng and the Go Kwan, there would be no end to the piratical depredations and the anarchy in Larut.[179] The first priority was thus to convince the Sin Heng to stop their acts of piracy. To this effect, Clarke sent Mr Pickering, an interpreter and junior colonial official who was fluent in Chinese and who commanded the respect of both the Go Kwan and the Sin Heng, to Larut. The headmen of the hard-pressed Sin Heng proved easy to convince and, according to Pickering, even pleaded with the British to take over the country.[180] On 4 January, Pickering telegraphed to Singapore: 'SINHENGS gladly sign agreement; give boats, everything to your disposal in seven days, meantime beg orders; Speedy to hold his hand. Boats being given up they cannot escape death; agreement broken, then let Speedy do his worst.'[181]

Upon receiving the telegram, Clarke immediately sent the steamer *Johore* to Larut and began to distribute food to the starving Sin Hengs. He also arranged for the Chinese headmen to bring their row-boats and arms to the Dinding Islands – supposedly a well-known pirate haunt off the coast of Perak – ten days later. There Clarke received them in person and oversaw the signing of the two agreements of the Pangkor Engagement. Steamers with plenty of food on board took the disarmed Chinese to Penang or Singapore, where the government was to provide them with temporary work until the mines could be reopened.[182] Meanwhile, steamers were sent into the rivers to raze the stockades, and Speedy, who reportedly was generally respected by all parties to the conflict, was appointed resident to Larut in order to assist the local

---

[177] Clarke to Earl of Kimberley, 26 January 1874, PP C.1111 (1874), 70.
[178] Gullick, 'Captain Speedy of Larut', 34–6.
[179] Clarke to Earl of Kimberley, 26 January 1874, PP C.1111 (1874), 70–1.
[180] Pickering to Governor, 5 January 1874, PP C.1111 (1874), 153–4.
[181] Pickering to Government, 4 January 1874, PP C.1111 (1874), 74; see also Pickering to Governor, 5 January 1874, PP C.1111 (1874), 153–4, for the full report of the negotiations.
[182] Birch to Pickering, 5 January 1874, PP C.1111 (1874), 74.

government in restoring order.[183] As the head of a 'Residency Guard' of about 185 men, he was charged with the responsibility of disarming the remaining combatants, including large numbers of fighting men who had been recruited and brought from China by the warring sides in preceding years.[184]

In view of the protracted unrest in Perak over the preceding two years, the object of restoring a reasonable level of peace and order and suppressing piracy was achieved within a remarkably short period of time, and Governor Clarke was complimented in the Straits Settlements for devising and implementing the successful scheme.[185] Aside from Clarke's personal role, three aspects of the policy stand out as instrumental for its success. First, the superior military power of the British was used not so much to chase after the pirates or destroy their vessels and land bases as to put pressure on the warring sides, particularly the Sin Heng, who were responsible for most of the piratical depredations. As in other examples of gunboat diplomacy, the threat of violence served as a strong incentive to accept British peace proposals.

Second, several of the old hands among the officials of the Straits Settlements played key roles in the negotiations, and many of them possessed a relatively good understanding of the social, political and cultural context in Perak and the other Malay states. Clarke was seconded in the negotiations by Auditor-General C. J. Irving and Attorney-General Thomas Braddell, both of whom had long served in the colony and had substantial knowledge of local affairs.[186] Braddell, who was also reputedly an amateur scholar of Malay history and culture, was central in the forging of the Pangkor Engagement.[187] In the negotiations with the warring Chinese factions, the role of the interpreter Pickering likewise stands out as crucial.

Third, the suppression of piracy was achieved by means of amnesty and appeasement combined with immediate disarmament rather than by the deployment of violence. There was no attempt to hold the perpetrators of the atrocities of the preceding years to account, and they were offered immediate relief from their dire situation in the form of food supplies and government employment in return for giving up their arms and boats.

---

[183] Clarke to Earl of Kimberley, 26 January 1874, PP C.1111 (1874), 85–6.
[184] Gullick, 'Captain Speedy of Larut', 38, 41.
[185] E.g., 'The Straits of Malacka', *The Times* (London), 11 March 1874.
[186] Parkinson, *British Intervention*, 119.
[187] See Makepeace, 'Concerning Known Persons', 425; Parkinson, *British Intervention*, 120. The appointment of J. W. W. Birch, who spoke neither Malay nor Chinese and was widely perceived as both arrogant and ignorant of local customs, as resident to Perak, on the other hand, was later regretted by Clarke and eventually ended in the murder of the deeply unpopular resident; see Anson, *About Others*, 323, quoting a letter from Clarke, where he expressed his annoyance over Birch's performance as resident. Birch's murder in November 1875 subsequently triggered the Perak War (1875–6), but piracy was not a prominent part of that conflict.

By thus employing qualified interpreters and negotiators who had an understanding of the culture, language and society of the opposing sides, and by combining the threat of violence – gunboat diplomacy in other words – with positive incentives, the British were able to bring a swift end to piratical activity and unrest in Perak, at least for the time being.

'The Most Daring and Bloodthirsty of All'

While the disturbances in Perak were developing in 1872–74, conditions in Selangor continued to be unstable, but in contrast to Perak there were very few reports of piratical activities emanating from Selangor during the two years after the incident in mid 1871. At the end of 1873, however, a brutal attack on a small Malay trading boat off the mouth of the Jugra River in Selangor gained widespread attention, not only in the colonial press, but also in leading metropolitan newspapers such as the London *Times* and the *New York Times*.[188] The details of the attack were unusually detailed due to the testimony of a member of the crew, a Malay named Mat Syed, who survived the attack.

According to Mat Syed, their boat left Bandar Langat on Selangor on the morning of 16 November with a crew of six Malays, including the skipper and owner of the boat, and three Chinese passengers, plus a cargo of rattan and $2,000 in specie.[189] Around noon they called on the stockade at the mouth of the Jugra River, which was occupied by a son of Sultan Abdul Samad, Raja Yakob, and his followers. The traders showed their pass and proceeded about a mile out to sea, where they anchored and waited for a favourable wind. Around five o'clock they saw two boats with some twenty men that set out from the stockade and headed in the direction of the anchored boat. Mat Syed asked the skipper who they were, and he replied that they were friendly boats from the stockade. The two boats came alongside and four or five men, including the leader, a Malay named Musa, came on board, saying they were about to go fishing. They talked amicably for a while, but as dusk began to set in, around six o'clock, Mat Syed heard shots being fired from the two boats, probably killing the skipper. Musa called out for his followers to run 'amok' – a traditional martial tactic used in the Malay world, consisting of a surprise attack and the frenzied, wholesale massacre of the enemy.[190] The aggressors shot or stabbed all the members of the crew and the three passengers, with the exception of Mat Syed, who escaped by jumping into the water and concealing himself under the boat, holding on to the rudder. After dark he let go of the

---

[188] *The Times* (25 May 1874); republished in *New York Times* (14 June 1874).
[189] The narration is based on the testimony that Mat Syed gave at the trial, published in McNair, *Perak and the Malays*, 283–6.
[190] See Spores, *Running Amok*, 20–7.

rudder and quietly floated to the shore, where he hid under the jetty of the stockade. About an hour later the attackers landed with the pirated vessel. Mat Syed heard a man, who came out from the stockade, ask the pirates if it was all over (*Sudah habis?*), to which they replied affirmatively, adding that they were taking the property to Tunku Allang, a nickname for Raja Yakob. The pirates then went up the river in their boats with the pirated boat in tow. They returned about an hour later without the latter boat.

With the help of a Bugis boat that was anchored close to the jetty, Mat Syed was able to reach Langat and eventually Melaka. By chance, around three weeks later, Mat Syed saw some of the pirates and identified them to the police, who arrested nine men altogether. Mat Syed also claimed that some of the plundered property – an anchor, a sarong and some weapons – was on board the boats of the arrested men.

While the alleged perpetrators of the Jugra River piracy were thus in custody, another maritime raid, believed to have been launched from the same part of the Selangor coast, occurred. On 11 January the lighthouse at Cape Rachado (Tanjung Tuan), which the British had constructed in 1863, was attacked by a small party of men who were suspected to be followers of Raja Mahmood, a Selangor chief who, together with Raja Mahdi, had been implicated in the attack on the *Kim Seng Cheong* in 1871. The raid on the lighthouse was in itself trifling: the raiders seem to have had their minds set on the monthly payroll for the staff of the lighthouse, less than a hundred dollars in total, but they were chased away by the light-keeper, armed with a carbine, before they were able to lay their hand on any plunder.[191]

Despite the minor nature of the incident, however, it was quickly seized upon by the Straits authorities. The assault on the lighthouse was useful because it could be represented as an affront to British pride and to the efforts of the British to bring progress and civilisation to the region. For the colonial authorities the attack, combined with the Jugra River piracy two months earlier, was aptly timed because, with order restored in Perak, they were able to turn their full attention to Selangor. As in Perak, and in accordance with his instructions from London, Governor Clarke envisioned an arrangement with a permanent British resident to Selangor.

The attempted raid on the lighthouse also nearly coincided with the arrival in the Strait of Malacca of the commander of the China Squadron of the Royal Navy, Vice-Admiral Shadwell, who brought an unusually large concentration of men-of-war to the area. Clarke requested the assistance of the squadron for the purpose of intervening in Selangor in order to put a stop to the civil unrest and the piratical activity. Using a highly securitising rhetoric, the governor said

---

[191] Parkinson, *British Intervention*, 143; for the full report, including testimonies, of the attack, see PP C.1111 (1874), 99–103.

that 'these attacks have at last reached a point when they are threatening the peaceful navigation of the Straits, the great highway between Europe and China'.[192] Attorney-General Thomas Braddell threw in his weight as a reputed expert on the Malay world, describing Selangor as a particularly dangerous and pirate-infested part of the archipelago:

The Salangore pirates are distinguished in the Malayan seas as the most daring and bloodthirsty of all. They are said to be supported by nobles, and even by members of the Royal Family, and are led by men of rank, of Bugghese descent, who are superior in warlike qualities to the ordinary Malayan Chiefs.

...

The coasts of Salangore are peculiarly well situated as a refuge and haunt for pirates ... The numerous rivers, great and small, between the Salangore and Lingie Rivers, afford shelter for pirates, who have stockaded defences up the creeks, from which they sally forth to attack the boats which pass close to their stations, making for the Calang Straits. When their work is done, the pirates retire to their strongholds, which are out of sight, and, practically, out of reach of the men-of-war cruizing in these seas.

...

The piratical practices at Salangore differed from those in other parts of the peninsula, in this; that they were continuous, well organized, and more daringly carried out; showing that they were not, as in other places, caused by temporary difficulties in the country, and ceasing with those difficulties, but were the result of long-continued lawlessness in the people, and protected, if not caused, by persons of rank in the country.[193]

In February 1874 Clarke, accompanied by Shadwell and a number of senior colonial officials, headed for Abdul Samad's capital at Langat on board the *Pluto* and followed by three men-of-war. The purpose of the expedition was to make the sultan cooperate with the British in the suppression of piracy, including seizing Raja Yakob and other suspected pirate chiefs and destroying all their stockades along the Selangor River. In addition, however, the unofficial purpose was to make the sultan agree to have a British resident appointed to his court.[194]

Arriving at the capital the British found the Sultan's palace heavily fortified with big guns and 'covered with some hundreds of very villainous-looking Malays armed to the teeth', according to Clarke.[195] The impression conjured

---

[192] Clarke to Shadwell, 1 February 1874, PP C.1111 (1874), 92–3; cit., 92.
[193] Braddell, Continuation of Report on the Proceedings of Government relating to the Native States in the Malay Peninsula, 18 February 1874, PP C.1111 (1874), 184–95; cit., 185–6. On Braddell's reputation as an expert on Malay history and culture, see Makepeace, 'Concerning Known Persons', 425–6.
[194] Clarke to Shadwell, 1 February 1871, PP C.1111 (1874), 92–3.
[195] Quoted in Makepeace, 'Concerning Known Persons', 426.

sat well with British expectations of Langat as the headquarters of the vicious Selangor pirates and of the royal family as 'thoroughgoing pirates'.[196]

Sultan Abdul Samad, for his part, apparently believed that the British had come with their gunboats to seize and imprison him and his sons and to install Tunku Kudin as sultan. After an initial tense standoff, however, the sultan agreed to come on board the *Pluto*, where he was reportedly well treated, and negotiations followed over the following days.[197]

Piracy was one of the main items on the agenda of the British, but the sultan was obviously less concerned with the problem than the British. At one point he told Braddell with regard to piracy off the Selangor coast: 'Oh! those are the affairs of the boys (meaning his sons), I have nothing to do with them.'[198] This attitude conformed with British expectations and understanding of traditional Malay culture, as demonstrated, for example, by Governor Clarke's characterisation of Malay piracy as 'bona fide' (in good faith), in contrast to the piracies committed by the Chinese in Perak.[199]

Regardless of the Sultan's good faith, the British were adamant that he and his chiefs should understand the importance of committing themselves to combat piracy. On his second meeting with the sultan, Clarke raised the 'unpleasant' subject of piracy and explained that the piratical acts emanating from Selangor risked bringing down the 'reprobation of the whole civilized world' on the sultan. It must be apparent to him as a ruler of his country, Clarke said, that these acts of piracies must cease and that it was clearly in the Sultan's own interest that this be achieved. Clarke called on Abdul Samad to take every possible measure to end piracy in Selangor and offered the assistance of British warships for the purpose. According to Braddell, who was present at the meeting, the governor's address appeared to make a deep impression on those present, many of whom, in the attorney-general's view, doubtless saw it as foreshadowing the end of their careers as pirates.[200]

In addition to securing the cooperation of Sultan Abdul Samad in suppressing piracy, the British expedition had a further concrete purpose in relation to it, namely to persuade the sultan to hold a trial of the suspected perpetrators of the Jugra River piracy in Selangor. There were two reasons for holding

---

[196] Clarke to Anson, 16 February 1874, quoted in Sadka, 'The Residential System in the Protected Malay States, 1874–1895', 79.

[197] Braddell, Continuation of Report on the Proceedings of Government relating to the Native States in the Malay Peninsula, 18 February 1874, PP C.1111 (1874), 189.

[198] Sultan as quoted by Braddell; insertion in brackets in original; Continuation of Report, 18 February 1874, PP C.1111 (1874), 194.

[199] Clarke to Shadwell, 1 February 1874, PP C.1111 (1874), 92.

[200] Braddell, Continuation of Report, 18 February 1874, PP C.1111 (1874), 193–4.

the trial in Selangor rather than in a British port. First, Governor Clarke feared that a British court might order the release of the suspected pirates because the crime had taken place outside British jurisdiction. Second, he was of the opinion that any punishment inflicted by a British court and in British territory, far removed from the sight and knowledge of the pirates' fellow countrymen and associates, would not have any permanent deterrent effect.[201] Clarke thus hoped to be able to set an example by prosecuting and punishing the pirates in their own homeland.

The trial was held immediately after Clarke had returned to Singapore, in mid February 1874. Tunku Kudin presided over the negotiations, which were also attended by two British commissioners appointed by Clarke: a respected Singapore lawyer named J. G. Davidson and John McNair. Both were good Malay speakers with firsthand knowledge of the Malay world, and had a reputation for integrity. Their instructions were to assist the court, which apart from Tunku Kudin and the two Britons consisted of three local notables, in order to secure a full and fair enquiry. The British officials were not to take any active part in the trial itself, although in the end Davidson, in particular, came to play a prominent role in the proceedings. The outcome of the three-day trial was that all of the eight accused pirates were convicted, and all but one, a teenager who was pardoned, were executed. Sultan Abdul Samad, to the satisfaction of the British, insisted that he provide the kris with which the punishment was effected. The trial and the executions thus appeared to show that the salutary effect that Clarke had intended had been achieved.

The trial, however, suffered from several structural weaknesses, and it is uncertain if those who were executed were in fact responsible for the Jugra River piracy. Frank Swettenham, who served as an assistant-resident and resident to Selangor for several years, later came to the conclusion that those executed were not so responsible and that the actual perpetrators remained at large. Moreover, the court found no evidence of the involvement of Raja Yakob, even though he was widely believed to have been the instigator of the piratical attack and was, in Braddell's view, a 'lawless cruel Chief'.[202]

---

[201] Clarke to Earl of Kimberley, 24 February 1874, PP C.1111 (1874), 181.
[202] Gullick, 'Kuala Langat Piracy Trial'; Swettenham, *British Malaya*, 184; cit. Braddell, Continuation of Report, 18 February 1874, PP C.1111 (1874), 194–5. Raja Yakob was heard at the trial but succeeded in dissociating himself from his followers, who stood accused of piracy and murder, and the court found that there was no evidence that they had acted on the orders of Raja Yakob; see Minute of the Proceeding of a Court held at Qualla Jugra, 13–15 February 1874, PP C.1111 (1874), 208.

The End of Piracy in the Straits Settlements

Piracy was an important part of the official rhetoric used to justify the intervention and extension of British influence in both Perak and Selangor at the beginning of 1874. The new policy was met with great approval, above all in the Straits Settlements, but also in London. As in 1871, however, there were critical voices. For example, a motion was presented in the House of Lords to reject Clarke's policy in the Malay Peninsula, although it was not adopted by the House.[203]

The nemesis of the Straits Government, Peter Benson Maxwell, also once again came forward to criticise the intervention and to question the colonial government's allegations of piracy. In a pamphlet entitled *Our Malay Conquests*, published in 1878, he wrote:

> The Parliamentary Books of 1872 and 1875, are so full of general assertions about piracy in the Straits, that they give the reader the impression that the Malay States of the Peninsula were little better than nests of pirates ... Two States are especially singled out for this bad eminence, Perak and Salangore. I read all those general statements with wonder, for I had filled a judicial office in the Straits Settlements for fifteen years without hearing of those formidable pirates or their misdeeds; and after searching the Parliamentary papers and other sources for information, I have no hesitation in asserting that the accusation is unfounded.[204]

With regard to Selangor, Maxwell found that there had been but three cases of piracy in the years preceding the Jugra River incident: the attack on the *Kim Seng Cheong* in 1871 – which, as we have seen, seems to have been committed by passengers who boarded the vessel from a British port and did not emanate directly from Selangor; the abortive raid on the Cape Rachado lighthouse in early 1874; and an attack on a small schooner from Melaka, also in the beginning of 1874, in which no one was injured or killed.[205]

Like his article in *The Times* in the aftermath of the Selangor incident, Maxwell's book was not well received in the Straits Settlements, where Clarke's interventionist policies were broadly popular. The *Straits Times* criticised Maxwell for being one-sided and unfair to Clarke and the other colonial officials responsible for the intervention The newspaper was also of the opinion that Maxwell had already been proven wrong by the stark contrast between the previous disorder in Perak and the present peaceful conditions.[206]

There were few piratical attacks in the vicinity of the Malay Peninsula during the remainder of the British colonial period up until the Japanese

---

[203] Cowan, *Nineteenth-Century Malaya*, 204.   [204] Maxwell, *Our Malay Conquests*, 119.
[205] Ibid., 122.
[206] *Straits Times Overland Journal* (11 April 1878). The British intervention in Perak led to the Perak War of 1875–76, however, in which Britain was directly involved.

occupation of Malaya in 1942. A rare case occurred in May 1884, however, when a small *tongkang* (light wooden boat) anchored off Singapore was attacked by five Malays, who killed five Chinese crew members and seriously wounded another. While loading off their booty, which consisted of some sacks of rice, they were spotted by a harbour pilot, Captain Davies, who was on his way to meet the incoming steamer *Glengarry*. Believing that the pirates were about to board his steam launch, Davies rammed the pirate boat and sank it. The pirates made it to a nearby reef, where they were arrested on the orders of a local Malay headman. The latter then headed for Singapore with his followers in three boats to deliver their captives to the police, but upon approaching the *Glengarry* the boats were fired upon by the crew, who believed that they were being attacked by pirates. The boats turned away and made it to Singapore to deliver the men. Although he received an apology, the headman was reportedly very indignant at the treatment he had received from the steamer and especially for being mistaken for a pirate.[207] The incident caused great excitement in the British colony because it was the first serious case of piracy in the vicinity of Singapore for a long time. The five perpetrators were sentenced to death for murder and executed by hanging at the beginning of August.[208]

The last major act of piracy in the vicinity of British Malaya before the end of the colonial era seems to have been an attack on a Chinese junk off Johor in 1909. A group of Malay and Chinese pirates robbed and killed five people and seriously injured four others, and made off with a small amount of cash and valuables.[209] Three of the perpetrators were arrested and sentenced to death, but for judicial reasons the verdict was altered to penal servitude for life, reportedly to the regret of the accused, who would rather have been put to death.[210] The case received some attention in the press, both in the Straits Settlements and other colonies and in London, but the colonial authorities, obviously embarrassed by the negative publicity that the incident brought to the colony, tried to tone down the importance of the affair.[211]

Piracy and the Aceh War

In the southern and western parts of the Strait of Malacca piratical activity receded after the Dutch strengthened their control over the Riau Archipelago around the middle of the nineteenth century. The sporadic acts of piracy that nevertheless continued and were reported by the Dutch colonial authorities

---

[207] *Straits Times* (6 May 1884, 14 May 1884).
[208] *Straits Times Weekly Issue* (23 July 1884; 6 August 1884).
[209] Brooke, 'Piracy', 299–300; *Singapore Free Press and Mercantile Advertiser* (12 April 1909).
[210] *Singapore Free Press and Mercantile Advertiser* (5 August 1909).
[211] Cf. *Singapore Free Press and Mercantile Advertiser* (3 June 1909).

happened mainly along the east and west coasts of the middle of Sumatra, between the Dutch colonial territory in the south and the Sultanate of Aceh in the north.[212]

In 1858 the Dutch took control over the Sultanate of Siak and its dependencies in the middle of Sumatra, leaving Aceh as the last significant indigenous power on the island. To the Dutch, Aceh was reputed to be a nest of pirates. Like elsewhere in the Malay Archipelago, the piratical inclinations of the Acehnese were linked to their adherence to Islam, which combined with the country's geographical position to make it a particularly prominent hotbed of piracy. According to the leading Dutch authority on the history and culture of the Acehnese in the nineteenth century, Christian Snouck Hurgronje:

> From Mohammedanism (which for centuries she is reputed to have accepted) she really only learnt a large number of dogmas relating to hatred of the infidel without any of their mitigating concomitants; so that the Achehnese made a regular business of piracy and man-hunting at the expense of the neighbouring non-Mohammedan countries and islands, and considered that they were justified in any act of treachery or violence to European (and latterly to American) traders who came in search of pepper, the staple product of the country. Complaints of robbery and murder on board ships trading in Achehnese parts thus grew to be chronic.[213]

In line with this characterisation of the Acehnese, Dutch colonial officials tended to see Aceh as a robber state (*roofstaat*), and they believed that the sporadic piracy that occurred along the east and west coasts of Sumatra, mainly to the south of Aceh, was committed by Acehnese.[214] There was very little piratical activity around the Acehnese coast for most of the 1860s and early 1870s, however, and in 1871 a Dutch gunboat, which cruised the northeast coast of Sumatra and visited several places on the Acehnese coast, reported that a 'desirable tranquillity' reigned everywhere.[215]

When the Dutch in 1873 decided to invade Aceh, piracy was thus not a credible *casus belli*. In fact, the piratical activity that still occurred along the east coast of Sumatra seemed mainly to reflect badly on the colonial authorities rather than on Aceh. One of the detractors of the Aceh War in the Netherlands, the lawyer and writer John Eric Bancks, for example, argued that because the colonial authorities to date had not been able to suppress piracy efficiently in the Dutch East Indies, it was unreasonable to demand that Aceh should succeed where the colonial authorities had failed.[216] The liberal colonial

---

[212] à Campo, 'Asymmetry, Disparity and Cyclicity', 55.
[213] Snouck Hurgronje, *Achehnese*, 1, vii–viii.
[214] à Campo, 'Patronen, processen en periodisering', 104; à Campo, 'Asymmetry, Disparity and Cyclicity', 55.
[215] à Campo, 'Patronen, processen en periodisering', 99, 104; *Java-bode* (11 July 1873).
[216] Banck, *Atchin's verheffing en val*, 53–4.

newspaper *Java-bode* went even further in its criticism of the authorities. The paper argued that the Dutch failure to suppress piracy around the coasts of Sumatra violated the terms of a treaty concluded between Aceh and the Netherlands in 1857, which obliged both parties to cooperate in the suppression of piracy, thereby actually providing the sultan of Aceh with a *casus belli* against the Dutch.[217]

The main reason for the Aceh War was thus not piracy or maritime raiding, but to prevent other colonial powers from settling on Sumatra. By the early 1870s, moreover, pressure to invade was mounting from Dutch businessmen who were jealous of Aceh's flourishing pepper trade with Penang. Consequently, even Snouck Hurgronje, who, as we have seen, had no doubts about the long-standing piratical character of the Acehnese, admitted that the suppression of piracy and the slave trade was but an auxiliary reason for the Dutch decision to invade Aceh. Paradoxically, piracy thus played a subordinate role in the outbreak of the Aceh War, despite the well-established colonial image of Aceh as a pirate or robber state.[218]

The attempted Dutch invasion in 1873 met with fierce resistance from the Acehnese and soon turned into a protracted guerrilla war that was to go on for more than three decades. There were worries from the outset among the Dutch that the war itself might trigger a resurgence in piracy, particularly after three minor piratical incidents were reported in the vicinity of Aceh shortly after the Dutch attack in 1873. As in most instances the main victims were small local traders. The three attacks, however, were not followed by a major resurgence in piracy along the Acehnese coast, although sporadic attacks occurred, such as in 1876, when a small Chinese-owned junk based in Penang, *Sin Soon Seng*, was brutally attacked and looted off the coast of Pulau Weh in Aceh.[219]

More serious piratical activity began to occur only in the 1880s and the 1890s, after the Dutch began to enforce a selective blockade of the coasts of Aceh as part of a more offensive war strategy.[220] Many of the attacks against small local vessels either went unreported or failed to attract much attention, but a number of spectacular attacks against steamships owned or commanded by Europeans did gain widespread public attention, both in the Dutch East Indies and in the Straits Settlements.

The first of these attacks occurred in 1883, when the British steamer *Nisero* ran aground near Panga on the west coast of Aceh. The local district chief (*ulèëbalang*), Teuku Imam Muda of Teunom, reportedly saw the grounded

---

[217] *Java-bode* (19 March 1873).
[218] Missbach, 'Aceh War', 43; Trocki, 'Political Structures', 100–1. See further Reid, *Contest for North Sumatra*, 91–7, for the immediate motives.
[219] *Java-bode* (19 March 1873, 17 April 1873); Tagliacozzo, *Secret Trades*, 113–14.
[220] à Campo, 'Asymmetry, Disparity and Cyclicity', 59.

vessel as a gift from God. He seized the ship's cargo of sugar and took the twenty-nine crew members, most of whom were British, hostage. Pressured by the British, the Dutch authorities tried but failed to free the hostages, and the crew was only released ten months later, after a substantial ransom had been paid to Teuku Imam.[221]

In 1886, a more brutal attack occurred at Rigas, also on the west coast of Aceh. On 14 June the Penang-based steamer *Hok Canton* was attacked by forty Acehnese, who boarded the ship, which was at anchor to conduct business with the local headman, Teuku Umar. The attackers, who were followers of Teuku Umar, tried to seize the European officers on board, and two of them, a German mate and the Scottish engineer, were killed when they tried to defend themselves. The Danish captain was wounded and died in captivity a few days later from lack of medical care. After plundering the ship, the pirates brought the captain's wife, a British second engineer and six Malay crew members to shore, where they were held hostage for almost three months. The Dutch, once again unsuccessfully, tried to free the hostages, and they too were released only after a ransom had been paid at the beginning of September.[222]

Despite the brutality of the attack and the fact that one British officer was killed and another taken prisoner, the Straits government tried to downplay the issue, possibly because the *Hok Canton* was not registered in the British colony, although the owner was based in Penang.[223] More importantly, however, the British had no desire to get mixed up in the conflict in Aceh, which was outside the British sphere of interest according to the Anglo–Dutch treaties concluded in 1870–71. Details of the piracy and the subsequent efforts to have the hostages released were reported in the colonial press in the Straits Settlements, but, compared with the public outrage in connection with the acts of piracy off Perak and Selangor in the previous decade, there was relatively little interest in the activity emanating from Aceh.[224]

Attacks on British vessels continued over the following years.[225] The most brutal incident took place in July 1893, when the *Rajah Kongsee Atjeh*, a steamer owned by the same company that owned the *Hok Canton*, was attacked off the east coast of Aceh. The attack was perpetrated by eight Acehnese, one of whom was a member of the crew, while the other seven were passengers who boarded the vessel in the port of Idi on the east coast of

---

[221] Reid, *Contest for North Sumatra*, 218–49.
[222] Snouck Hurgronje, *Achehnese*, 2, 113, n. 1; Reid, *Contest for North Sumatra*, 261–2.
[223] Reid, *Contest for North Sumatra*, 261.
[224] For example, in November the *Penang Gazette* lamented the fact that there was no collection to support John Fay, one of the hostages who had arrived in Penang after being released; *Straits Times Weekly Issue* (29 November 1886).
[225] Kruijt, *Atjeh-oorlog*, 51; Reid, *Contest for North Sumatra*, 268–9, n. 2.

Aceh. The attackers killed most of the other crew members, including the English captain and his mate, and several passengers. In all, twenty-four people were killed and another twenty drowned when they tried to escape in an overcrowded boat that capsized. The pirates made off with 5,000 Dutch guilders in cash and eight hostages.[226]

The attack was, as the *Straits Times* put it, 'one of the most disastrous cases of piracy that has occurred for many years in Eastern waters'. The paper, however, did not believe that the incident had any political significance but that it was motivated mainly by the desire for plunder. However, the paper thought that it was possible that the attack had been 'indirectly and remotely' a result of the combative spirit that had been fostered among the Acehnese by twenty years of military resistance to the Dutch. There was also a racial side to the problem, according to the *Straits Times*. The *Rajah Kongsee Atjeh*, like other cargo steamers in the region, was in the custom of taking on board large numbers of Asian passengers. With most crew members being Asian as well, the Europeans on board were generally greatly outnumbered, a circumstance that the newspaper believed was a potential security problem. Because it was not possible, on account of the construction of the steamers, to confine Asian passengers to the lower deck, it was all the more necessary to make them understand that piracy was an 'unforgiveable offence' that would surely lead to capital punishment.[227]

The last major attack in Acehnese waters occurred in 1897, when the British steamer *Pegu* was attacked in a similar manner to the *Rajah Kongsee Atjeh*, an incident that left three British officers and five Asian crew members dead.[228] Thereafter piratical activity subsided as the Aceh War came to an end in the first years of the twentieth century.[229]

Summary

Maritime raiding was a central part of the political dynamic of the Strait of Malacca and maritime Southeast Asia in precolonial times, and a coastal ruler's power depended largely on his or her ability to enlist the support of large raiding fleets. In times of political decentralisation and upheaval, piracy and maritime raiding tended to increase and become dispersed, as happened after the Portuguese conquest of Melaka in 1511. The arrival of the Portuguese

---

[226] *Straits Times* (28 July 1893); *Java-bode* (31 July 1893).
[227] *Straits Times Weekly Issue* (25 July 1893). In southern China, Chinese passengers on river steamers were confined to the lower deck and separated from other parts of the vessel by iron fences and armed guards in order to prevent pirates disguised as passengers from committing robberies and murders; e.g., Eklöf Amirell, 'Tools of Terror', 187–90.
[228] *The Times* (10 August 1897).
[229] à Campo, 'Patronen, processen en periodisering', 104–5; cf. Tagliacozzo, *Secret Trades*, 115.

in Southeast Asia brought about an increase in maritime violence and raiding, perpetrated both by Portuguese and Malays. As in the Indian Ocean, the onset of European expansion thus led to a deterioration in maritime security, particularly for Asian seafarers and coastal communities. The arrival of the Dutch from the turn of the seventeenth century resulted in a further increase in maritime violence and coercion, and triggered a long-term decline for indigenous traders and producers of spices and other commercial commodities.

From the turn of the eighteenth century – at around the same time that England began actively to try to shed its worldwide reputation as a nation of pirates – the Dutch East India Company began to take increasingly decisive measures against piracy and maritime raiding in the Malay Archipelago. In the same period, however, Dutch commercial activities and demand for slaves stimulated piratical activity and slave- raiding. From the end of the eighteenth century, under the influence of Enlightenment ideas of race and civilisation, piracy in the Strait of Malacca, as in the Spanish Philippines and elsewhere in the Malay Archipelago, also became increasingly linked to ethnicity, race and religion. In the eyes of British and Dutch observers, the maritime culture of the coastal Malays, combined with their presumed racial characteristics and adherence to Islam, seemed to make them natural and inveterate pirates, more or less on a par with the Iranun, Sama and Tausug of the southern Philippines.

The use of the term *piracy* by the Dutch and British to describe entire communities of Malay and other Southeast Asian seafarers served to legitimise the use of often indiscriminate maritime violence, particularly in the first half of the nineteenth century. Such rhetoric and the antipiracy operations that the Dutch and British undertook in the Strait of Malacca and other parts of the archipelago served to justify territorial expansion and the acquisition of commercial advantages. Ironically, however, much of the piratical activity that the Europeans set out to suppress was triggered by intensified European expansion and commercial penetration, which served to integrate maritime Southeast Asia in the global commercial system, fuelling the demand for slaves and export products from the region, and creating an influx of firearms and munitions that were used for raiding purposes. European trading stations in the region, particularly Singapore, also provided suitable landbases for pirates and markets for pirated goods and captives.

As the monopolistic commercial policies of the Dutch East India Company gave way to the free trade regime promoted by the British after 1815, piracy began to be seen, particularly by the British, but also by the Dutch, as a serious threat to the commerce and prosperity of the region. Although Europeans were only to a small extent the direct targets of piratical attacks, the British in particular had a strong economic interest in the protection of indigenous trade, which was a cornerstone of the prosperity and success of Singapore and the other Straits Settlements. The provision of commercial opportunities to indigenous traders and producers was also seen as a way of weaning piratical Malays and other indigenous groups away from their vile occupation.

The problem of piracy was particularly acute in the Strait of Malacca in the 1830s and 1840s, leading colonial officials, military officers and others to adopt a highly securitising discourse on piracy. Chinese, Malay and other Asian businessmen based in the Strait Settlements were also among the leading proponents of decisive measures to suppress piracy. The outcome was that numerous brutal antipiracy campaigns were launched, often involving the wholesale killing and destruction of allegedly piratical villages and communities. The campaigns were most intense and lethal in north Borneo in the 1840s, but they were also conducted in and around the Strait of Malacca by both Dutch and British authorities.

From the mid nineteenth century the increased use of steam navigation and improved intelligence for the suppression of piracy brought about a decline in the large-scale organised raiding by Malay (if not Chinese) perpetrators. In just a couple of decades, in the 1840s and 1850s, the back of the traditional Malay system of maritime raiding was broken and replaced by the maritime security regime set up by the colonial powers. Whereas the new system certainly was exploitative and biased in favour of the European colonisers, it did bring about a significant improvement in maritime security for most seafarers and coastal populations in the Strait of Malacca and other parts of maritime Southeast Asia. In several respects, intensified colonial expansion from the middle of the nineteenth century constituted an important break with the past, but its significance with regard to maritime security should not be exaggerated. Political stability and the centralisation of power had historically on several occasions led to improved maritime security and a decline in piratical activity in the Strait of Malacca, for example, under the hegemony of Srivijaya or the Sultanate of Melaka.

Although piracy had ceased to be a security threat in the Strait of Malacca by the 1860s, it continued to be used to justify colonial expansion, particularly in the 1870s, both by the British in Selangor and Perak, and by the Dutch in Aceh. As in previous decades, the business community, particularly in the Straits Settlements, was among the most vocal advocates of decisive measures, including military intervention and colonisation, in order to suppress piratical activity. Many senior colonial officials were also leading proponents of intervention, although others, such as Peter Benson Maxwell, were not. Consequently, in both the British and the Dutch contexts, there were critical voices, both in the colonies and in the metropoles, who questioned the way dubious allegations of piracy were used as a pretext for intervention and territorial expansion. The strategy of invoking piracy as a security threat thus always risked backfiring, as was most clearly demonstrated by the public criticism in London against the British intervention in Selangor in 1871.

Particularly in the British context – where there was great sensitivity about the use of excessive violence to suppress piracy after the brutal campaigns in north Borneo in the 1840s – such criticism seems to have had a tempering effect and served to restrain the use of maritime violence to deal with the sporadic piratical activity that remained, or resurged, in the Strait of Malacca after the middle of the nineteenth century. In contrast to the Dutch, French and Spanish, the British also tended to use negotiations and gunboat diplomacy, rather than direct military violence or wars of colonial conquest, in order to achieve their political and commercial objectives in the Malay Peninsula during most of the second half of the nineteenth century.

4 Indochina

Just like the Sulu Sea and the Strait of Malacca, the coast and waters off present-day Vietnam have a long history of piratical activity. Maritime raiding was an important part of the political dynamic of Champa, a loosely integrated kingdom of largely independent polities in central and southern Vietnam between the second and seventeenth centuries, and maritime raiding played a similar role in Champa as in the Malay world. Much of the raiding was aimed at capturing slaves, and it was both a means of waging war and an important source of social, economic and political power for the Cham rulers.[1]

In addition to Cham raiders, freebooters from northern Vietnam also frequently harassed the commercial traffic between Vietnam and southern China in precolonial times. Many of the pirates who throughout history raided the coasts of China originated from Vietnam, and, conversely, many Chinese raiders were active in Vietnamese waters. The European maritime influence, by contrast, was limited for much of the early modern period, and it was not until the second half of the eighteenth century that the increased maritime trade in East and Southeast Asia and the influx of European firearms began more directly to stimulate piratical activity in Vietnamese waters.[2]

Chinese, Vietnamese and French Pirates

Toward the end of the eighteenth century maritime raiding surged in Vietnamese and southern Chinese waters as a result of the political instability in Vietnam. In 1771 the Tay Son Rebellion, a popular uprising that led to the fall of the ruling Le Dynasty, broke out. Within a few years the Tay Son leaders had gained control over most of the country and set about to redistribute land and to eliminate official corruption. Meanwhile, opposition against the Tay Son was led by the Nguyen family, who, aided by Siamese and Chinese troops, struggled for three decades to overthrow the rebels.[3]

---

[1] Wheeler, 'Maritime Logic'; see further Wheeler, 'Maritime Subversions'.
[2] Antony, *Like Froth*; Li Tana, 'Water Frontier', 4.   [3] See Dutton, *Tay Son Uprising*.

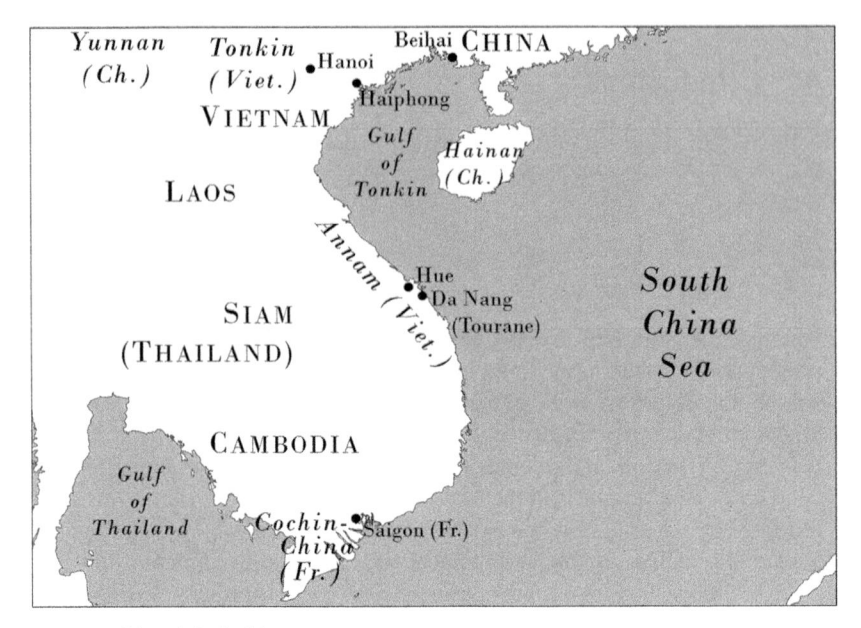

Map 4: Indochina

In order to enhance their military capacity, the Tay Son leaders enlisted the support of maritime mercenaries, mainly of Chinese origin. In European sources these mercenaries were usually called 'Chinese pirates', but arguably they were more akin to what Europeans called privateers. The Tay Son provided the Chinese raiders with official recognition, land bases and markets in exchange for military and financial support. This accommodation led to the development of a plunder-based economy in which Chinese raiders constituted the backbone of the Tay Son's maritime forces and contributed substantially to the revenues of the regime. Under the protection of the Tay Son, the raiding bands thus thrived and grew in size and strength. After the rebellion collapsed in 1802 the raiders lost their official support but continued to engage in piratical activities, and the vast fleets were still for several years a formidable maritime force in the South China Sea and the Gulf of Tonkin.[4]

The Chinese and Vietnamese authorities, aided by British and Portuguese bounty hunters, tried for several years during the first decade of the nineteenth century in vain to defeat the pirates. In 1809, however, a series of defeats spelled the beginning of the end for the raiders, and over the next couple of

---

[4] Antony, 'Maritime Violence'; Antony, *Like Froth*, 43–53.

years the Qing authorities, through a double strategy of coercion and appeasement, and aided by internal dissension among the pirate bands, managed more or less to end large-scale piratical activity in Chinese waters. With the restoration of peace and the consolidation of the Nguyen Dynasty in Vietnam, moreover, the bands were deprived of their markets and safe havens. The result was that for close to fifty years, until the middle of the nineteenth century, the Gulf of Tonkin and most of the Vietnamese coast were relatively free from organised piratical activity, even though petty coastal depredations continued to occur.[5]

During the Tay Son Rebellion, the French interests also increased in Vietnam. Although contacts between France and Vietnam dated back to the seventeenth century, it was only after a French missionary, Pierre-Joseph-Georges Pigneau de Béhaine, assisted the Nguyen Dynasty in defeating the Tay Son that a more permanent French presence in the form of Catholic missions was established in the country. Once in power, however, the conservative Nguyen Dynasty proved mostly hostile to the French missionaries' attempts to spread Christianity. After 1820 the Nguyen emperors pursued a vehemently anti-Christian policy and tried to hinder the expansion of European interests in East and Southeast Asia. Several officially sanctioned waves of persecution of Christians took place, for example in the 1830s and 1850s, which led the French Navy to intervene in order to protect the French missions.[6]

Toward the middle of the nineteenth century piratical activity began to increase in Vietnamese waters after the relative calm following the defeat of the Chinese bands that had supported the Tay Son. Again the perpetrators were mainly Chinese, and the reasons were the same as those that led to the outbreak of junk piracy in the Strait of Malacca and in the vicinity of Singapore around the same time, that is, the end of the Opium War and the decline of the Qing Dynasty in China. The increased China trade in the aftermath of the war also combined with the corruption and inefficiency of the British authorities in Hong Kong to create favourable conditions for piracy in the South China Sea. Moreover, as we have seen, arms and munitions were readily available in the British free ports of Hong Kong and Singapore, where many of the heavily armed pirate junks that roamed the South China Sea were fitted out. The situation was further exacerbated by the disorder that resulted from the Taiping Rebellion after the middle of the century.[7]

---

[5] Wheeler, 'Maritime Subversions', 151–2; Antony, *Like Froth*, 43–53.
[6] Cady, *Roots of French Imperialism*, 9–15.
[7] Antony, 'Piracy on the South China Coast', 41–2; Fox, *British Admirals*, 85–142; see also Tarling, *Piracy and Politics*, 214ff.

164   Indochina

The Nguyen Dynasty, weakened by internal dissension and French incursions, had limited means at their disposal by which to secure their coasts and river deltas in the face of the depredations. In 1850, a French missionary stationed in Tonkin, Monsignor Retord, reported that the whole coast of Tonkin and Cochinchina was infested by pirates organised in fleets that each numbered between fifty and sixty small boats (*barques*). These fleets consisted of both large and heavily armed boats that were used for attacks and smaller vessels that carried women and children and were used for the transportation of pillaged goods. Fortunately, according to Retord, two British steamers arrived to search for the pirates and destroyed or sank over sixty pirate vessels, killing and drowning many people.[8]

After the departure of the British steamers, however, the surviving pirates began to reunite and recommenced their exploits. Over the following years the situation deteriorated, and in 1852 another French missionary stationed in Tonkin, Abbé Taillandier, reported that the pirates conducted horrible ravages, attacking local merchants and even vessels belonging to the Vietnamese emperor. At the same time, moreover, bands of Chinese and Vietnamese brigands were growing in strength in the northern parts of the country, where the imperial forces were unable to control the territory.[9]

There are relatively few surviving firsthand accounts of the attacks by Chinese pirates in the South China Sea in the 1850s. An exception is the account by a French woman, Fanny Loviot, who experienced an attack at sea in 1854 and later published a book about her experiences. There she vividly described the night attack on the *Caldera*, on which she was a passenger:

Three junks, each manned by thirty or forty ruffians, surrounded the 'Caldera'. These creatures seemed like demons, born of the tempest, and bent upon completing our destruction. Having boarded the 'Caldera' by means of grappling-hooks, they were now dancing an infernal dance upon deck, and uttering cries which sounded like nothing human. The smashing of the glass awoke our whole crew, and the light which we had taken for a fire at sea was occasioned by the bursting of fiery balls which they cast on deck to frighten us. Calculating upon this method of alarming their victims, they attack vessels chiefly in the night, and seldom meet with any resistance ... They were dressed like all other Chinese, except that they wore scarlet turbans on their heads, and round their waists broad leather belts garnished with knives and pistols. In addition to this, each man carried in his hand a naked sword.[10]

Loviot survived the attack and her captivity among the pirates, apparently without being physically abused or harmed. She was rescued, quite

---

[8] Retord, 'Missions de Tong-King', 277.
[9] M. l'abbé Taillandier de Montjean to M. l'archiprêtre de la Trinité, *Journal des débats politiques et littéraires* (14 July 1852).
[10] Loviot, *Lady's Captivity*, 63–4.

undramatically, along with the rest of the *Caldera*'s crew by a British steamer less than a fortnight after the attack. Many other victims were less fortunate, however, and it was feared that Europeans were especially susceptible to being killed in order for the pirates to avoid persecution or revenge by the colonial authorities.[11]

The missionary testimonies about the surge in piracy in Vietnamese waters around the middle of the century are corroborated by reports in the colonial press. For example, in 1855 the *Pok Heng*, a junk from Hylam, Johor, carrying livestock, salt, fish, rice, lard, eggs, oil and tamarinds, with eighteen passengers and thirteen crew members on board, was attacked and hijacked by Chinese pirates off the coast of Cochinchina. The junk landed in Singapore a few days later, apparently still in the hands of the pirates. The ship was identified by the *nakoda* (captain) and some members of the original crew, who had escaped the attack by jumping into the water and swimming ashore. According to the *Straits Times*:

They left Anam on the 6th day of the 2nd Moon and on the 17th day when abreast of Chin Sey, on the coast of Cochin China, a Junk came up to them having on board about 40 Macao Chinese; they went close along side, threw stink pots and boarded the Hylam Junk; and being well armed, they commenced an attack upon the crew. The mate and three of the passengers were killed and thrown overboard, all the others jumped overboard. Seven of the crew succeeded in reaching the shore by clinging to a large plank which fell from the Pirate vessel, but what became of the rest is not known: the attack was made within a very short distance of the shore, and the whole of the rest must have perished or those that reached the shore must have seen something of them.[12]

The attack largely followed the pattern of the junk piracy in the waters around Singapore at the same time. The pirates seem to have operated all along the western rim of the South China Sea, from Hainan to Singapore, and, as we have seen, their depredations brought about a sharp decline in the volume of the junk trade between Singapore and Cochinchina in the 1850s.

To the French, however, the piratical activity was of less importance than the persecution of French missionaries in Vietnam. The French Navy was charged with the task of protecting them, but it was in a weak position to do so. In 1840 an attempt was made to strengthen French sea power in East Asia through the creation of the Naval Division of the Chinese Seas (Division navale des mers de Chine), but the capacity of the division was limited, and France still lacked a permanent naval base in East Asia. Consequently, and

---

[11] Duval, *Souvenirs militaires*, 111.
[12] *Straits Times* (1 May 1855), 4. The Straits police boarded the ship but were unable to apprehend the pirates. See also *Straits Times* (22 April 1851; 29 April 1851) for further reports of attacks by Chinese pirates off Vietnam.

because of the naval hegemony of the Royal Navy, any action that the French might contemplate in Asia depended on the consent of the British.[13]

Following an abortive move in 1845 to gain a foothold in the southern Philippines, French interests in Southeast Asia shifted decisively toward Cochinchina (southern Vietnam), which was seen as a possible target for French colonisation.[14] The increasing trade with China after the end of the Opium War in 1842 and the Treaty of Whampoa in 1844, which opened up the Chinese market to French commercial interests, fuelled calls in France for the establishment of a colony in East or Southeast Asia as a means of supporting French commercial activities. The Chamber of Commerce in Marseilles presented a vision of Saigon as a French Singapore in the region, and an official Commission for Cochinchina was established in 1857, charged with the task of drawing up a blueprint for strengthening the French colonial presence in southern Vietnam. The purpose was to ensure that France kept up with Britain and other colonial powers in the race for political and economic advantage in Asia.[15]

In the 1850s pressure from commercial and Catholic groups in France thus combined with the interests of the Navy to push the balance toward a more interventionist policy in Indochina. The French naval engagement in Asia was also part of a broader effort to strengthen the French Navy and to transform it into a powerful marine force with a global reach. This was achieved through a series of major naval building programmes around the mid nineteenth century, which turned the French Navy into a modern navy comparable, at least numerically, to the British.[16]

Before the last years of the 1850s French expansion in Vietnam was subordinated to the efforts to advance French interests in China. Consequently, to the extent that piracy is mentioned in the reports and correspondence of the French Navy in East Asia around the mid nineteenth century, it refers mainly to the situation in and around the coasts of China.[17] The main task of the French Navy in Indochina was instead the protection of the Catholic missions, and for these purposes French warships visited Vietnam on several occasions during the 1840s and 1850s. Even though the persecutions continued, the demonstrations of French military supremacy had a deterrent effect on the anti-Christian campaigns of the Vietnamese regime.[18] In contrast to the British, thus, the gunboats of the French Division of the Chinese Seas did not prioritise the suppression of piracy in Vietnamese waters.[19]

---

[13] Priestley, *France Overseas*, 112; Brocheux and Hémery, *Indochina*, 21–3.
[14] Nardin, 'Français à Basilan'; Cady, *Roots of French Imperialism*, 59.
[15] Brocheux and Hémery, *Indochina*, 14, 22–3; Cady, *Roots of French Imperialism*, 17.
[16] Brocheux and Hémery, *Indochina*, 21.
[17] E.g., BB 4 658, Archives de la Marine, Service historique de la Défense (SHD), Vincennes.
[18] Cady, *Roots of French Imperialism*, 73.   [19] Tarling, *Piracy and Politics*, 214.

The difference in priorities and concerns between the French and the British was linked to the difference in commercial interests and the extent to which maritime security was seen as an important objective in itself. Whereas Britain had strong commercial interests in Asia that depended on the security of trade and navigation at sea – not only for British vessels but also for the local traders who were crucial for the commercial success of the Straits Settlements – there were few immediate reasons for the French to uphold maritime security in Indochina. With no permanent base in the region and relatively small commercial interests, the major aim of French naval operations in Vietnam before the end of the 1850s was instead to put pressure on the Nguyen regime to guarantee the security of the Catholic missionaries in the country.[20]

As for the Nguyen Dynasty, their capacity for and interest in the suppression of piracy were limited. In the first decades of the nineteenth century the suppression of piracy, particularly with regard to the supporters of the Tay Son, had been an important objective of the new dynasty. Its first emperors gave high priority to the country's marine forces, which probably consisted of close to a thousand armed vessels of different sizes. After the South China Sea had been cleared of pirates, however, there seemed to be little reason for the Vietnamese government to maintain a large standing navy, and as a result the naval capacity of Vietnam deteriorated quickly after the 1820s. By the middle of the century the Vietnamese government no longer had the capacity to suppress piracy and maritime raiding around its coasts.[21]

From the point of view of the Nguyen Dynasty the main security threats were not the ravages of the Chinese pirates on the Vietnamese coast, but, on the one hand, internal rebellions on land, mainly in the north, and, on the other the European – particularly the French – incursions on the coasts. Several French naval visits to Vietnam in the 1840s resulted in tense standoffs and at times in violence, such as in April 1847, when the French sank five European-style vessels and about one hundred junks belonging to the Vietnamese Marine in the Bay of Da Nang (Tourane).[22] The event obviously contributed further to a decline in naval capacity on the part of the Vietnamese authorities.

---

[20] Taboulet, *Geste française*, 1, 415.
[21] A country study of Vietnam, published in 1859, stated that the Vietnamese Navy in 1825 consisted of 200 boats armed with 16, 18, 20 or 22 cannons, 500 small galleys with 40 to 44 oars and armed with stone catapults and a small canon in front, and 100 large galleys with 40 to 70 oars and armed with catapults, cannons and a large cannon in front; Girard, *Étude sur la Tourane et la Cochinchine*, 34. The author indicated, however, that the marine forces had deteriorated by the 1850s; cf. Postel, *L'Extrême Orient*, 244.
[22] *Histoire militaire de l'Indochine*, 1 (Hanoi: Impr. d'Extrême-Orient, 1930), 24; Septans, *Commencements de l'Indo-Chine française*, 131–3.

168   Indochina

The Nguyen Dynasty consistently rejected French invitations to establish diplomatic relations and tried, often unceremoniously, to curb French attempts to increase their influence in the country. For example, ahead of a French embassy to Da Nang in 1856, Emperor Tu Duc (r. 1847–83) issued a memorandum to his senior officials in which he ordered the French to be denied any official honours. In accordance with the memorandum, a French request that a letter be delivered to the emperor was refused under humiliating circumstances. The French Navy retaliated by attacking and capturing the fort at Da Nang but was forced to withdraw after a month without having succeeded in forcing the Vietnamese into submission. The withdrawal was seen as a major victory by the Vietnamese, and as the French departed, they displayed large signs that echoed the words of Emperor Tu Duc ahead of the French visit: 'The French bark like dogs and flee like goats.'[23] The emperor also accused the French of piracy, saying that the French 'roam the seas like pirates, establishing their lair on deserted islands, or hide on the coasts, in the depth of valleys, and from there foment troubles and revolutions in the neighbouring countries'.[24]

The persecution of Christian missionaries and converts intensified after the debacle at Da Nang, and Monsignor Retord now urged the French government to abandon such half-measures that, according to him, only aggravated the plight of the missionaries. France, Retord argued, should either intervene decisively or leave the missionaries in Vietnam to their unhappy fate.[25]

The trigger for a more decisive French intervention occurred in mid 1857, when the Vietnamese authorities had a Spanish Dominican missionary decapitated. The French government ordered Admiral Charles Rigault de Genouilly to lead a major naval expedition to Cochinchina in order to seek redress and to establish favourable conditions for French interests in the country. In a letter to the Minister for the Marine, the Minister of Foreign Affairs, Alexandre Colonna-Walewski, specifically emphasised two grievances of the French in Vietnam: the persecution of French missionaries and the constant refusal of the Vietnamese government to establish relations of friendship and commerce. Rigault de Genouilly's instructions were broad: he was to occupy Da Nang, but he was then given the mandate to decide, in view of the situation, whether to establish a French protectorate over Cochinchina or to negotiate a treaty with the Vietnamese.[26] Piracy, on the other hand, was not mentioned in the instructions or in the official letters preceding the expedition, despite the

---

[23] Launay, *Histoire ancienne*.
[24] Lettre de Mgr Retord, *Annales de la propagation de la foi*, 30 (1858), 226.
[25] Cady, *Roots of French Imperialism*, 187.
[26] Walewski to Hamelin, 25 November 1857, in Taboulet, *Geste française*, 1, 416.

prevalence of junk piracy in the region at the time. The French expedition in 1858 was thus not charged with the task of combatting piracy and seems not to have undertaken any such operations.

French troops again seized the fort at Da Nang in August 1858, but Rigault de Genouilly was unable to achieve either of the objectives of establishing a protectorate or negotiating a treaty with Vietnam. The admiral then decided to attack Saigon, which, in contrast to the Vietnamese capital, Hue, was within reach of French naval forces. The renewed war in China, however, forced the French to abort the intervention and sail for China in March 1860.[27] Once again, the Vietnamese celebrated what they saw as a victory over the French, and in a widely published decree issued shortly after the French departure, Tu Duc gave his opinion of the French: 'Pirates, equally incompetent and cowardly, they were defeated by our valiant soldiers and saved themselves like dogs with their tails between their legs.'[28]

Describing his enemies as pirates (and dogs) obviously served the rhetorical purposes for the Nguyen Dynasty, but in view of the French incursions and acts of aggression in the preceding years it was not an unreasonable accusation. The attacks on Da Nang and Saigon in 1858–60 reinforced the Vietnamese perception that the French were sea bandits or rebels rather than lawful enemies. Similar accusations were later repeated in appeals to resistance against the French after their invasion of Tonkin in 1883.[29] The notion that European navigators were pirates had a long history in Asia, dating back, as we have seen, to the onset of European maritime expansion in Asia in the sixteenth century. Against that background, the characterisation of the French as pirates probably made more than just rhetorical sense in Vietnam around the middle of the nineteenth century.

Colonial Expansion and River Piracy in Cochinchina

The Vietnamese triumph after the French evacuation of Da Nang turned out to be short-lived. Following the signing of the peace treaty with China in October 1860, French warships returned to Vietnam. Saigon was captured in early 1861, and French gunboats began to penetrate the river system of Cochinchina. The imperial troops were pushed back, and the Nguyen Dynasty, which also was under pressure from unrest in the north, was forced to negotiate with the French. In June 1862 the Treaty of Saigon was signed on terms that were highly unfavourable to the Vietnamese. Vietnam was forced to cede three of

---

[27] *Histoire militaire de l'Indochine*, 1, 26–7.
[28] 'Cochinchine', *Annales de la propagation de la foi*, 33 (1861), 71.
[29] Proclamation of the Can Vuong found in 1890, in Mat-Gioi [A. de Pouvourville], *Politique indo-chinoise*, 207; cit. in Brocheux and Hémery, *Indochina*, 59.

her southern provinces to France, which came to form the colony of French Cochinchina, and to give up her nominal sovereignty (shared with Siam) over Cambodia. The treaty also opened up three Vietnamese ports to French and Spanish commercial interests, and granted freedom of navigation for all French vessels, including warships, on the Mekong and its tributaries. This provision was important to the French because they hoped that the Mekong would provide direct access to the interior of China, a prospect that seemed to hold great commercial potential. The treaty also gave all French, Spanish and Vietnamese subjects the right to practise the Christian faith in Vietnam and set a large indemnity to be paid by Vietnam over ten years. In contrast to the treaties made by other colonial powers in Southeast Asia at the time, however, the Saigon Treaty did not mention any obligation on the French or the Vietnamese to cooperate in the suppression of piracy. The only mention of piracy in the treaty was in Article 9, according to which the two countries promised to extradite to the other country all 'brigands, pirates or trouble makers' who caused mischief in one territory and then escaped to the other.[30]

The first governor of French Cochinchina, Admiral Louis-Adolphe Bonard, initially tried to implement a system of indirect rule, according to which low-ranking Vietnamese officials and village heads were to continue to exercise local authority, supervised by French inspectors. The scheme was difficult to implement, however, because most of the mandarins who were the backbone of the civil administration in Vietnam chose to leave Cochinchina as the French took over power. In order to fill their places, inspectors and other high-ranking officials in the colony were recruited among the officers of the French Navy. However, most naval officers had no experience of civil administration, and virtually none of them had any deeper knowledge about or understanding of region's culture or language. The only interpreters available were the missionaries and their students, some of whom knew a bit of Latin. French administration of indigenous affairs in Cochinchina was thus often conducted in Latin during the first years of the colonial period.[31]

The colonial administration tried to downplay the security problems in the new colony, and piracy was described as a matter of minor concern. An official report in early 1863 optimistically claimed that piracy, the 'scourge of the Far East', probably still existed in some parts of the colony, but that it would not be able to resist long the energy of the French marines, who penetrated all rivers and creeks with their small gunboats in pursuit of the pirates. 'The destruction of these bandits can thus no longer be but a matter of perseverance', the report

---

[30] Taboulet, *Geste française*, 2, 474–6. For French attempts to reach China by the Mekong, see Osborne, *River Road to China*.
[31] Osborne, *French Presence in Cochinchina and Cambodia*, 35; Cultru, *Histoire de la Cochinchine française*, 297.

claimed.[32] Another report, published a few years later in the official journal of the Ministry for the Marine and the Colonies, praised the stable, patriarchal social system of Vietnamese society and concluded that those who took to piracy did so out of extraordinary local circumstances and because they lacked traditional ties to family and village. The pirates, according to the report, were thus degenerates, such as exist, unfortunately, in all societies, even in those with the most advanced levels of civilisation.[33]

In reality, however, the inexperience, inefficiency and lack of legitimacy of the new regime resulted in a sharp deterioration of the security situation and the breakdown of law and order in many parts of the colony, particularly in the region around the Mekong Delta. River piracy, extortion, banditry and violent attacks on French officials and interests were common. In order to police the Mekong and its delta and tributaries, the French relied on a system set up by the Nguyen Dynasty, which consisted of a fleet of small sailing junks, *lorchas*. Under the French administration the *lorchas* were charged specifically with the task of suppressing piracy. Each *lorcha* was manned by an indigenous crew and commanded by a junior French naval officer (*enseigne* or *maître de la flotte*). Captured pirates were sentenced – usually to immediate execution without the possibility of appeal – by the inspectors or other district officers holding judicial powers.[34] Harsh and arbitrary sentences passed on loose grounds by junior officers who had little knowledge of legal matters were common. The following case, presented to the governor of Cochinchina by a local French official, is one of several examples collected by Charles Le Myre de Vilers, who served as the first civilian governor of French Cochinchina from 1879 to 1882:

Considering that the three accused have come to surrender themselves, but only two days after the execution of Huan [an alleged rebel executed by the authorities] and that, judging from their *physical constitution* [*leur physique*], they seem to have been born to piracy and rebellion, and that they have made but incomplete confessions;

[We] declare them guilty of rebellion, etc., etc., and judge all three of them to decapitation and ask that their punishment be commuted to ten years' detention at Poulo-Condore.

X ...

Judgement approved without commutation of punishment: proceed immediately to execution.

GOVERNOR[35]

---

[32] 'Extraits de l'éxposé de la situation de l'empire, 13 January 1863', *Revue maritime et coloniale*, 7 (1863), 168.
[33] d'Aries, 'La Cochinchine française', 193.
[34] Cultru, *Histoire de la Cochinchine française*, 194.
[35] Le Myre de Vilers, *Institutions civiles de la Cochinchine*, 68–9; italics in original. Poulo Condore was a French penal colony on the island of Con Son, off the coast of mainland Cochinchina.

The arbitrary administration of justice continued throughout the era of naval administration in Cochinchina. Even in the 1870s alleged pirates and other criminals of Asian descent – in contrast to French citizens and fellow Europeans – did not have the right to appeal for mercy to the President of the Republic. This provision was justified by the extraordinary security situation in the colony and was abolished only with the transition to civil rule in Cochinchina in 1879.[36]

The authorities also took measures to ensure that the sentences passed on pirates and other brigands received as much publicity as possible. Indigenous courts were instructed to translate extracts from all sentences passed on those sentenced to death for piracy or brigandage into Vietnamese and Chinese and display them on high-visibility coloured paper in all villages in their district, in the most public places.[37]

Governor Bonard asked for reinforcements from Paris in order to deal with the security problems, but he was on the whole unable to establish an efficient administration in most of the colony during his two years in office.[38] In several letters to the Minister of the Marine, the governor expressed his despair at the chaotic situation and even asked to be relieved of his duties. He did not, however, explicitly mention in his letters piracy as a major cause of the troubles but rather pointed to 'brigands and rebels' who terrorised the population.[39]

Although there was a good deal of confusion initially among French colonialists as to who was a brigand and who was a rebel, some of the more experienced officers tried to clarify the distinction based on the motives and social background of the perpetrators. According to Lieutenant Francis Garnier, a naval officer who served in Cochinchina and published two influential reports on the social, economic and political situation in the colony in the 1860s, the rebel leaders were educated men (*lettrés*), who had preserved their prestige among the population and had not at all 'descended, as elsewhere, to the simple rank of pirates and common murderers'.[40]

Regardless of the motives and character of the alleged pirates and other troublemakers, the French colonial authorities became convinced that in order to establish efficient control over the Mekong basin they had to control Cambodia. Essentially, thus, the French pursued the same tributary strategy with regard to Cambodia that the Vietnamese emperors had done since the eighteenth century.[41] Meanwhile, Cambodia's King Norodom (r. 1860–1904) fought to save his dynasty against a series of internal rebellions and his country

---

[36] Fonssagrives and Laffont (eds.), *Répertoire alphabétique de législation*, 4, 75.
[37] Ibid., 647.   [38] Taboulet, *Geste française*, 2, 478.   [39] Ibid., 478–81.
[40] G. Francis [Francis Garnier], *La Cochinchine française en 1864*, 13.
[41] Brocheux and Hémery, *Indochina*, 27.

from being divided between Vietnam and Siam. To that end he approached the French and asked to be placed under French protection, and in August 1863 a Treaty of Friendship and Commerce was signed between the two countries. In contrast to the peace treaty with Vietnam signed the year before, the one with Cambodia contained two detailed and reciprocal but otherwise identical articles on the suppression of piracy:

> In the case of French vessels being attacked or plundered by pirates in waters governed by the Kingdom of Cambodia, the local authority in the closest location, as soon as it gains information about the event, shall actively follow the perpetrators and not spare any effort in order that they be arrested and punished according to the law. The seized cargo, regardless of in which place it is found or in what condition, shall be returned to the owners, or, in their absence, to the hands of a French authority that will take responsibility for its return. If it is impossible to seize those responsible or to recover all of the stolen objects, the Cambodian officials, after having proved that they have done their utmost to obtain this goal, shall not be held financially responsible.[42]

The pledges of the Cambodians to do their utmost to suppress piracy, however, were of little practical value, because the Cambodian government lacked the means by which to control the country. The French authorities were also unable to uphold security, and piracy was rife on the Mekong and its tributaries, particularly in Dinh Tuong (My Tho; today the province of Tien Giang), which formed the central province of French Cochinchina and potentially was one of the richest parts of the colony. According to Garnier, Dinh Tuong suffered heavily from attacks by pirates, who took refuge and found protection in Cambodia.[43]

Despite wearying and costly gunboat patrols, the French authorities were unable to protect the population of the region from the depredations, arsons and killings committed by the river pirates. The result was that after four years of French rule more than half of the population of the province had fled to Vietnamese territory, and whole villages and towns were deserted. There was no denying, Garnier argued, that these unfortunate circumstances derived more or less from the peculiar borders of the French possessions in Cochinchina. The solution, he advocated, was the extension of French sovereignty in southern Vietnam in order to improve the security situation.[44]

Such a course of action was adopted in mid 1866, when Bonard's successor as governor, Admiral Pierre-Paul de la Grandière, backed by the French Emperor Napoleon III, but not by the Foreign Ministry, suddenly occupied

---

[42] Extract from Article 13, Traité entre S. M. l'Empereur des Français et S. M. le Roi du Cambodge, 11 August 1863, printed in Fonssagrives and Laffont (eds.), *Répertoire alphabétique de législation*, 2, 77. Article 14 was reciprocal in favour of the Cambodians but otherwise identical.

[43] G. Francis [Francis Garnier], *De la Colonisation de la Cochinchine*, 9–10.

[44] Ibid., 9–10; cf. Petit, *Francis Garnier*, 80–1.

174   Indochina

the Vietnamese western provinces of the Mekong Delta. Ignoring the protests of the Nguyen court, de la Grandière then went on to annex the southernmost three Vietnamese provinces, Vinh Long, Chau Doc and Ha Tien, thereby considerably extending the territory under French control in Indochina.[45] The governor justified his move with reference to the security needs of the French colony, claiming that the three provinces under Vietnamese domination had served continuously as a refuge for rebels, both against the Cambodian government and the French colony, and provided them with both manpower, arms and munitions.[46] The Governor did not mention piracy in his official explanation, but it was widely reported in the French press that the provinces had served as a refuge for pirates and other troublemakers.[47]

The treaty with Cambodia and the annexation of the three Vietnamese provinces were meant to bring about an improvement in the security situation in French Cochinchina. To some extent this objective was achieved, and in 1871 the governor, Admiral Marie-Jules Dupré, claimed that the colony enjoyed perfect tranquillity with no signs of trouble or agitation on any side.[48] Although the claim was probably somewhat exaggerated, piracy began to be brought under control in the colony from the beginning of the 1870s.[49]

Piracy and Banditry in the North

Whereas piracy thus declined in the French-controlled southern part of Vietnam, the situation in the northern parts became increasingly unstable. The Nguyen Dynasty was weakened because of internal rebellions and an influx of Chinese bandits linked directly or indirectly to the Taiping Rebellion, particularly after the rebels were defeated in China in 1864. The Chinese government dispatched regular troops to assist Vietnam in quelling the anarchy. The reliance on foreign troops, however, served to further erode the authority of the Nguyen Dynasty in the northern parts of the country, and the support of the Chinese troops added to the financial difficulties of the regime.[50]

With the Nguyen Dynasty thus occupied with rebellions and banditry in the north and with trying to counter the French invasions in the south, Chinese

---

[45] Brocheux and Hémery, *Indochina*, 27.
[46] Ordre de l'Amiral, 15 June 1867, in Taboulet, *Geste française*, 2, 513–14; see also Proclamation de l'Amiral, 25 June 1867, in ibid., 514.
[47] E.g., *Le Figaro* (10 August 1867); *Journal de l'An* (12 August 1867). Both newspapers quoted the official journal for the French colonies in India, *Le Moniteur* (9 August 1867), as the source.
[48] L'Amiral Dupré au Ministre de la Marine, 12 October 1871, in Taboulet, *Geste française*, 2, 528; see also footnote 1, in ibid., 588.
[49] Cf. Postel, *Sur les Bords du Mé-Không*, 80, who claimed that contingents of pirates and bandits continuously roamed the region between 1861 and 1872.
[50] Davis, 'States of Banditry', 70.

pirates congregated in increasingly large numbers on the Vietnamese coast and on the islands of the Red River Delta from where they launched attacks on maritime traffic and coastal villages. The purpose of the raids was both robbery and the abduction of people, particularly Vietnamese girls and women, who were trafficked to China, where they were sold as concubines, prostitutes or domestic slaves.[51] Pirate bands based on Hainan also harassed the junk trade between Cochinchina and Tonkin.

The increase in piratical activity in the Gulf of Tonkin and around Hainan was in part due to the increasingly efficient suppression of piracy in other parts of Asia, particularly in the South China Sea, along the South China coast and in the Strait of Malacca.[52] Pressured from both sides, Chinese pirates thus took refuge to Hainan and the coasts and islands of Tonkin, where no major naval power undertook to uphold maritime security.

In early 1872, however, the French sent the dispatch boat (*aviso*) *Bourayne* to Tonkin. Officially the mission was to gather information about the geography and political situation in northern Vietnam, but covertly the expedition was to prepare for a possible French military intervention in Tonkin. Many of the senior naval officers stationed in Cochinchina, including Governor Dupré, believed that only the wholesale annexation of the rest of Vietnam would produce political stability and favourable conditions for trade and investment in Indochina. Piracy, in that context, was less of an obstacle to maritime commerce than a convenient pretext for territorial expansion.[53]

While surveying the Cat Ba Archipelago off the Red River Delta in early February 1872, the *Bourayne* encountered a fleet of pirate junks at sea. The French took up the chase and captured one of the junks after it was abandoned by the crew, whereas another junk was crushed against the cliffs after being hit by French cannon fire. The chase led the *Bourayne* to a natural port, sheltered by the islands surrounding it, where between 150 and 200 junks were anchored. According to the commander of the *Bourayne*, Captain Senez, the place was well known to local officials and people in general as a major nest of Chinese pirates. The port was completely hidden from sight from the sea, however, and impossible to find without prior knowledge of the location of the entrance. One could not, Senez claimed, find a more suitable location for the development and protection of piracy. He argued that the first step to be taken in order to eradicate piracy in the area must be to occupy Cat Ba, or at the

---

[51] Lessard, 'Cet ignoble trafic'; Anonymous, 'Commerce de la France', 242–3. See also Lessard, *Human Trafficking*, Ch. 1.
[52] See Chapter 3; Blue, 'Piracy on the China Coast', 75–7; Antony, 'Piracy on the South China Coast', 44; Chappell, 'Maritime Raiding', 10–14.
[53] See Dutreb, *L'Amiral Dupré*, 7–8; McLeod, *Vietnamese Response*, 101.

very least make such frequent appearances in the archipelago that the pirates should no longer feel safe.[54]

Despite the *Bourayne*'s victorious encounter with Chinese pirates, the expedition did little to improve the general maritime security situation in the waters of Tonkin. In May 1872 pirate fleets reportedly blocked most of the ports on the Vietnamese coast south of the Red River Delta.[55] At the same time, French business interests pressed for the extension of French control over northern Vietnam. The Red River seemed to hold great prospects for an expansion of French commercial interests to the interior of China, particularly Yunnan Province. The British, however, also appeared to be interested in the river, through which they hoped to be able to connect their interests in China with those in India and Burma. Imperial rivalry in Tonkin was further enhanced by Chinese military intervention in the north and – as in the Strait of Malacca around the same time – fears of German advances in the region.[56]

One of the keenest advocates of French intervention in Tonkin was Jean Dupuis, a businessman, adventurer and longtime resident of East Asia. Stopping in Cochinchina on his way from Paris in 1872, Dupuis persuaded the Acting Governor to dispatch yet another naval expedition to Tonkin for the purpose of further exploring the possibilities of a French intervention, but now also officially for the suppression of piracy.[57] In October 1872 the *Bourayne* was thus once again despatched to Tonkin, where it cruised for fifty days and engaged on three occasions in combat against Chinese pirates. The fiercest battle took place on 21 October, when two pirate junks opened fire on the *Bourayne* off the island of Hon Tseu. The French retaliated and eventually, after a battle that lasted for two hours, sank one of the junks and captured the other. According to Senez, the pirates fought with unexpected vigour and a 'bravery worthy of a better cause'. Three hundred pirates perished in the battle, whereas only two Frenchmen were wounded. Six days later, the *Bourayne* once again encountered and sank four small pirate junks, killing an estimated 120–50 Chinese, and the following morning yet another junk was destroyed, killing between 100 and 120 men.[58] Proudly summarising the results of the expedition, Senez claimed that it had rendered the Vietnamese government a service by unblocking its ports and 'beaten, sunk or burnt seven pirate junks carrying altogether more than 100 cannons and manned by 700 or 800 men, more than 500 of whom were killed'.[59]

---

[54] Senez, 'De Saigon au nord du Tonquin', 354–5. [55] Senez, 'Rapport nautique', 32.
[56] Priestley, *France Overseas*, 216–17; Cady, *Roots of French Imperialism*, 284.
[57] *Histoire militaire de l'Indochine*, 1, 45. [58] Senez, 'Rapport nautique', 12–15; cit., 13.
[59] Ibid., 32.

The news of the outcome of the expedition was greeted enthusiastically in France. Senez was promoted and widely praised in the press for having exterminated the pirates for no more than seven wounded French soldiers.[60] The contrast is striking with the criticism that James Brooke's expeditions in north Borneo had provoked in Britain some twenty years earlier, or the controversy surrounding the British (much less violent) intervention in Selangor the year before. In France there was hardly any questioning of the loss of life involved among the alleged pirates, despite the fact that many leading politicians and intellectuals were strongly opposed to further colonial adventures, wishing instead to concentrate on strengthening France's international standing in Europe in the wake of the humiliating defeat in the Franco–Prussian War of 1870–71.

The perceived success of the expedition of the *Bourayne* notwithstanding, it seemed to have little effect on piratical activity in Vietnamese waters. The year after the expedition, an apostolic missionary stationed in eastern Tonkin reported:

The pirates are mainly Chinese, but there are also Vietnamese among them. Their base is around a port called Cat-Ba, close to Dâu-son [Dô-son]. When these bandits want to make their expeditions they assemble a greater or smaller number of boats [*barques*] according to the difficulty of the enterprise. Then they enter abruptly the rivers, without fear either of the mandarins or the royal troops, and they go from village to village, wherever it pleases them to carry out their depredations. If the people resist, they burn, pillage, massacre, causing countless calamities; nevertheless they spare and abduct in captivity the beautiful women and children.[61]

Intervention in Tonkin

Despite the overwhelmingly positive response that the expedition of the *Bourayne* received in France, there was still no official support for military intervention in or annexation of northern Vietnam. Jean Dupuis, however, was determined to open up the Red River for commerce, with or without official French support. To that effect he assembled a private force, consisting of two gunboats, a steamship and a junk manned by altogether 175 men, and without bothering to secure the authorisation of the Vietnamese authorities, he headed off upstream on the Red River.

Most of the river and the territory around it was under the control of two rival bands of Chinese bandits, the Black Flags and the Yellow Flags, both of

---

[60] 'Le "Bourayne" et les pirates chinois', *L'Illustration: Journal universel*, 61 (1873), 170; 'L'aviso Le Bourayne et son commandant', *Le voleur* (28 March 1873).
[61] 'Lettre de Mgr Colomer, Vicaire Apostolique du Tonkin Oriental, 26 August 1873', in Taboulet, *Geste française*, 2, 681.

which had their origins in the defeated Taiping Rebellion. Even though he was a longtime resident of the region and spoke fluent Chinese, Dupuis failed to understand the complexity of the situation in upper Tonkin. By siding with the Yellow Flags – which before Dupuis' intervention was a relatively obscure band that for several years had been fighting a losing battle against the Black Flags – Dupuis managed to further alienate Vietnamese officials, who already regarded him as a pirate and a troublemaker. Obviously unbeknown to Dupuis, moreover, the Nguyen Dynasty covertly sanctioned the Black Flags in order to maintain at least nominal control over northern Vietnam in the face of open rebellions, the defiance of senior officials and Chinese incursions. Dupuis also mistakenly believed that the Yellow Flags were in the business of protecting the local highland population and claimed that they sought to live in peace with the Vietnamese. By contrast, he regarded the Black Flags as composed for the most part of 'pirates and bandits' who terrorised the local population.[62]

Dupuis' attempt to open up the Red River for commerce ended in failure as his mission came in conflict with the Black Flags. Although this should have made him aware of the power of the Black Flags, he managed to convince the French Navy that the band did not constitute any significant threat. He also secured unofficial support from Paris for his plans to open up commerce with China on the Red River, despite the generally cautious attitude of the French government (particularly the Foreign Office) at the time with regard to engagements in further imperialist adventures. At the same time Governor Dupré, advised by the ambitious and pro-imperialist Francis Garnier, was keen to intervene in Tonkin. An intervention seemed motivated by the weakness of the Nguyen Dynasty and its obvious impotence in dealing with the rebels, bandits and pirates in the country, some of whom spilled over into the French colony in the form of smuggling, piracy, and social and political unrest. In addition, a priority for Dupré was to terminate the protracted negotiations with Hue over the formal cessation of the French provinces in Cochinchina, which had been achieved de facto in 1867, but had not been settled by treaty. A further reason for intervention were the indications of increasing British as well as German interest in Vietnam.[63]

In this situation a window of opportunity opened up for the French Navy to intervene in Tonkin. In July 1873 the Vietnamese government sent two requests to Governor Dupré asking for his assistance to expel the troublesome Dupuis. Ignoring the hesitation of the central government in Paris, the governor dispatched a small expeditionary corps to Tonkin under the command of

---

[62] Davis, 'State of Banditry', 70–1, 140, 158; McLeod, *Vietnamese Response*, 103; Dupuis, *L'Ouverture du fleuve rouge*, 40–1.
[63] Davis, 'State of Banditry', 151; Cady, *Roots of French Imperialism*, 282–4.

Lieutenant Garnier. Officially the object was to assist the Vietnamese government to expel Dupuis, by force if necessary. In addition, however, Dupré secretly instructed Garnier to occupy the citadel of either Kecho or Hanoi and one of the Vietnamese strongholds on the coast in order to put pressure on the Vietnamese government to agree to a settlement of the territorial question. Although they were premeditated, the occupations were to be represented as sprung from necessity in order to quell the anarchy and rebellions that plagued the country, which the Vietnamese authorities were unable to deal with.[64]

The small and ill-equipped expedition, initially consisting of fewer than a hundred men and two small vessels, one of which sank on the way, reached Hanoi at the end of October. Within a few weeks Garnier got in touch with Dupuis, stormed and occupied the citadel at Hanoi – allegedly because of the uncooperative attitude of the Vietnamese officials – and unilaterally declared the Red River open to commerce. As the French had hoped, popular disaffection with the Nguyen Dynasty surged, and pro-French elements, mainly consisting of people loyal to the former Le Dynasty and Catholics, took control over the coastal provinces.[65]

By early December the intervention appeared to have achieved its objectives, and the Vietnamese government seemed willing to settle the territorial question. The Vietnamese, however, tried to weaken the French by using the Black Flags to assault them, and on 21 December a band of Black Flags attacked the citadel at Hanoi. The attack was repulsed, but Garnier, who led a small detachment in pursuit of the attackers, was killed in an ambush, along with three French soldiers. The event prompted the end of French intervention in Tonkin. The expedition withdrew, and the occupied citadels and other strongholds were returned to the Vietnamese.[66]

Although piracy was mentioned in the correspondence between Dupré and the Minister of the Marine as a reason for the military intervention of 1873, it was not officially identified as a major reason for the intervention. In Dupré's instructions to Garnier the suppression of piracy was mentioned merely as a secondary task, to be exercised only if opportunity arose.[67] Following the death of Garnier, however, the French colonial and metropolitan press eagerly seized on the theme of piracy. The *Courrier de Saïgon*, for example, claimed that Garnier had been obliged to take control over Hanoi and other provinces in order to make the pirates and rebel bands respect the authority of the

---

[64] Dupré to the Minister of the Marine, 28 July 1873, in Dutreb, *L'Amiral Dupré*, 30–5.
[65] Cady, *Roots of French Imperialism*, 286; *Histoire de la militaire de l'Indochine*, 1, 46.
[66] Davis, *State of Banditry*, 177–8.
[67] Dupré to the Minister of the Marine, 28 July 1873, in Dutreb, *L'Amiral Dupré*, 33; Dupré to Garnier, 10 October, in Dutreb, *L'Amiral Dupré*, 48.

180   Indochina

Vietnamese king, even though the Black Flags were described as a band of Chinese rebels rather than pirates.[68] The official gazette of the French Republic, meanwhile, claimed that the attack on the citadel in Hanoi was prompted by the concentration of pirates and rebels interested in plunder, and the Black Flags who had attacked the citadel on 21 December 1873 were described as 'Chinese pirates'. The gazette also reported that the expedition had sunk twenty-six pirate junks at the entrance of the Red River.[69]

The French withdrawal from Tonkin was followed by diplomatic negotiations, resulting in the signing in March 1874 of the Giap Tuat Treaty between France and Vietnam, which in effect replaced the Saigon Treaty of 1862. For France, the major gain was Hue's unconditional acknowledgement of French sovereignty over the southern provinces and several provisions that served to open up Vietnam to French economic interests. The treaty implied a French protectorate over Vietnam, but the very word *protectorate* was not mentioned in the treaty text. France acknowledged the full sovereignty and independence of Vietnam while pledging to 'render necessary support [to the Vietnamese king] for him to maintain order and peace in his territory, to defend him against any attack and to destroy the piracy that ravages part of the coasts of the Kingdom'. Such support was to be given only at the request of the Vietnamese king and for free. The Vietnamese government was also to receive from France (again for free) five fully armed steamers for the purpose of suppressing piracy along the Vietnamese coast.[70]

In Paris, however, Parliament was reluctant to ratify the new treaty. Garnier's death and the failure of his expedition seemed to demonstrate the perils of further colonial expansion in Indochina. The government, on the other hand, presented the new treaty as a necessity in order to assist the Vietnamese king to uphold law and order. According to the motivation, read by Senator Admiral Bénjamin Jaurès to Parliament in July 1874:

The Kingdom of Annam is today exposed to two types of dangers that paralyse all its resources. Tonkin, the richest of its provinces, has for some years been penetrated both by Chinese rebels pushed out of their territory and by regular Chinese troops dispatched to pursue them. The coasts are at present forbidden to commerce, less because of legal prohibitions that ban its access than by the pirates who form veritable naval squadrons in these provinces and against whom we ourselves, on several occasions, for the security of the seas, have had to undertake costly and bloody expeditions.[71]

---

[68] *Courrier de Saigon* (5 January 1874).
[69] *Journal officiel de la République française* (13 February 1874, 27 February 1874).
[70] Treaty of 15 March 1874 between France and Vietnam, in Taboulet, *Geste française*, 2, 743–7; cit., 744. See also Ageron, *France coloniale ou parti colonial?*, 103; *Journal officiel de République française* (4 August 1874).
[71] *Journal officiel de République française* (4 August 1874).

The suppression of piracy, moreover, was framed both in highly securitising terms and as part of the French and European civilising mission. Continuing the plea, Jaurès said:

France, after having, in concert with England, opened new ports in China to European commerce, has recently continued its work of civilisation and progress by obtaining the opening of ports in Vietnam. This kingdom will, moreover, be the first to reap the fruits of its concession; for everywhere European commerce penetrates, it carries with it peacefulness and respect for property as well as transactions. The south of Tonkin will soon see the disappearance of these bands of insurgents who there have brought about a state of permanent disorder.

Our protective vessels will soon have finished off this pirate fleet which, since time immemorial has carried out ravages on the coasts and prevented all sorts of vessels, all commerce and even the fishing from which the populations of the littoral to a great extent make their living, descending in hordes of bandits who penetrate the interior and engage in pillaging of all sorts, abducting the men to deliver them to the coolie recruiting agents and selling the women in order to fill the houses of debauchery in China.[72]

The conservative majority that dominated Parliament, however, was tied to the policy of so-called continental patriotism, meaning that the main foreign policy priority for France should be to defend her interests in continental Europe. In addition, the conservatives were strongly opposed to colonial expansion in Vietnam because it might lead to a conflict with China.[73] Among left-wing politicians, opposition to colonial expansion was even more pronounced. One of the most vocal anti-imperialists in Parliament, the Radical Socialist Georges Périn, argued that the task of maintaining peace and order among an estimated 15 to 20 million Vietnamese would be insurmountable and foolhardy. Why, Périn asked, should France risk the lives of her soldiers in order to police the Kingdom of Vietnam? The task, according to Périn, was not just to keep order among the Vietnamese, but also among the foreigners, in particular the pirates who infested the entrance of the Red River. 'When we shall have defended the south of Tonkin against the pirates, we shall have to defend the north, on the border to Yunnan, against the Chinese Muslims, who the Chinese Buddhists try to push toward Tonkin.'[74]

Despite the protests the treaty was ratified and shortly afterwards followed up by a commercial treaty, signed on 31 August 1874, which in turn was ratified the following year. In the commercial treaty, France renewed its promise to assist the Vietnamese government in the suppression of piracy.

---

[72] *Journal officiel de République française* (20 August 1874).
[73] Brocheux and Hémery, *Indochina*, 29.
[74] *Journal officiel de République française* (5 August 1874).

However, whereas the first treaty, as we have seen, spoke of suppressing the 'piracy that ravages part of the coasts of the Kingdom' – thus limiting the mandate to the sea and coastal regions – the commercial treaty spoke of the French obligation to 'make all efforts to destroy the pirates of the land and the sea, particularly in the vicinity of the towns and ports open to European commerce'.[75] The difference may not have seemed like a major one to the Vietnamese, because there was little distinction in the Vietnamese language between bandits on land and pirates or bandits at sea. The provision of the commercial treaty nevertheless gave France a stronger mandate to intervene in the affairs of Vietnam in the (likely) event that the Vietnamese government would prove unable to uphold security on land or at sea.

The five steamers that France had promised to donate to the Vietnamese government were delivered in July 1876, and at the request of the Vietnamese each of the five vessels was put under the command of a French captain, recruited from the merchant navy.[76] Relations between the French captains and the Vietnamese officials, however, were from the outset plagued by cultural and linguistic misunderstandings and mutual distrust, which effectively prevented the steamers from fulfilling their purpose. The commander of one of the gunboats, *Scorpion*, Jules-Léon Dutreuil de Rhins, found it extremely difficult to know whether a junk was a pirate vessel or not. According to the captain, the Vietnamese themselves could not see a junk without suspecting that it was engaged in piracy, and for his own part he believed that all of them were, given the opportunity. He was also convinced that Vietnamese officials colluded with the pirates, particularly the Chinese pirates, who were more feared than the Vietnamese and who seemed to enjoy complete impunity. When a pirate junk was captured, Dutreuil de Rhins asserted, the perpetrators were taken before the authorities in Hue, where they were immediately released on condition that they agreed to put their forces at the government's disposal and henceforth only pillage 'in good company', as the captain put it.[77]

In contrast to the spectacular battles of the *Bourayne* a few years earlier, the five gunboats that France gave to the Vietnamese government do not seem to have encountered or defeated any pirates. All five captains resigned within a few months, allegedly because of the misconduct of Vietnamese officials. The boats were subsequently either abandoned or wrecked along the Vietnamese coast.[78]

---

[75] Article 2, Treaty of 15 March 1874; Article 28, Treaty of 31 August 1874, in Ministère des affaires étrangères, *Affaires du Tonkin*, 1, 1, 23.
[76] Taboulet, *Geste française*, 2, 748, n. 3.   [77] Dutreuil de Rhins, *Royaume d'Annam*, 117.
[78] Postel, *L'Extrême Orient*, 243; Taboulet, *Geste française*, 2, 748, n. 3.

Piracy and Trafficking

Although the fiasco of Garnier's expedition was held up as warning against further colonial expansion by anti-imperialists in France, the 1870s saw a gradual strengthening of procolonial sentiments in France. Toward the end of the decade the colonial project showed an unprecedented capacity to mobilise supporters, thereby setting the stage for the occupation of what remained of the Vietnamese Kingdom.[79]

Piratical activity continued in Vietnamese waters throughout most of the 1870s but fluctuated and seems at times to have been relatively sparse. With little naval capacity of its own, the Vietnamese government had little choice but to welcome the assistance given by France, and the Vietnamese came to rely almost exclusively on French patrols to maintain a reasonable level of maritime security. In 1877, Hue even asked France to build a fort with a permanent garrison on Cat Ba, the major base for the pirates off the Tonkinese coast.[80] The French government – reportedly to the great disappointment of the Vietnamese – declined but continued to patrol Vietnamese waters. The naval presence seems to have brought about a substantial decrease in piratical activity. According to a French naval report, largely based on information provided by Vietnamese officials, piracy around Cat Ba and other places along the Tonkinese coast seemed to have all but disappeared in 1878:

> The 9 [February 1878] at 9 o'clock in the morning we again dropped anchor at Cacba [Cat Ba], where the tranquillity still was perfect. According to the French missionaries and the Annamite mandarins, no pirate had been seen in these waters for several months; this fortunate development is generally attributed, on the one hand certainly, to the cruises of the French warships, but more particularly to the destruction of the village of Traly, the centre for selling stolen goods, procurement and the place of refuge for the pirates.[81]

The problem soon resurfaced, however, and several naval expeditions were dispatched from Cochinchina to Tonkin in 1879–80. The expeditions destroyed several pirate junks and killed or captured some of the perpetrators, but the depredations nevertheless continued. According to the French consul in Haiphong, government officials and some Chinese businessmen seemed to be colluding with the pirates, and the consul suspected that the pirates who were captured by the French expeditions and turned over to the Vietnamese authorities for punishment were frequently allowed to escape or bribe themselves

---

[79] Hémery and Brocheux, *Indochina*, 30–1.
[80] Governor of Cochinchina to the Minister of the Marine and the Colonies, 21 March 1878, in Ministère des affaires étrangères, *Affaires du Tonkin*, 1, 79–80.
[81] 'Notes sur le Golfe du Tonkin', *Revue maritime et coloniale* 57 (1878), 706–7; cit., 710.

free.[82] The French cruises thus appeared to have the effect of containing some of the piratical depredations but did little to disrupt the networks and support that underpinned them.[83]

The most lucrative part of the pirates' business was the trafficking of abducted people, and this trade involved the complicity of both Chinese and Vietnamese businessmen and officials, as well as European merchants and ship captains in East Asia. The surge in piratical activity in Vietnam can thus not be understood in isolation, or just as the last vestiges of the civil unrest in China around the middle of the century. The raiding and the abductions were deeply embedded in regional and even global commercial networks, and local businessmen and notables often profited from the piratical activity. In contrast to the situation in the Straits Settlements, thus, pressure to end piracy and trafficking in Vietnam did not come so much from the local business community as from local missionaries and humanitarians in France.

The trade in humans seems to have begun in the 1860s and quickly developed to become the major source of revenue for the pirates.[84] The trafficking of young women and girls for the purpose of prostitution or other forms of sexual abuse was particularly repulsive to the French missionaries in Indochina. They frequently reported on the problem in letters, many of which were published in France, thus drawing public attention to the problem in the metropole.

Hundreds and possibly thousands of people were abducted from Vietnam each year from the 1860s until the end of the nineteenth century. Many victims were simply seized by force while fishing or travelling by boat, or when working, walking or playing on the beach, whereas others were tricked into captivity. The methods employed by the pirates to capture their victims varied. According to Monsignor Colomer, some Chinese pirates colluded with Vietnamese brokers – 'perverse Annamites', as he called them – who out of vile interests tricked their brothers into traps where they were caught and delivered as slaves to Chinese buyers.[85] One gang of pirates, captured in 1880, sent

---

[82] Governor of Cochinchina to the Minister of the Marine and Colonies, 6 March 1880; Consul, Haiphong to Governor of Cochinchina, 24 March 1880, both in Fonds ministérielles, Série géographique: Indochine A50(5), Carton 22, Anciens fonds (Centre des Archives d'Outre-Mer (CAOM), Aix-en-Provence).

[83] Consul of Haiphong to Governor of Cochinchina, 5 December 1880, Fonds ministérielles, Série géographique: Indochine A50(5), Carton 22, Anciens fonds (CAOM); see also Governor of Cochinchina to Minister of the Marine and the Colonies, 24 January 1880, in Ministère des affaires étrangères, *Affaires du Tonkin*, 1, 132.

[84] Watson, 'Transactions in People', 233. On the question of when the trafficking started, see Lessard, *Human Trafficking*, 5–6, citing several near-contemporary estimations of when the kidnappings started, and ibid., 103, mentioning a report from as early as 1863.

[85] Lettre de Mgr Colomer, 26 August 1873, in Taboulet, *Geste française*, 2, 681. In 1887 Colomer estimated that the number of abducted people to date in the small province of Bac-Ninh alone was around 15,000; Colomer, 'Les Missionnaires dominicains espagnols au Tonkin', *Annales*

forward a female member of the band to capture children onshore, a method that was seen as particularly objectionable both in Vietnamese and French eyes. The woman was found guilty to a higher degree than her accomplices by the Vietnamese court that handled the case, and she was sentenced to execution by strangling, rather than decapitation, which was the punishment that the other members of the band received.[86]

Colomer claimed that the majority of the victims were women and children, and most contemporary reports – both by missionaries and naval officers – seem to corroborate this impression. The trafficking of women was much more profitable than the trafficking of men, as young women commanded substantially higher prices. Young women who were considered attractive could be sold at a premium of up to two or three times as much as young men, according to the information obtained by a French gunboat commander.[87] The vast majority of freed victims were also women and children, including both boys and girls.[88]

Even though the majority of victims were thus probably women and children, it is likely that a large number of captured men went underreported. Kidnapped men were more difficult to identify because of the flourishing coolie trade in East and Southeast Asia, by which poor people, mostly men from southern China and India, were recruited as indentured labourers to work on plantations, mines and construction sites on the West coast of America or in the European colonies in the Caribbean, Southeast Asia and East Africa and elsewhere. Asian brokers were engaged by European and American merchants who transported the coolies to their destination. Whereas the trade in coolies generated large profits for the merchants and brokers, it was often less advantageous for the coolies. Many were made to sign long contracts, typically ranging from five to eight years, usually for a modest one-off payment in cash, and to labour under slave-like conditions.

According to contemporary missionary reports, the onset of the abductions in the 1860s was linked to the boom in the coolie trade.[89] Chinese pirates operating in Vietnam realised that they could make larger profits if they bypassed the brokers and did away with all appearances of a voluntary arrangement. Instead they simply abducted Vietnamese men and transported them as captives on their junks to colonial ports or treaty ports in China, where they were sold on to European and American coolie traders. Vietnamese men who had been abducted by Chinese pirates were taken to Macau, where they had their heads shaved in order to pass off more easily as Chinese. From

---

catholiques (11 September 1887), 583. On the modus operandi of the abductors, see also Lessard, *Human Trafficking*, 8; Baudrit, *Bétail humain*.
[86] Gros-Desveaux, 'Mission au Tonkin', 116.   [87] Ibid., 117.
[88] Colomer, 'Missionnaires dominicains', 582.   [89] Grimley, 'Traité des Annamites', 133–4.

Macau the coolies were promptly dispatched to Cuba or California, from where no one, according to a contemporary observer, ever returned. Other major ports for the coolie trade in East and Southeast Asia, apart from Macau, were Canton, Penang and Singapore.[90]

In contrast to the men, most of the abducted women and children were trafficked to China, where demand was great for domestic servants, concubines and prostitutes. According to André Baudrit, who wrote the first systematic study of human trafficking in Indochina and China, there were four principal reasons the Chinese turned to Vietnam for the supply of human cargo, apart from the geographical proximity and the existing networks of trade and contacts. First, the abducted Vietnamese were generally unfamiliar with the geography, language and culture of China and thus unlikely to fend for themselves or try to escape. Second, many Chinese looked upon the Vietnamese as an inferior and less civilised race, and consequently saw them as suited to low-status occupations, such as prostitution and domestic servitude. Third, the Chinese owners of Vietnamese slaves could mistreat their subjects with impunity, because neither neighbours nor the authorities were likely to take an interest in their fate. Last, it was cheaper to buy a Vietnamese wife or domestic servant than a Chinese one due to the racial prejudices against the Vietnamese in China.[91]

The abductions, however, cannot be understood only from the Chinese perspective. The trafficking of Vietnamese in the late nineteenth and early twentieth centuries was linked to the colonial networks of maritime commerce and traffic, regionally as well as intercontinentally. The governor of Cochinchina, Charles Le Myre de Vilers, for example, suspected that, apart from Vietnamese officials, European captains participated in the trafficking of Vietnamese.[92] At the very least, European coolie merchants, like the authorities in Macau and other colonial ports, turned a blind eye to any indication that the coolies delivered by Chinese pirates might have been forcibly abducted rather than made to sign a disadvantageous but legally binding and in theory voluntary contract.

On several occasions French vessels seized pirate junks and freed dozens of Vietnamese, mainly women and children who had been abducted in raids on local boats or on the coast and islands of Tonkin. The commander of the gunboat *La Massue*, L. Gros-Desveaux, described the conditions that the abducted Vietnamese of one pirate junk, captured in Tonkin in 1880, were forced to endure during the passage to China:

---

[90] Ibid.; Lessard, *Human Trafficking*, 22.   [91] Baudrit, *Bétail humain*, 106.
[92] Governor of Cochinchina to Minister of the Marine and the Colonies, 4 August 1880, Fonds ministérielles, Série géographique: Indochine A50(5), Carton 22, Anciens fonds (CAOM).

These 44 women and children were squeezed in one upon another, on stones, half dead from bad treatment, misery and hunger. These unfortunates, who between them occupied but a fifth of a junk of 11 meters, had not got ten any air or daylight except but by a hole of 4 square centimetres drilled in the deck since they were torn from their homes a fortnight ago, some by violence and some by trickery ... Three of them had perished from suffocation since departure.[93]

Although French patrols probably reduced the number of raids and abducted people somewhat, the French Navy only had one dispatch boat and two gunboats permanently stationed in Indochina, which clearly was insufficient to uphold maritime security. In Paris, meanwhile, efforts to secure additional funding for the Navy in Indochina met with resistance, both in the government and in Parliament. A further problem was that the French, according to the 1874 Treaty with Vietnam, did not have the right to search foreign vessels in Tonkinese ports.[94]

In July 1881 Parliament eventually decided to approve an increase in funds for the Navy in Tonkin by adding two dispatch boats, two gunboats and three river boats, all heavily armed. The purpose was for France to fulfil her obligations according to the 1874 Treaty, particularly with regard to the suppression of piracy, and to render safe communications with the interior of China on the Red River, which was still blocked by the Black Flags.[95]

The decision to release the funds was contested because it seemed to set France on the path of a more aggressive policy of colonisation in Indochina, thereby adding to the expansionist policies already pursued in North and West Africa. Georges Périn again emerged as the most vocal opponent of the bill in the Chamber of Deputies. He argued that France should not continue its course toward an increasingly colonial foreign policy. 'Our politics must not be colonial to the point that it ceases to be continental', Périn argued rhetorically in a bid to appeal to the conservative majority of the Chamber. In response to Périn's question as to why France should seek to extend her territory overseas, the Minister for the Marine and the Colonies, Vice-admiral Georges Charles Cloué, vehemently denied that the government had any plans to conquer Tonkin. The government, according to Cloué, only wished to have an 'honourable situation' in which law and order prevailed. The debate was followed by a vote in which an overwhelming majority of 310 deputies voted for the bill and only 86 against.[96]

---

[93] Gros-Desveaux, 'Mission au Tonkin', 115.
[94] *Journal officiel de la République française* (13 May 1880); Governor of Cochinchina to Minister of the Marine and the Colonies, 4 August 1880; see also Procès-verbal, Haiphong, 3 July 1880, Fonds ministérielles, Série géographique: Indochine A50(5), Carton 22, Anciens fonds (CAOM); Taboulet, *Geste française*, 2, 757.
[95] *Journal officiel de la République française* (13 May 1880).
[96] 'Gazette de la Chambre', *Le Figaro* (22 July 1881).

Piracy and Colonial Expansion in Tonkin

For those in France who favoured further colonial expansion, the fact that piracy and the trafficking of women and children continued in Tonkin served as a strong argument for invention. A Republican politician and author, Paul Deschanel, for example, wrote a pamphlet entitled 'The question of Tonkin' in which he lamented the insufficient efforts on the part of the French Navy to suppress piracy in Vietnamese waters. Upholding maritime security in Tonkinese waters, Deschanel argued, was both a matter of dignity for France and a matter of furthering her interests in Eastern Asia. He also worried that the prevalence of piracy in Indochinese waters might serve as a pretext for other countries, notably Britain or Germany, to intervene and thus threaten French hegemony in the region.[97] In the view of Deschanel and other proponents of colonial expansion, the suppression of piracy and human trafficking in Indochina thus united several of the key objectives of France in the East: the assertion of national dignity and the spread of French civilisation, the promotion of French economic interests, and the furthering of the country's geopolitical interests, particularly in relation to other imperialist nations in Europe.

The weakness of the Nguyen Dynasty and the continuing unrest in Tonkin combined with the increasing imperial scramble among the European powers to set the stage for further French colonial expansion in Indochina. In France the policy of colonial expansion began to acquire more of a clear sense of direction from the end of the 1870s, notwithstanding the protestations of the anticolonial opposition. The influence of these critical voices, however, weakened as pressure for further colonial expansion mounted from several influential and partly overlapping groups: naval and army officers, businessmen, missionaries, scientific societies and politicians.[98]

As the colonial camp thus gained momentum, the central question shifted from whether or not France should extend its influence in Indochina to by what means and how quickly colonial expansion should progress. Indochina was a distant and relatively obscure place for most people in France, and although it occupied centre stage in the debates about colonialism in the 1870s and 1880s, it was far from the top foreign policy priority. French cabinets, moreover, were mostly short-lived, and changes in government led to frequent shifts in foreign policy orientation. As a consequence, official French policy in Indochina often lacked a clear sense of purpose and was largely formulated more or less ad hoc as events unfolded.[99]

---

[97] Deschanel, *Question du Tonkin*, 66–7.   [98] Brocheux and Hémery, *Indochina*, 30–3.
[99] Taboulet, *Geste française*, 2, 787. On the rise of the colonial idea in France from late 1870s, see Brocheux and Hémery, *Indochina*, 30–4; see also Andrew, 'French Colonialist Movement'.

By the beginning of the 1880s it seemed clear, both to the advocates of colonial expansion and to its detractors, that the middle position that France occupied in Indochina – with a colony in the south and a quasi-protectorate in the north – was untenable in the long run.[100] The dream of developing the commercial potential of the Red River and reaching the interior of China was also strong but failed to materialise, apparently because of the lack of social and political stability in Tonkin and the control that the Black Flags had over the river.

Against this background, Governor Le Myre de Vilers began to argue for a restrained and peaceful, as far as possible, intervention in Tonkin. He was convinced that France needed to take swift action in order to prevent other imperial powers from establishing a foothold in Vietnam or for the country to disintegrate completely, which he believed were the two most likely scenarios should France abstain from intervention. His proposition, put forth in a letter to the Minister for Commerce and the Colonies in 1881, was to send a small force of marine infantry to Hanoi, where they would occupy the citadel – like Francis Garnier had done in 1873 – and take over the administration of the city and its environments. The governor, optimistically, estimated that the customs and farm revenues from Hanoi and its hinterland would be enough to cover the cost of the French intervention. The Vietnamese government would probably protest, Le Myre de Vilers foresaw, but this was of little consequence, given its weakness. Other European powers, meanwhile, would probably be uninterested or, in the case of Britain, even approve. The only major power that might object was China, but the country would probably abstain from intervening, given that France was not to declare war and could justify her intervention with reference to the 1874 Treaty. The only major foreseeable obstacle to the success of the expedition, according to Le Myre de Vilers, were the Black Flags, who controlled much of Hanoi and the Red River. These were to be dealt with through the inflicting of serious punishment early on. He suggested shelling one or two of their strongholds with gunboat artillery while avoiding disembarking or engaging the Black Flags in close combat, because, the governor argued, even 'the smallest defeat could be harmful to us'.[101]

Assuming that he had the support of the government, Le Myre de Vilers proceeded to dispatch a small armed force to Tonkin in early 1882. In his instructions to the commander of the expedition, Captain Henri Rivière, the governor emphasised the need to avoid any contact, direct or indirect, with the

---

[100] The impossibility of this position was recognized by those opposed to colonial expansion such as Géorges Périn; see 'Gazette de la Chambre', *Le Figaro* (22 July 1881); 'Latest Intelligence: France', *The Times* (22 July 1881).

[101] Governor of Cochinchina to the Minister for Commerce and the Colonies, 21 December 1881, in Taboulet, *Geste française*, 2, 763–4.

Black Flags. If such contact nevertheless could not be avoided, the instructions were specific: the Black Flags were to be dealt with as pirates, yet treated humanely in order to demonstrate the magnanimity and good intentions of France:

> You must not have any relations, direct or indirect, with the Black Flags. To us, they are pirates, and you shall treat them as such, if they place themselves in your way; however, as we must demonstrate that we spare human lives, instead of executing them, you shall dispatch them to Saigon and I will have them imprisoned at Poulo-Condore.[102]

In contrast to his previously laid-out plan, however, the governor did not instruct Rivière to occupy the citadel at Hanoi, and he was to use as little force as possible. Rivière was also to survey the Red River, but the instructions did not explain how Rivière was to proceed on the river without confronting the Black Flags.[103]

Rivière arrived in Hanoi in March 1882 with 400 men. Officially his mission was to ensure the security of French citizens in Vietnam. In a letter that Rivière delivered to the Vietnamese emperor, the governor drew attention to the anarchy in Tonkin, and he specifically mentioned the harassment of two French mining engineers in January by the leader of the Black Flags, Luu Vinh Phuoc (Liu Yongfu), whom Le Myre de Vilers described as the 'Chinese pirate chief'.[104]

As tensions mounted between the Vietnamese and the French in Hanoi in the weeks following the arrival of the French troops, Rivière decided to take the citadel with force. He did so in April but was unable to move against the Black Flags. Neither could he undertake the planned survey expedition on the Red River because the water was too low for the French gunboats. For several months Rivière and his troops were thus confined to the citadel at Hanoi, awaiting, on the one hand, further instructions from Paris or Saigon and, on the other, the rains that would flood the river and make it navigable for the French vessels. Meanwhile, the French troops were besieged by the Black Flags, and it seemed to the French that the country was teeming with pirates.[105] On 18 May 1883 Rivière instructed one of his subcommanders to concern himself as little as possible with piracy. 'In a country where everybody is a pirate, it is a question which constantly reappears and which bores me', he wrote, obviously somewhat despondently.[106]

---

[102] Governor of Cochinchina to M. Rivière, 17 January 1882, in Taboulet, *Geste française*, 2, 767.
[103] Ibid.
[104] Le Myre de Vilers to His Majesty Tu-Duc, 13 March 1882, in Taboulet, *Geste française*, 2, 768. On the expedition by the two French engineers, see further Davis, 'State of Banditry', 214ff.
[105] Priestley, *France Overseas*, 219; Lettre particulière du Commandant Rivière, 4 June 1882, in Taboulet, *Geste française*, 2, 781.
[106] Rivière to the Commander-in-charge of Nam-Dinh, 18 May 1883, in Rivière, *Correspondance politique*, 252.

The day after he wrote the letter Rivière was killed when he led a sortie against the Black Flags, not far from where Garnier had fallen under similar circumstances ten years earlier. In contrast to the swift withdrawal of the French expedition after Garnier's death, however, the killing of Rivière hardened French resolve to intervene in Tonkin. A month before the commander's death the French government had laid a bill before the Chamber of Deputies demanding additional credit for the expedition in Tonkin. As in 1881, the object of the intervention was motivated in terms of the need to uphold peace and order, which was expressly linked to the national pride and dignity of France. The French government was careful not to represent the intervention as directed against the Vietnamese government, but instead emphasised that the object was to suppress piracy on the Red River and thereby secure freedom of commerce and traffic. According to the motivation of the bill, which the Minister of Foreign Affairs Paul-Armand Challemel-Lacour read to the Chamber:

The Red River has never, in fact, been open to commerce, its banks continuing, in several places, to be occupied by the pirates known by the name of Black Flags, who prevent the traders from moving freely. On several occasions, French travellers, having entered the country after having complied with all requirements of the treaty, have been molested, without our chargé d'affaires in Hue having been able to obtain satisfaction ...

With the authorization of the joint instructions of the Ministry of Foreign Affairs and the Marine, the Governor of Cochinchina had, in the month of January 1882, decided upon certain measures for the purpose of emphasizing our protectorate over the Annamite Empire. It was not, however, about a conquest of Tonkin, or even a venture that could lead us to intervene in the internal administration of this country. The proposition was only to dispatch on the Red River the naval forces necessary to go after the Black Flags, who occupy the river banks, and thereby to secure commercial freedom. It was thus not, properly speaking, a military expedition that we undertook, because our troops were only to act against the pirates.[107]

Pursuing the argument, the government's demand for a further increase in funding for the Navy in Tonkin – this time of 5,300,000 francs, more than twice the amount approved by the Chamber in 1881 – was also motivated in terms of the need to maintain the peace and specifically to rid Tonkin of all 'bands of pillagers and fleets of pirates that oppress it'.[108] The bill was passed, first before the death of Rivière, with a vote of 351 for and 48 against, and then once more after his death, unanimously, with even vocal anti-imperialists such as Périn closing ranks behind the government and demanding that the death of Rivière be avenged.[109]

---

[107] 'Exposé des motifs', in Ministère des affaires étrangères, *Affaires du Tonkin* 2, 95.
[108] Ibid., 97.   [109] Taboulet, *Geste française*, 2, 798; Périn, *Discours politiques*, 481.

In the atmosphere of injured national pride and unity there was little room for questioning the styling of the Black Flags as pirates. Their name became virtually synonymous in France with pirates, and the association was probably facilitated by the fact that their very name invoked the image of the classical, mostly black, skull-and-crossed-bones flags used during the Golden Age of Atlantic piracy.[110] The lack of maritime capacity on the part of most of the alleged pirates was no obstacle to using the *pirate* label. The Black Flags were seen as uncivilised brutes who constituted the main obstacle against the opening up the Red River for commerce, which, the French believed, would lead to a flourishing and profitable commerce with the interior of China. For those who had an interest in this commerce – and they included politicians, civil and military officials, businessmen and explorers – labelling the Black Flags 'pirates' served as a powerful rhetorical device that strengthened the case for decisive military intervention in Tonkin. National pride and the wish to revenge the killing of Rivière further fanned opinion in favour of annihilating the Black Flags.[111] Compared with the suppression of piracy and trafficking on the coast, however, humanitarian motives were of less importance with regard to the need to suppress the Black Flags.

Sino–French Rivalry

The French government was aware that a full-scale military intervention in Tonkin was likely to invite a hostile response from China, which in the preceding years had made efforts to assert its influence in Vietnam. Historically, Vietnam was a tributary of China and from the Chinese point of view the increasingly strong French presence and influence in Vietnam threatened China's traditional supremacy in the region. The Vietnamese Emperor Tu Duc, moreover, actively sought the support of the Qing Dynasty in order to counterbalance French influence. In 1868 he resumed paying regular tribute to the Chinese emperor, a practice that had been suspended for fourteen years during the havoc of the Taiping Rebellion. He also asked China to send regular troops to assist the Vietnamese in putting down the rebellions and reassert its influence in northern Tonkin, a request to which the Qing government agreed.[112]

The result was that tensions mounted between France and China at the beginning of the 1880s, particularly as the Chinese began to send naval vessels

---

[110] See Fox, *Jolly Rogers*.
[111] E.g., Extraordinary envoy of France to China M. Tricou to Minister of Foreign Affairs, Annex to the dispatch of 1 September 1883, in Ministère des affaires étrangères, *Affaires du Tonkin*, 2, 248.
[112] Yu Insun, 'Vietnam–China Relations', 90.

to Tonkinese waters. Ostensibly the purpose was to suppress piracy, but the expeditions also served the purpose of sending a message to France that China was not prepared to give up its interests in Vietnam or accept a French protectorate over the country. Internationally, Chinese patrols were an embarrassment to France because they seemed to demonstrate that the French Navy was unable to suppress piracy in Vietnamese waters as stipulated by the two treaties of 1874. The French also worried that the Chinese patrols were compromising French supremacy in the eyes of the local population. As the treaties had failed to establish a formal French protectorate over Vietnam, however, the French could not forcibly turn away the Chinese gunboats or demand through diplomatic channels that China withdraw them.[113]

In the wake of the killing of Rivière, China tried to take a firm stance against France and warned that any attempt to occupy Tonkin would mean war. The French maintained that military intervention was necessary in order to suppress piracy in Tonkin, which according to the French government had not declined but rather shifted locations, thereby implying that the pirates had moved inland, from the seaboard to the Red River and its tributaries to the north of Tonkin.[114] The intervention on land could thus be framed as an extension of French naval patrols on the coast in previous years, although there was little that indicated that the pirates on the coast were in fact identical to or linked with the Black Flags.

The French argued that the intervention was not a war of conquest and that the only enemies of France in Tonkin were pirates, 'banned by the nation and whom no civilised people could take in defence', in the words of the French foreign minister in a letter to the Chinese Ambassador to France, Zeng Jize (Marquis de Tseng or Tseng Chi-tse).[115] The French maintained that they had no intention of occupying Tonkin, but only of cleaning out the Red River basin and then negotiating with China to open up trade with Yunnan on the river.[116] These arguments met with little understanding among the Chinese, and Zeng Jize protested vehemently against the French intrusions, including the

---

[113] Governor of Cochinchina to Minister of the Marine and the Colonies, 7 January 1881; Minister of the Colonies to the Minister of Foreign Affairs, 19 February 1881; see also Extrait d'une dépêche adressée à M. le Capitaine de Vaisseau, Chef de Division, Commandant la D:on N:le de Cochinchine à Saigon, 17 October 1879, all in Fonds ministérielles, Série géographique: Indochine A50(5), Carton 22, Anciens fonds (CAOM).

[114] Minister of the Marine and the Colonies to the Governor of Cochinchina, September 1881, in Ministère des affaires étrangères, *Affaires du Tonkin*, 1, 191.

[115] Minister of Foreign Affairs to the Minister of France in China, 7 July 1882, in Ministère des affaires étrangères, *Affaires du Tonkin*, 1, 273.

[116] Conversation du marquis Tseng, ministre de Chine à Paris, avec M. Jules Ferry, président du conseil etc., Paris, 21 June 1883, in Ministère des affaires étrangères, *Affaires du Tonkin*, 2, 145.

194   Indochina

occupation of the citadel at Hanoi. In an interview, published in *Le Figaro* in June 1883, he also rejected the designation of the Black Flags as pirates:

> The Black Flags ... are what is left of the Taiping rebels. They are in the service of Annam. In France, they are turned into a bogeyman and the Black Flags are used to fool the French people. In Paris, they are called pirates. Well, they are neither pirates nor bandits outside the law. They are regular soldiers in the service of King Tu Duc, who appoints their leader, almost always a Chinese. It is thus not possible for China to join forces with France to combat them.[117]

China, obviously wary of French imperialist ambitions, continued to assert its suzerainty over Vietnam. A compromise, according to which France and China were to share a protectorate over Vietnam, was rejected by France, and in mid 1883, an army of 4,000 men was dispatched from Cochinchina to occupy Hanoi and to set up a French protectorate over the Red River delta region. China responded by sending regular troops to reinforce the Black Flags, and the war was a fact, even though it was not formally declared.

Meanwhile in Hue Emperor Tu Duc died on 17 July 1883, leaving no apparent heir to the throne. A period of dynastic instability followed that played into the hands of the French, who now took to the offensive. In August, the newly appointed Commissioner for France in Vietnam, François-Jules Harmand, issued an extremely frank ultimatum to the Vietnamese court, in which he cited numerous griefs that the Vietnamese government had caused France, including its support for the Black Flags:

> The Red River has remained closed, absolutely closed to Europeans. Instead of punishing the Black Flags as bandits by profession, as they merit, you have served yourselves with their crime-contaminated hands. Without fear of the ignomiy of such a procedure, you have taken them in your pay. The High Officer [*Thoung-Bac*] and your consuls at Saigon have admitted as much on several occasions, and this fact is thus proven; you have driven the lack of respect against yourselves and against us to the point of giving military ranks to the leaders of these pirates; these very same pirates, encouraged by you, have collected arbitrary customs duties at the border of Yunnan and internally in the provinces of Tonkin.[118]

The Vietnamese were given forty-eight hours to accept the French ultimatum, which, among other things, demanded that they accept a French protectorate over the whole of Vietnam, or face complete annihilation. On 25 August, the Vietnamese government signed a provisional convention, in which it acknowledged French suzerainty and renounced all rights to an independent foreign policy. In contrast to the treaties of 1874, the convention did not mention the

---

[117] 'Une entrevue avec le marquis de Tseng', *Le Figaro* (16 June 1883). The interview was made by a correspondent of the *New York Herald* in Moscow and published on the same day in the American newspaper.
[118] Ultimatum Harmand à la Cour de Hué, August 1883, in Taboulet, *Geste française*, 2, 805.

suppression of piracy, but gave France the right to establish military posts along the Red River and to build permanent fortifications wherever it deemed necessary in the country. France also promised to defend the Vietnamese king against all external aggression, as well as against internal rebellions. The colonial authorities took upon themselves to chase the 'bands known under the name of Black Flags' from Tonkin and to guarantee security and commercial freedom on the Red River.[119]

The following year the provisional convention was replaced by a permanent treaty, which formally abolished the two treaties of 1874 and reaffirmed Vietnam's protectorate status and France's economic, political, military and administrative rights in the country. As in the provisional convention, there was no mention in the new treaty of any French obligation to suppress piracy, and explicit mention of the Black Flags was also omitted. Obviously France henceforth saw herself as entitled to govern Vietnam and undertake whatever military operations necessary without the consent of the court at Hue.[120] Piracy on the coast, moreover, seemed to contemporary observers to have been relatively efficiently suppressed by French naval patrols in the preceding years, and the remaining 'pirates' that caused problems for the French were for the most part land-based bandits and rebels.[121]

In late 1883 and early 1884 French troops successfully fought the Black Flags – the latter reinforced by regular Chinese troops – and after a series of losses the Chinese were forced to negotiate for peace. In May 1884 the Tianjin (Tientsin) Accord, also known as the Li-Fournier Convention, was concluded, according to which China promised to respect all past or future treaties between France and Vietnam and to withdraw its troops from Vietnam. The agreement, however, was not ratified by the Chinese government, and negotiations broke down in August 1884. The French then attacked China's new Southern Fleet, which consisted of eleven warships, and destroyed all of which were in less than one hour. The French also set fire to the docks at Fuzhou, leaving a total of over 500 Chinese dead (against 4 French). The war continued on land until March 1885, but despite some Chinese victories on the ground, the outcome was a victory for France.[122] China was forced to accept the terms of the Tianjin Accord, thereby acknowledging French rights in Vietnam and renouncing its sovereignty over the country.

---

[119] La convention Harmand, 25 August 1883, in Taboulet, Geste française, 2, 808–9.
[120] Le traité Patenôtre, 6 June 1884, in Taboulet, Geste française, 2, 809–12.
[121] On the efficiency of French efforts to suppress piracy in the first half of the 1880s, see Paulus, 'L'Esclavage en Indo-Chine', 342. Cf. also the report by French Resident-general in Hué, Journal officiel de la République française (9 March 1885).
[122] Spence, Search for Modern China, 221.

The Golden Years of Tonkinese Piracy

The victory, and the withdrawal of the Chinese army, did not mean that France controlled the north of Vietnam. A report on the 'Piracy Situation' at the time of the conclusion of the peace with China stated that beyond French lines the country had been given over to anarchy after the evacuation of the Chinese troops.[123] The Resident-General and Commander-in-Chief of the military in Vietnam, General Henri Roussel de Courcy, reported to the Minister of War that the Chinese Army, upon leaving Tonkin, had fomented disorder, which he believed was carefully entertained by the hostile mandarins of the Court at Hue. The Chinese also left numerous deserters behind, as well as many well-armed soldiers belonging to the Yunnan Army. The majority of the Black Flags refused to evacuate together with the Chinese Army, as had been presumed (if not stated explicitly) in the peace treaty, and thus remained in Vietnam. To these groups were, according to the general, added the unfortunate Vietnamese who had had their villages burnt and ransacked and saw no other way of surviving than by taking to brigandage.[124]

These and other troubles notwithstanding, Roussel de Courcy believed that it would be possible, given that the necessary reinforcements were provided, to obtain the pacification of Tonkin in a single blow and thereby avoid a drawn-out campaign over several years. He asked France to make 'one last sacrifice' and send more troops and resources. With these, the general believed that he would be able to pacify Tonkin completely in a few months. In May the following year most of the French troops would be repatriated, and France's military obligations in Tonkin would then gradually diminish over the coming years, just as had been the case in Cochinchina.[125]

Roussel de Courcy's plan was first to eliminate those mandarins and members of the royal family who were hostile to French rule, including the 14-year-old Emperor and his two regents, Ton That Thuyet and Nguyen Van Tuong. For this purpose, Roussel de Courcy made repeated provocations against the imperial court in Hue, which at the beginning of July succeeded in triggering an armed attack by Vietnamese soldiers on the French legation. The attack was repulsed by the French forces, and the Emperor and the regents fled with their followers to the mountains on the border with Laos. On the

---

[123] Situation de la Piraterie, 9 June 1885, GR 15 H 93, Service historique des troupes de la Marine (SHD).

[124] Ibid; Commander-in-Chief, Corps du Tonkin to the Minister of War, 12 June 1885; 10 H 21 d. 1 (SHD).

[125] Commander-in-Chief, Corps du Tonkin to the Minister of War, 18 June 1885, 10 H 21 d. 1 (SHD). de Courcy is generally described in historiography as an archetypical brutal and arrogant colonialist; e.g., Marr, *Vietnamese Anticolonialism*; Brocheux and Hémery, *Indochina*, 48.

way they issued calls for general resistance against the French, to help the King (Chieu Can Vuong, as the proclamation of the 13 July was entitled). Even though support for the resistance movement in the royal family and the highest echelons of the mandarins quickly evaporated, the call to resistance was heeded throughout the country and signalled the start of a veritable national insurrection against colonial rule, known as the Can Vuong ('Help the King') movement.[126]

The French authorities tried to downplay the importance of the Can Vuong movement and did not recognize it as a national resistance movement. Instead they insisted on calling the movement 'pirates', as they had done with the Black Flags and other bandits in the region. Like Roussel de Courcy, most French officers in Tonkin had little understanding of Vietnamese society, history or culture. It seemed to be of no consequence to the French whether the 'pirates' were Chinese bandits, whose main object was plunder and kidnapping, or Vietnamese *literati*, who fought for the restoration of Vietnamese sovereignty and the Nguyen Dynasty. The failure on the part of the French to understand the character of the resistance against their rule and the differences between the various groups of 'pirates', however, hampered the efforts to pacify Vietnam and led the French to prioritise military rather than political solutions to the problems in the country.

General Roussel de Courcy received the requested troop reinforcements, and by the end of 1885 the so-called expeditionary corps of the French Army in Vietnam consisted of 42,000 men. The troops, however, were of mediocre quality and chronically ravaged by epidemics, and these circumstances, combined with the French officers' lack of understanding of the local situation, rendered the so-called pacification campaigns largely inefficient. For several years, throughout the second half of the 1880s and the first years of the 1890s, the harsh military campaigns failed to yield lasting results, and the arbitrary killings, destruction of property and forced recruitment of labourers by the colonial army served instead to strengthen popular support for the Can Vuong.[127]

In northern Tonkin the Black Flags and other bands of Chinese outlaws continued to plunder and ransack local villages. Although French troops on several occasions attacked the bandits and caused them to suffer tangible losses, the French were on the whole unable to uphold law and order. The repeated but increasingly costly French successes were, in the words of the commander-in-chief in Indochina, 'purely local and were not followed by any durable results'.[128]

---

[126] Ibid., 48–9; see further Marr, *Vietnamese Anticolonialism*, 44–76; Fourniau, *Vietnam*.
[127] Brocheux and Hémery, *Indochina*, 57–8.
[128] Commander-in-Chief of the military in Indochina to the Governor-General, 26 April 1891, Fonds ministérielles, Série géographique: Indochine, A50(17), Carton 23, Anciens fonds (CAOM).

Against that background, Governor-General Jules Georges Piquet, in 1889, proposed a scheme by which the bandits – who he believed largely consisted of former regular Chinese troops who had been made redundant from their regiments in Yunnan and thus forced to seek their livelihood from banditry – could be persuaded to give up their criminal ways and take up farming in some of the vast uncultivated areas of northern Vietnam. The Commander-in-Chief of the army in Indochina, General Anicet-Edmond-Justin Bichot, however, was strongly opposed to the idea. He believed that the outlaws would never be content to earn their living by working, given, as they were, to a life of adventure and constant alerts. Besides, the general argued – probably erroneously – the Chinese pirates were acting at the instigation of the leader of the Can Vuong movement, the former regent, Ton That Thuyet.[129]

The differences in opinion between the Governor and the military over which strategy to deploy in order to pacify the country led to frequent clashes. In February 1890 Governor Piquet gained the upper hand after he succeeded in convincing the government in Paris to give him full military powers in the colony. Over the next six months he tried to implement his policy of appeasement. He negotiated a settlement with Luong Tam Ky, the leader of the Yellow Flags, according to which Luong and his followers were to receive 150,000 francs a year for maintaining order in their area of control in the eastern parts of upper Tonkin. However, while Luong feigned loyalty to the French, he continued to support other pirate bands, and many of his followers used the area controlled by the Yellow Flags as a base for conducting raids into neighbouring regions. Critics of the appeasement policy, moreover, pointed to the great expense involved and the obvious dangers that Luong once again might decide to turn against the French.[130]

Piquet for the most part confined the military to their quarters and abstained from the campaigns that in previous years had been conducted annually during the cool season. The result was that the depredations increased and that many bands, unrestrained by French military campaigns, were able to consolidate their forces.[131] The bandits were thus given virtually free rein in the years 1890–91. Jean Marie Antoine de Lanessan, who took office as governor-general in June 1891, described the situation at the beginning of the year:

---

[129] Governor-General of Indochina to the Under-secretary of State for the Colonies, 16 September 1889, Fonds ministérielles, Série géographique: Indochine, A50(11), Carton 23, Anciens fonds (CAOM); Brocheux and Hémery, *Indochina*, 54.

[130] Brocheux and Hémery, *Indochina*, 58; Charles-Lavauzelle (ed.), *Piraterie au Tonkin*, 28–9; Situation de la piraterie au moment de l'arrivée de M. de Lanessan, June 1891, GR 15 H 93, d. 3, Service historique de l'Armée de terre (SHD).

[131] Charles-Lavauzelle (ed.), *Piraterie au Tonkin*, 6.

In all of the mountainous parts of Tonkin, situated east of the Red River, the Chinese pirates were the absolute masters of the country. The rare inhabitants of these regions regularly paid them tribute; our troops were, so to speak, encircled by them in their posts; they could not prevent them from moving between Tonkin and China, or protect the delta against their depredations.

They came there constantly and in a hundred places each time, stealing rice, buffaloes and women, whom they would exchange in China for opium, munitions and arms. The latter were easily disposed of in the delta among villains and rebels.[132]

Meanwhile, the pirates based in the Delta region – a region considered pacified, although not completely secure[133] – were believed to consist of around twenty bands of all together 2,000 men with 1,500 rapid-fire arms. In addition, the more numerous pirates outside the Delta region, mainly Chinese outlaws, were believed to possess around 10,000 good rifles, at least 7,000 of which were rapid-fire arms. They obtained their arms and munition from Hong Kong, where British and German firms readily sold them to Chinese merchants, who in turn forwarded them to Tonkin by junk or small steamer. Another important market for arms was the Chinese port of Beihai (Pakhoi) on the southwest coast of China, where Chinese officials encouraged the commerce. The arms were mainly paid for by the sale of kidnapped Vietnamese women and children.[134]

As a result of the increased trade in arms and munitions (and opium), kidnapping and trafficking resurged around 1890. According to figures collected by historian Micheline Lessard from newspaper reports, 333 women and children were either freed or reported kidnapped during 1891 alone, but the actual number of trafficked Vietnamese was obviously many times higher.[135] French efforts to suppress the trade were largely inefficient, and the colonial administration was accused of trying to conceal the problem from the French public and the outside world rather than dealing with it.[136]

After the failure of Piquet's strategy, the French began to put more effort into understanding the diversity of the 'pirates' that were causing trouble in different parts of the country. General Bichot commanded a study of the

---

[132] de Lanessan, *Colonisation française en Indo-Chine*, 3–4. See also Lessard, *Human Trafficking*, 63, for numerous examples of the depredations carried out by Chinese 'pirates' in the late 1880s and early 1890s.
[133] Charles-Lavauzelle (ed.), *Piraterie au Tonkin*, 41.
[134] Governor-General to undersecretary of state for the Colonies, 29 September 1891; Fonds ministérielles, Série géographique: Indochine, A50(12), Carton 23; Commander-in-Chief of the military in Indochina to the Governor-General, 26 April 1891, Fonds ministérielles, Série géographique: Indochine, A50(17), Carton 23, Anciens fonds (CAOM); *The Times* (22 December 1890).
[135] Lessard, *Human Trafficking*, 78; in addition, seven men were freed or reported kidnapped during the same year.
[136] Ibid.

different groups of troublemakers, which resulted in a brief report that listed the major groups by their respective geographic areas of operation. The study analysed the different bands with regard to their composition, leadership, area of operations, modus operandi and the possibilities for suppressing them. Eight major groups of rebels or 'pirates' were identified: the Rebels of the Southwest; the Pirates of the Black River; the Pirates of Hungh Hoa; the Pirates of Son-la; the Regulars of Hoang-si Phi; the Pirates of the North; the Pirates of the Northeast; and the Pirates of the East.[137]

The security situation in Tonkin improved from the second half of 1891, as new policies that combined the use of military force against the outlaws with social, economic and political measures designed to create long-term stability and prosperity in the affected territories. A string of military posts, connected by telegraph, was erected on the border with China in order to stop the illicit movements of bandits and rebels between China and Vietnam. The number of locally recruited soldiers was also increased, and the practice of paying ransoms for kidnapped colonists was discontinued. Villages were provided with arms in order to defend themselves against depredations, and some bands were pacified by turning their leaders into district officers (*soumissionnaires*) charged with the responsibility of upholding law and order in their respective districts. Several measures were also implemented in order to stimulate economic recovery and development, including the distribution of seeds and the provision of subsidies for agriculture, the establishment of markets for farm products and other daily necessities, and improvements in infrastructure. Combined with improved relations with China from the middle of the 1890s, which allowed the French to close the access of the Chinese bands in the north to their safe havens in Yunnan, these measures finally enabled the colonial authorities to extend their control to upper Tonkin.[138]

The new strategy was associated with an important and lasting change in the thinking of the French military with regard to its role in Indochina and other colonies. Known as the Gallieni–Lyautey method, after the architects of the new strategy, Joseph Gallieni and Hubert Lyautey, the method emphasised the need for social, economic and political action rather than repressive military campaigns in order to take control over and govern the colonies. To the extent that military force was to be used, it was primarily to be in the form of a creeping occupation, likened to the way oil inexorably spreads on water. Local military commanders, in this context, were to unite military and civil powers, and oversee both the upkeep of law and order and social and economic development in their regions.[139]

---

[137] Charles-Lavauzelle (ed.), *Piraterie au Tonkin*.
[138] *Histoire militaire de l'Indochine*, 2, 9–10; Taboulet, *Geste française*, 2, 895.
[139] The method was presented by Lyautey in his article 'Du Rôle colonial de l'armée' in *Revue des deux mondes* (15 January 1900). See also Finch, *Progressive Occupation?*

In 1895 and 1896 French troops defeated most of the remaining opponents of colonial expansion, and over the following year the French, for the first time, could claim to control all of Vietnam. Piracy nevertheless continued to be invoked and used to refer to both banditry and nationalist and other anticolonial protest movements. The colonial authorities – both military and civilian – continued to produce numerous dossiers and reports about the operations against alleged pirates. For example, the so-called Boudet Files, kept at the Archives nationales d'outre-mer in Aix-en Provence, which indexes the archives of the Admiralty and General Government of Indochina from the 1860s until 1945, contain hundreds of files classified under the labels 'piracy' or 'pirates'. The number of such dossiers peaked in 1908–10, when several uprisings against French rule took place, most of which were principally political in their nature.[140]

Pirates of the Land and the Sea

The terms *pirate* and *piracy* were more or less broadly defined in all colonial contexts in Southeast Asia in the nineteenth century, but their use was most ubiquitous in French Indochina, particularly from the time of the French intervention in 1883. Ironically, the label seemed to become more widely used after piracy had ceased to be a major maritime security threat for France and other colonial powers in the region. This unique development was linked to the French colonial imagination and to the usefulness of the label *piracy* for justifying colonial expansion.

Piracy, as we have seen, was not a major concern for the French in Indochina before the establishment of French Cochinchina in 1858 and played a relatively subordinate role until the beginning of the 1870s. The contrast is striking with Britain, which was more active than France (or any other nation) in the efforts to suppress piracy in Indochinese waters in the 1850s and early 1860s.

After the establishment of the French colony in Cochinchina in 1858, the term *pirate* was confined in principle to the irregular bands of armed robbers who used some form of water transportation, whether at sea, on the coast or on the rivers of Cochinchina and Cambodia. At that time the term was not used to signify anticolonial resistance. Francis Garnier, for example, distinguished between, on the one hand, the educated Vietnamese who resisted French domination in southern Vietnam on political grounds and, on the other hand, those whom he considered to be simple 'pirates and common murderers'.[141]

---

[140] Fonds des Amiraux/Gouvernement général de l'Indochine: Fichier Boudet, Indo, GGI (CAOM). For a map of the major rebellions against French rule in Vietnam after 1900, see Brocheux and Hémery, *Indochina*, 290.

[141] Francis, *Cochinchine française*, 13. Cf. also the definition of pirates given by the explorer and diplomate Xavier Brau de Saint Pol Lias; 'Affaires coloniales', *La Gazette Géographique*, 1 (1885), 305.

For Garnier, moreover, there was nothing glamorous about chasing pirates, or fighting the resistance led by the *literati*. Instead he believed that the exploration of the interior of Indochina promised to yield 'more fruitful results and more glorious discoveries than the sterile pursuit of evasive pirates or all too unequal combats against an already vanquished enemy'.[142]

The securitisation of piracy in Indochina only occurred from the 1870s. The well-published expeditions of the *Bourayne* in 1872 did much to establish Indochina as a pirate-infested region in the French imagination. Captain Senez's reports of the two expeditions to Tonkin were conveyed to the general public in France through the Navy's journal, *Revue maritime et coloniale*, and news and images of the expedition were also disseminated in other media, including popular newspapers and magazines.[143]

Before the 1870s the treaties between France and Vietnam had not mentioned piracy or its suppression, but the treaties concluded in the aftermath of the abortive French intervention of 1873 did so. In the Commercial Treaty of 1874 the label was extended to include not only maritime piracy but also terrestrial activities, as manifested in the obligation of the French to assist Vietnam in combating the 'pirates of the land and the sea'.[144] This wording was different from the treaty of peace and friendship signed the previous year, which more conventionally had confined the label *piracy* to the maritime sphere. The extension of the term *piracy* to encompass land-based banditry may have been a concession to the Vietnamese understanding of piracy, or *giặc*, which can be translated as *pirate*, but more accurately as enemy, invader or raider and referring to a person beyond the borders of law and civilisation, regardless of whether at land or at sea.[145] From the French point of view, moreover, a broad definition of piracy was obviously advantageous, as it served to extend the French mandate to intervene militarily in Vietnam.

The treaties did not diminish the differences in perception between the French and the Vietnamese with regard to the Black Flags. Whereas the French saw them as despicable pirates, the Nguyen Dynasty sanctioned and relied upon them as a bulwark against the French and as a mercenary force. In doing so, the Nguyen Dynasty endorsed what Bradley Camp Davis has called a 'bandit culture of power in the far north'.[146]

The main source of income for the Black Flags was the tribute they levied on the commercial traffic on the Red River, a privilege granted to them by the

---

[142] Garnier, *Voyage d'exploration*, 2.
[143] Senez, 'De Saigon au nord du Tonquin'; 'Rapport nautique'. For other examples of the reporting about the antipiracy operations of the *Bourayne*, see *Le Monde illustré* (22 February 1873); *Le Voleur* (28 March 1873); *Le Temps* (16 May 1873).
[144] Article 28, Treaty of 31 August 1874, in Ministère des affaires étrangères, *Affaires du Tonkin*, 1, 23.
[145] Brocheux and Hémery, *Indochina*, 51, 57.   [146] Davis, 'State of Banditry', 71.

Vietnamese government in exchange for their loyalty and military support.[147] The French, however, saw the tributes as a serious impediment to commerce. According to the French consul in Hanoi, Alexandre de Kergaradec, who made a reconnaissance trip on the Red River in 1876–77, the ransoms demanded by the Black Flags were exorbitant to the point of stifling the trade in tin and other commodities. The consul described the Black Flags in very negative terms, calling their leader, Luu Vinh Phuoc, an 'ignorant, savage and suspicious brigand who had lived for twenty years of plunder in the mountains'. According to the consul, not even the payment of the ransoms meant that the merchants were protected from the arbitrary seizure of their boats by Luu and his band.[148]

With the death of Henri Rivière at the hands of the Black Flags in 1883 the accusations of piracy intensified in the colonial and metropolitan press. As the Black Flags operated mainly on land, the extended definition of piracy used in the 1874 Treaty gained renewed currency and served to legitimise French military intervention. In that context, it did not matter that few of the alleged pirates operated at sea or even close to the sea. For example, in the study mentioned earlier of different pirate groups commissioned by General Bichot, sea pirates were only discussed briefly in the last section of the report and under the broader heading 'Pirates of the East', which mainly described the bands operating on land in the coastal regions of Tonkin and the delta. It is emblematic of the French use and understanding of the word *pirate* in Indochina that less than a page and a half out of fifty-two pages was dedicated to what were called 'Sea pirates' (*Pirates de mer*).[149]

Sea piracy, moreover, declined with the improved political situation in China and the consolidation of colonial power in Indochina and the neighbouring regions, particularly maritime Southeast Asia and the South China Sea. Consequently, according to the study, the sea pirates' main base was still in Cat Ba off the Red River Delta, but in contrast to when the *Bourayne* had chased after them in 1872, they now reportedly consisted only of very small groups, described as poor and lacking in maritime capacity.[150]

Some Frenchmen reacted against the unconventional use of the label *piracy* in Indochina. For example, a former governor-general of Indochina, Ernest Constans, tried to nuance the image of the colony's pirates in an address to the Chamber of Deputies in 1888:

---

[147] Ibid., 194.
[148] de Kergaradec, 'Rapport sur le reconnaissance', [1], 345, cit. 346; 'Rapport sur le reconnaissance', [2], 40.
[149] Charles-Lavauzelle (ed.), *Piraterie au Tonkin*, 44–5.   [150] Ibid., 44–5.

These pirates, ... are actually often given a somewhat pompous name and one which sometimes has the feel of the language of comic opera. I have seen these pirates. I was on board one of our gunboats, the *Henri-Rivière*, with a very amiable commander.

One came to inform us, at night, that there were pirates on board a cagna. There had been turmoil. We realised what had happened. Actually, two Annamites had come and tried to steal a cow. These are the kinds of acts of theft that occur in the faubourgs of Paris, and not acts of piracy.[151]

Colonel Henry Frey, a French officer who served in the District of Yen-Thé and later published a book about his experiences, likewise explained to his readers:

[I]n Indochina, Europeans indiscriminately mix up under the label 'pirate' not only marauders, highway robbers and smugglers, but also adventurers of all sorts who, yielding to the lure of a roaming life and defying the impotence of the laws, carry out their depredations, in armed bands, on land, on the coast or on the rivers of Tonkin; but also the natives who, rising up against the French domination, fight to regain national independence.[152]

In time the colonial authorities became increasingly knowledgeable about the character, composition and modus operandi of their different adversaries. Particularly from around 1890 both military and civilian officials began to give more attention to the differences between, on the one hand, 'pirates' in the sense of essentially nonpolitically motivated bandits and, on the other hand, rebels in the sense of politically motivated nationalists or proto-nationalists such as the Can Vuong.[153] In the early 1890s, for example, Governor de Lanessan spoke of a 'general movement of the Annamite people' against French colonial rule, quoting his predecessor, Acting Governor François Marie Léon Bideau, who said, 'This is no longer piracy, this is rebellion.'[154]

At the same time, there are indications that many Vietnamese regarded the French colonial administrators as just as piratical as the Black Flags or other bandits. According to a French officer who spent several years in Tonkin:

For the Annamites [Vietnamese], the word 'pirate' equally has this general meaning. A pirate is anyone who lives or enriches himself at the expense of others; the adventurer, as well as the French administrator who, in the place of the Annamite government collects a tax, as regularly and equitably as ever; and finally the leader of the Chinese band who extorts contributions from the inhabitants of the region in which he has settled, where he rules as the uncontested master for many years, are all pirates just alike.[155]

---

[151] Address of Ernest Constans to the Chamber of Deputies, 20 November 1888, cited in Ferry, *Tonkin et la mère-patrie*, 269–70.
[152] Frey, *Pirates et rebelles*, 39–40.   [153] Cf. Davis, 'State of Banditry', 8–9, 11.
[154] de Lanessan, *Colonisation française*, 2; cf. Harmand, *Indo-Chine française*, 11, for a similar assessment.
[155] Frey, *Pirates et rebelles au Tonkin*, 40.

Even though French colonial officials were aware of the impropriety of the wide application of the term *piracy*, it continued to be used throughout the colonial period, for three reasons. First, the narratives and images of pirates in Indochina resonated with a popular cultural demand in France for thrilling stories about the savage and exotic. In this sense, piracy was a major theme in the colony's function in French national culture as an 'imagined elsewhere' (*ailleurs rêvé*), in the words of Nicola Cooper.[156] In that context the depredations of the Tonkinese pirates were exaggerated, dramatized and even romanticised. Numerous books on the subject were published in French in the late nineteenth and early twentieth centuries, with titles such as *La Piraterie au Tonkin*, *Pirates et rebelles*, *Au Tonkin: Milices et piraterie*, *Chez les pirates*, *Chasseur de pirates* and *La Chasse aux pirates*.[157] Many of these books were written by officers and soldiers who had taken part in the so-called pacification campaigns in Tonkin, and they generally focused on the adventure, hardship and heroism of the French troops in their efforts to put down piracy.

In addition to these purportedly truthful accounts of antipiracy operations in Indochina the theme of piracy also flourished in contemporary French fiction. Louis Malleret, in his comprehensive study of Indochinese exoticism in French literature, has argued that the literature on piracy was part of a genre of epic colonial literature that emphasised the heroic aspects of the pacification campaigns in Tonkin. Moreover, fictional works on piracy in Indochina could be regarded as a 'horror literature' (*littérature d'horreur*), although in general, the streak of adventure and romanticism was stronger than the horror theme.[158] Hoang Hoa Tham (De Tham), a bandit turned rebel who eluded the French for several decades before he was killed in 1913, for example, acquired the image, not only of a pirate but also of a romantic rebel or Indochinese Robin Hood, in both Vietnam and France.[159]

Second, and perhaps most important, the pirate label served to justify French colonialism in Indochina and to deprive those who resisted it of any vestiges of political legitimacy. By lumping together nationalist rebels with simple bandits and calling all of them pirates, proponents of colonialism in France could effectively deny any suggestion that the unrest in the colony was motivated by anticolonialism or a nationalist spirit and instead suggest that they were driven by debauchery and greed or possibly desperation.[160] In denying the

---

[156] Cooper, *France in Indochina*, 2.
[157] Charles-Lavauzelle (ed.), *Piraterie au Tonkin*; Frey, *Pirates et rebelles*; Bevin, *Au Tonkin*; Mat-Gioi [A. de Pouvourville], *Chez les pirates*; de Pouvourville, *Chasseur de pirates*; Carpeaux, *Chasse aux pirates*.
[158] Malleret, *Exotisme indochinois*, 87–124.
[159] Marr, *Vietnamese Anticolonialism*, 194; see also Rabinow, *French Modern*, 146.
[160] This was, for example, the position taken by Jules Ferry, who served as prime minister in 1880–81 and 1883–85 but never set foot in Vietnam; Ferry, *Tonkin et la mère-patrie*, 275.

Vietnamese any capacity for nationalist sentiment, moreover, the common people of the colony could be cast as victims of piracy and banditry and in need of French protection.[161]

Lastly, the use of the label *piracy* in Indochina – as in other colonial contexts – served to dehumanise those who were accused of engaging in such activities. It was part of a colonial discourse on race that legitimised violence against non-Europeans, in the context of which brutal and even lethal violence could be used by the colonial state with impunity. The discourse on piracy also combined with the anxiety and feeling of vulnerability of the French colonial community in Indochina, particularly in the early years of the French colonial period. This anxiety manifested itself in public displays of extreme violence, such as public executions and the dissemination of gruesome images of beheaded pirates on postcards.[162]

Because of its usefulness, the concept of piracy continued to be frequently invoked in French Indochina long after sea piracy had ceased to be a significant problem in the waters of the colony. It continued to be used, albeit with less frequency, until the end of the French colonial era. Even the Vietnamese nationalists who declared independence in August 1945 were called pirates in some of the official reports.[163]

Summary

The increase in French interests in Indochina around the middle of the nineteenth century coincided with a surge in Chinese piracy in the South China Sea following the end of the Opium War and the outbreak of the Taiping Rebellion. As the British, Dutch and eventually Chinese authorities took measures to suppress piracy in the Strait of Malacca and on the South China Coast the perpetrators crowded increasingly into Vietnamese waters, where the Nguyen Dynasty, weakened by internal rebellions and French incursions, lacked the naval capacity to uphold maritime security. The Vietnamese authorities were obviously more concerned with French naval aggression – which they, not unreasonably, regarded as piratical – than with the Chinese pirates who congregated on the coast and islands of northern Vietnam.

In that context it may seem strange that the French did not make the suppression of sea piracy in Indochinese waters a major priority, at least not before 1872, because the actions taken by the British, Dutch and Spanish in other parts of Southeast Asia around the same time suggested that the

---

[161] Fourniau, 'Colonial Wars before 1914', 73.
[162] Vann, 'Of Pirates, Postcards, and Public Beheadings'; cf. Osborne, *From Conviction to Anxiety*; Kleinen, 'Piracy through a Barbarian Lens'.
[163] de St-André, *Tour du monde*, 435; Deroo and Vallaud, *Indochine française*, 7.

Summary 207

suppression of piracy could serve as a convenient excuse for intervention and territorial expansion. French policy in Indochina, by contrast, was more land-oriented, and in particular the protection of the Catholic missions from prosecution by the Nguyen Dynasty was of greater importance than the upkeep of maritime security. In contrast to the Straits Settlements, where maritime security and the protection of maritime commerce, including local vessels, was the foundation of the colony's prosperity, the French initially had little incentive to protect or encourage indigenous commerce in Indochinese waters. Even after the French gained a foothold in Cochinchina in 1858, their main priority was to gain control on land – including on the rivers that served as important communication lanes – rather than at sea. The combined result of the French lack of interest in the suppression of piracy and the incapacity of the Nguyen Dynasty to uphold maritime security in its waters was that piracy and coastal raiding were allowed to thrive for several years in the Gulf of Tonkin, even after such activities had been efficiently suppressed in other parts of Southeast Asia. Organised piracy flourished particularly from the 1860s, when the abduction and trafficking of Vietnamese men, women and children took off, driven by a demand for prostitutes and domestic servants in China and for coolie labourers in America and in European colonies around the world.

Only from the 1870s, as pressure from French businessmen and other proponents of colonial expansion for intervention in northern Vietnam increased, did piracy begin to be invoked as a reason for intervention. The well-published operations of the *Bourayne* against Chinese pirates in 1872 contributed to convey an image of Indochina as a pirate-infested country in the French colonial imagination, and this perception was reinforced over the following decades as France intervened more decisively in northern Vietnam. The Black Flags were described as the most dangerous pirates, particularly after their killing of Henri Rivière in 1883. In the excited atmosphere following Rivière's death it was of little consequence that the Black Flags had virtually no maritime capacity and no connection to the pirates who roamed the Vietnamese coast and the Gulf of Tonkin.

As the French annexed Vietnam and faced resistance both from bandit groups, such as the Black Flags, and anticolonial nationalists, such as the Can Vuong, the *piracy* label was extended even further. French officers and administrators in Indochina were aware of the unconventional use of the term *pirate* in the region, but it was in many ways useful, as it allowed the French to portray themselves as fighting a noble cause against the enemies of mankind. In doing so, the French could argue that they brought progress and civilisation to the Vietnamese population by clearing the country of pirates. The reality was obviously far more complex, but the official rhetoric, combined with the French cultural imagination of Indochina as a land of pirates, served its purpose.

Compared with the British and Dutch contexts there was little questioning in France of how the label *piracy* was used to justify colonial expansion. In this sense the situation in France resembled that of Spain in the Sulu Archipelago. In contrast to Great Britain, and to a lesser extent the Netherlands, moreover, the considerable loss of human life on the part of the alleged pirates as a result of French antipiracy operations did not lead to widespread criticism or controversy in the metropolis.

Conclusion

Piracy in Asian and European Perspective

Studies of the European expansion in Asia, particularly during the nineteenth century, have generally treated the concept of piracy as part of a colonial discourse aimed at justifying European imperialism and domination. The thrust of the argument is that European colonisers inappropriately applied an essentially alien, European concept to the Asian context and that indigenous perceptions of maritime raiding and violence were fundamentally different from the European ones. This book, however, has shown that whereas the concept of piracy undeniably was part of the colonial discourse and frequently was used as a pretext for colonisation, these circumstances do not preclude there being indigenous terms in Asian languages that in some respects corresponded to the European understanding of piracy. Many contemporary nineteenth-century actors and observers of both Asian and European origin were also aware of the conceptual differences and understood that what was considered legitimate maritime violence varied between different social, political and cultural contexts.

The idea that pirates, by definition, were the enemies of mankind was indeed a distinctly European idea that originated in Roman Republican times. The understanding of piracy in this sense developed over a long period in European law, politics and culture, particularly during the early modern era, when European overseas expansion stimulated different forms of illicit or unregulated maritime violence around the world. The exploits of the pirates of the early modern age and the efforts to suppress them led to the emergence of the so-called piratical paradigm, which was established in Western Europe in the eighteenth century. This paradigm involved a complex set of ideas and implicit connotations related to piracy as a subversive and particularly serious form of maritime violence, which was associated both with debauchery, greed and extreme cruelty, and with liberty, romance and adventure.

From around 1730 European nation states were mostly, for the first time in history, able to control maritime violence emanating from their territories or perpetrated by their subjects against the vessels and coasts of other countries.

In contrast to the notorious pirates and privateers of the sixteenth, seventeenth and early eighteenth centuries, most of whom were of European nationality, piracy from the second half of the eighteenth century became increasingly associated with non-European peoples and allegedly lawless or uncivilised nations beyond European control.

In confronting a surge in maritime raiding and violence in Southeast Asia in the second half of the eighteenth century and the first half of the nineteenth century, the piratical paradigm proved useful for the European colonisers in the region because it projected an image of the raiders as barbarians and a threat to progress and prosperity. Thus applied to the Southeast Asian context, the piratical paradigm justified the use of extraordinary measures, including the deployment of extremely brutal and indiscriminate forms of maritime violence against allegedly piratical communities.

Although accusations of piracy were frequently used by European colonisers to obscure less noble motives for sending naval expeditions to foreign countries, it was not necessarily inappropriate to describe the ravages of Iranun, Sama, Malay, Chinese and other raiders in nineteenth-century Southeast Asia as piracy, at least not in the vernacular European sense of the word. Just as the concept of slavery could be (and was) applied in Southeast Asia, what European and American colonisers in the nineteenth century labelled piracy often involved abhorrent violence and abuses to human life and dignity that from an ethical perspective were repulsive to Asians and Europeans alike.

The concept of piracy, in the sense of the illegitimate use of maritime violence for the sake of plunder and material gain, was also well known throughout Asia's modern history, not least against the background of the maritime depredations by European navigators. The frequent violent displays by European navies, trading companies and freebooters in Asian waters from the turn of the sixteenth century onward gave Europeans a solid reputation as pirates throughout the ports and coasts of the Indian Ocean and East and Southeast Asia. Many Asian languages, including Malay, Chinese and Japanese, had specific terms that signified illegitimate and violent maritime activities, such as armed robbery against ships or raids on coastal regions by descent from the sea. Such activities were well known throughout Asia long before the arrival of Europeans, and the use by the latter of maritime violence to further their commercial and political interests were readily described in those terms, which then in turn were translated into European languages as *piracy*. When early modern Europeans worried that they were seen as pirates in Asian eyes, they were thus often correct, even if the connotations of the various terms that were translated into European languages as *piracy* differed in some respects from those embedded in the European piratical paradigm.

Asians were also capable of understanding the European concept of piracy and were at times able to appropriate it and use it to their advantage in their contacts with the colonial powers, for example, by committing themselves – whether earnestly or only ostensibly – to cooperate with the colonial powers in the suppression of piracy or by using the accusation against their enemies. Some Asian sovereigns, such as Emperor Tu Duc of Vietnam, even accused Europeans of piracy, an accusation that seemed to carry some weight in view of their long-standing reputation as pirates in Asian seas.

By comparison, the French casting as pirates all who resisted colonial domination in Vietnam after the invasion of Tonkin at the beginning of the 1880s seems more far-fetched. The French extended the *pirate* label to include marauders on land as well as at sea, the former comprising the vast majority of so-called pirates. Moreover, the Black Flags, which initially was the main group of pirates in terrestrial Tonkin according to official French rhetoric, was not just a band of land-based river pirates or outlaws, but part of the irregular forces of the Nguyen Dynasty, which sanctioned them in order to maintain nominal control over the Red River region and other parts of northern Vietnam. The French also subsequently extended the accusations of piracy to Nguyen Dynasty loyalists among the *literati* and supporters of the Can Vuong nationalist resistance movement, most of whom probably never set foot on a ship and whose main motivation was political rather than economic.

Designating the Black Flags and other opponents of French colonialism as pirates and thus as enemies of mankind may not have been appropriate from a factual point of view, but it served the purpose of drumming up support in France for colonial expansion in Vietnam. The discourse also gave rise to a literary genre of both fiction and nonfiction about the pirates of Tonkin, which resonated with a popular cultural demand in France for tales of the savage and exotic. With regard to piracy, the discrepancy between the colony's function as an *ailleurs rêvé* in French national culture and the reality in Indochina could hardly have been greater. The colonial imagination nonetheless served French colonial interests well by diverting attention from the security problems and lack of legitimacy that characterised French colonial rule in Vietnam, particularly before 1895. In that context it did not matter that the *pirate* label was stretched beyond recognition and applied not only to land-based bandits such as the Black Flags, but also to the Vietnamese anticolonial resistance movement.

Colonial officials in the Malay world were well aware that piracy was seen by some of the perpetrators in the region, particularly traditional Malay chiefs and noblemen, as a legitimate and even honourable way of securing wealth, social status and political influence. Those colonialists who took more than a passing interest in Malay history and society, such as Van Angelbeek, Raffles and Crawfurd, however, also realised that such notions were not shared by the majority of the indigenous population of Southeast Asia, who were the main victims of the piratical depredations. In other words, although the perpetrators and sponsors of maritime raiding in the Malay Archipelago may have argued, and possibly sincerely believed, that their activities were just and morally defensible, most Southeast Asians probably did not think the robbing and killing of peaceful traders, fishermen and other seafarers, or the wanton abduction of coastal populations, were legitimate or honourable.

As the naval dominance of the colonial powers was gradually extended throughout maritime Southeast Asia, particularly from the 1840s, many Asian sovereigns who previously had sponsored piratical activities realised that the tide was turning against the pirates, and they tried to adapt their policies and economic activities accordingly. Although European colonists frequently doubted the sincerity of the efforts by Southeast Asian rulers, such as the Sultans of Sulu, Selangor and Aceh, to distance themselves from what the colonisers saw as their old piratical habits, there is little to indicate that any of the major Southeast Asian sovereigns actively sponsored or encouraged piratical activity after the mid nineteenth century. Their failure to suppress piracy emanating from their territory was unsatisfactory from the European or colonial point of view, however, and often served as a pretext for military intervention. The principal aim of such intervention was more often than not to further the commercial or political interests of the colonisers rather than the suppression of piracy in itself. Southeast Asian rulers in the second half of the nineteenth century and the beginning of the twentieth century were for the most part shrewd enough to understand that the European colonisers used the concept of piracy for such purposes. Realising the threat that piracy, from that perspective, posed to their power and autonomy, many of them also tried, with varying success, to suppress piratical activities in or around their territories.

Race and Religion

The eighteenth century saw the end of the classical age of European piracy and a shift of most of the main theatres of piracy in the world from the West Indies and the Indian Ocean to East and Southeast Asia. In Southeast Asia, maritime raiding increased sharply from around 1770, and the Iranun, based in the southern Philippines, emerged as a distinct ethnic group with a formidable reputation for it. By the end of the century the word *lanun*, derived from Iranun, had entered the Malay language as a generic term for pirate, in addition to several other terms, including those derived from the names of other ethnic groups engaged in maritime raiding throughout the Malay Archipelago.

From the second half of the eighteenth century British, Dutch and Spanish colonisers began to use the concept of piracy more frequently to describe the raids of various indigenous ethnic groups of maritime Southeast Asia, particularly the Iranun and Sama of the southern Philippines. Piracy came to be seen as intrinsic to the Malay Archipelago in general, where the natural geography, with its many small islands, sheltered coves and shallow rivers, seemed to have stimulated the development of piratical habits among the population since the dawn of history, if not before.

In that context, and under the influence of Enlightenment ideas about race, civilisation and stadial theory, the concept of piracy, from the European perspective, began to be increasingly associated with race. In contrast to the French buccaneers of the seventeenth century or the British and other European pirates of the so-called Golden Age of Atlantic piracy at the beginning of the eighteenth century, most pirates around the world after the mid eighteenth century seemed to be non-Europeans. Colonial officials and observers consequently began to associate the presumed piratical habits of various ethnic groups in Asia with their allegedly inherent racial traits or deficiencies. The association between piracy and race, however, was not only – and possibly not even primarily – based on empirical observation. It was also an essential part of the emerging colonial discourse on piracy and race, according to which whole villages and even nations were defined as piratical and thus became susceptible to extinction. The suppression of piracy was the principle concern of colonial navies in Southeast Asia after 1815, and it was seen as necessary to stamp out piracy everywhere, regardless of the cost in human lives among the alleged enemies of mankind. By labelling whole nations or 'races' piratical, the use of wholesale and arbitrary violence to combat them could be justified and even be regarded as necessary or inevitable. Large-scale massacres of alleged pirate communities, in which hundreds of people, frequently including not only fighting men but also women, children, elderly people and slaves, were killed, could from this perspective be understood as legitimate and even progressive, although such claims did not always pass unchallenged by European humanitarians and other critics of imperialism.

The racial discourse was strengthened over the course of the nineteenth century. Malays in particular came to be seen as prone to piracy, and according to John Crawfurd, who by the mid nineteenth century was the leading authority in Great Britain on Malay history and culture, virtually all peoples of the archipelago were more or less addicted to piracy, bar the major settled agricultural peoples, such as the Javanese, Balinese and Christian Filipinos. The racial discourse was most pronounced in the Spanish colonial context, however, where there was virtually no questioning of the designation of the Muslims of the southern Philippines as pirates by nature. The terms *Moro* and *pirate* became more or less synonymous in the course of the nineteenth century, and the standard histories of the protracted Moro Wars, written toward the end of Spanish rule over the Philippines, described the Moros in almost exclusively negative terms, casting them as cruel, vengeful and deceitful by nature.

The racial lens of colonialism tended often to obscure the heterogeneity of the members of the ethnic groups that were labelled pirates. Even though it must have been obvious, for the most part, to colonial observers and officials that most members of any given nation in Southeast Asia did not engage in piracy, they were still collectively labelled as piratical, and all were seen either as pirates or potential pirates, or as accomplices in piratical activity. As a consequence, the rule of law was frequently subordinated to the racist paradigm, which made it possible for colonial officials to assume guilt and even pass death sentences on suspected pirates only by judging them on their looks and physique.

The great majority of the victims of piracy in Southeast Asia were Asians. This circumstance, however, did not stop European and American colonisers from expressing their concern for the suffering of the victims of piratical attacks and coastal raids, particularly not when doing so enabled them to argue for decisive measures to suppress piratical activity. Much was made, for example, of the reported murder of thirty-four Chinese passengers on the junk *Kim Seng Cheong* in 1871. It is doubtful, however, if the concern was based on any deeper felt sympathy or sincere care for the loss and suffering of the victims, all of whom remained unnamed, both in official correspondence and reports and in contemporary newspapers. Only rarely were Malay or Chinese victims of piracy named, and the media instead tended to focus on the gruesome details of the piratical deeds rather than the subsequent fate of the victims. That the ethnicity of the victims was consequential is also clear from the attempts by American officials in the early twentieth century to downplay the problem of piracy in Tawi-Tawi because it was supposedly only committed by the inhabitants of the islands upon each other.

All of this was in sharp contrast to when Europeans or Americans occasionally fell victim to attacks by pirates or alleged pirates, such as happened in Tonkin in 1883, when the French commander Henri Rivière was killed by the Black Flags, or in Basilan in 1907, when an American timber merchant and his Dutch business partner were hacked to death, together with their Chinese associate. Both incidents triggered loud calls for revenge among Europeans and Americans, and the Basilan murder caused manifest displays of solidarity and an outpouring of racist sentiments in the colonial press. Echoing earlier Spanish stereotypes about the Moros, they were described in sweeping racist terms as being by nature cruel and treacherous.

Racism was part of the colonial discourse everywhere, and the characterisation of whole nations as piratical is found in the Spanish, Dutch, British, French and American colonial contexts. However, the racial explanations tended to be more generalised and conspicuous where relations between colonisers and the allegedly piratical races were openly hostile, or when ignorance of the other group's culture and society was great. Such was the case, most obviously, with regard to Spanish relations with the Moros, but the tendency is also manifest in the Dutch scholar Snouck Hurgronje's view of the Acehnese as arch-pirates or in American perceptions of the Moros as pirates by nature. Among the British and Dutch, however, the racial discourse was to some extent mitigated by senior colonial officials, such as Johan Christiaan Van Angelbeek, Thomas Stamford Raffles, James Richardson Logan, Thomas Braddell, Peter Benson Maxwell, John McNair and Frank Swettenham, all of whom served long periods in Southeast Asia and developed an intimate knowledge of and sometimes even sympathy for the Malay language, culture and history. Some of them were able to some extent to go beyond the racial stereotypes and identify differences of opinion and character among the Malays with whom they dealt, although Braddell's claim – which was forcefully rejected by Maxwell – that the Selangor pirates were the most daring and bloodthirsty of all in the Malayan seas was patently false, a circumstance of which Braddell was probably well aware. The claim was obviously intended to resonate with the racial stereotypes of the Malays as inveterate pirates in order to legitimise a British intervention in Selangor.

Religious adherence to Islam intersected with race in colonial attempts to explain piracy in Southeast Asia. To many colonial observers, Islam also seemed to be relevant with regard to the other two regions of the world that in the first half of the nineteenth century were seen as the most pirate-infested, the Mediterranean (north Africa) and the Persian Gulf (the Oman coast). In all three regions the pirates were for the most part followers of Islam, and contemporary reports held that the fact that most Malays – like the Arabs who were implicated in piracy in the other two regions – were Muslims explained their piratical habits. Islam, it was claimed, sanctioned piracy, slavery and other forms of violence, robbery and deceitful behaviour by Muslims against non-Muslims.

The attempt to explain piracy with reference to Islam is found among the representatives of all the colonial powers in the Malay Archipelago, including among generally well-informed students of the region, such as Raffles, Ferd. Blumentritt, P. J. Veth and Snouck Hurgronje, all of whom pointed to the role of Islam in encouraging piratical activity among the Malays. The connection between piracy and Islam was also manifest among the Spanish. Piracy and maritime raiding emanating from the southern Philippines was interpreted against the background of the Moro Wars, which since the sixteenth century had been regarded by the Spanish – and, largely, by the Moros as well – as part of a global struggle between Christianity and Islam. Maritime raiding, in that context, was used by both parties to the conflict as a means of warfare. However, it was only from the second half of the eighteenth century and above all during the nineteenth that the Spanish began to describe their Muslim enemies as generic pirates.

The typical image of the pirate in popular history and culture around the world today is still a white man, generally a European. The most famous historical pirates, such as Henry Morgan, François l'Olonnais, William Kidd, Edward Teach and Bartholomew Roberts, were also Europeans. Against this background, an auxiliary purpose of this book has been to highlight the names of some of the lesser-known pirates and pirate chiefs of non-European origin who have made a name for themselves in the history of Southeast Asia, at least locally and in their own time: Pak Ranti, Raja Yakob, Taupan, Selungun and Jikiri, to mention some of the more prominent maritime marauders who have appeared on the pages of this book. There is little reason to suppose that their exploits and characters were more noble or honourable than their European counterparts, but they may be just as worthy of attention as some of the Europeans who occupy the pirates' hall of fame today.

Explanations

By the middle of the nineteenth century the navies of Great Britain, the Netherlands and Spain had broken the back of the large raiding fleets that had ravaged the coasts and seas of Southeast Asia since the late eighteenth century. Piracy continued on a smaller scale, however, throughout the second half of the nineteenth century and in some places well into the twentieth.

In the Straits Settlements occasional attacks by Malay pirates based in southern parts of the Strait of Malacca, including the Riau-Lingga Archipelago and the small islands near Singapore and on the coasts of some of the Malay Peninsula, constituted a minor problem for several decades after the mid nineteenth century. Although it was difficult to suppress completely, such piratical activity was for the most part relatively efficiently contained by British patrols, sometimes in collaboration with the Dutch colonial authorities or independent Malay states such as Johor and Terengganu. The most serious outbreak of piracy perpetrated by pirates who were indigenous to the region occurred in the 1880s and early 1890, when several brutal attacks on British ships took place in the context of the Aceh War, which was caused by the Dutch attempt to subjugate the Sultanate from 1873.

A problem of much greater importance to the commerce and security of the Straits Settlements was the depredations of heavily armed Chinese pirate junks. There were two major outbreaks of Chinese piracy affecting the Straits Settlements during the second half of the nineteenth century. The first, which mainly affected the trade between Singapore and Indochina, occurred in the 1850s, and the second occurred in 1872–74 and emanated from Perak, affecting the trade in and out of Penang and threatening public order in the colonial port. The first of these two waves of piracy was the most serious and protracted. As in Indochina at around the same time, the so-called junk piracy was linked to the upheaval in China, mainly the outbreak of the Taiping Rebellion. It flourished in the Strait of Malacca and along the east coast of the Malay Peninsula, largely because Singapore was an excellent land base for the pirates. The trade in arms was an important part of the port city's commerce, and pirates could easily obtain arms and munitions there, as well as general provisions, crew members and information for carrying out their depredations. Pirated goods could also be easily marketed and disposed of in Singapore. By providing these advantages to the pirates, the British inadvertently encouraged piratical activity emanating from the very centre of British power in maritime Southeast Asia, at the same time as Great Britain claimed to be the international leader in the struggle to suppress piracy there and in the rest of the world. The irony and hypocrisy did not go unnoticed by contemporary observers, but efforts to pass stricter laws and curb the arms trade in order to deal with the problem were slow to come about and largely insufficient.

Piracy in the rivers and on the coasts of Indochina in the 1860s and 1870s was essentially part of the same wave of Chinese piracy, the origins of which was the breakdown of law and order in southern China during the Taiping Rebellion. When piracy was suppressed with increasing vigour and efficiency, both on the south China coast and in the Strait of Malacca, many pirate junks seem to have taken refuge in the coast and islands of northern Vietnam, where the maritime geography, combined with the political and military weakness of the Nguyen Dynasty, created favourable conditions for piracy and maritime raiding. Robbery of trading junks and other local vessels seems at first to have been the main activity of the pirates, but from the 1860s they turned increasingly to the abduction and trafficking of Vietnamese women and children to China, where most of the victims were sold as domestic slaves, concubines or prostitutes. Vietnamese men were also abducted and trafficked as involuntary coolie labourers to colonial plantations, mines and other workplaces around the world.

In the Sulu Archipelago piratical activity continued for about a decade after the Spanish destruction of the Sama raiding base on Balangingi in 1848, albeit on a smaller scale than before. Many survivors of the attack moved to the periphery of the Sulu Archipelago, particularly the Tawi-Tawi group of islands, from where they continued to conduct raids, occasionally on a relatively large scale, to neighbouring islands in the Philippines, as well as to north Borneo and the eastern parts of the Dutch East Indies. From the end of the 1850s, and especially during the following decade, Spanish efforts to suppress piracy in the Sulu Archipelago became increasingly efficient. Occasional piratical activity continued to occur throughout the Spanish colonial era, but were on the whole relatively efficiently contained by Spanish naval patrols.

It was only in the early twentieth century, when the American colonial authorities began to implement a program of economic development, which led to increased maritime commerce and traffic and to a decline among the indigenous pearl fishers of Sulu, that piracy again resurfaced on a large scale in the southern Philippines. For eighteen months, from the end of 1907 until the middle of 1909, a band of outlaws led by Jikiri, a former member of the entourage of Sultan Jamalul Kiram II, brought terror to the Sulu Archipelago and Basilan, and almost brought maritime trade and pearl-fishing in the region to a standstill.

In all of these outbreaks of piracy were traces of the impact of colonialism and the changes brought about by the economic and political transformations due to the intensified imperial expansion in Asia in the nineteenth century. British free trade policies in maritime Southeast Asia and the South China Sea facilitated piratical activities to the extent that even the centre of British power in the region, Singapore, became a well-known pirate haunt. In the context of the unrest in Perak in the first half of the 1870s, Penang similarly functioned as a catalyst for piratical activities, although on a smaller scale and during a more limited period of time.

Raffles and other European observers of Southeast Asia in the nineteenth century frequently explained piracy in the region in terms of the decline of the indigenous economy caused by the European expansion of the early modern period, particularly the monopolistic practices of the Dutch East India Company. Although this so-called decay theory has in part been superseded by more sophisticated explanations as to the large-scale maritime raiding emanating from the southern Philippines in the late eighteenth and early nineteenth centuries, it still carries some explanatory value with regard to the outbreaks of piracy in Southeast Asia after the mid nineteenth century. The ravages of Chinese pirates off the coast of northern Vietnam, for example, were only possible because of the weakness of the Nguyen Dynasty, which to a significant extent was due to French advances and aggression from the 1840s. More broadly, the surge in Chinese piracy affecting the South China Sea, Vietnam and the Strait of Malacca was linked to the instability and civil war in southern China, particularly the Taiping Rebellion, which also to a large extent was triggered indirectly by European incursions into China during the first half of the nineteenth century. The Opium War played an important part in triggering junk piracy, as numerous privateers who had fought on the side of the Qing Dynasty took to piracy after the end of the war.

Perhaps the most clear-cut example of piracy caused by the decline of indigenous power and prosperity due to Western imperialism was the ravages of Jikiri and his followers in Sulu between 1907 and 1909. In a desperate attempt to counter the injustice and flawed implementation of a colonial law aimed at facilitating the exploitation of the pearl beds of the Sulu Archipelago by foreigners, Jikiri attacked the interests of those who, in contrast to himself and many indigenous Sulu Moros, seemed to gain from colonial efforts to transform the region's economy. The latter groups included European and American colonisers, overseas-owned pearl luggers, Japanese pearl fishers and Chinese merchants, all of whom fell victim to Jikiri's attacks. Against this background it has been suggested that Jikiri's motives were political rather than economic, but it is difficult to interpret his actions as anything but those of a disaffected desperado, whose main interest lay in plunder and violence and in gathering a large following in order to conduct ever more daring and spectacular raids. Nevertheless, behind the outbreak lay widespread discontent among the Joloanos with the American policy, which in part explains why the Americans had such difficulties defeating Jikiri and his band.

Plunder was the main motive for most of the outbreaks of piracy that occurred in Southeast Asia after the middle of the nineteenth century, even when piratical activity was directly linked to war and other politically motivated hostilities, such as in China and the Malay Sultanates in the Strait of Malacca. The suggestion that the concept of piracy would be inappropriate in Southeast Asia on the grounds that the cultural and political context was different from that of Europe cannot, therefore, on the whole, be sustained, at least not after the middle of the nineteenth century. Whether triggered by misery or opportunity – push or pull, in other words – the main goal of the pirates during Southeast Asia's age of empire was in virtually all instances material gain, possibly combined with the prospect of increased social status.

The main exception to this conclusion is Vietnam, where the acts of violence, robbery and extortion perpetrated by the Black Flags were political in the sense that they were sponsored by the Vietnamese government and used, among other things, as a bulwark against the French incursions in Tonkin in the 1870s and early 1880s. The Black Flags and the other predominantly Chinese bands that controlled most of northern Vietnam were nonetheless bandits or brigands more than anything else, and their main interest lay in activities such as plunder, extortion and trafficking. By contrast, the Can Vuong was an anticolonial resistance movement whose main aim was political, that is, to expel the French colonisers and restore the sovereignty of Vietnam under the Nguyen Dynasty. The supporters of the Can Vuong were thus not so much pirates or bandits as nationalist resistance fighters, despite the fact that they were described as pirates in the French colonial discourse and in the French cultural imagination.

Sovereignty, Security and the Suppression of Piracy

By the 1850s piracy had in principle ceased to be a major security threat for the colonial powers in Southeast Asia. Even though petty piracy continued to occur in many parts of Southeast Asia it was no longer a threat to European maritime commerce or the security and prosperity of the colonial centres in the archipelago. On several occasions between the middle of the nineteenth and the early twentieth centuries the threat of piracy was nonetheless brought to the fore and securitised by various actors, including senior colonial officials, military officers, local merchants and the victims of various acts of maritime violence. The securitising moves involved concerted attempts to draw attention to the problem of piracy by describing such activity in strong words as a serious and even existential threat to, for example, maritime commerce, the colonial community, law and order, or civilisation. The thrust of the argument was that piracy was not just an ordinary crime, but a threat so grave as to require the urgent use of extraordinary measures, such as punitive naval expeditions, and wars of conquest and colonisation. The antipiracy operations of James Brooke to north Borneo in the 1840s were examples of such extraordinary and often brutal measures, as was the destruction of Balangingi by the Spanish in 1848.

The fact that piracy was no longer a security threat in most parts of Southeast Asia after the middle of the nineteenth century did not put an end to the efforts of various actors to securitise it. By looking beyond the securitising rhetoric and analysing the motives of those involved, however, a deeper understanding of the reasons for the invocation of piracy as a security threat emerges. Most conspicuously, the securitisation of piracy was linked to the assertion of sovereignty over territories suspected or accused of harbouring pirates. In all three geographic regions under study here, the suppression of piracy was thus accompanied by colonial expansion and the loss of sovereignty for indigenous Southeast Asian states.

Despite these general similarities there was considerable variation with regard to the actors, motives and measures implemented to deal with piratical activity, both between the three areas under study and within each of them. These differences had an impact on the timing and character of the adopted antipiracy measures, which were often accompanied by colonial territorial expansion, as well as on the colonial imagination and the long-term relations between colonisers and colonised.

In the Strait of Malacca, piracy was not securitised to any significant degree in the 1850s and 1860s, despite the relatively serious problems that junk piracy caused for maritime commerce in the Straits Settlements. Local merchants demanded naval protection and improved legislation to deal with the problem, but such measures were only adopted slowly and partially. Furthermore, because Singapore, for good reasons, was suspected of being the main land base of the pirates in the area, securitising the issue risked drawing negative attention to the British colonial authorities and exposing their failure to uphold law and order in their own backyard. Suggestions to curb the arms trade in order to stop the pirates from getting access to arms and munitions, meanwhile, were rejected because of the negative consequences that such measures might have for Singapore's commerce.

In 1871, by contrast, the reported attack on the *Kim Seng Cheong*, in which thirty-four people were said to have been brutally murdered at sea by a gang of Chinese pirates after leaving Penang, led to a securitising move by the acting governor of the Straits Settlements, Edward Anson. Upon receiving news of the attack Anson dispatched a naval expedition to Selangor, which led to skirmishes between the British and local Malay bands, and eventually to the destruction by the British of the fort at Selangor, which they, on dubious grounds, claimed to be a major nest of pirates. The main objective of the intervention, however, was not the suppression of piracy but to put an end to the ongoing civil war in Selangor and bring about a transfer of power from the apparently inept Sultan Abdul Samad to his son-in-law, the British-friendly Tunku Kudin. The involvement of fifty of Kudin's followers in a recent case of piracy on the Selangor coast notwithstanding, senior government officials and influential merchants in the Straits Settlements both believed that he, with British support, would be able to bring political stability and favourable conditions for trade and investment to Selangor. Piracy was used as a motive for the military intervention in the Sultanate, despite the fact that the attack on the *Kim Seng Cheong* – if indeed it happened as reported – had been launched from the British port of Penang and not from Selangor.

The scheme ultimately failed because of a countermove by the recently retired Chief Justice of the Straits Settlements, Peter Benson Maxwell, to de-securitise the threat of piracy in the Strait of Malacca. In doing so he challenged both the legality and morality of the British intervention. In an article in *The Times*, Maxwell sharply criticised Anson's handling of the affair, and his criticism contributed to a more cautious, noninterventionist policy on the part of the colonial government and the Royal Navy in relation to the Malay states in subsequent years. In contrast to Anson, Governor Harry Ord, who returned to the Straits Settlements in March 1872, sought to downplay the threat of piracy emanating from the coasts of the Malay Peninsula, despite a surge in piratical activity in Perak, which to some extent affected British interests in Penang. This policy, among other things, contributed to widespread discontent with his administration, both in the colony and in London.

At the end of 1873 Ord was replaced by Andrew Clarke as governor of the Straits Settlements. Under the new governor, and in concert with several of the old hands in the colonial administration, many of whom took a great personal interest in the problem of piracy, the threat was again securitised and used to motivate British military and political interventions, first in Perak and then in Selangor. The condition for the success of the securitising moves, in contrast to 1871, was the policy change in London, where the government – still under the generally nonexpansionist Prime Minister William Ewart Gladstone – now had come to support a more interventionist British policy in the Malay Peninsula. Consequently, Clarke carried with him instructions by the Colonial Secretary to take measures for the protection of British commerce with the Malay states, much in contrast to the noninterventionist policy under Clarke's predecessor. Although piracy was not explicitly mentioned in the new governor's instructions, the threat was once again mobilised in order to justify intervention in both Perak and Selangor. The theme of piracy was highlighted both in the colonial press and in official reports about the current situation in the Malay states, particularly in Perak, where raiding by Chinese bands involved in the conflict in Larut did cause a deterioration in maritime security and affected local traders and fishermen. The reports used a highly securitising rhetoric in order to justify not only increased antipiracy patrols and other policing measures, but also increased British political control over the Malay states through the appointment of a permanent British resident, first to Perak and then to the other sultanates on the Malay peninsula.

In contrast to Perak there had been very few reported pirate attacks emanating from Selangor in the preceding years, but this circumstance did not prevent senior government officials and the colonial press from describing Selangor as a hotbed of piracy. In that context, an attack on a small trading boat off the Selangor coast in November 1873, in which five Malays and three Chinese were killed, apparently on the orders of a son of the sultan of Selangor, was quickly seized upon by the colonial government as a reason for intervening in Selangor.

Although the measures taken by the British to deal with the problem of piracy in Perak and Selangor in the first half of the 1870s were extraordinary compared with the previous policy of nonintervention, they were far less violent than earlier British antipiracy campaigns, particularly those of the late 1830s and 1840s, in which thousands of real and imagined pirates were killed. The Straits Government now instead used gunboat diplomacy, combining more or less overt threats of violence with negotiations and offers of rewards for complying with British demands. The negotiations were largely conducted by colonial officials who were familiar with the language and culture of their negotiation partners and commanded their respect and possibly even a measure of trust. The threat of violence was often direct and clear, but the British also offered clear benefits to their counterparts, such as immediate food relief for the Sin Heng in Perak or the prospect of increased British trade and investment in Selangor.

The first half of the 1870s was unique in the Straits Settlements in that it was the only time after the mid nineteenth century that piracy was successfully securitised. By contrast, when several British ships were attacked by Acehnese pirates in the 1880s and 1890s in the context of the Dutch war of conquest in

Aceh, the issue was not securitised, despite the fact that several British officers and other Europeans – in addition to an even larger number of Asian crew members and passengers – were killed. The attacks on the *Hok Canton*, *Rajah Kongsee Atjeh* and *Pegu* were among the most brutal to befall British ships in the Strait of Malacca in the second half of the nineteenth century, but neither the colonial government, the government in London nor the general public in the Straits Settlements were interested in securitising the issue. There were no plans for a British intervention in the bitter and protracted Aceh War, nor was there any interest in a fallout with the Dutch over their failure to curb piracy emanating from their territory. The piratical attacks were thus treated by the British as tragic events and criminal acts, but not as a threat to the security of the Straits Settlements or its commerce.

Whereas the perceived seriousness of the threat of piracy thus subsided among the British in the Strait of Malacca after the mid 1870s, piracy started to become increasingly seen as a security threat by the French in Indochina from around the same time. French missionaries in the region had drawn attention to the problem since the middle of the century, but the suppression of piracy in Indochina was not a major concern for the French Navy before the 1870s. Moreover, although river piracy was rife in French Cochinchina from the establishment of the colony in 1858 until the end of the 1860s, the naval officers who administered the colony tended to downplay the problem rather than to securitise it. Doing so would obviously have reflected poorly on the Navy and its ability to maintain law and order in the colony, for which it was responsible. Just like the British did not want to draw attention to the Chinese pirates operating out of Singapore in the 1850s, the French authorities in Cochinchina had no wish to call attention to the prevalence of river piracy or other forms of disorder in the colony.

Whereas the problem of piracy was thus toned down in official correspondence and reports from Cochinchina, it was dealt with internally by a combination of regular patrols taken over from the Vietnamese and an extremely harsh and arbitrary system of justice in which death sentences were frequently passed on suspected pirates and other criminals, often on very loose grounds and by junior naval officers who lacked both training in judicial matters and understanding of the cultural and linguistic context of Cochinchina. The harsh measures were motivated by the extraordinary security situation in the colony and were terminated only with the transition to civilian rule in 1879.

Sea piracy increased on the coast and around the islands of northern Vietnam in the 1860s and early 1870s as numerous Chinese pirates were drawn to the area after being pushed out of the Strait of Malacca and much of the South China Sea. A French businessman and adventurer, Jean Dupuis, who had commercial interests in northern Vietnam and sought to expand his operations to the Yunnan province of southwest China, urged the French Navy in Cochinchina to take on a greater responsibility for suppressing piracy on the coast of northern Vietnam while simultaneously exploring the possibilities for further French colonial expansion. In 1872 the dispatch boat *Bourayne* was sent to Tonkin for the dual purpose of exploring the region and suppressing piracy. Even though piracy in northern Vietnam was not seen by the French as a security issue at the time, the second expedition of the *Bourayne* in October turned out to be one of the most brutal antipiracy campaigns in Southeast Asia after the middle of the nineteenth century, leaving more than 500 alleged pirates dead.

Rather than trying to securitise the problem of piracy and banditry in Tonkin, however, Dupuis downplayed the threat, particularly with regard to the Black Flags, who controlled the Red River and obstructed the passage of commercial traffic with Yunnan. Consequently, a small and ill-prepared French expedition was dispatched to Tonkin in 1873, officially for the purpose of expelling the troublesome Dupuis, but actually for the purpose of putting pressure on the Vietnamese government to settle a territorial dispute with France in the south. The intervention ended in disaster for the French, however, after the commander of the expedition, Lieutenant Francis Garnier, was killed by the Black Flags. The failure of Dupuis and the colonial authorities to securitise the depredations of the Black Flags, combined with the European orientation of French foreign policy at the time, contributed to the decision to withdraw French troops from Tonkin and to a more noninterventionist French policy in Indochina over the following years.

To anti-imperialists in France, Garnier's death seemed to demonstrate the perils of further colonial adventures. The government had to use a highly securitising rhetoric to get Parliament to ratify the treaty of peace and friendship, which was negotiated with Vietnam in 1874. According to the treaty, France promised to assist the Vietnamese emperor in suppressing piracy, an obligation that was represented by the government as part of France's civilising mission in Asia. In the end the treaty was ratified, despite the attempts by anti-imperialists to desecuritise the threat of piracy in Indochina with regard to French interests.

In the following years, missionary and official reports contributed to securitising piracy and trafficking in Vietnam, particularly with regard to the trafficking of women and girls to prostitution in China, which by the 1870s had developed to become the main source of income for the pirates. The reports contributed to strengthening procolonial sentiments in France, and by the early 1880s there was a strong opinion in favour of annexing the rest of Vietnam. Against that background – and in sharp contrast to the French withdrawal from Tonkin after the killing of Garnier in 1873 – the killing of the commander of another French expedition to Tonkin in 1883, Henri Rivière, by the Black Flags triggered loud and virtually unanimous calls in France for intervention. Vietnam was described as infested by pirates, of whom the Black Flags were the most barbarous and dangerous.

The rhetoric of piracy became firmly entrenched in French colonial discourse in the aftermath of the events of 1883 and continued to be used throughout the French colonial era in Vietnam. In the second half of the 1880s and first half of the 1890s the allegations of piracy were extended to include virtually anybody who resisted French domination in Indochina with little regard for the diversity of the groups that were labelled piratical. The rhetoric contributed to a sense of emergency that justified the use of repressive military action against so-called pirates in various locations, including, and even, from around 1890s, predominantly, on land. The extraordinary measures taken by the French authorities included the dispatch of tens of thousands of troops to Indochina, as well as arbitrary killings, the destruction of property and the forced recruitment of labour to support the colonial war effort. The securitisation of piracy in French Indochina lasted well into the twentieth century, but it was most pronounced until the middle of the 1890s, when the back of anticolonial resistance and the power of the Black Flags and other bandit gangs was broken.

Piracy was also securitised by the Vietnamese authorities to draw attention to the existential threat that the French incursions constituted to the country from the middle of the nineteenth century. Emperor Tu Duc accused the French of being cowardly pirates who sought to foment disorder in his realm, and by the beginning of the 1870s, Dupuis was regarded by Vietnamese officials as a pirate after he tried to force the Red River open for commerce without official authorisation. The appeals to resistance after the French invasion of Tonkin in 1883 also called for the Vietnamese to rise up and expel the French pirates. Even though the connotations of the Chinese or Vietnamese terms may have differed from the European ones, there were similarities in that pirates in both contexts were seen as subversive and treacherous. Describing the French in such terms served not only to defame them but also to cast them as an existential threat to the Vietnamese nation. In that sense, the Nguyen Dynasty's use of the *pirate* label to refer to the French was arguably more appropriate than the corresponding French discourse, according to which all who resisted French advances in Indochina were cast as pirates.

Of the major colonial powers in Southeast Asia, Spain was probably the most consistent when it came to the securitisation of piracy. In contrast to the Straits Settlements, where piracy after the mid nineteenth century only briefly emerged as a security threat at the beginning of the 1870s, and in comparison with Indochina, where the securitisation of piracy by the French emerged only gradually before coming into full swing after 1883, the Spanish perception of the Moros of the southern Philippines as a security threat was more pronounced throughout most of the nineteenth century. The Spanish understood

Moro culture and society against the background of the global historical struggle between Islam and Christianity, and the Moros were thus seen as the arch-enemies of the Spanish. The frequent slave raids that seafaring Moros undertook to the islands of the Spanish colony also constituted a significant and persistent security threat for the Spanish authorities and the coastal populations for much of the Spanish colonial period. From that point of view, Spanish descriptions of the Moros as inveterate pirates were more empirically based than, for example, the exaggerated British accounts of the allegedly dangerous and bloodthirsty Selangor pirates or the sweeping use of the label *piracy* by the French in Indochina.

As the slave raids emanating from the southern Philippines intensified toward the end of the eighteenth century and during the first decades of the nineteenth, piracy emerged as a major theme in Spanish rhetoric about the Moros. The large-scale raiding expeditions of the Iranun and Sama affected not only the Philippines but large parts of the rest of maritime Southeast Asia as well. The raids led British and Dutch (and later American) colonisers in Southeast Asia to concur with the Spanish impression of the Moros as pirates, and such perceptions were reinforced by the racial and stadial theories that emerged around the same time in Europe. The Iranun and Sama in particular gained a reputation for being the most dangerous pirates in Southeast Asia, and by the early nineteenth century they were widely seen as a threat to the security of human life and maritime commerce throughout the Malay Archipelago.

With Moro piracy thus being seen as a persistent security threat by the Spanish, extraordinary measures, such as the dispatch of major naval expeditions, invasion attempts and the destruction of alleged pirate fleets and land bases, were implemented with relative frequency during the protracted struggle of the Moro Wars. The arrival of steam navigation from the 1840s gave the Spanish Navy a decisive advantage over the Moros, as demonstrated by the destruction of the Sama raiders' base at Balangingi in 1848. The attack was followed by the despatch of another major naval expedition to Jolo in 1851. The assault was to some extent motivated by the need to suppress piracy, but its purpose was above all to preclude further British attempts to compromise the Spanish claim to sovereignty over the Sulu Sultanate after the conclusion of the Brooke Treaty between Britain and Sulu in 1849. Jolo was thus attacked after raiding had declined substantially in the wake of the destruction of Balangingi in 1848 and after Sultan Muhammad Fadl Pulalun had begun to distance himself from the Iranun and Sama raiders.

Further Spanish naval expeditions were dispatched to the Sulu Archipelago in the 1850s in order to suppress piracy emanating from Tawi-Tawi islands, which were close to the Dutch and British possessions in Borneo. The Spanish, however, rejected suggestions to cooperate with the naval forces of their colonial neighbours, demonstrating again that for the Spanish the main security threat in the Sulu Archipelago after the middle of the nineteenth century was no longer Moro piracy or raiding in itself but the prospect of other colonial powers gaining a foothold in the region. The securitisation of piracy thus served to justify further naval patrols in and expeditions to the southern Philippines. The main purpose was to assert Spanish sovereignty over the Sulu Archipelago, both in relation to other colonial powers and to the apparently insubordinate Sulu Sultanate.

Securitisation of piracy in the Sulu Archipelago intensified in the 1870s, when the Spanish began to implement a fully fledged policy of maritime warfare directed at Moro shipping not only for the purpose of suppressing piracy but also in order to destroy the commerce of the Sultanate. In 1876 a large military expedition was dispatched to Jolo to occupy the capital of the Sultanate and suppress, once and for all, piracy emanating from the archipelago. The Spanish conquered the capital at Jolo and established a Spanish garrison there, and naval expeditions were sent out throughout the Sulu Archipelago to chase down alleged pirates. The conquest of Jolo was hailed as a great victory in Spain, and the histories of the Moro Wars published in subsequent years described the Moros as a race of inveterate pirates, thereby reproducing and disseminating the securitising colonial discourse about Moro piracy and justifying Spanish colonial expansion in the southern Philippines.

When the United States took over the Philippines from Spain in 1899, piracy was initially not seen as a major security problem, despite occasional attacks against local traders and fishermen. As long as the number of attacks was limited and the victims were Asian, piracy was seen as one among many forms of violent crime that were prevalent among the Moros. However, when two white settlers were murdered on Basilan at the end of 1907, the problem was immediately securitised. The colonial press called for extraordinary measures and even suggested that a massacre, such as the one on Bud Dajo on Jolo in 1906, in which close to 1,000 Moros had been killed by the US military, should be staged in order to teach the Moros a lesson.

The raid on Basilan triggered a massive effort on the part of the US Army and the Philippine Constabulary to exterminate the pirates. The governor of Moro Province, Tasker Howard Bliss, was blamed by his superiors for the deteriorating security situation, but his efforts to maintain law and order were hampered by the lack of naval support. When such support eventually, in February 1909, came forth, the authorities were at last able to put an end to the raids and restore maritime security in the Sulu Archipelago. Despite the plea for a wholesale massacre of Moros in the colonial press, and in contrast to the brutality of the military expeditions under Bliss's predecessor as governor of Moro Province, Leonard Wood, the operations of 1908–09 were relatively restrained, and few innocent Moros or other people seem to have been killed or injured by the colonial troops.

To sum up, piracy was securitised in all three regions under study after the mid nineteenth century, but for different reasons, most of which did not have to do with the problem of piracy or other forms of maritime violence, at least not on its own. The threat of piracy tended to be invoked when there was a desire on the part of the agents of colonialism, such as colonial officials, naval officers, journalists and merchants, to extend colonial sovereignty or influence to nearby autonomous states and territories, such as Selangor, Perak, Aceh, Sulu and Vietnam. Piracy was rarely securitised, however, when it occurred in or emanated from an area over which the colonial powers exercised sovereignty (real or nominal) already, such as Singapore or French Cochinchina. The securitisation of piracy in the southern Philippines under American colonial rule in 1907–09 stands out as an exception in this context because of the strong emotions that the killing of white men triggered in the local colonial community.

The timing of most of the successful cases of securitisation of piracy after the mid nineteenth century is also significant. The first half of the 1870s saw the rise of the last major wave of antipiracy operations in Southeast Asia, with major interventions, ostensibly for the suppression of piracy, in all three regions under study: the British attack on Selangor following the reported attack on the *Kim Seng Cheong* (1871), the antipiracy cruises of the *Bourayne* in Vietnam (1872), the Dutch invasion of Aceh (1873), the onset of the Spanish attacks on Moro shipping (1873), and the British interventions in Perak (1874) and Selangor (1874). All of these events occurred more or less concurrently within a period of just three years, which coincided with the intensified scramble for colonies among the established and emerging imperial powers, including the rising Germany. In that context, allegations of piracy were useful in order to obscure self-interested motives for imperial expansion on the part of the colonial powers in Southeast Asia.

If the motives for securitising piracy thus for the most part depended on factors other than the threat of piracy in itself, it was still essential, in order for the securitising moves to succeed, that there was some empirical ground for the allegations of piracy. In other words, piracy was a *sine qua non* for the securitisation of piracy. Even in Indochina, where the label was stretched beyond recognition, the securitisation of piracy after 1883 could probably only have taken place against the background of earlier reports about piracy and trafficking in the region and the well-published antipiracy operations in Vietnam in the 1870s.

Last, there were substantial differences between the colonial powers under study with regard to which types of extraordinary measures they implemented to suppress piracy and to extend or assert their sovereignty. After the middle of the nineteenth century the gunboat diplomacy employed by the British involved limited military expeditions that resulted in relatively few casualties on both sides. The French and Spanish antipiracy measures, by contrast, often involved much larger contingents and expeditions, and were considerably more costly in human lives, particularly on the side of the alleged pirates but sometimes also among the colonial troops. The American efforts to chase down Jikiri and his band involved relatively large numbers of military and constabulary personnel over a long period of time (eighteen months) but nevertheless – in contrast to many other American military operations in the region around the same time – avoided extensive destruction of human lives.

Maritime Violence and the Civilising Mission

Time and again during the nineteenth and early twentieth centuries the suppression of piracy was framed as part of the obligation of the European and American colonisers to bring civilisation and progress to the rest of the world. Regardless of whether piracy was understood as part of the nature of certain piratical 'races', a cultural habit, a religiously sanctioned practice or the result of economic and political decay, those who engaged in piracy were, by definition, regarded as uncivilised.

For colonial observers and agents the inclination to piracy was not linked to the individual perpetrator's degree of civilisation but to the stage of civilisation achieved by the race or nation to which he (or, very rarely, she) belonged. Colonial rule, it was assumed, would eventually lift up even the most barbarous tribes and nations to a reasonably civilised level, although it might be necessary to kill off a substantial number of the most depraved pirates first in order to teach the community as a whole a lesson. The survivors would then hopefully come to their senses and abandon their piratical habits and adopt more civilised and sedentary ways of life.

Against this background, the application of the European concept of piracy to the Southeast Asian context was not, from the perspective of the colonisers, misguided or inappropriate but part of Europe's and the United States' civilising mission. By suppressing indigenous forms of maritime violence in Southeast Asia, European and American colonisers believed that they were bringing improvement and progression to the region, particularly with regard to the free flow of maritime commerce and the human security of the Asian seafarers and coastal populations who were the main victims of the piratical attacks. Awareness of the fact that there were differences between European and Asian understandings of piracy, and that some of the perpetrators may have regarded piracy and maritime raiding as legitimate and even honourable pursuits, did not alter the conviction of the colonisers that piracy was an immoral and uncivilised practice. By siding with the victims, moreover, the colonial agents could project themselves as altruistic saviours of the majority of the population, who bore the brunt of the depredations. Smug as this attitude may have been, human security did improve significantly in the course of the nineteenth century due to the antipiracy campaigns of the colonial powers – even if colonialism obviously gave rise to other forms of oppression, exploitation and insecurity.

The civilising discourse is found among all the colonial powers under study here but with some variations. For the Spanish, the piratical Moros were to be civilised through conversion to Catholicism, combined with the adoption of agriculture. The British, by contrast, did not seek to convert the Malays to Christianity, and they believed the best road to civilisation was a combination of economic and commercial development, the rule of law and the demise of the traditional Malay nobility, which was understood for the most part to be made up of oppressive pirates, brigands, parasites or tyrants. The Americans, upon taking over the Philippine colony from Spain, largely shared the British view and did not actively seek to convert the Moros to Christianity. In Indochina, meanwhile, the focus for the French was on bringing law and order to the colony by exterminating or driving out the pirates, in order for the majority of the population to return to their peaceful, mainly agricultural, pursuits. In contrast to the Spanish, however, and despite the long-standing strong presence of Catholic missionaries in Indochina, the French did not seem to harbour any great hopes of making the Chinese and Vietnamese pirates and other outlaws in the region abandon their ways by converting them to Christianity.

Piracy was often a prominent subject in treaties and negotiations between Asian sovereigns and European colonisers, and the latter frequently called attention to the necessity of meeting the international standard of civilisation when it came to the suppression of piracy. The Malay states were largely seen by paternalistic European and American colonisers as rude or barbarian, and even if they were sincere in their commitment to combat piracy, they were generally deemed to be lacking both the legal institutions and the necessary repressive capacity for dealing effectively with the problem. In European eyes, a state's ability to suppress piracy and other forms of illicit violence emanating from its territory was essential in order to be respected and seen as civilised by other nations of the world. This reasoning seems to have convinced at least some Southeast Asian sovereigns, such as the Sultans of Johor, Terengganu and Sulu, and King Norodom of Cambodia, of the need to cooperate with the colonial powers in order to suppress piracy. The Vietnamese Emperor Tu Duc and other members of the Nguyen Dynasty, meanwhile, seem in principle to have shared the European understanding of pirates as being uncivilised – although, of course, Emperor Tu Duc held that it was the French who were pirates, along with the Chinese and other bandits who ravaged his country.

Finally, the suppression of piracy frequently involved the use of indiscriminate and arbitrary violence, particularly during the 1830s and 1840s, when the British, Dutch and Spanish antipiracy campaigns sank the fleets and destroyed the land bases of the alleged pirates, often killing several hundreds of people in a single encounter. In Britain, but less so in the other colonial metropoles, the massacres gave rise to sharp criticism from anti-imperialist groups. From around the middle of the nineteenth century, such criticism brought about more restricted policies and practices with regard to British antipiracy operations in Southeast Asia and elsewhere.

The public displays of concern for the lives and rights of alleged pirates were less prominent in the Netherlands and seem to have been altogether absent in France and Spain, as indicated by the praise that Senez and Malcampo received in the wake of their successful campaigns against the alleged pirate bases in Cat Ba (1872) and Jolo (1876), respectively. Both campaigns involved significant destruction of human lives and property, none of which reflected negatively on the expeditions or their commanders in the eyes of the domestic public or policymakers in the metropoles. If anything, they were commended for exterminating the enemies of mankind in such great numbers, with few casualties among the French and Spanish troops.

By contrast, the relatively limited use of violence by the British in Selangor and Perak in 1871–74 gave rise to criticism and controversy in Britain. Maxwell's warning that the unjust and wanton intervention in Selangor in 1871 would cause England's name to stink in Asian idiom may not have been shared by most members of the general public in Britain and certainly did not meet with much sympathy in the Straits Settlements. But it demonstrated that there were differences of opinion with regard to the standard of civilisation among the colonial powers, whose self-imposed task it was to bring civilisation to the rest of the world by exterminating piracy.

Epilogue: Piracy and the End of Empire

For around half a century, from around 1900 until the end of the colonial era in the mid twentieth century, there was relatively little piratical activity in Southeast Asia. As the colonial states took control over the coasts, islands and estuaries where the pirates used to have their bases, piracy and maritime raiding ceased, for the most part, to be a viable way to gain material wealth, social status or political power. Piracy did continue in Chinese waters throughout the first half of the twentieth century, until more socially and politically stable conditions developed after the People's Republic of China was established in 1949. Apart from a few spectacular attacks carried out by passengers on ferries in the South China Sea and the Strait of Malacca, however, the activities of twentieth-century Chinese pirates rarely affected Southeast Asia.[1]

By contrast, in the wake of World War II and after most former colonies in Southeast Asia gained independence, several outbreaks of piracy have occurred in various parts of the region, including in the Strait of Malacca in 1945–46, in the southern Philippines and north Borneo in the 1950s and first half of the 1960s (and later), in the Gulf of Thailand in the 1970s and 1980s, in the South China Sea in the 1990s, and again in the Strait of Malacca in the 1980s, 1990s and early 2000s. As a result, particularly of the successive waves of piracy and armed robbery against ships in the Strait of Malacca, Southeast Asia has gained a reputation for being one of the most pirate-infested regions in the contemporary world.

It might be tempting – particularly for apologists of colonialism – to explain the resurgence in piracy in the region after independence as a result of the demise of colonial power and law and order. A message from the British Legation in Manila to London in 1950, for example, claimed that after the Americans had left the Philippines, and with the Philippine authorities not being capable of maintaining the same standard of law and order, the Moros were 'reverting to type', again 'finding in piracy and smuggling an easy way of

---

[1] See Miller, *Pirates of the Far East*, 153–84, for piracy in the South China Sea in the twentieth century.

making a living'.[2] Such analyses echo nineteenth-century views of the Malays and other maritime groups in Southeast Asia as natural and inveterate pirates, who could be expected to take every opportunity to resume their piratical habits as soon as imperial law enforcement and vigilance were relaxed.

However, although anthropological evidence from Jolo to some extent supports the notion of a cultural continuity and a sanctioning of maritime raiding among the Tausug, the explanations as to the renewed piratical activity in Southeast Asia after independence – as elsewhere in the postcolonial world – are not so much linked to cultural endurance or continuity with the pre-colonial era as to more recent changes in the global economy, technology and the international shipping industry.[3] For example, the reduction in the number of crew members aboard commercial vessels, combined with the increase in maritime trade and lax security onboard ships, have all served to create new opportunities for piracy in Southeast Asia and elsewhere. Another, often overseen, explanation is the motorisation of water transportation in the twentieth century, particularly the availability of inexpensive but powerful outboard engines suitable for use in piratical attacks.

These explanations may not be directly linked to the end of imperialism in Southeast Asia in the decades following the end of World War II, but in at least three other respects colonialism and its legacies are at the heart of the explanations for the resurgence of piracy in the region. The first of these is war and its aftermath, particularly with regard to World War II and the Vietnam War. Petty piracy affecting the local junk trade increased in the Strait of Malacca during the Japanese occupation between 1942 and 1945, and in the southern Philippines the proliferation of arms and military surplus engines after the end of World War II encouraged maritime raiding and led to a surge in piracy. The end of the Vietnam War in 1975, meanwhile, led to another – and more serious – outbreak of piratical activity that targeted the refugees who fled by boat across the Gulf of Thailand from southern Vietnam and Cambodia to Thailand and Malaysia.[4] In all of these instances, piratical activity increased as a result of the decline in law and order due to major wars.

The second explanation concerns the national borders in maritime Southeast Asia, all of which are legacies of colonialism. Smuggling cigarettes over the maritime border between British North Borneo and the southern Philippines, for example, stimulated piracy and maritime raiding after the Philippines gained independence in 1946. Subsequently, after North Borneo became a

---

[2] British Legation, Manila to the Minister of State for Foreign Affairs, 24 March 1950, FO 371/84337 (TNA).
[3] Kiefer, *Tausug*, 85; see further Liss, *Oceans of Crime*; Eklöf Amirell, *Pirates in Paradise*, for these and other more recent explanations of piracy in Southeast Asia.
[4] Ibid., 17–34.

part of Malaysia in 1963, mutual suspicion and hostility between Malaysia and the Philippines due to the territorial dispute over Sabah, the eastern part of Malaysian Borneo, effectively hampered collaboration between the two countries to suppress piracy and maritime raiding. As a consequence, pirates based in the Sulu Archipelago could conduct raids with relative impunity, targeting Indonesian and Malaysian victims at sea as well as towns and settlements on the east coast of Sabah. Such piratical activity emanating from the Sulu Archipelago has continued more or less unabated until the present, many of the perpetrators being members of or associated with militant Islamist or sessecionist groups based in the southern Philippines.[5]

The maritime border established by the British and Dutch through the Strait of Malacca is also part of the explanation for piracy in that part of the region. Shortly after independence, in the 1950s, Indonesian regular and irregular troops began to undertake frequent piratical attacks on fishing boats from British Malaya. Some of the attacks appear to have involved the killing of the victims, but more often they consisted of thefts of nets, engines, stores and money or, more rarely, the confiscation of boats and arrests of men.[6] Officially sponsored piracy was also used at the beginning of the 1960s by Indonesia in the context of her policy of Confrontation (*Konfrontasi*) against Malaysia, which the Indonesian government saw as a neocolonial construction. In 1963 Malaysia's Prime Minister, Tunku Abdul Rahman, directly accused the Indonesian Navy of robbing Malaysian fishermen of their catch and equipment, setting their boats on fire and physically assaulting them, both in Malaysian and international waters.[7]

More recently, since the beginning of the 1980s, piracy in the Strait of Malacca has surged on several occasions, in part because of the lack of naval cooperation and intelligence-sharing between the three littoral states in the Strait, Indonesia, Malaysia and Singapore. By contrast, when efforts have been made to conduct coordinated antipiracy operations and share information between the law-enforcement authorities of the three countries, piracy has generally been brought under control without much difficulty, for example in 1992 and 2005.[8]

---

[5] Eklöf Amirell, 'Suppressing Piracy in Asia'; Liss, 'Contemporary Piracy'. In 2017 the International Maritime Bureau reported that kidnappings by Philippine militants in the Sulu Sea and the Celebes Sea had stopped due to the efforts of the Philippine military, although it remains to be seen whether the improved maritime security situation can be maintained in the long run; ICC International Maritime Bureau, 'Piracy and Armed Robbery against Ships', 21–2.
[6] C-in-C Far Eastern Station to Admiralty, 20 November 1953, AIR 2/12136 (TNA).
[7] Abdul Rahman, Address to the Malaysian Parliament, 12 November 1963, in Winks and Bastin (eds.), *Malaysia*, 436.
[8] Eklöf Amirell, *Pirates in Paradise*, 133–42.

Lastly, the differences in priority between the colonial and postcolonial states go some way to explain why piracy has occasionally surged in Southeast Asia after independence. Whereas a key priority of the colonial states was law and order and the promotion of economic development, mainly for the benefit of foreign traders and investors largely based in the metropoles, the postcolonial states in Southeast Asia have often been more concerned with nation-building and with trying to improve the economic and social conditions of the indigenous population. These priorities have frequently led to nationalistic economic policies and efforts to control and exploit natural resources, both on land and at sea. In terms of maritime policies, this shift has meant that the protection of international maritime commerce from petty piracy has often been of less importance than the assertion of maritime sovereignty and control over maritime resources. Such considerations have been particularly important for Indonesia, the largest maritime state in Southeast Asia, but also for the Philippines and, to a lesser degree, Malaysia. Against that background, the main reason the Indonesian authorities at times since the 1980s have allowed piracy to flourish is not the country's lack of sea power, but its maritime priorities. Controlling the Indonesian Archipelago against illegal fishing and smuggling has, for example, frequently been seen as more important than the suppression of piracy.[9]

Despite much talk about Southeast Asia being one of the most piracy-prone regions of the world over the past few decades, there has actually been relatively little piratical activity in the region – at least in historical comparison – and the waves of piracy that have occurred have, for the most part, been relatively limited and of low intensity, with the exception of the gruesome attacks on the boat refugees from southern Vietnam and Cambodia in the Gulf of Thailand in the 1970s and 1980s. The postcolonial states have also, on several occasions, shown that they are able to suppress piracy and armed robbery against ships and to uphold maritime security. The necessary conditions for doing so have been peace, and international cooperation built on mutual trust and political will. In these respects, the conditions for maintaining maritime security in postcolonial Southeast Asia differ little from those of the colonial period.

---

[9] Ibid., 162–3; on the fishing policies of Indonesia and other Southeast Asian states, see Butcher, *Closing of the Frontier*.

Bibliography

Manuscripts and Archival Sources

France

Centre des Archives d'outre-mer (CAOM), Aix-en-Provence
Anciens fonds: Fonds ministérielles
    Série géographique: Indochine
Fonds des Amiraux/Gouvernement général de l'Indochine
    Fichier Boudet

Service historique de la Défense (SHD), Vincennes
Archives de la Marine
    Série BB: Service général (1790–1913)
Service historique de l'Armée de terre
    Sous-série 10H: Indochine (1867–1956)
    Sous-série 15H: Centre militaire d'information et de documentations sur l'Outre-mer

Spain

Archivo General de Indias (through the online Portal de Archivos Españoles (PARES))
FILIPINAS: Audiencia de Filipinas (1564–1850)

United Kingdom

The National Archives (TNA), Kew
Air Ministry, the Royal Air Force and related bodies
    AIR2: Air Ministry and Ministry of Defence: Registered Files (1887–1991)

Colonial Office
Straits Settlements, Original Correspondence (1838–1946)
CO 882: War and Colonial Department and Colonial Office: Confidential Print Eastern (1843–1970)

Foreign Office
FO 71: Political and Other Departments: General Correspondence before 1906, Sulu Islands (1849–1888).

FO 371: Political Departments: General Correspondence (1906–1966).
WO 203: South East Asia Command: Military Headquarters Papers, Second World War (1932–1949).

United States

National Archives and Records Administration (NARA), Washington, DC
RG 45: Naval Records Collection of the Office of Naval Records and Library Navy Subject Files (1775–1927)
M617: Returns from US Military Posts (1800–1916)

Manuscript Division, Library of Congress (MDLC), Washington, DC
Hugh Lenox Scott Papers (HLSP)
John J. Pershing Papers
Tasker Howard Bliss Papers (THBP)

Legislation, Official Print and Reports

Compilations of Legislations and Treaties

Aitchison, C. U. (ed.), *A Collection of Treaties, Engagements, and Sunnuds, relating to India and Neighboring Countries*, 1 (Calcutta: Savielle and Cranenburgh, 1862).
British International Law Cases: A Collection of Decisions of Courts in the British Isles on Points of International Law 3 (London: Stevens and Sons, 1965).
Fonssagrives, J.-B. and E. Laffont (eds.), *Répertoire alphabétique de législation et de réglementation de la Cochinchine*, 2, 4 (Paris: A. Rousseau, 1890).
Hertslet, G. E. P. (ed.), *Hertslet's China Treaties: Treaties etc., between Great Britain and China in Force on the 1st January, 1908* 1, 3rd edn. (London: Harrison and Sons, 1908).
Isambert, F.-A., *Recueil général des anciennes lois françaises, depuis l'an 420 jusqu'à la Révolution de 1789* 14 (Paris: Belin-Leprieur, 1829).
Lauterpacht, H. and J. F. Williams (eds.), *Annual Digest and Reports of Public International Law Cases* (London: Longmans, Green and Co., 1932).
Liaw Yock Fang, *Undang-undang Melaka* (The Hague: Martinus Nijhoff, 1976).
Recopilación de leyes de los Reinos de las Indias 2 (Madrid: Boix, 1841).
The Laws of the Straits Settlements 1 (London: Waterlow and Sons, 1920).
United Nations Convention on the Law of the Sea (United Nations General Assembly, 1982; entered into force 1994).
Winstedt, R. and P. E. De Josselin De Jong, 'The Maritime Laws of Malacca', *Journal of the Malayan Branch of the Royal Asiatic Society*, 29:3 (1956), 22–59.

United Kingdom: Parliamentary Papers (PP) and Debates

PP HC.114 (1850): Pirates. Return of bounties paid for the capture and destruction of pirates, under the act 6 Geo. 4, c. 49.
PP HC.238 (1850): Malay pirates. Return of the names of any British vessels attacked or plundered by Malay or Dyak pirates, from 1839 to 1849.

PP C.466 (1872): Papers (with a map) relating to recent proceedings at Salangore consequent upon the seizure by pirates of a junk owned by Chinese merchants of Penang; and the murder of the passengers and crew.

PP C.1111 (1874): Correspondence relating to the affairs of certain native states in the Malay Peninsula, in the neighborhood of the Straits Settlements.

House of Commons Debate, 10 July 1851. Commons and Lords Hansard, Official Report of Debates in Parliament, vol. 118, cc 498–9.

United States: Official Reports

Annual Report of Major General Arthur MacArthur, U.S. Army, Commanding, Division of the Philippines 1 (Manila: P.I., 1901).

Annual Report of the Governor of the Moro Province (*ARGMP*) (Zamboanga: The Mindanao Herald Pub. Co., 1903–10).

Annual Report of the Philippine Commission (*ARPC*) (Washington, DC: Government Printing Office, 1903–08).

Annual Reports of the Navy Department: Report of the Secretary of the Navy: Miscellaneous Reports (*ARSN*) (Washington, DC: Government Printing Office, 1900–03).

Annual Reports of the War Department (*ARWD*) (Washington, DC: Government Printing Office, 1899–1909).

Other Miscellaneous Official Print and Reports

House of Commons, Statement exhibiting the Moral and Material Progress and Condition of India, 1861–62 (London: House of Commons, 1863).

ICC International Maritime Bureau, 'Piracy and Armed Robbery against Ships: Report for the Period 1 January–31 December 2017' (London: ICC International Maritime Bureau, January 2018), available at www.icc-ccs.org/reports/2017-Annual-IMB-Piracy-Report.pdf (downloaded 4 June 2018).

Ministère des affaires étrangères, *Affaires du Tonkin* 1–2 (Documents diplomatiques) (Paris: Impr. nationale, 1883).

Philippine Claim to North Borneo 1 (Manila: National Government Publication, 1963).

United States Congress, *Treaty with the Sultan of Sulu*, US Congress 56, 1st session, Senate doc 136.

Newspapers and Periodicals

Annales catholiques (Paris).
Annales de la propagation de la foi (Paris).
Courrier de Saigon (Saigon).
The Economist (London).
El Globo (Madrid).
Java-bode (Batavia).
Journal de l'An (Bourg).
Journal des débats politiques et littéraires (Paris).

Bibliography 239

Journal of the Indian Archipelago and Eastern Asia (Singapore).
Le Figaro (Paris).
La Gazette Géographique (Paris).
Journal officiel de la République française (Paris).
L'Illustration: Journal universel (Paris).
Manila Times (Manila).
Mindanao Herald (Zamboanga).
Le Monde illustré (Paris).
Le Moniteur (Paris).
New York Herald (New York).
New York Times (New York).
Penang Argus (Penang).
Penang Gazette (Penang).
Philippine Inquirer (Manila).
Revue des deux mondes (Paris).
Revue maritime et coloniale (Paris).
Singapore Free Press (Singapore).
Singapore Free Press and Mercantile Advertiser (Singapore).
Straits Times (Singapore).
Straits Times Overland Journal (Singapore).
Straits Times Weekly Issue (Singapore).
Le Temps (Paris).
The Times (London).
Le Voleur (Paris).

Other Printed Sources

[Anonymous], 'Cochinchine', *Annales de la propagation de la foi* 33 (1861), 71–4.
   'Extraits de l'éxposé de la situation de l'empire, 13 January 1863', *Revue maritime et coloniale* 7 (1863), 165–90.
   'Le Commerce de la France dans l'Extrême orient', *Revue maritime et coloniale* 33 (1872), 221–56.
   'The Piracy and Slave Trade of the Indian Archipelago', *Journal of the Indian Archipelago and Eastern Asia* 3 (1849), 581–8.
Abdul Rahman, Tunku, 'Speech before the Malaysian Parliament', in R. W. Winks and J. Bastin (eds.), *Malaysia: Selected Historical Readings* (Kuala Lumpur: Oxford University Press, 1966), 434–7.
Ageron, C.-R., *L'Anticolonialisme en France de 1871 à 1914* (Paris: Presses universitaires de France, 1973).
Ali Haji ibn Ahmad, *The Precious Gift [Tuhfat al-Nafis]: An Annotated Translation by Virginia Matheson and Barbara Watson Andaya* (Kuala Lumpur: Oxford University Press, 1982).
Anson, A. E. H., *About Others and Myself, 1745 to 1920* (London: John Murray, 1920).
d'Aries, M., 'La Cochinchine française: Son organisation', *Revue maritime et coloniale* 31 (1871), 165–202.
Ayala, V., *Discurso que, en la solemne acción de gracias al Todo Poderoso por la victoria que en los días 28 de febrero y 1º de marzo del presente año consiguió del*

pérfido pirata Joloano el valiente y leal ejército de Filipinas bajo las órdenes inmediatas del escelentísimo señor capitán general D. Antonio de Urbiztondo, marqués de La Solana, pronunció el M.R.P. Fr. Vicente Ayala (Manila: D. M. Ramirez, 1851).

Banck, J. E., *Atchin's verheffing en val* (Rotterdam: Nijgh and Van Ditmar, 1873).

Barrantes, V., *Guerras piráticas de Filipinas contra mindanaos y joloanos* (Madrid: Manuel G. Hernandez, 1878).

Bevin, E., *Au Tonkin: Milices et piraterie* (Paris: Limoges: H. Charles-Lavauzelle, 1891).

Blumentritt, F., 'Versuch einer Ethnographie der Philippinen', *Ergänzungsheft 67 zu Petermanns Mittheilungen* (Gotha: Justus Perthes, 1882).

Bresnahan, R. J., *In Time of Hesitation* (Quezon City: New Day Publishers, 1981).

Carpeaux, L., *La Chasse aux pirates* (Paris: B. Grasset, 1913).

Charles-Lavauzelle, H. (ed.), *La Piraterie au Tonkin* (Paris and Limoges: H. Charles-Lavauzelle, 1891).

Cloman, S. A., *Myself and a Few Moros* (Garden City, NY: Doubleday, Page and Co., 1923).

Colomer, Mgr, 'Les Missionnaires dominicain espagnol au Tonkin', *Annales catholiques* (11 September 1887), 581–4.

Cornets de Groot, J. P., *Notices historiques sur les pirateries commises dans l'archipel Indien-oriental* (La Haye: Belinfante Frères, 1847).

Crawfurd, J., *A Descriptive Dictionary of the Indian Islands and Adjacent Countries* (London: Bradbury and Evans, 1856).

History of the Indian Archipelago: Containing an Account of the Manners, Art, Languages, Religions, Institutions, and Commerce of its Inhabitants 1, 3 (Edinburgh: Archibald and Co., 1820).

'Malay Pirates', Extract from the Singapore Chronicle, republished in *The Asiatic Journal and Monthly Register for British India and Its Dependencies* 19 (1825), 243–5.

Dalrymple, A., *An Historical Collection of the Several Voyages and Discoveries in the South Pacific Ocean* 1 (London: J. Nourse etc., 1770).

Davidson, W. H., 'Jikiri's Last Stand', *Quartermaster Review* (July–August 1935), 14–16.

Deschanel, P., *La Question du Tonkin* (Paris: Berger-Levrault, 1883).

Dupuis, J., *L'Ouverture du fleuve rouge au commerce* (Paris: Challamel aîné, 1879).

Dutreuil de Rhins, J.-L., *Le Royaume d'Annam et les Annamites* (Paris: Librairie Plon, 1889).

Duval, C., *Souvenirs militaires* (Paris: Imprimerie des arts et manufactures, 1900).

Exquemelin, A., *De Americaensche zee-rovers* (Amsterdam: Jan ten Hoorn, 1678).

Fa-hsien, *The Travels of Fa-hsien* (London: Routledge and Kegan Paul, 1956).

Ferry, J., *Le Tonkin et la mère-patrie* (Paris: V. Havard, 1890).

Finley, J. P., 'The Commercial Awakening of the Moro and Pagan', *The North American Review* 197:688 (1913), 325–34.

Francis, G. [Francis Garnier], *La Cochinchine française en 1864* (Paris: E. Dentu, 1864).

De la Colonisation de la Cochinchine (Paris: Challamel aîné, 1865).

Frey, H., *Pirates et rebelles au Tonkin* (Paris: Hachette, 1892).
Garnier, F., *Voyage d'exploration en Indo-Chine* (Paris: Hachette et Cie, 1885).
Girard, A., *Étude sur la Tourane et la Cochinchine* (Paris: Corréard, 1859).
Grimley, Mgr, 'La Traite des Annamites', *Les Missions catholiques* (21 March 1873), 133–4.
Gros-Desveaux, L., 'Une Mission au Tonkin sur la canonnière la Massue, 1879', *Bulletin Société bretonne de géographie* 2 (1883), 109–43.
Harmand, J., *L'Indo-Chine française* (Paris: Impr. de C. Pariset, 1887).
de Hollander, J. J. (ed.), *Handleiding bij de beoefening der land- en volkenkunde van Nederlandsch Oost-Indië* 1 (Breda: Broese and Comp., 1874).
Jansen, A. J. F., 'Aanteekeningen omtrent Sollok en de solloksche zeeroovers', *Tijdschrift voor Indische taal-, land- en volkenkunde* 7 (1858), 211–43.
Jarman, R. L. (ed.), *Annual Reports of the Straits Settlements 1855–1941* (Cambridge: Archive Editions, 1998).
Johnson, C. and D. Cordingly, *A General History of the Robberies and Murders of the Most Notorious Pirates* (London: Conway 1998 [1724]).
Keppel, H., *A Visit to the Indian Archipelago, in H. M. Ship Maeander* 1 (London: Richard Bentley, 1853).
The Expedition to Borneo of H.M.S. Dido for the Suppression of Piracy (New York: Harper and Brothers, 1846).
de Kergaradec, M., 'Rapport sur la reconnaissance du Fleuve Rouge du Tonkin' [1], *Revue Maritime et Coloniale* 54 (1877), 321–52.
'Rapport sur la reconnaissance du Fleuve Rouge du Tonkin' [2], *Revue Maritime et Coloniale* 55 (1877), 20–42.
Kruijt, J. A., *De Atjeh-oorlog* (The Hague: Loman and Funke, 1896).
de Lanessan, J.-L., *La Colonisation française en Indo-Chine* (Paris: F. Alcan, 1895).
Le Myre de Vilers, C.-M., *Les Institutions civiles de la Cochinchine (1879–1881)* (Paris: E. Paul, 1908).
Logan, J. R., 'Malay Amoks and Piracies', *Journal of the Indian Archipelago and Eastern Asia* 3 (1849), 463–7.
Loviot, F., *A Lady's Captivity among Chinese Pirates* (London: Routledge 1859).
Lyautey, H., 'Du Rôle colonial de l'armée', *Revue des deux mondes* (15 January 1900), 308–28.
Mackenzie, H., *Storms and Sunshine of a Soldier's Life* (Edinburgh: D. Douglas, 1884).
Mat-Gioi [A. de Pouvourville], *La Politique indo-chinoise* (Paris: A. Savine, 1894).
Chez les pirates (Hanoi: Impr. de l'Indo-Chine française, 1898).
Maxwell, P. B., *Our Malay Conquests* (Westminster: P. S. King, 1878).
McNair, J. F., *Perak and the Malays* (Kuala Lumpur: Art Printing Works, 1972 [1878]).
Montero y Vidal, J., *Historia de la piratería malayo-mahometana en Mindanao, Joló y Borneo* 1–2 (Madrid: Manuel Tello, 1888).
Osborne, S., *My Journal in Malayan Waters or the Blockade of Quedah* (London: Routledge, Warne and Routledge, 1860).
Paulus, A., 'L'Esclavage en Indo-Chine', *La Gazette géographique* 1 (1885), 337–42.

Périn, G., *Discours politiques et notes de voyages* (Paris: Societé nouvelle de librairie et d'édition, 1905).

Postel, R., *L'Extrême Orient* (Paris: Degorce-Cadot, 1882).

Sur les Bords du Mé-Không (Paris: Libr. générale de vulgarisation, DL 1884).

de Pouvourville, A., *Chasseur de pirates* (Paris: Editions du 'Monde moderne', 1928).

Raffles, S., *Memoir of the Life and Public Services of Sir Thomas Stamford Raffles* (London: John Murray, 1830).

Raffles, T. S., *The History of Java* 1 (London: John Murray, 1817).

Retord, Mgr, 'Lettre de Mgr Retord, vicaire apostolique', *Annales de la propagation de la foi* 30 (1858), 201–45.

'Missions de Tong-King', *Annales de la propagation de la foi* 23 (1851), 268–89.

Rivière, H., *Correspondance politique du commandant Rivière au Tonkin* (avril 1882–mai 1883) (Hanoi: Le-Van-Tan, 1933).

Santiago Patero, D., *Sistema que conviene adoptar para acabar con la piratería* (Madrid: Miguel Ginesta, 1872).

Sawyer, F. H., *Inhabitants of the Philippines* (New York: Charles Scribne's Sons, 1900).

Scott, H. L., *Some Memories of a Soldier* (New York: The Century Co., 1928).

Senez, 'De Saigon au nord du Tonquin: Voyage du Bourayne (23 janvier – 16 février 1872)', *Revue maritime et coloniale* 34 (1872), 346–60.

'Rapport nautique sur l'exploration des côtes de Cochinchine et du golfe du Tonquin (octobre et novembre 1872)', *Revue maritime et coloniale* 37 (1873), 5–32.

Snouck Hurgronje, C., *The Achehnese*, 1–2 (Leiden: Brill, 1906).

de St-André, L., *Le Tour du monde* (Paris: Librairie Hachette, 1913).

St Augustine of Hippo, *City of God*, transl. by M. Dods (Peabody, MA: Hendrickson Publ., 2009).

St John, S., *The Life of Sir James Brooke* (Edinburgh: William Blackwood and Sons, 1874).

Stibbe, D. G., 'Zeeroof', in D. G. Stibbe (ed.), *Encyclopædie van Nederlandsch-Indië* 4 (The Hague: Martinus Nijhoff, 1921), 821–6.

Swettenham, F. A., *British Malaya: An Account of the Origin and Progress of British Influence in Malaya* (London: John Lane, 1907).

Taboulet, G., *La Geste française en Indochine* 1–2 (Paris: Librairie d'Amérique et d'Orient, 1955–56).

Taillandier de Montjean, M. l'abbé, 'M. l'abbé Taillandier de Montjean to M. l'archiprêtre de la Trinité', *Journal des débats politiques et littéraires* (14 July 1852).

Temminck, C. J., *Coup d'oeil général sur les possessions néerlandaises dans l'Inde archipélagique* 2 (Leide: A. Arnz and Comp., 1847).

Veth, P. J., 'De heilige oorlog in den Indischen Archipel', *Tijdschrift voor Nederlandsch Indië* 4:1 (1870), 167–76.

Wallace, A. R., *The Malay Archipelago: The Land of the Orang-utan and the Bird of Paradise: A Narrative of Travel, with Studies of Man and Nature* (Auckland: The Floating Press, 2014 [1869]).

de Wilde, A., *Nederduitsch–Maleisch en Soendasch woordenboek* (Amsterdam: Johannes Müller, 1841).
Worcester, C., *The Philippine Islands and Their People* (New York: Macmillan, 1898).
Xavier Brau de Saint Pol Lias, [M. F.], 'Affaires coloniales', *La Gazette géographique* 1 (1885), 305–6.

Literature

Abel, S. C., 'A Covert War at Sea: Piracy and Political Economy in Malaya, 1824–1874', unpubl. Ph.D. thesis, Northern Illinois University (2016).
Ageron, C. R., *France coloniale ou parti colonial?* (Paris: Presses universitaires de France, 1978).
Amoroso, D. J., 'Inheriting the "Moro Problem": Muslim Authority and Colonial Rule in British Malaya and the Philippines', in J. Go and A. L. Foster (eds.), *The American Colonial State in the Philippines: Global Perspectives* (Durham, NC: Duke University Press, 2003), 118–47.
Andaya, B. W., 'The Anak Raja in 18th-Century Kedah: A Case Study from Eighteenth-Century Kedah', *Journal of Southeast Asian Studies* 7:2 (1976), 162–86.
  To Live as Brothers: Southeast Sumatra in the Seventeenth and Eighteenth Centuries (Honolulu: University of Hawai'i Press, 1993).
Andaya, B. W. and L. Y. Andaya, *A History of Malaysia* (London: Macmillan, 1982).
  A History of Malaysia, 3rd edn. (Houndmills, Basingstoke: Palgrave Macmillan, 2017).
Andaya, L. Y., *The Heritage of Arung Palakka* (The Hague: Martinus Nijhoff, 1981).
Andrew, C. M., 'The French Colonialist Movement during the Third Republic: The Unofficial Mind of Imperialism', *Transactions of the Royal Historical Society* 26 (1976), 143–66.
Anjum, N. A., 'Indian Shipping and Security on the Seas in the Days of the Mughal Empire', *Studies in People's History* 2:2 (2015), 155–68.
Antony, R. J., 'Introduction: The Shadowy World of the Greater China Seas', in R. J. Antony (ed.), *Elusive Pirates, Pervasive Smugglers: Violence and Clandestine Trade in the Greater China Seas* (Hong Kong University Press, 2010), 1–14.
  Like Froth Floating on the Sea: The World of Pirates and Seafarers in Late Imperial South China (Berkeley, CA: Institute for East Asian Studies, University of California, 2003).
  'Maritime Violence and State Formation in Vietnam', in S. Eklöf Amirell and L. Müller (eds.), *Persistent Piracy: Maritime Violence and State-Formation in Global Historical Perspective* (Houndmills, Basingstoke: Palgrave Macmillan, 2014), 113–30.
  'Piracy on the South China Coast through Modern Times', in B. A. Elleman, A. Forbes and D. Rosenberg (eds.), *Piracy and Maritime Crime: Historical and Modern Case Studies* (Newport, RI: Naval War College Press, 2010), 35–50.
Arnold, J. M., *The Moro War: How America Battled a Muslim Insurgency in the Philippine Jungle, 1902–1913* (New York: Bloomsbury Press, 2011).

Barnard, T. P., 'Celates, Rayat-Laut, Pirates: The Orang Laut and Their Decline in History', *Journal of the Malaysian Branch of the Royal Asiatic Society* 80:2 (2007): 33–49.

Barth, B. and J. Osterhammel (eds.), *Zivilisierungsmissionen: Imperiale Weltverbesserung seit dem 18. Jahrhundert* (Constance: UVK Verlagsgesellschaft, 2005).

Barth, V. and R. Cvetkovski (eds.), *Imperial Co-operation and Transfer, 1870–1930: Empires and Encounters* (London: Bloomsbury, 2015).

Baudrit, A., *Bétail humain: Rapt, vente, infanticide dans l'Indochine française et dans la Chine du Sud* (Paris: Connaissances et Savoirs, 2008 [1943]).

Beckman, R. and M. Page, 'Piracy and Armed Robbery against Ships', in M. Gill (ed.), *The Handbook of Security* (Houndmills, Basingstoke: Palgrave Macmillan, 2014), 234–55.

Belmessous, S. (ed.), *Empire by Treaty: Negotiating European Expansion, 1600–1900* (Oxford University Press, 2014).

Benton, L., *A Search for Sovereignty: Law and Geography in European Empires, 1400–1900* (Cambridge University Press, 2010).
  'Legal Spaces of Empire: Piracy and the Origins of Ocean Regionalism', *Comparative Studies in Society and History* 47:4 (2005), 700–24.

Bessire, F., 'Le Beauchêne de Lesage ou la discrète accession du pirate au rang de Héros de roman', in S. Requemora and S. Linon-Chipon (eds.), *Les Tyrans de la mer: Pirates, corsaires et flibustiers* (Paris: CELAT/Presses de l'Université de Paris-Sorbonne, 2002), 349–56.

Blue, A. D., 'Piracy on the China Coast', *Journal of the Hong Kong Branch of the Royal Asiatic Society* 5 (1965), 69–85.

Bonura, C and L. J. Sears, 'Introduction: Knowledges that Travel in Southeast Asian Area Studies', in L. J. Sears (ed.), *Knowing Southeast Asian Subjects* (Seattle: University of Washington Press, 2011), 3–32.

Boxer, C. R., 'Piracy in the South China Sea', *History Today* (December 1980), 40–4.

Brands, H. W., *Bound to Empire: The United States and the Philippines* (New York: Oxford University Press, 1992).

Brinton, D. G., 'Professor Blumentritt's Studies of the Philippines', *American Anthropologist* 1:1 (1899), 122–5.

Brocheux, P. and D. Hémery, *Indochina: An Ambiguous Colonization, 1858–1954* (Berkeley: University of California Press, 2009).

Brooke, G. E., 'Piracy' in W. Makepeace, G. E. Brooke and R. St. J. Braddell (eds.), *One Hundred Years of Singapore* 1 (Singapore: Oxford University Press, 1991), 290–300.

Brydon, D., P. Forsgren and G. Fur (eds.), *Concurrent Imaginaries, Postcolonial Worlds: Toward Revised Histories* (Leiden: Brill, 2017).

Burgess Jr., D. R., 'Piracy in the Public Sphere: The Henry Every Trials and the Battle for Meaning in Seventeenth-Century Print Culture', *Journal of British Studies* 48 (2009), 887–913.

Butcher, J. G., *The Closing of the Frontier: A History of the Marine Fisheries of Southeast Asia c. 1850–2000* (Singapore: Institute of Southeast Asian Studies, 2004).

Buzan, B., O. Wæver and J. de Wilde, *Security: A New Framework for Analysis* (Boulder, CO: Lynne Rienner, 1998).

Byler, C., 'Pacifying the Moros: American Military Government in the Southern Philippines, 1899–1913', *Military Review* 85:3 (2005), 41–5.
Cady, J. F., *The Roots of French Imperialism in Eastern Asia* (Ithaca, NY: Cornell University Press, 1967).
Calanca, P., 'Wokou: Un terme au long cours?', in M. Battesti (ed.), *La Piraterie au fil de l'histoire: Un défi pour l'État* (Paris: Presses de l'Université Paris-Sorbonne, 2014), 63–80.
à Campo, J. N. F. M, 'Asymmetry, Disparity and Cyclicity: Charting the Piracy Conflict in Colonial Indonesia', *International Journal of Maritime History* 19:1 (2007), 35–62.
  'Discourse without Discussion: Representations of Piracy in Colonial Indonesia 1816–25', *Journal of Southeast Asian Studies* 34:2 (2003), 199–214.
  'Patronen, processen en periodisering van zeeroof and zeeroofbestrijding in Nederlands-Indië', *Tijdschrift voor sociale en economische geschiedenis* 3:2 (2006), 78–107.
Chakrabarty, D., *Provincializing Europe: Postcolonial Thought and Historical Difference* (Princeton University Press, 2000).
Chappell, J., 'Maritime Raiding, International Law and the Suppression of Piracy on the South China Coast, 1842–1869', *International History Review* 40:3 (2017), 473–92.
Cheng, Wei-chung, *War, Trade and Piracy in the China Seas (1622–1683)* (Leiden: Brill, 2013).
Chérif, D., 'Pirates, rebelles et ordre colonial en Indochine française au XIXe siècle', *Insaniyat* 62 (2013), 11–42.
Chew, E., *Arming the Periphery: The Arms Trade in the Indian Ocean during the Age of Global Empire* (Houndmills, Basingstoke: Palgrave Macmillan, 2012).
Chomsky, N., *Pirates and Emperors* (Brattleboro, VT: Amana Books, 1986).
Clulow, A., 'European Maritime Violence and Territorial States in Early Modern Asia, 1600–1650', *Itinerario* 33:3 (2009), 72–94.
Coats, G. Y., 'The Philippine Constabulary in Mindanao and Sulu, 1903–1917', *Bulletin of American Historical Collection* 8 (1975), 7–32.
Cooper, N. J., *France in Indochina: Colonial Encounters* (Oxford: Berg, 2001).
Cowan, C. D., 'Early Penang and the Rise of Singapore 1805–1832', *Journal of the Malayan Branch of the Royal Asiatic Society* 23:2 (1950), 2–210.
  Nineteenth-Century Malaya: The Origins of British Political Control (London: Oxford University Press, 1961).
Cultru, P., *Histoire de la Cochinchine française* (Paris: A. Challamel, 1910).
Davis, B. C., 'States of Banditry: The Nguyen Government, Bandit Rule, and the Culture of Power in the Post-Taiping China-Vietnam Borderlands', unpubl. Ph.D. thesis, University of Washington (2008).
Deroo, É. and P. Vallaud, *Indochine française, 1856–1956: Guerres, mythes et passions* (Paris: le Grand livre du mois, 2003).
Dickinson, E. D., 'Is the Crime of Piracy Obsolete?', *Harvard Law Review* 38:3 (1925), 334–60.
Doyle, L., 'Inter-imperiality: Dialectics in a Postcolonial World History', *Interventions* 16:2 (2014), 159–96.
Dutreb, M., *L'Amiral Dupré et la conquête du Tonkin* (Paris: Au siège de la Société, 1924).

Dutton, G. E., *The Tay Son Uprising: Society and Rebellion in Eighteenth-Century Vietnam* (Honolulu: University of Hawaii Press, 2006).

Earle, P., *The Pirate Wars* (London: Methuen, 2003).

Eklöf Amirell, S., '"An Extremely Mild Form of Slavery" … "of the Worst Sort": American Perceptions of Slavery in the Sulu Sultanate (Southern Philippines), 1899–1904', in H. Hägerdal (ed.), *Slavery and Slave Trading in the Indian Ocean World and Beyond* (Athens: Ohio University Press, 2020).

'Civilizing Pirates: Nineteenth-Century British Ideas of Progress and the Suppression of Piracy in the Malay Archipelago', *HumaNetten* 41 (2018), 25–45.

'Pirates and Pearls: Jikiri and the Challenge to Maritime Security and American Sovereignty in the Sulu Archipelago, 1907–1909', *International Journal of Maritime History* 29:1 (2017), 1–24.

Pirates in Paradise: A Modern History of Southeast Asia's Maritime Marauders (Copenhagen: NIAS Press, 2006).

'Political Piracy and Maritime Terrorism: A Comparison between the Straits of Malacca and the Southern Philippines', in G. G. Ong-Webb (ed.), *Piracy, Maritime Terrorism and Securing the Malacca Straits* (Singapore: Institute of Southeast Asian Studies, 2006), 52–67.

'Suppressing Piracy in Asia: Decolonization and International Relations in a Maritime Border Region (the Sulu Sea), 1959–63', in J. Kleinen and M. Osseweijer (eds.), *Pirates, Ports, and Coasts in Asia: Historical and Contemporary Perspectives* (Singapore: Institute of Southeast Asian Studies, 2010), 222–36.

'The Tools of Terror: Technological Development and Modern Piracy', in M. Battesti (ed.), *La Piraterie au fil de l'histoire: Un défi pour l'État* (Paris: Presses de l'Université Paris-Sorbonne, 2014), 185–96.

Eklöf Amirell, S. and L. Müller, 'Introduction: Persistent Piracy in World History', in S. Eklöf Amirell and L. Müller (eds.), *Persistent Piracy: Maritime Violence and State-Formation in Global Historical Perspective* (Houndmills, Basingstoke: Palgrave Macmillan, 2014), 1–23.

Elleman, B. A., 'The Taiping Rebellion, Piracy and the Arrow War', in B. A. Elleman, A. Forbes and D. Rosenberg (eds.), *Piracy and Maritime Crime: Historical and Modern Case Studies* (Newport, RI: Naval War College Press, 2010), 51–78.

Ericson Wolke, L., *Lasse i Gatan: Kaparkriget och det svenska stormaktsväldets fall* (Lund: Historiska media, 1997).

Ewing, J. F., 'Juramentado: Institutionalized Suicide among the Moros of the Philippines', *Anthropological Quarterly* 28:4 (1955), 148–55.

Federspiel, H. M., 'Islam and Muslims in the Southern Territories of the Philippine Islands during the American Colonial Period (1898 to 1946)', *Journal of Southeast Asian Studies* 29:2 (1998), 340–56.

Fillafer, F. L., 'A World Connecting? From the Unity of History to Global History', *History and Theory* 56:1 (2017), 3–37.

Finch, M. P. M., *A Progressive Occupation? The Gallieni-Lyautey Method and Colonial Pacification in Tonkin and Madagascar, 1885–1900* (Oxford University Press, 2013).

Fisher, M. H. 'Indirect Rule in the British Empire: The Foundations of the Residency System in India (1764–1858)', *Modern Asian Studies* 18:3 (1984), 393–428.
Fourniau, C. 'Colonial Wars before 1914: The Case of France in Indochina', in J. A. de Moor and H. L. Wesseling (eds.), *Imperialism and War: Essays on Colonial Wars in Asia and Africa* (Leiden: Brill, 1989), 72–86.
  Vietnam: Domination coloniale et résistance nationale, 1858–1914 (Paris: Les Indes savantes, 2002).
Fox, E. T., *Jolly Rogers: The True History of Pirate Flags* (Middletown, DE: Fox Historical, 2015).
Fox, G. E., *British Admirals and Chinese Pirates* (London: K. Paul, Trench, Trubner, 1940).
Frake, C. O., 'The Genesis of Kinds of People in the Sulu Archipelago', in A. S. Dil (ed.), *Language and Cultural Description: Essays* (Stanford University Press, 1980), 311–32.
Fulton, R. A. *Moroland: The History of Uncle Sam and the Moros 1899–1920* (Bend, OR: Tumalo Creek Press, 2009).
Fur, G. 'Concurrences as a Methodology for Discerning Concurrent Histories', in D. Brydon, P. Forsgren and G. Fur (eds.), *Concurrent Imaginaries, Postcolonial Worlds: Toward Revised Histories* (Leiden: Brill, 2017), 41–68.
Gallagher, J. and R. Robinson, 'The Imperialism of Free Trade', *Economic History Review* 6:1 (1953), 1–15.
Gaynor, J. L., *Intertidal History in Island Southeast Asia: Submerged Genealogy and the Legacy of Coastal Capture* (Ithaca, NY: Cornell University Press, 2016).
  'Piracy in the Offing: The Law of Lands and the Limits of Sovereignty at Sea', *Anthropological Quarterly* 85:3 (2012), 817–57.
Glete, J., *Navies and Nations: Warships, Navies and State Building in Europe and America, 1500–1860* (Stockholm: Almqvist and Wiksell, 1993).
  Warfare at Sea, 1500–1650: Maritime Conflicts and the Transformation of Europe (London: Routledge, 2000).
Gong, G. W., *The Standard of 'Civilisation' in International Society* (Oxford: Clarendon Press, 1984).
Gowing, P. G., 'Mandate in Moroland: The American Government of Muslim Filipinos, 1899–1920', unpubl. Ph.D. thesis, Syracuse University (1968).
  'Muslim–American Relations in the Philippines, 1899–1920', in P. G. Gowing and R.D. M. Amis (eds.), *The Muslim Filipinos; There History, Society and Contemporary Problems* (Manila: Solidarided, 1974).
Graham, G. S., *Great Britain in the Indian Ocean: A Study of Maritime Enterprise 1810–1850* (Oxford University Press, 1967).
Gullick, J. M., *A History of Selangor, 1742–1957* (Singapore: Eastern Universities Press, 1960).
  'Captain Speedy of Larut', *Journal of the Malayan Branch of the Royal Asiatic Society* 26:3 (1953), 3–103.
  'The Kuala Langat Piracy Trial', *Journal of the Malaysian Branch of the Royal Asiatic Society* 69:2 (1996), 101–14.
  'Tunku Kudin in Selangor (1868–1878)', *Journal of the Malaysian Branch of the Royal Asiatic Society* 59:2 (1986), 5–50.

Guyon, G., 'Les Coutumes pénales des Roles d'Oléron', in Centre d'études et de recherches en droit des affaires et des contrats, Université Montesquieu-Bordeaux IV (ed.), *Études à la mémoire de Christian Lapoyade-Deschamps* (Presses Universitaires de Bordeaux, 2003), 327–43.

Hägerdal, H., *Hindu Rulers, Muslim Subjects: Lombok and Bali in the Seventeenth and Eighteenth Centuries* (Bangkok: White Lotus, 2001).

Hal, K. R., *Maritime Trade and State Development in Early Southeast Asia* (Honolulu: University of Hawaii Press, 1985).

Harding, C. 'Hostis Humani Generis: The Pirate as Outlaw in the Early Modern Law of the Sea', in C. Jowitt, *Pirates? The Politics of Plunder, 1550–1650* (Houndmills, Basingstoke: Palgrave Macmillan, 2006), 20–38.

Harrington, F. H., 'The Anti-imperialist Movement in the United States', *The Mississippi Valley Historical Review* 22:2 (1935), 211–30.

Hawkley, E. P., 'Reviving the Reconquista in Southeast Asia: Moros and the Making of the Philippines, 1565–1662', *Journal of World History* 25:2 (2014), 285–310.

Heller-Roazen, D., *The Enemy of All: Piracy and the Law of Nations* (New York: Zone Books, 2009).

Higgins, R. L., 'Japanese Piracy in China', in A. T. Embree (ed.), *Encyclopedia of Asian History* 3 (London: Collier Macmillan, 1988), s.v. 'Piracy', 261–2.

Hill, C. 'Radical Pirates?' in M. C. Jacob and J. Jacob (eds.), *The Origins of Anglo-American Radicalism* (London: Allen and Unwin, 1984), 17–32.

Histoire militaire de l'Indochine 1–2 (Hanoi: Impr. d'Extrême-Orient, 1930).

Hobsbawm, E., *Bandits* (New York: Delacorte Press, 1969).

Howe, S., *The New Imperial Histories Reader* (London: Routledge, 2010).

Hurley, V., *Jungle Patrol: The Story of the Philippine Constabulary* (Salem, OR: Cerberos Books, 2011 [1938]).

  Swish of the Kris: The Story of the Moros (Salem, OR: Cerberos Books, 2010 [1938]).

Junker, L. L., *Raiding, Trading, and Feasting: The Political Economy of Philippine Chiefdoms* (Honolulu: University of Hawaii Press, 1999).

Kaiser, W. and G. Calafat, 'Violence, Protection and Commerce: Corsairing and *ars piratica* in the Early Modern Mediterranean', in S. Eklöf Amirell and L. Müller (eds.), *Persistent Piracy: Maritime Violence and State-Formation in Global Historical Perspective* (Houndmills, Basingstoke: Palgrave Macmillan, 2014), 69–92.

Kathirithamby-Wells, J. and C. Hall, 'The Age of Transition', in N. Tarling (ed.), *The Cambridge History of Southeast Asia* 1:2 (Cambridge University Press, 1992), 228–75.

Kempe, M., '"Even in the Remotest Corners of the World": Globalized Piracy and International Law, 1500–1900', *Journal of Global History* 5:3 (2010), 353–72.

Ken, W. L., 'The Trade of Singapore, 1819–96', *Journal of the Malayan Branch of the Royal Asiatic Society* 33:4 (1960), 4–315.

Khalilieh, H. S., *Islamic Maritime Law* (Leiden: Brill, 1998).

Kiefer, T. M., *The Tausug* (New York: Holt, Rinehart and Winston, 1972).

  'The Tausug Polity and the Sultanate of Sulu', *Sulu Studies* 1 (1972), 19–64.

Kleinen, J., 'Maritime Piracy through a Barbarian Lens: Punishment and Representation (the SS Naoma Hijack Case [1890–91])', in J. Kleinen and M. Osseweijer (eds.), *Pirates, Ports, and Coasts in Asia: Historical and Contemporary Perspectives* (Singapore: Institute of Southeast Asian Studies, 2010), 99–127.

Knapman, G., *Race and British Colonialism in South-East Asia, 1770–1870: John Crawfurd and the Politics of Equality* (New York: Routledge, 2017).

Konstam, A. and R. M. Kean, *Pirates: Predators of the Seas* (New York: Skyhorse Publishing, 2007).

Koskenniemi, M., *The Gentle Civilizer of Nations: The Rise and Fall of International Law 1870–1960* (Cambridge University Press, 2001).

Kratoska, P. and B. Batson, 'Nationalism and Modernist Reform', in N. Tarling (ed.), *The Cambridge History of Southeast Asia* 2:1 (Cambridge University Press, 1999), 245–320.

Kuder, E., 'The Moros in the Philippines', *Far Eastern Quarterly* 4:2 (1945), 119–26.

LaFeber, W., *The New Empire: An Interpretation of American Expansion, 1860–1898* (Ithaca, NY: Cornell University Press, 1963).

Lane, J. C., *Armed Progressive: General Leonard Wood* (San Rafael, CA and London: Presidio Press, 2009).

Lapian, A. B., *Orang laut, bajak laut, raja laut* (Depok: Komunitas Bambu, 2009).
  'Violence and Armed Robbery in Indonesian Seas', in J. Kleinen and M. Osseweijer (eds.), *Pirates, Ports, and Coasts in Asia: Historical and Contemporary Perspectives* (Singapore: Institute of Southeast Asian Studies, 2010), 131–46.

Launay, A., *Histoire ancienne et moderne de l'Annam, Tong-King et Cochinchine* (Paris: Challamel aîné, 1884).

Layton, S., 'Discourses of Piracy in an Age of Revolutions', *Itinerario* 35:2 (2011), 81–97.

Lessard, M., 'Cet ignoble trafic', *French Colonial History* 10:1 (2009), 1–34.
  Human Trafficking in Colonial Vietnam (London: Routledge, 2015).

Lester, A., 'Imperial Circuits and Networks', *History Compass* 4:1 (2006), 124–41.

Li Tana, 'The Water Frontier: An Introduction', in N. Cooke and Li Tana, *Water Frontier* (Singapore University Press, 2004), 1–17.

Lieberman, V. B., *Strange Parallels: Southeast Asia in Global Context, c. 800–1830: 2. Mainland Mirrors: Europe, Japan, China, South Asia, and the Islands* (Cambridge University Press, 2009).

Linn, B. M., *Guardians of Empire: The US Army and the Pacific, 1902–1940* (Chapel Hill: University of North Carolina Press, 1997).
  The Philippine War, 1899–1902 (Chapel Hill: University of North Carolina Press, 2000).

Liss, C., 'Contemporary Piracy in the Waters off Semporna, Sabah', in J. Kleinen and M. Osseweijer (eds.), *Pirates, Ports, and Coasts in Asia: Historical and Contemporary Perspectives* (Singapore: Institute of Southeast Asian Studies, 2010), 237–68.
  Oceans of Crime: Maritime Piracy and Transnational Security in Southeast Asia and Bangladesh (Singapore: Institute of Southeast Asian Studies, 2011).

Llanos, M. B. B., 'Piratas y cautivos en las Filipinas de 1898', in M. L. Talaván, J. J. Pacheco Onrubia and F. Palanco Aguado (eds.), *1898: España y el Pacífico* (Madrid: Asociación española de estudios del Pacífico, 1999), 39–52.

Lloyd, C. *The Navy and the Slave Trade* (London: Routledge, 2012).

Lombard, D., 'Regard nouveau sur les "pirates malais" (1ère moitié du XIXème siècle)', *Archipel* 18:1 (1979), 231–50.

MacCormack, G., 'Studies in the Traditional Chinese Law of Forcible Threat', *Journal of Comparative Law* 7:2 (2012), 207–57.

MacIntyre, D., 'Britain's Intervention in Malaya: The Origin of Lord Kimberley's Instructions to Sir Andrew Clarke in 1873', *Journal of Southeast Asian Studies* 2:2 (1961), 47–69.

Majul, C. A., *Muslims in the Philippines* (Quezon City: University of the Philippines Press, 1999).

Makepeace, W., 'Concerning Known Persons', in W. Makepeace, G. E. Brooke and R. St J. Braddell (eds.), *One Hundred Years of Singapore* 2 (London: John Murray, 1921), 416–64.

Mallari, F., 'The Spanish Navy in the Philippines, 1589–1787', *Philippine Studies* 37:4 (1989), 412–39.

Malleret, L, *L'Exotisme indochinois dans la littérature française depuis 1860* (Paris: L'Harmattan, 2014).

Manning, P., *Navigating World History: Historians Create a Global Past* (Houndmills, Basingstoke: Palgrave Macmillan, 2003).

Marr, D. G., *Vietnamese Anticolonialism 1885–1925* (Berkeley: University of California Press, 1971).

Marshall, A. G., *Nemesis: The First Iron Warship and Her World* (Singapore: Ridge Books, 2016).

Mathonnet, D., 'L'Évolution du droit de la piraterie en France', in M. Battesti (ed.), *La Piraterie au fil de l'histoire: Un défi pour l'État* (Paris: Presses de l'université Paris-Sorbonne, 2014), 49–62.

McIntyre, David W., *The Imperial Frontier in the Tropics, 1865–75: A Study of British Colonial Policy in West Africa, Malaya and the South Pacific in the Age of Gladstone and Disraeli* (London: Macmillan, 1967).

McKechnie, P., *Outsiders in the Greek Cities in the Fourth Century B.C.* (London: Routledge, 1989).

McLeod, M. W., *The Vietnamese Response to French Intervention* (New York: Praeger, 1991).

Miller, D. G., 'American Military Strategy during the Moro Insurrection in the Philippines, 1903–1913', unpubl. MA thesis, US Army Command and General Staff College, Fort Leavenworth, KS (2009).

Miller, H., *Pirates of the Far East* (London: Robert Hale and Company, 1970).

Mills, L. A., 'British Malaya, 1824–67', *Journal of the Malayan Branch of the Royal Asiatic Society* 33:3 (1960 [1925]), 1–424.

Milner, A. C., *Kerajaan: Malay Political Culture on the Eve of Colonial Rule* (Tucson: University of Arizona Press, 1982).

Missbach, A., 'The Aceh War (1873–1913) and the Influence of Christiaan Snouck Hurgronje', in A. Graf, S. Schröter and E. Wieringa (eds.), *Aceh: History, Politics and Culture* (Singapore: Institute of Southeast Asian Studies, 2010), 39–62.

Moor, G. (eds.), *Pirates and Mutineers of the Nineteenth Century: Swashbucklers and Swindlers* (Aldershot: Ashgate, 2011), 255–71.
de Moor, J. A., 'Warmakers in the Archipelago: Dutch Expeditions in Nineteenth-Century Indonesia', in J. A. de Moor and H. L. Wesseling (eds.), *Imperialism and War: Essays on Colonial Wars in Asia and Africa* (Leiden: Brill, 1989), 50–71.
Myrdal, J., 'On Source Criticism in World History', in A. Jarrick, J. Myrdal and M. Wallenberg Bondestam (eds.), *Methods in World History* (Lund: Nordic Academic Press, 2016), 45–83.
Nambiar, *The Kunjalis, Admirals of Calicut* (London: Asia Publishing House, 1963).
Nardin, D., 'Les Français à Basilan', *Archipel* 15:1 (1978), 29–40.
Netzloff, M., 'Sir Francis Drake's Ghost', in C. Jowitt, *Pirates? The Politics of Plunder, 1550–1650* (Houndmills, Basingstoke: Palgrave Macmillan, 2006), 137–50.
Ormerod, H. A., *Piracy in the Ancient World* (Baltimore, MD: Johns Hopkins University Press, 1997 [1924]).
Osborne, M., *From Conviction to Anxiety: Reassessing the French Self-Image in Vietnam* (Bedford Park, SA: Flinders University of South Australia, School of Social Sciences, 1976).
  River Road to China: The Mekong River Expeditions, 1866–73 (London: George Allen and Unwin, 1975).
  The French Presence in Cochinchina and Cambodia (Ithaca, NY: Cornell University Press, 1969).
Osterhammel, J., 'Approaches to Global History and the Question of the "Civilizing Mission"', Working Paper 3, Osaka University, Program on Global History and Maritime Asia (2007).
Ouellet, R., 'Fiction et réalité dans *Nouvelles de l'Amérique* (anonyme, 1678) et *l'Histoire des aventuriers* (1686) d'Exquemelin', in S. Requemora and S. Linon-Chipon (eds.), *Les Tyrans de la mer: Pirates, corsaires et flibustiers* (Paris: Presses de l'Université de Paris-Sorbonne, 2002), 283–96.
Paige, T., 'Piracy and Universal Jurisdiction', *Macquarie Law Journal* 12 (2013), 131–54.
Parkinson, C. N., *British Intervention in Malaya 1867–1877* (Singapore: Malaya University Press, 1960).
Pearson, M., 'Piracy in Asian Waters: Problems of Definition', in J. Kleinen and M. Osseweijer (eds.), *Pirates, Ports, and Coasts in Asia: Historical and Contemporary Perspectives* (Singapore: Institute of Southeast Asian Studies, 2010), 15–28.
Pelner Cosman, M. and L. G. Jones, *Handbook to Life in the Medieval World* 1 (New York: Infobase, 2008).
Pennell, C. R. 'Introduction: Brought to Book: Reading about Pirates' in C. R. Pennell (ed.), *Bandits at Sea* (New York University Press, 2001), 3–24.
Pérotin-Dumon, A., 'The Pirate and the Emperor: Power and Law on the Seas, 1450–1850', in C. R. Pennell (ed.), *Bandits at Sea: A Pirates Reader* (New York University Press, 2001), 25–54.
Petit, É., *Francis Garnier, sa vie, ses voyages, son oeuvre, 1839–1874* (Paris: M. Dreyfous et M. Dalsace, 1894).
Potter, S. J. and J. Saha, 'Global History, Imperial History and Connected Histories of Empire', *Journal of Colonialism and Colonial History* 16:1 (2015), 1–38.

Bibliography

Prétou, P., 'Du "larron écumeur de mer" aux "pirathes"', in M. Battesti (ed.), *La Piraterie au fil de l'histoire: Un défi pour l'État* (Paris: Presses de l'université Paris-Sorbonne, 2014), 37–48.

Priestley, H. I., *France Overseas: A Study of Modern Imperialism* (New York: Octagon Books, 1966).

Pringle, R., *Rajahs and Rebels: The Ibans of Sarawak under Brooke Rule, 1841–1941* (London: Macmillan, 1970).

Putnam, L., 'The Transnational and the Text-Searchable: Digitized Sources and the Shadows They Cast', *American Historical Review* 121:2, 377–402.

Rabinow, P., *French Modern: Norms and Forms of the Social Environment* (University of Chicago Press, 1995).

Reber, A. L., 'The Sulu World in the 18th and Early 19th Centuries', unpubl. PhD thesis, Cornell University (1966).

Rediker, M., *Villains of All Nations: Atlantic Pirates in the Golden Age* (London: Verso; 2004).

Reid, A., 'Economic and Social Change, c. 1400–1800', in N. Tarling (ed.), *The Cambridge History of Southeast Asia* 1:2 (Cambridge University Press, 1999), 116–63.

  Southeast Asia in the Age of Commerce: 1: The Lands below the Winds (New Haven, CT: Yale University Press, 1988).

  Southeast Asia in the Age of Commerce: 2: Expansion and Crisis (New Haven, CT: Yale University Press, 1993).

  The Contest for North Sumatra: Atjeh, the Netherlands and Britain, 1858–1898 (Kuala Lumpur: Oxford University Press and University of Malaya Press, 1969).

  'Violence at Sea: Unpacking "Piracy" in the Claims of States over Asian Seas', in R. J. Antony (ed.), *Elusive Pirates, Pervasive Smugglers: Violence and Clandestine Trade in the Greater China Seas* (Hong Kong University Press, 2010), 15–26.

Reynolds, C. J., 'A New Look at Old Southeast Asia', *Journal of Asian Studies* 54:2 (1995), 419–46.

Rigaud, Ph. (ed.), *Pirates et corsaires dans les mers de Provence, XVe–XVIe siècles: Letras de la costiera* (Paris: Éditions du CTHS, 2006).

Risso, P., 'Cross-Cultural Perceptions of Piracy: Maritime Violence in the Western Indian Ocean and Persian Gulf Region during a Long Eighteenth Century', *Journal of World History* 12:2 (2001), 293–319.

Ritchie, R. C., *Captain Kidd and the War against the Pirates* (Cambridge, MA: Harvard University Press, 1986).

  'Government Measures against Piracy and Privateering in the Atlantic Area, 1750–1850', in D. J. Starkey, E. S. van Eyck van Hesling and J. A. de Moor (eds.), *Pirates and Privateers: New Perspectives on the War on Trade in the Eighteenth and Nineteenth Centuries* (University of Exeter Press, 1997), 10–28.

Rodger, N. A. M., *The Command of the Ocean: A Naval History of Britain, 1649–1815* (London: Penguin, 2006).

Rubin, A. P., *Piracy, Paramountcy and Protectorates* (Kuala Lumpur: Penerbit Universiti Malaya, 1974).

  The Law of Piracy (Irvington-on-Hudson, NY: Transnational Publishers, 1998).

Sachsenmaier, D., *Global Perspectives on Global History* (Cambridge University Press, 2011).

Sadka, E., 'The Residential System in the Protected Malay States, 1874–1895', unpubl. PhD thesis, Australian National University (1960).
Said, E., *Orientalism* (New York: Pantheon Books, 1978).
Saleeby, N. B., *Studies in Moro History, Law and Religion* (Manila: Bureau of Public Printing, 1905).
  The History of Sulu (Manila: Bureau of Printing, 1908).
Salman, M., *The Embarrassment of Slavery: Controversies over Bondage and Nationalism in the American Colonial Philippines* (Berkeley: University of California Press, 2001).
Scott, W. H., *Slavery in the Spanish Philippines* (Manila: De La Salle University Press, 1991).
Semmel, B., *The Governor Eyre Controversy* (London: Kee 1962).
Septans, A., *Les Commencements de l'Indo-Chine française* (Paris: Challamel aîné, 1887).
Sidel, J. T., *Capital, Coercion and Crime: Bossism in the Philippines* (Stanford University Press, 1999).
Sinn, D. and N. Soares, 'Historians' Use of Digital Archival Collections', *Journal of the Association for Information Science and Technology* 65:9 (2014), 1764–1809.
Slack, E. R., 'Philippines under Spanish Rule, 1571–1898', Oxford Bibliographies in Latin American Studies, www.oxfordbibliographies.com/view/document/obo-9780199766581/obo-9780199766581-0164.xml (accessed 27 February 2017).
Smith, J., *The Spanish–American War: Conflict in the Caribbean and the Pacific, 1895–1902* (London: Longman, 1994).
Somer, J. G., *De korte verklaring* (Breda: Corona, 1934).
de Souza, Ph., 'Piracy in Classical Antiquity: The Origins and Evolution of the Concept', in S. Eklöf Amirell and L. Müller (eds.), *Persistent Piracy: Maritime Violence and State-Formation in Global Historical Perspective* (Houndmills, Basingstoke: Palgrave Macmillan, 2014), 24–50.
  Piracy in the Graeco-Roman World (Cambridge University Press, 1999).
Spence, J. D., *The Search for Modern China* (New York: W. W. Norton, 1990).
Spores, J. C., *Running Amok: An Historical Inquiry* (Athens, GA: Ohio University Center for International Studies, 1988).
Starkey, D. J., 'Pirates and Markets', in C. R. Pennell (ed.), *Bandits at Sea: A Pirates Reader* (New York University Press, 2001), 107–24.
Starkey, D. J., E. S. van Eyck van Hesling and J. A. de Moor (eds.), *Pirates and Privateers: New Perspectives on the War on Trade in the Eighteenth and Nineteenth Centuries* (Exeter University Press, 1997).
Stoler, A. L., *Along the Archival Grain: Epistemic Anxieties and Colonial Common Sense* (Princeton University Press, 2009).
  Duress: Imperial Durabilities in Our Times (Durham, NC: Duke University Press, 2016).
Stoler, A. L. and F. Cooper, 'Preface', in A. L. Stoler and F. Cooper (eds.), *Tensions of Empire: Colonial Cultures in a Bourgeois World* (Berkeley: University of California Press, 1997).
Stritzel, H., *Security in Translation: Securitization Theory and the Localization of Threat* (Houndmills, Basingstoke: Palgrave Macmillan, 2014).

Subramanian, L., 'Of Pirates and Potentates: Maritime Jurisdiction and the Construction of Piracy in the Indian Ocean', in D. Ghosh and S. Muecke (eds.), *Cultures of Trade: Indian Ocean Exchanges* (Newcastle: Cambridge Scholars Publishing, 2007), 19–30.

Tagliacozzo, E., 'Kettle on a Slow Boil: Batavia's Threat Perceptions in the Indies' Outer Islands, 1870–1910', *Journal of Southeast Asian Studies* 31:1 (2000), 70–100.

Secret Trades, Porous Borders: Smuggling and States along a Southeast Asian Frontier, 1865–1915 (New Haven, CT: Yale University Press, 2005).

Tan, S. K., 'Sulu under American Military Rule 1899–1913', *Philippine Social Sciences and Humanities Review* 32:1 (1967), 1–189.

Tarling, N., *Anglo–Dutch Rivalry in the Malay World, 1780–1824* (St Lucia, Queensland: Cambridge University Press and University of Queensland Press, 1962).

Britain, the Brookes and Brunei (Kuala Lumpur: Oxford University Press, 1971).

Piracy and Politics in the Malay World (Nendeln: Kraus Reprint, 1978 [1963]).

Sulu and Sabah: A Study of British Policy towards the Philippines and North Borneo from the Late Eighteenth Century (Kuala Lumpur: Oxford University Press, 1978).

'The Establishment of the Colonial Régimes' in N. Tarling (ed.), *The Cambridge History of Southeast Asia* 2:1 (Cambridge University Press, 1999), 1–74.

Teitler, G., 'Piracy in Southeast Asia: A Historical Comparison', *Maritime Studies* 1:1 (2002), 67–83.

Teitler, G., A. M. C. van Dissel and J. N. F. M. à Campo, *Zeeroof en zeeroofbestrijding in de Indische archipel (19de eeuw)* (Amsterdam: De Bataafsche Leeuw, 2005).

Thompson, W. W., 'Governors of the Moro Province', unpubl. PhD thesis, University of California, San Diego (1975).

Thomson, J., *Mercenaries, Pirates and Sovereigns: State-Building and Extraterritorial Violence in Early Modern Europe* (Princeton University Press, 1994).

Tilly, C., 'War Making and State Making as Organized Crime', in P. B. Evans, D. Rueschemeyer and T. Skocpol (eds.), *Bringing the State Back in* (Cambridge University Press, 1985), 169–91.

Tim Penysun Kamus, *Kamus besar Bahasa Indonesia* (Jakarta: Balai Pustaka, 1996).

Tompkins, E. B., *Anti-imperialism in the United States: The Great Debate, 1890–1920* (Philadelphia: University of Pennsylvania Press, 1980).

Tregonning, K. G., *A History of Modern Sabah* (University of Singapore Press, 1965).

Trocki, C., 'Political Structures in the Nineteenth and Early Twentieth Centuries', in N. Tarling (ed.), *The Cambridge History of Southeast Asia* 2:1 (Cambridge University Press, 1999), 75–126.

Prince of Pirates: The Temenggongs and the Development of Johor and Singapore, 1784–1885 (Singapore: NUS Press, 2012 [1979]).

Turley, H., *Rum, Sodomy and the Lash: Piracy, Sexuality, and Masculine Identity* (New York University Press, 1999).

Turnbull, C. M., 'Governor Blundell and Sir Benson Maxwell: A Conflict of Personalities', *Journal of the Malayan Branch of the Royal Asiatic Society* 30:1 (1957), 134–63.

A History of Singapore, 1819–1988 (Singapore: Oxford University Press, 1989).

Uckung, J. V., 'From Jikiri to Abu Sayyaf', *Philippine Inquirer* (9 June 2001).

Van Leur, J. C., 'Eenige aanteekeningen betreffende de mogelijkheid der achttiende eeuw als categorie in de Indische geschiedschrijving', *Tijdschrift voor indische taal-, land- en volkenkunde* 80 (1940), 544–67.

Indonesian Trade and Society: Essays in Asian Social and Economic History (The Hague: W. van Hoeve, 1955).

Van Schendel, W., 'Asian Studies in Amsterdam', in L. Douw (ed.), *Unsettled Frontiers and Transnational Linkages* (Amsterdam: VU University Press, 1997).

Vann, M. G., 'Of Pirates, Postcards, and Public Beheadings: The Pedagogic Execution in French Colonial Indochina', *Historical Reflections* 36:2 (2010), 39–58.

Vázquez R. and W. Mignolo, 'Decolonial AestheSis: Colonial Wounds/Decolonial Healings', *Social Text* 15 (2013).

Velthoen, E., 'Pirates in the Periphery: Eastern Sulawesi, 1820–1905', in J. Kleinen and M. Osseweijer (eds.), *Pirates, Ports, and Coasts in Asia: Historical and Contemporary Perspectives* (Singapore: Institute of Southeast Asian Studies, 2010), 200–21.

de Vere Allen, J., 'The Colonial Office and the Malay States, 1867–73', *Journal of the Malayan Branch of the Royal Asiatic Society* 36:1 (1963), 1–36.

Vink, M. '"The World's Oldest Trade": Dutch Slavery and Slave Trade in the Indian Ocean in the Seventeenth Century', *Journal of World History* 14:2 (2003), 131–77.

Vlekke, B. H. M., *Nusantara: A History of the East Indian Archipelago* (Cambridge, MA: Harvard University Press, 1945).

Wagner, T. S., 'Piracy and the Ends of Romantic Commercialism: Victorian Businessmen Meet Malay Pirates', in G. Moore (ed.), *Pirates and Mutineers of the Nineteenth Century: Swashbucklers and Swindlers* (Aldershot: Ashgate, 2011), 255–71.

Walker, J. H., *Power and Prowess: The Origins of Brooke Kingship in Sarawak* (Crows Nest, NSW: Allen and Unwin, 2002).

Warren, J. F., *Iranun and Balangingi: Globalization, Maritime Raiding and the Birth of Ethnicity* (Singapore University Press, 2002).

'Moro Wars', in A. T. Embree (ed.), *Encyclopedia of Asian History* 3 (London: Collier Macmillan, 1988), 40–1.

'The Balangingi Samal: "Pirate wars", Dislocation and Diasporic Identities', *The Great Circle* 33:2 (2011), 43–65.

'The Port of Jolo: International Trade and Slave Raiding' in J. Kleinen and M. Osseweijer (eds.), *Pirates, Ports, and Coasts in Asia: Historical and Contemporary Perspectives* (Singapore: Institute of Southeast Asian Studies, 2010), 178–99.

The Sulu Zone: The World Capitalist Economy and the Historical Imagination (Amsterdam: VU University Press, 1998).

The Sulu Zone, 1768–1898: The Dynamics of External Trade, Slavery, and Ethnicity in the Transformation of a Southeast Asian Maritime State (Singapore University Press, 1981).

Watson, J. L. 'Transactions in People: The Chinese Market in Slaves, Servants, and Heirs', in J. L. Watson (ed.), *Asian and African Systems of Slavery* (Oxford: Blackwell, 1980), 223–50.

Weatley, A. T., 'Historical Sketch of the Law of Piracy', *The Law Magazine and Review* 3 (1874), 536–55.

Webster, A., *Gentlemen Capitalists: British Imperialism in South East Asia 1770–1890* (London: Tauris Academic Studies, 1998).

Werner, M. and B. Zimmermann, 'Beyond Comparison: Histoire Croisée and the Challenge of Reflexivity', *History and Theory* 45:1 (2006), 30–50.

Wheatley, P., *The Golden Kherosonese: Studies in the Historical Geography of the Malay Peninsula before AD 1500* (Kuala Lumpur: University of Malaya Press, 1961).

Wheeler, C., 'A Maritime Logic to Vietnamese History? Littoral Society in Hoi An's Trading World c. 1550–1830', *World* 100 (2003).

  'Maritime Subversions and Socio-political Formations in Vietnamese History', in M. A. Aung-Thwin and K. R. Hall (eds.), *New Perspectives on the History and Historiography of Southeast Asia* (London: Routledge 2011), 141–56.

White, J. M., *Piracy and Law in the Ottoman Mediterranean* (Stanford University Press, 2018).

Whiteway, R. S., *The Rise of Portuguese Power in India* (Goa, Daman and Diu: Asian Educational Services, 1995 [1899]).

Wilkinson, R. J., *A History of the Peninsular Malays* (Singapore: Kelly and Walsh, 1923).

Wilson, H. H., 'Some Principal Aspects of British Efforts to Crush the African Slave Trade, 1807–1929', *American Journal of International Law* 44:3 (1950), 505–26.

Winichakul, T., *Siam Mapped: A History of the Geo-body of a Nation* (Honolulu: University of Hawaii Press, 1994).

Woods, R. G., 'Looking Back Thirty Years', *Khaki and Red: Official Organ of the Constabulary and Police* (July 1931).

Yazdani, K., *India, Modernity and the Great Divergence: Mysore and Gujarat (17th to 19th c.)* (Leiden: Brill, 2017).

Young, A. J., *Contemporary Maritime Piracy in Southeast Asia: History, Causes and Remedies* (Singapore: Institute of Southeast Asian Studies, 2007).

Yu Insun, 'Vietnam–China Relations in the 19th Century', *Journal of Northeast Asian History* 6:1 (2009), 81–117.

Zwick, J., *Mark Twain's Weapons of Satire: Anti-imperialist Writings on the Philippine–American War* (Syracuse University Press, 1992).

Index

abductions, 5, 175, 184–7, 199, 207, 217,
  See also trafficking
Abdul Rahman, Tunku, 234
Abdul Samad, 6, 128–9, 133–4, 147, 149–51, 221
Abdullah Muhammad Shah, 144
Abdullah, Raja, 124
Aceh, 6, 10, 97, 106, 159, 212, 215, 222, 228
  Aceh War, 153–7, 216, 223
Act for the More Effectual Suppression of Piracy, 30
Admiralty, 30, 109–10, 118, 135
  High Court of, 110
Africa, 24, 33, 185, 187, 215
agriculture, 78, 107, 198, 200, 213, 230
Aguinaldo, Emilio, 65
Aix-en-Provence, 201
Alexander the Great, 12
Algiers, 24, 111
America, 29, 207
American Civil War, 65, 69
amok, 147
Andromache, H.M.S., 109
Anglo–Dutch Wars, 30
Anglo–Spanish War, 27
Annam. *See* Vietnam
Anson, Edward, 125–7, 129–30, 132, 135, 137, 140, 144, 221
Antequera, Juan, 59
anti-imperialism, 213, 231
  in France, 183, 188, 224
  in Great Britain, 110, 177, 231
  in the United States, 65, 68, 76
Antiquity, 11, 21–3
appeasement, 144, 146, 163, 198
Arabic, 34, 40
Arabs, 96, 102, 106, 215
Arayat, 87
archives, 10–11, 15, 19
Archives nationales d'outre-mer, 201

arms, 66, 83, 87, 93, 115, 199–200
  embargo, 56, 58, 119, 140
  proliferation of, 42, 56, 95, 113, 116, 138, 158, 161, 163, 233
  trade in, 45, 60, 98, 116, 119–20, 199, 217, 220
  used in pirate attacks, 117, 199
ar-Rashid, Harun, 62
Aru, 39
Atlantic, 21, 27, 71, 102, 213
  Golden Age of piracy in, 30, 32, 192, 213
Audiencia de Filipinas, 44
Augustine of Hippo, 12, 21
Avery, Henry, 29–31
Avon, 142

bajak, 38
Balabac, 55
Balangingi, 52
  destruction of, 48–9, 53, 55, 101, 217, 220, 226
Bali, 102, 213
Balingki, 56
Bancks, John Eric, 154
Bandar Langat, 147
Bandholz, Harry Hill, 85
bandits, 5, 22, 33, 174, 206, 219, *See also* brigands
Banjarmasin, 100
Banka, 37
Barbary States, 24
Barrantes, Vicente, 60
Barros, João de, 27
Basilan, 47, 68, 80, 82–3, 87, 92, 214, 218, 227
Batang Marau, 111
Batavia, 97
Bates Agreement, 68–9, 75
  abrogation of, 77, 91–2
Bates, John C., 63, 68–9
Baud, J. C., 101
Baudrit, André, 186
beheadings, 36, 81, 171, 185, 206

257

Beihai, 199
Bellamy, Samuel, 33
Belli, Pierino, 25
Bencoolen. *See* Benkulu
Benga, Tan, 90
Bengal, 28–9, 40
Benkulu, 102, 105
Benton, Lauren, 25
Bichot, Anicet-Edmond-Justin, 198–9, 203
Bideau, François Marie Léon, 204
Birch, J. W., 128–9, 136, 146
Black Flags, 177–80, 189–97, 202, 204, 207, 211, 214, 219, 224–5
Black River, 200
Bliss, Tasker Howard, 79, 83, 86, 88, 91, 227
Blumentritt, Ferd., 61, 215
Blundell, Edmund, 116–19
Board of Commissioners for the Affairs of India, 119
Bombay, 119
Bonard, Louis-Adolphe, 170, 172
Bongao, 73–4, 86, 93
Borneo, 44–7, 54, 69, 95, 106, 109–11, 136, 159–60, 177, 217, 220, 226, 232
Bourayne, 175–7, 182, 202–3, 207, 224, 228
Braddell, Thomas, 146, 149–51, 215
brigands, 164, 170, 172, 219, 230, *See also* bandits
British North Borneo, 79, 233
Brooke, James, 7, 48, 53, 109, 111, 135, 137, 177, 220, 226
Brunei, 44, 55, 106
    Sultan of, 48
buccaneers, 32, 213
Buccaneers of America, 32
Bud Dajo, 78, 83, 227
Buddhists, 181
Bugis, 98, 106, 148–9
Bukutua, 49
Bulan, 49
Bunbun, 71
Burma, 105, 176
businessmen, 64, 90, 125, 129, 136, 143, 155, 159, 183, 188, 192, 207, 223

Cagayan Valley, 48
Calang Straits, 149
Calcutta, 103, 105, 109, 115, 117, 119
Caldera, 164
California, 186
Cambodia, 6, 8, 114, 170, 172–4, 201, 230, 233
Can Vuong, 197–8, 204, 207, 211, 219
Canton, 113, 186
Cape Rachado, 148, 152
capitalism, 16, 52

Caribbean, 27, 29, 32, 108, 185
cartaz, 27, 97
Cat Ba, 175, 183, 203, 231
Catholicism, 23, 35, 58, 94, 163, 230,
    See also Christianity, missionaries
cedula (head tax), 78, 92
Celebes. *See* Sulawesi
Challemel-Lacour, Paul-Armand, 191
Chamber of Deputies. *See* Parliament, French
Champa, 161
Chau Doc, 174
Chevalier, Robert, dit de Beauchêne, 32
children, 48, 130, 164, 185, 213
    victims of piracy and trafficking, 73, 125, 134, 177, 184–7, 199, 207, 217, 224
China, 120, 166, 176, 181, 185, 189, 192, 196, 199, *See also* Chinese, Ming Dynasty, Opium War, Qing Dynasty, Sino–French War, Taiping Rebellion
    concepts of piracy in, 35
    Navy, 192, 195
    origins of piracy, 113, 140, 146, 184, 200, 217–19
    piracy in, 29, 119, 232
    suppression of piracy, 162, 175, 193, 206, 232
    trade with, 45–6, 64, 102, 115–16, 161, 163, 166, 170, 178, 181, 192
    trafficking to, 186, 207, 224
Chinese, 62, 79, 88, 106, 124, 134, *See also* Mandarin
    bandits, 174, 197, *See also* Black Flags, Yellow Flags
    businessmen, 60, 64, 72, 86, 95, 103, 118, 129, 136, 143, 183–4
    pirates, 106, 113–20, 125, 131, 150, 153, 157, 159, 161–3, 165, 174–7, 182, 184–5, 198, 206–7, 216, 218, 222–3
    victims of piracy, 71–2, 81, 84–6, 126, 131, 137–8, 147, 153, 155, 214, 219, 222
Christianity, 27, 31, 35, 42–4, 46, 58, 64, 99, 111, 163, 170, 215, 226, 230, *See also* Catholicism, missionaries, proselytisation
Cicero, Marcus Tullius, 11, 21–2, 25
Cilicians, 22
civil war, 123, 137, 221, *See also* American Civil War
civilisation, 1, 7–8, 34, 58, 83, 94, 102, 104, 134, 150, 158, 171, 186, 192–3, 213, 220, 229–31
civilising mission, 7, 58, 76, 104, 181, 188, 207, 224
Clarke, Andrew, 143–6, 148–52, 221
Cloman, Sydney A., 73–4
Cloué, Georges Charles, 187

Index

Cobden, Richard, 111
Cochinchina, 114, 164–6, 168–75, 178, 183, 194, 196, 201, 207, 223, 228, *See also* Indochina, Vietnam
Coke, Edward, 26
Colomer, Monsignor, 184–5
Colonial Office (Great Britain), 135, 140, 143
Colonna-Walewski, Alexandre, 168
commerce. *See* trade
Commission for Cochinchina, 166
communis hostis omnium, 22, 26
Concurrences, 17, 19
Confrontation, 234
Congress. *See* United States, Congress
Conrad, Joseph, 7
Constans, Ernest, 203
coolies, 185, 207, 217
Cooper, Frederick, 16
Cooper, Nicola, 205
Copenhagen, 111
  School of Security Studies, 18, *See also* securitisation
corruption, 113, 161, 163, 183, 199
corsairs, 23, 31, 34
Cotabato, 73
Courrier de Saïgon, 179
Cowan, C. D., 126
Crawfurd, John, 37, 39, 102, 107, 112, 120, 211, 213
Cuba, 186

Da Nang, 167–9
Danes, 156
datus, 51–3, 61–2, 66–7, 72, 77–8, 80, 84, 91
Davidson, J. G., 151
Davis, Bradley Camp, 202
Davis, Natalie Zemon, 16
Dayaks, 106, 111
De Tham. *See* Hoang Hoa Tham
De Witt, F. S., 85, 87
decapitation. *See* beheadings
Denison, A. D. S., 139
Department of Mindanao and Sulu, 69–71, 75
dependency theory, 13
Deschanel, Paul, 188
Dewey, George, 66
Dhiauddin Zainal Rashid. *See* Kudin, Tunku
Dinas, 74
Dinding Islands, 145
Dinh Tuong, 173
diplomacy, 31, 133–4, 167, 180, *See also* gunboat diplomacy
Dominicans, 168
Dô-son, 177
Drake, Francis, 31

Dupré, Marie-Jules, 174–5, 178–9
Dupuis, Jean, 176–8, 223–5
Dutch East India Company, 28–9, 97–101, 103, 158, 218
Dutch East Indies, 2, 46, 49, 54, 71, 74, 94, 217
Dutreuil de Rhins, Jules-Léon, 182

Earle, Peter, 27
East China Sea, 28
East India Company Act, 103
Elizabeth I, 26
England, 26, 29–31, 41, 158, 181, *See also* English East India Company, Great Britain
English East India Company, 28–9, 97, 102, 104–5, 107, 109, 115, 119
Enlightenment, 94, 158, 213
Esk, 119
ethnicity, 15, 39, 61, 94, 158, 214, *See also* civilisation, race, racism
ethnohistory, 13
Eurocentrism, 9, 12–13, 15
European expansion, viii, 2, 12, 19, 21, 25, 40, 96, 101, 158, 163, 188, 209, 218, *See also* Dutch East India Company, English East India Company, France, Great Britain, Netherlands, Portugal, Spain, trading companies, treaties
executions, 30, 151, 153, 171, 185, 206, *See also* beheadings
exoticism, 205
Exquemelin, Alexandre, 32
extortion, 5, 171, 202, 204
Eyre, Edward John, 135–6

Fadl Pulalun, Muhammad, 48, 52, 55, 226
Fair Malacca, 138–40
Far East Station, 135, 142
Faxian, 96
Ferry, Jules, 205
Filipinos, 54, 61–2, 65, 71, 79, 213
Finley, John, 81
fishermen, 107, 121, 141, *See also* fishing, pearl fishing
  victims of piracy, 2, 73, 95, 110, 122, 184, 212, 222, 227, 234
fishing, 60, 73, 76, 78, 90, 235, *See also* fishermen, pearl fishing
flags, 59, 104, 138–9, 192
Flores, 54, 101
Forbes, William Cameron, 85
France, 8, 32, 133–4, 161–208, *See also* Paris; Tonkin, French intervention in
  Army, 197
  colonial expansion, 6, 47, 160, 211, 223–5

Index

France (cont.)
  imperial rivalry, 94
  Navy, 163, 165–6, 168, 170, 178, 187–8, 191, 193, 202, 223
  suppression of piracy, 5, 26, 171, 173, 175–6, 179–81, 187, 191, 223, 229
Franco–Prussian War, 177
French Division of the Chinese Seas, 166
Frey, Henry, 204
Fujian, 106
Fur, Gunlög, 16
Fuzhou, 195

Gabino, Datu, 81
Galang, 121
Gallagher, John, 105
Gallieni, Joseph, 200
Gang-i-Sawai, 29
Garnier, Francis, 172–3, 178–80, 183, 189, 191, 201, 224
Gatenhielm, Lars, 32
gender, 15, *See also* women
General History of the Most Notorious Pyrates, 32
Gentili, Alberico, 25
George Town, 102, *See also* Penang
Germany, 60, 90, 156, 199
  imperial rivalry, 59, 63, 94, 125, 144, 176, 178, 188, 228
giặc, 202
Giap Tuat Treaty, 180
Gladstone, William Ewart, 125, 135, 143, 222
Glengarry, 153
global history, 15, 17–18
Go Kwan, 138, 141, 144–5
Graaf, Laurens de, 32
Grandière, Pierre-Paul de la, 173
Great Britain, 8, 46, 56, 100–53, 156, 163, 166, 199, 208, 212–13, 230, *See also* London, Parliament: British
  colonial expansion, 6, 28, 49, 158–9, 217–18, 228
  imperial rivalry, 47–8, 52, 59, 63, 94, 176, 178, 188–9, 226, 234
  Royal Navy, 29–30, 54, 102, 106, 109, 113, 115, 119, 127, 133, 135, 145, 148, 166, 216, 221
  suppression of piracy, 11, 29, 54, 74, 102, 119, 136, 159, 162, 164–5, 167, 201, 206, 220–3, 229, 231
Greece, 21, 37
Greek, 21
Gros-Desveaux, L., 186
Guangzhou, 113
Gulf of Tonkin, 120, 162–3, 175
gunboat diplomacy, 133, 146–7, 160, 222, 229

gunboats, 48, 50, 56–8, 66, 71, 74, 79, 86, 90, 115, 118, 121, 130, 169–70, 173, 187, 190, 204

Ha Tien, 174
haifei, 35
Hainan, 165, 175
Haiphong, 183
Hanoi, 179, 189–90, 194, 203
harmads, 28
Harmand, François-Jules, 194
Hassan, Panglima, 77
head money, 56, 108–11
Heller-Roazen, Daniel, 31
Henri IV, 26
Henri-Rivière, 204
histoire croisée, 16
Hoang Hoa Tham, 205
Hoang-si Phi, 200
Hobsbawm, Eric, 33
Hodges, C. L., 92
Hok Canton, 156, 223
Hokkien, 141
Hon Tseu, 176
Hong Kong, 113, 116, 135, 163, 199
Hooghly, 119
Hornet, 139
horror literature, 205
hostis humani generis. *See communis hostis omnium*
Hoyt, Ralph W., 87
Hue, 169, 178, 182, 195–6
human rights, 34
human security, 229–30
Hungh Hoa, 200
Hurley, Vic, 63, 89
Hussein Shah, 13
Hylam, 165

Ibbetson, Robert, 107
Iberian Peninsula, 43
Ida, 86
Illana Bay, 39
Illanun. *See* Iranun
Illyrians, 22
Imam Muda, Teuku, 155
India, 27, 29–30, 102, 105, 115, 125, 145, 176, 185, *See also* Calcutta, English East India Company, Indians
Indian Ocean, 21, 27–9, 97, 158, 210, 212
Indian Rebellion, 120
Indians, 96, 103, 106, 129
Indochina, 5–6, 161–208, 211, 216–17, 223, 225–6, 228, 230, *See also* Cambodia, Cochinchina, Laos, Tonkin, Vietnam

Index 261

Indonesia, 8, 234–5
International Maritime Bureau, 5, 234
International Maritime Organization, 5
Iranun, 4, 7, 39, 45–6, 51–2, 54, 99, 101, 103, 106, 116, 158, 212, 226
Irving, J. C., 128, 130, 146
Islam, 31, 34, 42–4, 58, 67, 158, 226, *See also* Muslims, religion
  associated with piracy, 46, 94, 99, 102, 154, 213, 215–16, 234

Jakarta. *See* Batavia
Jamaica, 135
Jamal ul-Azam, 59
Jamalul Kiram II, 67, 71, 78, 89, 218
Japan, 29, 35, 80, 152, 233
Japanese, 40, 79, 85
Jaurès, Bénjamin, 180
Java, 37, 97, 99–100, 102–3
  Java War, 100
Java-bode, 155
Javanese, 213
Jenkins, Leoline, 30
jihad, 99
Jikiri, 82–90, 92, 95, 216, 218, 229
Johnson, Charles, 32
Johor, 6, 10, 13, 97, 99, 103, 106, 122, 130, 165, 216, 230
Johore, 145
Jolo, 45, 48, 52, 66–7, 71, 77–8, 80, 82, 84, 86, 90, 227, 233
  Spanish assault on, 50, 56, 61, 64, 226–7, 231
Jugra River, 147–8, 151–2
juramentados, 62, 77
Jurata, 86
jurisdiction, 24, 34, 72, 104, 114, 123, 151

Kecho, 179
Kedah, 6, 107, 129
Keppel, Henry, 53
Kergaradec, Alexandre de, 203
Kidd, William, 29–30, 32, 216
Kim Seng Cheong, 125–8, 131, 148, 152, 214, 221, 228
Kimberley, Earl of, 135
Klang, 124, 129
Kobbé, W. A., 69–70
Konfrontasi, 234
Kopagu, 82, 87
Korea, 35
Kuala Buka, 123
Kudin, Tunku, 129–32, 135–6, 150–1, 221
Kulan, 71
Kwangtung, 106

La Massue, 186
Labuan, 55, 58, 60
Lanao, 82
Lanessan, Marie Antoine de, 198, 204
Langat, 148–50
lanun, 38–9, 99, 212
Laos, 196
Lapian, Adrian B., 15, 38
Lapingan, 72
Larut, 123, 125, 137, 139–42, 144–5, 222
Larut River, 137–8
Latin, 170
Latin America, 15
Latuan, 87
laws. *See* piracy: laws pertaining to
Le Dynasty, 161, 179
Le Figaro, 193
Le Myre de Vilers, Charles, 171, 186, 189–90
Lessard, Micheline, 199
lettrés, 172
Leyte, 54
Liaoning, 106
Li-Fournier Convention. *See* Tianjin Accord
Lingga, 4, 100, 106, 109, 216
Liu Yongfu. *See* Luu Vinh Phuoc
Logan, D., 139
Logan, James Richardson, 9, 215
Lombok, 102
London, 10, 50, 90, 103, 110, 123, 125, 132–3, 137, 143, 152–3, 159, 221, 223
  1824 Treaty of, 105–7, 112
lorchas, 171
Louis Philippe, 47
Loviot, Fanny, 164–5
Luong Tam Ky, 198
Lushington, Stephen, 110
Luu Vinh Phuoc, 190, 203
Luzon, 46, 48, 57
Lyautey, Hubert, 200

Macau, 113, 138, 165, 185
Mackenzie, Colin, 109
Madrid, 10, 50
Maeander, 53
Maguindanao, 38–9
  Sultanate of, 42, 45
Mahdi, Raja, 124, 126, 128–31, 136–7, 148
Mahmood, Raja, 127–8, 130, 148
Maibung, 74, 84
Majul, Cesar Adib, 15
Makassar, 98
Malacca. *See* Melaka
  Strait of, 4, 46, 96–161, 163, 175–6, 206, 216–17, 219–23, 232–4
Malalis, Datu, 74

262 Index

Malay, 36–40
Malay Archipelago, 28, 33, 36–40, 96–7, 102, 119, 154, 158, 213, 215, 226
Malay Peninsula, 6, 96, 102, 105, 133, 143, 152, 160, 216–17, 221
Malaya, 153, 234
Malays, 96, 103, 106, 134, 136, 230
  perpetrators of piracy, 7, 13, 102, 111, 131, 153, 159, 213, 215
  victims of piracy, 13, 137, 141–2, 222
Malaysia, 8, 233–5
Malcampo y Monge, José, 60, 231
Malleret, Louis, 205
Malusu, 83
Mandarin, 35, 40
Manila, 16, 44, 49–50, 52, 58, 65–6, 83, 89, 93, 232
Manila Bay, 46
Manuc Manka, 93
maritime security, 63, 79, 92, 103, 159, 167, 175, 183, 201, 207, 222
Marseilles, 166
Mashoor, Syed, 130
massacres, 78, 109, 111–12, 176–7, 213, 227, 231, *See also* Batang Marau, Bud Dajo
Mat Syed, 147–8
Maxwell, Peter Benson, 132–6, 139, 152, 159, 215, 221, 231
McNair, John, 124, 151, 215
Mediterranean, 21–2, 24, 27, 35, 43, 102, 215
Mekong, 170–2, 174
Melaka, 37, 96–7, 105, 123–4, 129–30, 136, 148, 152, 157, *See also* Straits Settlements
  Sultanate of, 159
metropoles, 13, 15–16
Middle Ages, 23, 43
Middle East, 15
Midge, 140–1
Mignolo, Walter, 110
Mindanao, 39, 45, 47, 66, 68, 73–4, 78, 82
Mindanao Herald, 80–1, 83, 88
Ming Dynasty, 35
mining, 123, 137–8, 144, 185, 190, 217
Ministry for the Marine and the Colonies (France), 171
missionaries, 59, 64, 163–8, 170, 177, 183–4, 188, 207, 223–4, 230, *See also* proselytisation
Moghuls, 29
Mohr, 123
Moluccas, 54
Montero y Vidal, José, 61
moral relativism, 11, 14, 36
Morgan, Henry, 31–2, 216
Moro Province, 76, 88, 91

Moro Wars, 43–63, 93, 213, 215, 226–7
Morocco, 24
Moros, 43, 46, 67, 71, 213, 215, 225–6, 230, 232, *See also* Moro Wars
mother-of-pearl, 45, 76, 79, *See also* pearl, pearl fishing
Musa, Raja, 126, 134
Muslims, 181, *See also* Islam, Moros
My Tho, 173

Nancy, 86
Napoleon III, 173
Napoleonic Wars, 30, 46, 100, 108
Nassau, 56
nationalists, 205
  in the Philippines, 65–6, 68
  in Vietnam, 206–7, 211, *See also* Can Vuong
Naval Division of the Chinese Seas (France), 165
Netherlands, 8, 32, 46, 74, 93, 101–2, 116, 156, 208, 212, 231, *See also* Aceh: Aceh War, Anglo–Dutch War, Dutch East India Company, Dutch East Indies, treaties
  colonial expansion, 6, 28, 104, 158–60, 228
  imperial rivalry, 30, 47–8, 52, 94, 105, 107, 234
  Navy, 100, 216
  suppression of piracy, 54, 98, 104, 112–13, 120, 155, 206, 223
New Imperial History, 15
New York Times, 147
newspapers, 121, 214
Ngah Ibrahim, 137–40
Nguyen Dynasty, 161, 163–4, 167–9, 171, 174, 178–9, 188, 197, 202, 206–7, 211, 217–19, 225, 230
Nguyen Van Tuong, 196
Nine Years War, 27
Nisero, 155
Norodom, King, 172, 230
Norzagaray, Fernando, 56

olandez, 29
l'Olonnais, François, 32
Oman, 215
opium, 45, 102, 114, 117, 129, 199
Opium War, 36, 106, 113, 163, 166, 206, 218, *See also* Second Opium War
oral history, 13
Orang laut, 39, 100
Ord, Harry, 125, 137–41, 143, 221
Orientalism, 12, 15, 104
Osborne, Sherard, 107
Osterhammel, Jürgen, 7

Index

Otis, Elwell Stephen, 66, 69
Ottoman Empire, 24, 31
Ovando, Francisco José de, 45
Owen, Edward, 107

Pacific War. *See* World War II
pacification, 196–7, 205, *See also* appeasement
Pakhoi, 199
Palawan, 54, 80
Palembang, 10
Panga, 155
Pangkor, 142
    Engagement, 144–6
Papuans, 38
Paragua, 87
Parang, 85
Paris, 10, 172, 178, 187, 190, 194
Parliament
    British, 30, 49, 102–3, 108, 111, 115, 135, 152
    French, 180–1, 187, 191, 203, 224
paternalism, 77, 230
Patian, 84, 88
pearl fishing, 2, 85–6, 89–92, 95
pearls, 76, 94, 218, *See also* mother-of-pearl, pearl fishing
Pegu, 157, 223
Penang, 102, 105, 108, 114, 123, 125, 128, 131, 137–40, 142, 155, 186, 218, 221, *See also* Straits Settlements
Penang Guardian, 142
Perak, 6, 123–5, 137–48, 152, 156, 159, 216, 218, 221–2, 228, 231
Perak River, 142
Perak War, 146, 152
Périn, Georges, 181, 187, 191
perompak, 38
Persian, 34, 40
Persian Gulf, 33, 102, 215
Pettit, James S., 74
Philippine Constabulary, 85, 87, 93, 227
Philippine Pearling and Trading Company, 90
Philippine–American War, 65, 68, 70, 75–6
Philippines, 6–8, 18, 39, 42–95, 97–9, 102, 106, 158, 166, 213, 215, 217–18, 225–8, 230, 232–3, 235
Pickering, Mr, 145–6
Pigneau de Béhaine, Pierre-Joseph-Georges, 163
Pilas Islands, 80
Piquet, Jules Georges, 198–9
piracy
    definition of, 3, 10, 14, 21, 101, 158, 201, 206
    etymology of, 21–4

    Europeans accused of, 27–30, 168–9, 178, 211, 225, *See also* piratical imperialism
    explanations for, 99, 103, 107, 214, 216–19, 233
    historiography of, 8, 61
    in popular culture, 7, 23, 31–3, 40, 102, 205, 211
    laws pertaining to, 7, 23, 25–6, 30, 36–7, 72, 118, 139, *See also* trials
    sponsorship of, 6, 41, 45–6, 52, 77, 107, 124, 212, 234
    suppression of, 3, 6, 41, 100, 104, 133, 211–12, 231, *See also* China, France, Great Britain, Netherlands, Spain, Sulu Sultanate, United States, Vietnam
    translation of concept, 21–4, 34–40
piratical imperialism, 27–31, 101, *See also* piracy: Europeans accused of
piratical paradigm, 31–4, 40, 209–10
plantations, 78, 92, 185, 217
Pluto, 126–8, 135, 149–50
Pok Heng, 165
police, 114, 118, 121, 131–2, 134, 139, 145, 165
Polybius, 22
Pompeius Magnus, Gnaeus, 22
Pontianak, 100
Portugal, 24, 27–8, 35, 96–7, 157, 162
postcolonial studies, 15
Poulo-Condore, 190
praedones, 22
prahus, 48, 54, 107, 109, 133
privateering, 24, 26, 29–30, 34, 44, 162, 210, 218
proselytisation, 58, 94, 99, 230, *See also* missionaries
prostitution, 175, 184, 186, 207, 217, 224
protectorates, 62, 168, 180, 189, 193–4
Pulau Weh, 155

qiangdao, 36
Qing Dynasty, 35, 163, 192, 218
Quedagh Merchant, 29

race, 7, 15, 34, 69, 94, 99, 102, 158, 229, *See also* civilisation, ethnicity, racism, stadial theory
racism, 9, 88, 104, 110, 157, 186, 212–15, 226, *See also* civilisation, ethnicity, race, stadial theory
Rackham, Calico Jack, 33
Raffles, Thomas Stamford, 7, 13, 40, 89, 103–5, 211, 215, 218
Rajah Kongsee Atjeh, 156–7, 223
Ranti, Pak, 121, 216

Rayat Laut, 100
Reber, Anne Lindsey, 89, 104
Reconquista, 42
Red River, 175–81, 189–91, 193–5, 199, 202, 224–5
Red Sea, 29
Reid, Anthony, 12
religion, 34, 42–4, 58, 64, 78, 99, 158, See also Catholicism, Christianity, Islam
Renaissance, 25
residential system, 125, 144–6, 148–9, 222
Retord, Monsignor, 164, 168
Revue maritime et coloniale, 202
Riau, 4, 97, 99–101, 103, 105–6, 112–13, 116, 120–2, 153, 216
Ricketts, George Thorne, 58
Rigas, 156
Rigault de Genouilly, Charles, 168–9
Rinaldo, 127–8, 130, 137
Risso, Patricia, 11–12
Rivière, Henri, 189–93, 203, 207, 214, 224
Roberts, Bartholomew, 33, 216
Robin Hood, 205
Robinson, George, 127, 132
Robinson, Ronald, 105
Rolls of Oléron, 23
Rome, 22–3, 209
Roosevelt, Theodore, 77
Roussel de Courcy, Henri, 196–7
Royal Navy. *See* Great Britain: Royal Navy
Rubin, Alfred P., 21, 26

Sabah, 55, 234
Sabudin, 72
Said, Edward, 15
Saigon, 16, 166, 169, 190, 194
  Treaty of, 169, 180
sakoku, 29
Saleeby, Najeeb, 50
Salip Aguil, 81–2, 84
Sama, 7, 40, 45–6, 48, 51–2, 54, 101, 106, 158, 213, 217, 226
Samar, 54, 57
sampans, 121
San Bernardino Strait, 57
Sangir, 45
Santa Lucia, 60
Santiago Patero, D, 59–60
Sarawak, 48
Schück, Charlie, 90
Schück, Eddie, 90
science, 188
Scorpion, 182
Scott, Hugh Lenox, 89, 91
sea nomads, 39

Second Opium War, 120, 169
securitisation, 18, 22, 35, 137, 159, 181, 229
Selangor, 6, 123–38, 143–4, 147–52, 156, 159, 177, 212, 215, 221–2, 226, 228, 231
  Fort of, 127–8, 130, 132, 135
Selangor River, 126–9, 149
Selungun, 73–5, 216
Senez, Captain, 175–6, 202, 231
Serasan, 110
Serhassan, 110
Shadwell, Chas, 142, 148–9
Siak, 6, 10, 154
Siam, 115, 161, 170, 173, *See also* Thailand
Siamese, victims of piracy, 123
Siasi, 57, 63, 66–7, 73, 80, 86–7
Simunul, 87
Sin Heng, 138, 140–1, 144–6, 222
Sin Soon Seng, 155
Singapore, 8, 16, 90, 103, 105, 130, 138, 141–2, 145, 234, *See also* Straits Settlements
  landbase for pirates, 113, 116–20, 158, 163, 165, 217–18, 220, 223, 228
  piracy in, 4, 114–15, 124, 153, 163, 165, 216
  Strait of, 96, 116
  trade, 58, 60, 106, 114, 186, 216
Singapore Chamber of Commerce, 114, 136
Singapore Free Press, 118
Sino–French War, 192–6
Sitankai, 86
slavery, 4, 9–10, 14, 45–6, 65, 68, 94, 97, 109, 116, 158, 175, 210, 215
  abolition of, 76, 78, 116
  slave raiding, 38, 48, 52, 56, 71, 75, 77, 94, 98–9, 104, 161, 226
  slave trade, 75, 95, 102, 116, 155
smuggling, 58, 60, 66, 75, 178, 233, 235
Snouck Hurgronje, Christian, 154–5, 215
Socialists, 181
Son-la, 200
South Asia, 15
South China Sea, 2, 5, 28, 33, 111, 113–14, 119, 162–5, 167, 175, 206, 218, 223, 232
South Ubian, 79, 93
sovereignty, 1, 24, 47, 50, 55, 63, 94, 104, 112, 173, 180, 220, 226, 228, 235
Spain, 8, 42–64, 99, 102, 158, 170, 208, 212–13, 215, 225–7, 230, *See also* Madrid, Spanish–American War
  colonial expansion, 6, 24, 90, 93–5, 160, 227–8
  Navy, 66, 90, 95, 215–16, 226
  suppression of piracy, 4, 26, 51, 86, 104, 112, 206, 217, 220, 225, 229
Spanish–American War, 64–5, 90

Speedy, Tristram, 145
Sree Singapura, 129, 132
Srivijaya, 159
stadial theory, 104, 213, 226, *See also* civilisation, racism
steam navigation, 1, 47–8, 59, 159, 226
Steever, E. Z., 91
stinkpots, 139
Stoler, Ann Laura, 15–16
Straits Settlements, 101–53, 159, 167, 184, 207, 216, 220, 222–3, 225, 231, *See also* Great Britain: colonial expansion, Melaka, Penang, Singapore Legal Council, 141
Straits Times, 122, 131, 133–4, 152, 157, 165
Subrahmanyam, Sanjay, 16
subversion, 35
Sulawesi, 54, 74, 93, 98, 106
Sulu
  Archipelago, 6, 37, 45, 99, 217–18, 227, 234
  Sea, 3, 42–95, 105, 161
  Sultan of, 14, 57, 64, 66, 77, 90, 95, 212
  Sultanate, 42, 45, 226, 228
    piracy emanating from, 14, 45, 101
    suppression of piracy, 62, 69, 230
  Zone, 14
Sulug, 74
Sumatra, 6, 37, 97, 102–3, 105–6, 112–13, 120, 154
Sweden, 32
Sweet, Owen J., 70, 72
Swettenham, Frank, 141, 151, 215

Taft, William Howard, 76–7, 89
Tagliacozzo, Eric, 2
Tahil, 81
Taillandier, Abbé, 164
Taiping Rebellion, 113, 120, 163, 174, 178, 192, 194, 206, 217–18
Tampang, Datu, 48
Tanjung Tuan, 148
Tao Tila, 81, 84
Tarling, Nicholas, 8, 11, 61
Taupan, Panglima Julano, 53–5, 216
Tausug, 7, 40, 50, 158, 233
Tawi-Tawi, 56, 59, 63, 71–2, 74, 79, 87, 214, 217, 226
Tay Son Rebellion, 161, 163, 167
Teach, Edward, 33, 216
Teazer, 129
Telegrafo, 140
telegraph, 72, 200
Terengganu, 123, 216, 230
Ternate, 45
Teunom, 155

Thailand, 233, *See also* Siam
  Gulf of, 114, 232–3
Thalia, 140
Thames, 123
Thomson Janice E., 47
Thucydides, 37
Tiana, Leopoldo Canizato, 90
Tianjin Accord, 195
Tidong, 38
Tien Giang, 173
Times (London), 132–3, 135–6, 147, 152, 221
tin, 123–4, 137, *See also* mining
Tobelo, 38
Tokugawa, 29
Ton That Thuyet, 196, 198
Tonkin, 6, 174–83, 189, 196, 198, 200, *See also* Vietnam
  French intervention in, 169, 189, 191, 193, 202, 211, 214, 219, 224–5
  piracy in, 164, 183, 186, 202, 211
Tonze, 123
Tourane. *See* Da Nang
trade, 14, 27–8, 45, 64, 86, 96, 102, 104–5, 112, 114, 158, 167, 218, 222, *See also* arms: trade in, businessmen, slavery: slave trade. *See also* arms, trade in; coolies; slave trade; trading companies
  decline in because of piracy, 86, 114, 216
  embargo on, 58, 60
trading companies, 24, 26, 41, *See also* Dutch East India Company; English East India Company
Trafalgar, 111
trafficking, 5, 75, 184–8, 199, 207, 217, 224, 228, *See also* slarery: slave trade
transnational history. *See* global history
treaties, 100, 103–5, 169–70, 230
  between Aceh and the Netherlands, 155
  between Cambodia and France, 173
  between China and France, 166, 169, 195
  between France and Vietnam, 169, 178, 180–1, 187, 189, 193–5, 202, 224
  between Great Britain and Selangor, 128, 133
  between Great Britain and Sulu, 226
  between Great Britain and the Netherlands, 105–6, 156
  between Spain and Sulu, 49–50, 57, 62, 69
trials, 30–1, 92–3, 129, 131–2, 140, 150
Tripoli, 24
Trocki, Carl A., 38–9
Tseng, Marquis de. *See* Zeng Jize
Tu Duc, 6, 168–9, 192, 194, 211, 225, 230
Tukuran, 74

Tunis, 24
Tunkil, 49–50, 85

Ucbung, 82–4
ul-Azam, Jamal, 61–2
Umar, Teuku, 156
United Nations Convention on the Law of the Sea, 14
United States, 8, 185, 215, 229, 232
   Army, 42, 66, 85, 227
   colonial expansion, 6, 61, 227, 230
   Congress, 65–6
   Constitution, 68
   Navy, 66, 70, 75, 86, 88
   suppression of piracy, 64–93, 228–9
Urbiztondo, Don Antonio, 50

Van Angelbeek, Johan Christiaan, 100, 211, 215
Van den Broecke, Pieter, 29
Van Leur, J. C., 10–12, 14
Vasco da Gama, 27
Vazquez, Rolando, 110
Veth, Pieter Johannes, 99
Vietnam, 6, 8, 161–70, 173–5, 192, 211, 219, 223–5, 233, *See also* Cochinchina, Hue, Nguyen Dynasty, Sino–French War, Tonkin, Vietnam War, Vietnamese
   piracy in, 35, 114, 206, 217–18, 223, 228
   suppression of piracy, 162, 167, 180–1
Vietnam War, 233
Vietnamese, 184
   pirates, 177, 210
   victims of piracy and trafficking, 187
Vikings, 23
Vinh Long, 174
vintas, 74, 80, 85, 93

violence, 8–12, 14, 27, 34, 41, 76, 88, 114, 121, 144, 158, 160, 206, 210, 231, *See also* beheadings, massacres, piracy: suppression of

waegu. *See wokou*
wakō. *See wokou*
Wallace, Alfred Russel, 7, 39
war, 6, 12, 22, 27, 103, 108, 120, 132, 219
War of the Spanish Succession, 27, 30
War Office (Great Britain), 135
Warren, James F., 14, 39, 52, 54
Washington DC, 77
West Indies, 212, *See also* Caribbean
Whampoa, Treaty of, 166
Wilkinson, Richard, 124
Wodehouse, John. *See* Kimberley, Earl of
wokou, 29, 35
women, 48, 57, 88, 130, 164, 185, 213
   victims of piracy and trafficking, 73, 93, 125, 134, 175, 177, 184–7, 199, 207, 217, 224
Wood, Leonard, 76, 78–9, 227
Worcester, Dean Conant, 63
world systems theory, 13
World War I, 8
World War II, 65, 93, 95, 232–3

Yakob, Raja, 147–9, 151, 216, 222
Yangtze, 36
Yellow Flags, 177, 198
Yunnan, 176, 181, 193–4, 196, 198, 223

Zamboanga, 50, 55, 57, 60, 66–7, 71, 74, 80, 83, 86
Zebra, 138–9
Zeng Jize, 193